Phil Polley

TRENDS IN LITERATURE

BOOKS
by
JOSEPH T. SHIPLEY

As Translator
- YOU AND ME—PAUL GERALDY
- A NAKED KING—ALBERT ADES
- MODERN FRENCH POETRY (300 poems by 90 poets, with introduction and critical notes)
- *TO PABLO PICASSO—PAUL ELUARD

As Editor
- *DICTIONARY OF WORLD LITERATURE: Criticism—Forms—Technique
- *ENCYCLOPEDIA OF LITERATURE

As Author
- THE LITERARY ISMS
- THE ART OF EUGENE O'NEILL
- KING JOHN
- THE QUEST FOR LITERATURE
- RODIN (with Victor Frisch)
- *DICTIONARY OF WORD ORIGINS
- *TRENDS IN LITERATURE

*Published by the Philosophical Library

TRENDS IN LITERATURE

Joseph T. Shipley

PHILOSOPHICAL LIBRARY

New York

Copyright, 1949
by Joseph T. Shipley
All rights reserved.

Printed in the U. S. A.

To
Burke and Thorne

NOTE

After the body of this book will be found some pages of notes.

These notes contain:
1. Titles of books or names of persons alluded to in the text.
2. The original version of poems quoted from other languages.
3. Development of points pertinent to the book's thesis, but not relevant in such detail in the body of the book.

* * *

In order to leave the main flow unbroken, no indication of these notes is given in the text. They are intended to supplement rather than complement the main material.

PREAMBLE:
Confounded Confusions

"If any have wisdom, let him share it."

Much of our writing seems deliberately cloaked in abstruse terms, or couched in a special vocabulary, as though to be obscure were sign that one is profound.

Sometimes very simple ideas are smothered in phraseology. More often, perhaps, questionable notions are disguised in ponderous terms.

Let us examine what seems a recent instance of each.

In A Grammar of Motives (1945), Kenneth Burke builds upon "a pentad of terms ... we shall use five terms as generating principle of our investigation. They are: Act, Scene, Agent, Agency, Purpose." Again and again, Burke stresses the fundamental and pervasive character of these terms, their high value in explaining life and the philosophies. "The use of the pentad as a generating principle," he pontificates, "somewhat resembles the Kantian transcendentalism in one respect. Kant was concerned with the necessary forms of experience; and similarly the pentadic ratios name forms necessarily exemplified in the imputing of human motives." Figure that out— and then observe that Burke's potent pentad (save that he combines time and space) is what every elementary course in Journalism presents as the six questions a news item should answer: Who? What? Where? When? How? Why? Basic, naturally—because all-inclusive. Fruitful too, when the interrelations are examined. But why burke the reader with roundabout words? Journalist Rudyard Kipling pondered the potent pentad:

> I keep six honest serving men,
> They taught me all I know:
> Their names are What, and Why, and When,
> And How, and Where, and Who.

PREAMBLE

The science of signs—semiotic—is discussed by Charles Morris in Signs, Language, and Behavior (1946). He employs a score of new terms: *lansign; lexicative ascriptor; modor;* "*formator: a sign signifying how something is signified in an ascriptor.*" These may be helpful, to those willing to learn them; but so much stress is laid by these writers on the wide value of their field, that it seems a shame the public should be thus barred from its benefits!

Let us, nonetheless, examine Dr. Morris' definition of a sign. He tells of a landslide across a road, then of the spoken sounds of a man warning a traveler to detour because of the obstacle. "*If something, A, controls behavior towards a goal in a way similar to (but not necessarily identical with) the way something else, B, would control behavior with respect to that goal in a situation in which it were observed, then A is a sign. The spoken sounds are sign of obstacle.*" We may observe, in passing:

1. *The parenthesis pays little compliment to the expected reader, who might, indeed, know the difference between similarity and identity. This is a loose use of words.*

2. *The spoken sounds may be signs, not of an obstacle, but of a mistaken informant, a liar, a practical joker, or a hold-up man. This is a loose definition.*

More basically, "*the spoken sounds are sign of obstacle*" because Dr. Morris wills the former to be A; the latter, B. But, since either produces the effect without the other, it would as well fit the terms of his definition *if we reverse the letter-labels;* whereupon we reach the absurd conclusion that the obstacle is a sign of the spoken words. Surely we should expect more of a "science" of meaning and signs!

—*The present book is intended for the general reader, interested in the currents and tides that surge through our time. My observations may not be profound; I have at least endeavored to make them clear.*

TRENDS IN LITERATURE

CONTENTS

                                                                                       Page

POSTSCRIPT: DEFINITIONS
1. It all starts with life. 1
2. The Greeks put the questions. 4
3. It must strike home. 6
4. The philosopher holds up his glass. . . . 7
5. Herein the pattern is set. 11
6. The forces interplay. 13
7. You are recalled to life. 16

THE CLASSICAL
1. Time lays on its hand. 21
2. Variety abounds. 25
3. Unity abides. 26

THE NEO-CLASSICAL
1. Shakespeare shows the way. 31
2. French fashions cross the channel. . . . 34
3. The English behave by rule. 37
4. One device may serve two desires. . . . 42
5. Life bows to law. 54

THE ROMANTIC REBELLION
1. Laws invite their breaking. 57
2. Nature is behind us all. 60
3. Life is for conquest. 72
4. Imagination snaps the reins. 75
5. Emotion flowers. 77
6. — and goes to seed. 84
7. The hunt gallops wide. 87
8. Art gives a round-trip from life. 93
9. Realism is sibling to romance. 98

CONTENTS

10. Sidney Carton looks at Anthony Adverse . . . 102
11. Come take a journey! 105
12. The censor intrudes. 107
13. Fear leads us far. 114
14. Enter: woman, and love. 117
15. Foremost is form. 126
16. Freud's finger probes. 131
17. Goethe gathers all. 135

SYMBOLISM
1. Self puts on a social mask. 139
2. The Victorians muddle through. 142
3. The century eases onward. 149
4. France takes direction. 155
5. Baudelaire builds time's bridge. 158
6. The senses make sense. 165
7. Mind and heart reach out. 172
8. George Sand shows the pattern. . . . 181
9. America strikes up the band. 185

MONITORY INTERLUDE 193

POLITICAL PREAMBLING
A. The Hope of Democracy. 203
B. The Dilemma of Democracy. 211

TWAIN TURMOIL OF TODAY
1. Words bear, and bare, the trend. . . . 215
2. The single mind emerges. 220
3. — and subdivides. 239
4. Romanticism turns social. 240
5. Realism rips the skin. 244
6. Art looks beyond. 248
7. Reason runs awry. 274
8. God faces both ways. 293
9. Value arises. 297

Here we stand. 312
Art abides. 313

CONTENTS

OTHER FIELDS
  Our Conglomerate Age. 322
    1. We take the plunge. 323
    2. He restoreth the soul. 334
    3. Time brings the existentialist. 356
    4. The state swallows the man. 365
    5. Men point the way. 373
    6. Propaganda rears. 378
  Herein the pattern is named. 387
NOTES 389
  "History repeats itself." 391
  The Artist's Revolt. 415
  Modern Art. 424
INDEX 449

CONTENTS

Other Fields

Our Conglomerate Age 322
 1. We take the plunge. 323
 2. He restoreth the soul. 334
 3. Time brings the existentialist. . . . 356
 4. The state swallows the man. . . . 365
 5. Men point the way. 373
 6. Propaganda rears. 378

Herein the pattern is named. 387
Notes 389
"History repeats itself." 391
The Artist's Revolt. 415
Modern Art. 424
Index 449

POSTSCRIPT: DEFINITIONS

POSTSCRIPT: DEFINITIONS

1. It all starts with life.

READERS ask at the beginning: what is this book about? The author must tell them. In a work of art, he can do so without danger; the Greeks had a word for the device they used, of making sure the audience knew the story before the play began. Consider the ironic power that is added to the words Lady Macbeth utters upon the murder of the king:

> *A little water clears us of this deed*

when we know that soon she will piteously cry:

> *All the perfumes of Arabia will not sweeten this little hand.*

It is only in the potboiler, the quick mystery story or detective thriller, that a knowledge of what is coming spoils its arrival. It is one of the paradoxes of art that familiarity breeds contemplation and increased regard.

The case is quite different when the author's task is to argue or explain, especially if his ideas run counter to the generally accepted notions. Through the course of his book, he hopes to develop his position, to enfold it in sustaining tissue of logic, examples, fine persuasive figures, so that the readers will at length be lulled by his style, won by his rhetoric, convinced by his reason, so that his theme is accepted and his merit hailed. In the shelter of the ramparts he builds along the way, the writer may venture shots at venerable names and respected points of view. He trusts by then to have drawn the reader behind the same walls of interest, into at least a deferring of judgment. But bluntly to announce, at the beginning, the basic idea of the book, is to run the gauntlet of immediate scorn.

Readers ask at the beginning, nonetheless: what is this book about? The author must tell them.

The central thought of the present book may be simply

[1]

stated. Observing the many efforts at "definition" of the literary movements and schools, the author has turned with these back to life. He views their products, neither as separate creations carved in an ivory tower, nor as works produced on the spur of some other aspect of man's functioning, such as the economic; but rather as an integral part of the complex but single structure of government and food-supply and beauty man is forever rearing to shelter him from the cold and the dark.

The primary interest of this volume is the rearing of that structure in our own time. Glances at earlier periods are made only in the hope of observing our bricks while they are still clay and straw, of gaining perspective through watching from afar the forces that gather as they approach our heads. The ninety-odd chemical elements existed before they were named; the label alone, despite sympathetic magic, does not bring understanding, or command. The confusion of qualities, to those present in earlier periods now past and comfortably catalogued, may give us promise of ultimate order in our own chaotic stir. The consideration of other times is therefore fragmentary, entered into only as it may shed light upon the basic emphases of today, the warp and woof of the pattern of our time.

It is convenient, for the learning process, to isolate elements and operations. In the study of physics, for example, heat, light, energy are studied in turn; when gravity is exerted we neglect friction and the winds that blow through most of life; that's how the rules are formed. And often they are stated as though the forces acted in a vacuum, which is an emptiness man has only recently learned how to approximate, and would abhor even more than nature does if he were stuck in one.

Without this artificial simplification, we might not ever have derived any general principles; and however we may mistrust them, we must admit that scientific "laws" have their usefulness. I shall make simplifications too, no doubt, which may be seized upon as though they invalidate the thesis; but I hope some will discern value in what I mean to indicate as tendencies rather than set down as rules.

POSTSCRIPT: DEFINITIONS

After all, they will be drawn in the most democratic fashion possible: from the things concerned, and after the event. I am seeking to trace a process. Nor do I claim originality in the findings, any more than in the search. Art has been part of life for quite a while; many have woven a pattern of their inter-relationships. At best I am embroidering a new design with the old, unraveled threads. Without adding letters to the alphabet, however, one may coin fresh words. New applications or combinations of known elements have indeed revolutionized many fields of man's activity; think of steel, and relativity, and dynamite; the electric eye; light from the inert gases; nylon; cellophane. We have begun to work within the atom.

I promise nothing either explosive or unique; I hope merely that it will prove illuminating. Gunpowder was first used as a toy. In truth, only since a work of art became an article of commerce, protected by copyright, has originality been greatly prized. Cervantes in *Don Quixote* apologizes for being too lazy to gather his material in study. The Spaniard had his tongue in his cheek; but many of the Elizabethan writers invented Italian originals for their tales. The desire for originality is, as we shall see, one of the romantic aberrations. When a competent writer has felt his oats, he turns not to pastures new but to often ploughed fields; these are probably the most fertile ground. Both Masefield and E. A. Robinson have in our own day, and quite legally, taken blind Homer's story. Of those less assured, we may recall Donne's challenge:

> *For if one eat my meat, though it be known*
> *The meat was mine, the excrement is his own.*

"In aesthetics, that is to say, in the clouds"; quietly Anatole France pricks the bubbles of pretension. Although the points pressed here will be driven home (I trust), they form in my mind only a tentative, though I think a working, scheme; they are but a skeleton onto which the flesh of art and life must grow in the reader's mind. Regardless of the clouds of disputation, I shall try—despite the twinkling stars—to stay on earth. It is not the stars that twinkle.

2. *The Greeks put the questions.*

IT is always wise to examine a movement at its source. The quest of literature thus carries us to life, from which literature springs. Without turning either to the egg or to Adam, however, we may briefly consider those that, though not the first to create, were first to speculate upon the results of their creation. The Assyrians, the Egyptians, made their works of art, and worshipped them. The Israelites were restrained from idolatry by the command that they make no graven image. The Greeks rose from superstition to philosophy when they looked upon their statues not with reverence but with critical consideration. They checked this analysis with the implacable facts of life. Similarly, we must balance ancient and long accepted theory in the scales with present practice. Let us, then, accept the gifts of the Greeks; but let us look them in the mouth.

To the Greeks, art is the imitation of life; and whatever meaning—of photographic or of "idealized" transcription—we may give the Greek word *mimesis,* it follows that literature will reflect the problems of life. What, then, are the eternal aspects of man's being? Birth; the intermediate phase, the needs and the lusts of living; and final death. To the Greeks, the necessities of life were not problems, but facts. Facts out of which plots might grow, but beneath which lies the true field of man's exploration. Those Greeks that set the pattern of literature and of philosophy had little need of asking how they could satisfy their wants. The material needs they took for granted; their question was not How? but Why? Why must men beat against unbreachable barriers and walk however warily into the ultimate traps? To the Jew, to the Christian, these basic answers are given; their problems are the immediate, daily concerns: how to prevail, not why. Hence the emphasis of the Christian

POSTSCRIPT: DEFINITIONS

on conduct, of the Greek on contemplation. For to the Greeks the fundamental oppositions and limitations of life were continuous irritants. The centuries have threaded their pearls.

The most immediately noticeable oppositions in life are those of extremes: cold and heat; light and dark; birth and death; good and evil. Somewhere between these, in what we wistfully call the golden mean, most of our days wear on. Put these realities into more philosophic phrasing, and you move through Man (many men) and the multiform world without, yet also something common to all men, something common to all trees, and through their essential elements something common to all essences—to variety and unity, all lesser unities converging toward a basic One that is Rhythm, or Number, or God.

Among their oppositions the Greeks did not set religion and science; this battle, with its various truces, was not theirs. But the general problem of unity and variety was central to their systems of thought, gave rise to the rival schools of philosophy that still disturb the calm of the academic classroom. Logically subordinate, but a bit nearer home, pressed the problem of the ego and the universe—me, and rest of the world. Whether these divisions were considered complete and permanent or just a result of man's binary vision, is for the moment immaterial; what matters is that nature and all life were regarded as made up mainly of such conflicts and the attempt to find a way between.

As in man's living, so in his art. The basis of every drama and every novel, we are thus told, lies in the confronting of two seemingly irreconcilable forces; the plot strives on until their opposition is resolved. And art, we hear the Greek point of view caught in a sentence, art is the sensuous expression of unity in variety.

3. *It must strike home.*

ARISTOTLE maintained that "poetry is a more philosophical and higher thing than history; for poetry occupies itself in expressing the universal, history the particular. The particular is, for example, what Alcibiades did or suffered." Which of the two is "higher" depends upon what ladder you're climbing (beauty's, or truth's); but Aristotle goes on more wisely. Within poetry's universal vision, he continues, each of us must find himself. The hero must be *manlike*. We must feel ourselves capable of the protagonist's conduct, however exalted, however base. In ourselves must murmur or rumble an inner echo of his impulses, so that we may feel sympathy, and achieve understanding. We have been told that we should go from a novel or a play considering, of the main figure:

"There, but for the grace of God, go I."

This is retrospective thanksgiving; for through all literature, while it holds us in its spell, shines no such shielding grace. Which is its greater glory. "There go I."

POSTSCRIPT: DEFINITIONS

4. *The philosopher holds up his glass.*

THOUGHT since the Greeks has wrestled with the same problems. It has tried to unite, indeed, not merely these opposite poles of being, but the very philosophies (dualism and monism) that seek to explain them.

Religion, beyond its primordial rouse of the emotions in ritual, makes appeal because of its answers to the basic and eternal questions. It resolves the opposition of determinism and freedom of the will; it sweeps away the difficulties that cloud good and evil; with the after-world it wipes out man's greatest fear, assuring him that his end is but a more glorious beginning, for—as Francis Thompson words it:

For they are twain yet one, and Death is Birth.

With less popular success, philosophy has similarly striven. The principle of polarity explains that twilight makes one movement of night and day, that all behavior is a mortal mixture between the impossible extremes of absolute good and uttermost evil. Various shades of gray (in conduct if not in color) are the nearest we can come to black and white. Cheap fiction may give us the villain out of the ink-well, the heroine out of the white-wash pail; a good story, like life itself, has each a bit bespattered with the other.

A metaphysician declares that matter is merely the point of view of mind. A scientist retorts that mind is the result of a chemical reaction. Still more proclaim that energy and substance are one—and no one can tell which is which! An electron assumes mass through its probabilities of concentrated force; and if you can't understand that, try to digest the notion that light is neither a corpuscle nor a vibration, but at once the likelihood of either. Sir William Bragg declares that all the fundamental entities have this dual possibility, and behave sometimes like bodies, sometimes like waves.

These questions are by no means shuttlecocks in an academic game of badminton. Giving body to a word without reality behind it is a logical error set down in the text-books as hypostatization; but from its practice in life (as often through slogans) wars may spring. The cry of race-purity is such a beaten drum. The contorted pattern of the world today is woven of such threads.

Thus the logician warns us of the errors that may rise from the false separation of subject and object, the knower and the known—me, and the rest of the world. On the other hand, we are reminded that these opposites are complementary, one requires the other—we cannot know good unless there is also evil—but that, though they are inseparable, they are distinct. Some go so far as to say that from confused blending (as in empathy, as in a social sympathy that blames the sin not on the sinner but on the slums) rises most that is wrong in contemporary writing and thought. It's a skipping back and forth such as might bemuse even the Mad Hatter. Morris R. Cohen sees the snake of the ages swallow its tail: "ultimately all science goes back to the classical conception of nature, according to which the variation of phenomena is to be referred to some unitary law."

To all these disputations we return a twisted smile. The philosopher sits no longer in our council halls. Of the ancient culture, our legislators have retained but the rhetoric. Our poets, like the Greek tragedians, may march to battle or sing the triumph; but our generals do not put aside the sword to don their robes of philosopher and seer. Nor to set hand to plough. Both the army and the legislature are the worse therefor.

Diogenes, with his lantern and his barrel, would today be referred to the social worker, or the psychiatrist. Somewhere, no doubt, there is already a "case history" of his obsession, such

POSTSCRIPT: DEFINITIONS

as Freud himself has given of Leonardo's dream. Diogenes' counterpart in our comic-strip days is Mopey Dick. Philosophy works in a rarer atmosphere than the smoke and steel of daily life; dim dust of it sifts downward through the industrial fog, accepted—if not blessed—unawares. As over the crowds of The Great White Way, our artificial illumination blots out the very stars. We have a great light on the ground level, but intellectually our ceiling is little more than zero. The artist, along with his fellow-citizens, is bedazzled by this nearer brilliance. Instead of the arduous search for wisdom at her source, he turns (if at all) to the popular simplifications and gossipy distortions that in our day present "the story of philosophy" and "the art of living." Encouraged by these monosyllabic attempts to give us sugar-candy explanations of life's problems, the successful lord of industry blossoms forth as omniscient seer. The hero of a transoceanic solo flight, the champion at a game of cards, become the heralds of an international philosophy. Too often the public accepts them at their self-estimate.

For the serious aspects of his work, the artist is driven back upon his own feelings and speculations, as pummeled into him by the world around. Even more than his fellow-citizens, he responds to the active forces of society and of nature; in his everyday contacts, he is chafed by their binding, is beaten aware.

At once he is brought back to the ancient opposition. Equally strong today is the sense of separation:—me; and the rest of the world. The artist has often high imaginative powers; he may, in rare moments of great felicity, or more often in mystic exaltation, feel "at one" with all things. He may expiate what some call the "guilt" of personality in a social gaol or goal. Mary Baker Eddy reminds us that atonement means achieving "at-onement". This is a truly harmonious state; yet it is but an extension of the ego to embrace the world, and like as not the joy is made up partly of satisfaction at having attained such a union: and that satisfaction is still the mark of the separate mind. Ordinarily the awareness of a distinction is uppermost; man's struggle is to adjust himself to life's forces, or to wring them into the service of his needs and his desires.

Kenneth Burke, defending—who knows why?—romanticism from the charge of monism, declares that the romantic may also claim a dualistic system, its opposites being the principle he stands for and the principle represented by the society against which he revolts. His "individualism" never for a moment permits him to forget the "enemy". If not everyone is a rebel, surely everyone hopes to transform or to appease the world around.

In a mellower mood, one may see the world around in either of two aspects. It may mean primarily the nurse and parents from whom the infant draws its joy and pain; the family group; the teacher and fellow-pupils with whom the child aims for happiness and freedom; the society of his fellow-men, with which the individual must weave the stuff of harmony. This garment woven (however ill-fitting), "the world around" may mean not man but "the limit set to man": nature, the primal forces men must unite to tame to their many uses.

POSTSCRIPT: DEFINITIONS

5. *Herein the pattern is set.*

THIS much is apparent to immediate thought, despite its philosophic sanction. But whether we speculate upon them or not, the life of each of us is a continuous stirring of these conflicts. One of us may feel that his social conscience is at war with his animal instincts; another may fret that his personal desires are thwarted by an oppressive social order. However we align the forces, whatever armistice may be called, we are all and always in the fight.

The plot of a novel or play grows out of this conflict. But beneath the story, and in every work of art, the artist takes his stand. The literary "schools", romanticism, realism, and the rest, represent the different bivouacs in the unending struggle.

The battle that we call life can be looked upon from four cardinal points of view, occurring (like the compass points) in opposed pairs.

Down the ages, in pendulum swing of predominance as the periods pass, two attitudes are alternate. The individuals in an era tend to accept unconsciously, or to defend and justify, one of these points of view:

A. Concern chiefly with oneself; on a larger scale, with the individual, the separate objects and events that constitute the world—with the multiplicity, the variety, of things.

B. Recognition of the prime significance of the central core that is the same in all men, of (in either a mystic or a scientific comprehension) the single spirit, the integrating law, that binds all things in basic unity.

The many forms, or the one essence. Emphasis on one or the other of these ways of beholding life marks successive ages in the movement of mankind.

And within each age, whichever of these attitudes it prefers, another opposition urges. We may

1. deem the human individual, the human race, part of the single stream of nature.

2. consider men, mankind, somehow apart from and above other aspects of the world, endowed with free will therefore power of infinite progress.

Thus persons in various times, or various persons at one time, may be possessed of four main visions. They may consider:

> A1. men as equal drops in the waters of natural flowing;
> B1. humanity as bound by natural law;
> A2. men as endowed with free will of personal choice;
> B2. mankind as subject only to rule of common conscience, or common sense, or divine will.

Let us set the scheme down again, in more general terms.

The dominant mood of an era, with minority dissent, will be marked by either

> A. Concern with particulars, separate individuals; variety—or
> B. Concern with universals, the collective unity, the general law or essence.

In any period, this basic attitude is divided according as one has

> 1. Prime regard for nature (as all-inclusive).
> 2. Prime regard for man, as apart and above and free.

Out of these four attitudes toward life spring the literary schools. These are the basic distinctions; all else is derivative, incidental. Because these are the basic attitudes in all man's earthly doings. In their flow are borne not only his art, but his science, his ethics, his national being—the current state of his world.

POSTSCRIPT: DEFINITIONS

6. *The forces interplay.*

BEFORE tracing the distinctions as they appear in our times, it may be well to ponder a few prior considerations. First, to point out that the "absolute romanticist", or the "pure realist" would never create a work of art. The one would go off, like Rimbaud, to build great caravels of the desert, or like Werther and Sanine sink (or soar) into suicide; the other would become a research worker in biophysics, or a tramp. When muddled with a messianic urge, a "Christ-complex", the romanticist produces the "spoiled art" of a self-glorifying Hugo, a complacent Tennyson, a rebellious Hood.

Every work of art is indeed ultimately classic, in the sense that all that man deems art somehow impresses upon the variety of its material at least the unity of its form. Its "school" is determined by the direction from which it approaches the harmony; by the exuberances, the excesses, or the restraints, the refinings, that appear.

As this quality is no more than an emphasis in the work of art, so in the artist it may be only the most frequent tendency, so of an age it becomes the defining yet far from the single characteristic. Once a line of thought has been traced, it is never wholly obliterated, even on the shifting sands of time. Every attitude, once established, despite condemnation by ethics or annihilation by logic somehow persists. "Hitler" is a modern name, but marks an ancient behavior; and some even today remember Jesus. Not even in eighteenth century France were the literary rules held inviolate: the greater the tyrant, the stronger the impulse to rebel. And when that despot's finger is on the relentless hand of the hours—some time lags withal, with others gallops. Not only do various stages of development, many and often irreconcilable points of view and courses of conduct, exist side by side, but in the cycle of time extremes meet, and the advance guard overtakes the rear. Each for his own end, "radical" and "conservative" unite. The farmer who protests against the encroachments of industry is joined by the "intellectual" agrarian who cries out upon the mechanization of the times. Radical parades are swelled by those that march in personal dissatisfaction, beside the few with intelligent concern for the general good: the egocentric and the socially-minded lift the same torch. Politics has more than once conjoined *The Daily Worker* and *The Wall Street Journal*.

Do not expect an age to define itself. Seldom, for more than the reasons just indicated, seldom can it seem to its indwellers other than a teeming press of contradictions. Every age calls itself transitional, as of course it is; but tends to stage-design its travail into the death-bed of a culture and the maternity ward of a new civilization. Put children into the cars of a swift-swinging circus wheel, and they have the quivery thrill of the centrifugal force, the sense of flying away, while all the time there snuggles in them the comforting security of the chains they can see, holding them tightly to the central hub. Of an age, however, it is seldom save in retrospect that the centripetal force becomes clear, the solid hub that is its binding core. Think of the wide-ranging contrasts, the foaming chaos, of the period we now call Elizabethan without doubt that the name bears meaning. Yet such an age may be like our earth itself, with the sun supremely visible, yet with only a void for the equally potent twin focus around which our orbit takes its measure. The isolation of one characteristic, however important, is a falsifying simplification. No work of art is really a member of a school; it is itself, unique. If for convenience (as we herd sheep in flocks, and children in classroom grades) we set the work in a "literary school", we must remember that it is nonetheless a distinct entity, possessed of many qualities other than the ones we are selecting for our classification. Keep that in mind throughout this book—and after.

POSTSCRIPT: DEFINITIONS

And we must make the bases of our groups truly basic. "Romanticism always ill-defined", protested Hugo, adding another poor effort. The very multiplicity of definitions—scattered pitfalls—lends encouragement to the planning of a clean-cut way.

7. *You are recalled to life.*

ONE further reminder ploughs more deeply than such easy assumptions as Henry Hazlitt slips into, in speaking of the eternal alternation of "traditionalism and revolt. Behind this endless see-saw", he declares, "are two main causes. Either traditionalism or revolt, when it reaches a high point, tends to discredit itself by its own excesses. And even if it does not, critics tire of the old theories and the old gods and want new theories and new gods, if only for the sake of something fresh to talk about. Hence the present shouts of down with Mencken, down with Dreiser, down with Lewis, down with Cabell; hurrah for the youngsters under thirty and the critics over sixty! It is the same motive, at bottom, that periodically leads a bored and restless voting public to turn the Republicans out and put the Democrats in. This phenomenon is recurrent and immemorial, both in politics and literature. It deserves a special name. We might call it, after its most famous victim among the Greeks, the *aristidization* of old heroes." This is not simplification, it is misdirection. (The casual nature of these remarks, further betrayed by the careless English, while indicative of his general trend of thought, is not typical of the writer. The obiter dictum appears in a discussion of Humanism, of which Mr. Hazlitt thought little; his tone, waving the tempest into its tea-pot, breathes across the surface of the subject —which calls not for a napkin, but for a bathysphere.)

For—and this cannot be kept too firmly in mind—all art springs directly from life. The impulses that set a man to writing, that determine the spirit of his work, are mainly non-aesthetic. He may enter a contest to write a sonnet on a grasshopper and a cricket, yet out will peep his own preoccupation, and he will begin—if he is Keats:

The poetry of life is never dead.

POSTSCRIPT: DEFINITIONS

The artist may venture into the most out-of-the-way corners of the golden realm, he may leap beyond the valley of the shadow of the moon; still there clings to his feet the clay of earthly soil. His feet *are* clay.

However far a bird may fly, it takes its tail along.

The causes of change in literature are non-literary: the causes of movements in art are non-aesthetic. The surge of politics, of social, economic, industrial history—following philosophy as it spreads, and thins, to common sense, in the wake of pure science as it comes to be applied: the march of life takes its direction from causes diverse and often dimly seen, and always beyond exact description. Sometimes exultant in the van, sometimes earnest guardian in the rear, or bewildered or contented stray; sometimes beating against the oncoming force, more often one with the accepted flow—but always in immediate relation to life, and explicable in its current terms, art rears its works. What sets its character upon a period, determines its art.

THE CLASSICAL

1. *Time lays on its hand.*

THE many efforts to distinguish classicism from romanticism have produced a confusion the befogging effects of which it would be easy to spread. Stendhal declared that all good art was romantic in its day; Ramon Fernandez announces that romanticism in its essence is a classic achievement; Kenneth Burke asseverates that classicism might be called the flowering of a romantic excess. Goethe, who many believe created excellent examples of both schools, said bluntly:

> I call the classic *healthy,* the romantic *sickly* . . .
> If we distinguish classic and romantic by these qualities,
> it will be easy to see our way clearly.

—If the same doctor is called to diagnose every case!

Other critics use the word classic as indicating a work of such vitality that it remains always alive. In this sense, the term *the classics* brings to mind, first, the masterpieces of Greek and Latin literature and, secondly, the body of works that in modern languages have won survival. It would seem, therefore, that endurance is both a test and a prerequisite. A work must get its second wind. It must claim place upon the five-foot shelf.

No contemporary work is classical.

Time, however, does not confer the distinction upon a work. Uncounted readers may light candles as at a shrine, but there is danger that the drip-wax may harden into classroom study, and the book be condemned to required reading in a thousand schools, where a million children will shudder at its name. The passing of years, however, permits an important process. The intrinsic qualities of the work appear, as the shell of contemporary concerns is cracked. What was exciting because the readers' lives were tangled in its issues has died; then there lies clear what remains of worth. A widely sold book arguing for or against a third term for Franklin D. Roosevelt is likely in 1990 to have less interest, except for the historiographer, than a poem accepted, after seventeen rejection slips, by a nonpaying magazine of virtually no circulation. Most obvious in books like *Uncle Tom's Cabin* and in plays like *A Doll's House,* even in statues like those of Rodin and Epstein it is the expression of an urgent attitude that wins the attention of its time. The local habitation and the name mostly impress the man that dwells beside them. What strike him first (as with an unplaned wall) are the protuberances, the excesses, the prejudices, the very imperfections. Time will either toss these aside with the rest of the work, or smooth them down, lose them as details in a greater whole.

Every reader, of course, has his own cranial bumps upon which a work will make first impact. With a book or a painting of his own day, the rouse of his emotions by the issues involved provokes a double distortion. To a quiet fellow, who does not wish his hours or his income disturbed, *The Grapes of Wrath* may seem radical propaganda. To the "leftist", most Hollywood films are opium for the masses, drugs to make them forget their discontent with the status quo.

But of course the reader of our time requires no explanation of such devices as subways and jet propulsion planes; the term summons the picture. In New York today, reading a short story, if one finds his hero Herman coming out of the subway at Times Square, to look up and see that the President has called a special session, the author need hardly mention the racing dots of light that form letters around the Times Building. But try reading Dante: some of his words and references baffle even scholars that have given all their mature years to the study of *The Divine Comedy. Don Quixote,* Rabelais' writings, *Gulliver's Travels,* are full of contemporary allusions wholly lost on most readers today—and what if the nursery rhymes once were political jingles! Behind these details of local color and immediate reference lie more pervasive social habits, economic and political ways of being. How many of us know, when we hear a person described as graciously unbending, that *unbending* gets its meaning from the fact that when arrows were not being set to the bow, its string was loosened, the wood no longer taut? But that, when we hear a man pictured as stiff, unbending in his dignity, this opposite meaning is derived from the rigid ramrod of the muzzle-loading gun that supplanted the long-bow? In Roman comedy, one of the most familiar figures is the complaining hen-pecked husband. Why didn't he get a divorce? It was easier in Rome than in Reno. If you knew that, you might also know the further fact that most shrew-bitten husbands preferred to endure their wife's ever-wagging tongue—because back with the departing divorcee must go the dowry! We may wonder, too, at the crowd in these comedies of bawds and procurers and lively loose ladies; but there must be a female in a farce; the respectable Roman maiden was carefully guarded in seclusion and therefore was out of place on the stage, while the Roman youth sowed his wild oats in the stony field of schemed affairs before planting himself in the sheltered garden of arranged matrimony. What is of vital concern or ready assumption in one age, to a later generation may possess only an antiquarian interest, or be, without reconstruction, impossible to understand.

Not merely down the ages, but across the miles, these difficulties grow. The play *Another Language,* successful in the United States and there deemed an excellent contemporary picture, suffered a sea-change on its trip to England; there it seemed unreal, because families of that level would have hired servants. Books have been written to explain why Englishmen cannot appreciate French poetry.

The sand-blasting of the fronts of city buildings is a commercial, not an aesthetic, action. Old schools, olden cathedrals, often acquire a mellow beauty, ivy-grown. The patina of the years may enhance any work of art. It softens as its controversies lapse into memories. To be sure, each age views every work of art as contemporary, at least sees it through the glass of its own desires, praises in it the qualities that echo its own ideals. Homer has been considered, successively, a teacher of (bad) morals, a model of decorum, a prize of primitive simplicity, the closing token of a lengthy age. Specialists today also study how opinions in their field have shifted from age to age. Not merely attitudes, but interpretations. The early Christians found in Vergil a prophecy of Jesus' coming. The later English changed Shakespeare's Shylock from a beaten buffoon and minor figure to the central character, a deeply wronged and sorely suffering soul, so that it now seems almost incongruous to include *The Merchant of Venice* among the comedies. What matters more than such variations, however, is the fundamental shifting of emphasis from the contemporary features of a product of its time to the essential, the permanent, values of a work of art.

When it is said, then, that every good work is sure to become a classic, we may understand that after it has played its part in life's battles, from it may more peacefully emerge the thrill of art. Let us, then, look at "the classics".

THE CLASSICAL

2. *Variety abounds.*

As soon as we take more than a distant view of the classics, it becomes clear that the one term covers a multitude of very different works. They are diverse not only in their unique qualities as individual creations, but also in their underlying points of view. The Greeks were concerned with problems of belief; the Romans, with questions of conduct. The Athenian considered evil as opposed to beauty (proportion); the Roman, as opposed to good. Good was obedience to the law. There is a thrust to the heart of the Roman code in the story of the general who condemned his son to death for winning a victory against orders.

The Greek (with many diversities that further press our point) sought harmony through reason, through the inner balance of the individual, whether against the forces of nature or in battle with his own passions or defying the throng; in the anonymity of Oriental art a thousand men are as a single hand. The temple of India grows in the ritual mould; the individuality of the architect is no more than three drops of rain. The land is part of the Greek temple, built beside a grove, on a hilltop; between its columns flash the ocean and the stars. Like the gods, it has grown from nature. Its simplicity makes it one with the world around. The Gothic cathedral is constructed with relation only to itself, in the heart of the town, where needed; it is adorned with figures like an Elizabethan play. You have to move back, across a square, for proper view of it. Like God, it is above nature. It stands by itself, sufficient. Its very complexity makes it one.

The three great Greek tragedians trace a path from belief in the gods, from divine and human passions, to an agnostic realism that manipulates the emotions, and utilizes the deities as a dramatic device—the god from the machine—to bring about the ending. Yet all these notes along the scale, we call "the classics".

3. *Unity abides.*

Beneath the diversity glimpsed in these few words, lies an even more basic identity. The notes are in one scale. In terms almost as various as the works themselves, their essential sameness, the all that is in each, has been expressed. In ancient India and Egypt, says Elie Faure, the problem centered on the individual emerging from the social mass. (Europe today has reversed the calendar.) Moving westward, Faure follows art out of religion, observing that the statue breaks clear of the temple in proportion as man stands forth from the crowd. But Faure does not escape from his original figures; he pictures art as a conflict between the hero and the myth. The hero is always tragic because the myth is invincible, whether man move toward his fellow-men with knowledge (law, society, religion) or in love (self-control, freedom, individual will).

> The whole history of art is dominated and conditioned by this drama: the imperishable desire to retain the universal life that at every instant escapes us, in the image capable of defining it for all time. If one does not conceive this, no art form is intelligible save the narrowest naturalism. If one does conceive of this, the forms furthest from the appearance of life become at once and fully intelligible ... It is but the humble and marvellous image of the cosmic order itself, that state of provisional equilibrium between two chaos.

Having thus assured us that the road to comprehension exists, Faure leaves us to find it for ourselves.

Long before him, Plato gave voice to this doctrine of the alternation of opposites. The Greek sought equilibrium of the life within and the life without. There is a quest of the same goal in the Roman submission to a higher law, a life controlled by ordered principles. Some strive to adjust life to themselves;

THE CLASSICAL

others seek to adjust themselves to life: from either end the aim is harmony, the coordination of life's many contrary tuggings. In the Greek drama the protagonist was not a human, but rather that Necessity which drives us briefly within, and swiftly snatches us from, the mazy room of life. Shakespeare's concerns lay inside that crowded room; the war between good and evil that ends only with death is constantly waged in his dramas. And somehow out of the war rises the peaceful exaltation of great art. The eighteenth century emphasized the propriety that must govern human conduct, the decorum of the gentleman's code to which our baser passions must subscribe. The following generations, not

Content to dwell in decencies forever,

exalted the freedom an individual must achieve despite all social bindings. Each age may have its particular problem, its unique variation of the eternal theme. It struggles for a way of life within the opposed urgings. It seeks—or beats against—the eternal compromise. By its failures, by its deficiencies and its excesses, we may determine its point of departure. But in its art the harmony is attained.

In the substance of the universe we see a constant breaking down, and somewhere in the reaches of interstellar cold we begin to guess the atoms are reforming. Chemistry presents to us the two aspects of analysis and synthesis. Physiology brings it home to our hearts in systole and diastole. Biology leads us from the sexual cell to the organism to the cell, recurrently. So the history of races, of the human spirit, may be seen as a pit-and-pendulum movement, from the binding ties (of faith or quest of truth) with which men cleave to one another to the lightning flashes (of faith or quest of truth) that cleave them asunder. Always it is a quest, and in art a precarious capture, of an harmonious balance between the forces that join and the forces that sever man and nature, man and his fellows, man and himself.

THE NEO-CLASSICAL

THE NEO-CLASSICAL

THE NEO-CLASSICAL

1. *Shakespeare shows the way.*

WHEN Shakespeare wrote *Macbeth*, a son of Banquo sat on the throne of England. Not only had the play's prophecy thus more than come true, but its magic was up-to-the-minute news. The three weird sisters stirred their grisly pot just after the London publication of King James' book on *Demonology*, which led to the passing of more stringent laws against witchcraft, and had eerie echoes in the American colonies. It may be that Shakespeare was tempted by the task of rendering sympathetic an egregious villain, of capturing the audience's emotions in concordant flow with a soldier that slays his commander and king, a host that betrays his trusting guest, a friend that murders his benefactor and noble friend. This is a mighty task, boldly ventured and fully accomplished; but it is not fanciful to suppose that the playwright, actor, and theatre owner, whose dramas we may sometimes date by their timely allusions, who called one of his comedies *As You Like It,* was ever ready to supply what the public wants. Was he not engaged by the Crown to write national propaganda? He had a keenly open weather eye.

Beneath any casual reference to immediate events, runs the more constant current of an age. This spirit sets a more profound, though sometimes a subtler, mark upon the artistic products than any reasoned aesthetic code or borrowed creed. The same set of literary principles that was formulated in the Renaissance was formalized for the drier age that followed. Ronsard and Du Bellay, who in the Pléiade heralded the new birth of poetry in France, set down the concepts of which France for two centuries built its literary laws.

Of the poet, they emphasized the divine inspiration, whence followed his duty to himself, to make himself worthy of his

gift, and his duty to mankind as prophet and inspired teacher; as a result of these ensued his undying fame. Surely I need not quote from the Elizabethans instances of this triune conception; Sidney's *Apology for Poetry* grows out of it; it holds over as the basis of the self-dedication of Milton: "These abilities, wheresover they are found, are the inspired gift of God . . . to imbreed and cherish in a great people the seeds of virtue and public civility, to allay the perturbations of the mind, and set the affections in right tune . . . I might relate of thousands, and their names Eternize here on earth."
Speaking in his case of a singled one, Sidney also declares

My verse your virtues rare shall eternize.

Of the poem, the Renaissance manifestoes (continuing the medieval triplifying) considered three aspects, the invention or determining of the theme, the disposition or organizing of the image and ideas, and the elocution or style. In all of these, drunk with the heady draughts of newfound beauty, they hailed the rediscovered ancients, "the classics", as true guide. Follow nature, they cried; but as a medieval monk might seek the color of the sky not in the heavens but in the holy Book, so the Renaissance enthusiast declared nature spreads forth at her truest and best in the works of Greece and Rome. It was the dashing Elizabethans that tried to revive the classical meters in English verse. Young Spenser composed hexameters "extempore, in bed"; fortunately, he did not give his daytime hours to the practice. Sidney, whose prose treatise draws from Greek examples his justification of the poet as an inspired and deathless teacher, in his verse nobly recants:

"Fool", said my Muse to me, *"Look in thy heart and write!"*

and on another occasion issues the same command in sweeter terms:

Stella behold, and then begin t' endite!

Campion, who makes the last Elizabethan stand for the clas-

THE NEO-CLASSICAL

sical forms, observing of rhyme that it is a figure and therefore, like all tropes, "sparingly to be used, lest it offend the ear with tedious affectation", Campion has given us some of the loveliest English lyrics, in spontaneous, fertile rhyme.

2. *French fashions cross the channel.*

THE Renaissance preached restraint, but practiced freedom. Shakespeare, the exuberance and spontaneity of whose plays Jonson deplores—Jonson, who loved him as much as any man, "this side idolatry"—Shakespeare showed in one play, *The Tempest,* that if he pleased he could observe the dramatic unities. In all his others, they are blithely disregarded.

On the continent, it is true, there was even from the first more measured consideration, more control, seldom such complete scorn of classical precedent and rule. But in England . . .

England! Held by the Channel and her island state from long sense of union in a holy empire; freed from such ties in a sweeping gesture of a recent king, for personal reasons; growing thus conscious both of nationalism and of individual importance, personal pride and worth—wearing her freedom like the gantlet of a knight, ready to fling in challenge . . . Grown in the glory of a Virgin Queen the greatest of all nations, sweeping the farthest seas to bring back wealth from newfound lands; from the old, culling the best in costume, speech, in costly wares and courtly ways; in colorful profusion laying it all at the feet of her whom proudly they gave their loyalty and love, who was at once the monarch of England and the symbol of freedom and virtue—truly a faerie queene!—England had little use for formulae and restrictions.

What world too vast for the island might to conquer! What wooden O too small for loftiest art!

After Elizabeth, however—for our concern is not with these lusty folk, whose drive we shall find renewed in the romantic rebellion—love lapsed to gallantry, devotion hardened to duty. Roundhead and Cavalier tore the land with turmoil. Every man watched his neighbor, watched himself. Each, for fear of persecution, sought to conform; so that down the seven-

THE NEO-CLASSICAL

teenth century there gathered an emphasis on behavior, a yearning for peace and order. By a different pathway, France even more became the demesne of manners. The Academy, in 1635, rose out of the salons; the golden king grew patron of the arts. Life, centripetal to the court, was increasingly patterned after the code of courtly etiquette; every page had his daily practice with the period's Emily Post. In literature each genre held its patent of nobility or its menial state, from His Exalted Highness the Epic and His Excellency the Drama to henchman trope and varlet vulgar tongue. England loudly echoed, through Dryden, Rymer, Pope, the rules set down in France by Malherbe, Boileau, Rapin.

Are you familiar with the poems of Denham? of Waller? Yet Dryden declared that Denham's *Cooper Hill*, for the majesty of the style, "is, and ever will be, the exact standard of good writing"; while Waller brought our poetry to its first fair growth, for "our numbers were in their nonage until Waller came."

Denham and Waller spent Cromwell's years with the exiled Stuarts in France. St. Evremond, exiled from France in 1661, was buried in Westminster Abbey. For a century, Paris set the style for its neighbors. Pope pictures a repetition of the story of Greece and Rome:

We conquered France, but felt our captive's charms,
Her arts victorious triumphed o'er our arms.

Dryden at first hailed this supremacy: "I might find in France a living Horace and Juvenal, in the person of the admirable Boileau." But in his *Essay of Dramatic Poesy* he is less enthusiastic over this prowess; we learn where the shoe pinches when he complains that his dramas are weighed in the French scales: "I find that our *chedreux* critics form their judgment wholly by them."

In 1637 the French Academy, instigated by Cardinal Richelieu, condemned Pierre Corneille for refusing to couch *Le Cid* in the Procrustean bed of the three unities. The public,

TRENDS IN LITERATURE

ignorant of these dramatic laws, crowded to the play. As Boileau declared:

> *In vain 'gainst* Le Cid *does a minister league,*
> *Paris all views Chimène with the eyes of Rodrigue.*
> *In vain as one man the Academy sneers,*
> *The obstinate public, rebellious, reveres.**

But Corneille succumbed. He grumbled a bit; he wrote a play, *Clitandre,* "obeying all the rules of the drama, but having nothing in it"; he scoffed at the "rampant trade in sighs and flames" —but he became such a tradesman. He even wrote three *Discourses* supporting the Academy views. All of France followed. In the year of the battle of *Le Cid,* Descartes published his *Discourse on Method,* which sets as the universal criteria, reason and order. Richelieu was dictator until his death in 1642, and the next year inaugurated *le grand siècle* of Louis XIV, *Le Roi Soleil.*

---

* The original of poems from other languages will be found in the Notes.

THE NEO-CLASSICAL

3. *The English behave by rule.*

THE period these men mark has been given several names: the Augustan Age, the neo-classical; terms that imply a harmony with the ancient times. No deep study is required, however, to reveal that its works approach the classical harmony from one of the four attitudes earlier indicated. Most of its writers were caught in the emphasis I have labeled B1.

"The proper study of Mankind is man"; and all was ordered, codified, made general.

It was a little too early (and much too late) for man and nature to be considered a continuum; but the individual items of existence were submerged in the typical; objects animal, vegetable, and mineral were all subjected to inviolate law.

> *All nature is but art, unknown to thee;*
> *All chance, direction which thou canst not see;*
> *All discord, harmony not understood;*
> *A partial evil, universal good.*

This feeling that all things must be in accord with law, although it permeated the period, was of course most manifest in the excesses. It is usually the second-rate, the failure, that represents its era; the successes are not of an age but for all time. In the mediocre works of the Augustan age, imagination was tamed. Its impulse would carry each man on separate flight; therefore it must be trained to walk sedately on the common ground, even though thus in danger of stopping at the commonplace. It was subdued to fancy; just as humor was threaded through that finer eye of reason which is wit.

Good nature and good sense must ever join.

Common sense and good taste—which all were assumed to recognize, however actually uncommon—were the directors of action and the judges of art. They checked exuberance as a blotch on decorum; they strove to make deeds and works not individual but typical— never to count the streaks on the tulip. Artists, like all good citizens, must conform, must be proper members of a society attuned to good form,

Where even "I hate you" was tenderly breathed.

It is in this age that the word *vulgar,* referring to what is general, common, acquired the sense of *not belonging to good society, cheap, mean.*

When writers are limited to "what oft was thought", they are likely to try to make it "ne'er so well expressed" as in their work. It is inevitable that matter shall seem less important than style, that polish shall spread its glossy surface over pretentiousness and pretense, until goodness itself is suspected of ulterior motives. That age pricks a pin through its own bubble in which the phrase "tho' learned, well-bred" needs be written—and must be followed by the further praise "and tho' well-bred, sincere."

The very forms of literature are such as have a wide, a social, appeal. In poetry the "essay", the satire, share popularity with other didactic verse and with social drama. In the coffee-houses and clubrooms where, after the separate secrecies and intense partisanships of the wars, social amenities are being observed and general themes discussed, periodicals begin to appear. The novel now first claims its ever widening public.

In France, the dictatorship of the salons drove in the same direction. "The good form of the well-bred" was there most lavishly displayed. Poetry showed a tendency to become *vers de société.* The new novel in France (like Dryden's satires over-channel, and Pope's, and Butler's *Hudibras,* and later *Gulliver*) was a *roman à clef,* with personages of the time thinly disguised as imagined or historical figures. The conversation of the salons was brilliant but far from spontaneous; the courtier practiced his effects before the glass; the wit elaborated his retorts at home, then spun the talk so that he could weave them in.

THE NEO-CLASSICAL

The ladies, as Molière shows in several of his comedies (*Les Femmes savantes, Les Précieuses ridicules*), set challenging questions so that the men might display their grandiloquence and wit. Out of these fashionable games (in our days supplanted by treasure hunts, cross-word puzzles, bridge, gin rummy, the radio quiz, and Bingo!) sprang such works as the *Maxims* of Rochefoucauld. Perhaps the first of them was a sort of guide, or text-book of salon conversation, as the first English novel, Richardson's *Pamela*, was ordered as a model for letter-writing. They spread over the cake of life a frosting of general observation and prinked epigram, so that the nibblers felt they were enjoying courtly culture.

The works of the period are rich in studies of types and manners. These are deftly delineated in the comedies that gave Molière both official and popular fame: *L'Avare, Le Misanthrope, Le Bourgeois Gentilhomme,* and the rest. In the tragedies of Racine, the most academically respected, as in truth the sole vindication of the Academy's rigid rules, the depersonalization attains its snow-clad peak. The dialogue is stripped of all adornment until it grows strong through very understatement; while the characters move with feeling less human than, as it were, the distilled essence, the emphialed but cold concentrate of passion.

The ancient *character*—a sketch of "the serving-man", "the usurer", "the bawd", and other frequent figures described as types—became a popular form, developed by La Bruyère in France, Butler in England, and many more. Countless letters, memoirs, diaries, have come to us from this period, on both sides of the Channel. They differ significantly from the later *Confessions*. The Romantics wrote of their personal feelings and their own deeds—frequently their misdeeds; but the records of their private lives were intended for public perusal. The comments of the neo-classical age were less personal, less involved in intimate emotions, more concerned with public affairs; nor were they meant to be published. The writer was setting down what he saw of his age. The comments of the Cardinal de Retz, written in 1661, were not published until 1717. Pepys' diary, begun in 1660, was brought to light at the peak of the Romantic period, in 1825. The diary of Saint-Simon was issued seventy-five years after his death. "These facts", Laurie Magnus well observes, "may be taken to illustrate both the veracity and the intimacy of the study which was devoted in the seventeenth century to material for pictures of the times. It was hidden away behind a guise of fiction, or it was dressed in antique robes, or it was distilled through satire or fable, or it was laid by on a shelf." It was an age that, wanting peace, kept watch on itself and obeyed the laws.

In France, this obedience was enforced on the grounds of good taste and decorum; in England, it was insisted on as good conduct. The French politeness overglossed the ethical aspect of art; but the British kept clear its function as education and uplifting force. Pope declared roundly that "no writing is good that does not tend to better mankind in some way or other"; and the commentators that from one another quote Dryden's remark that "delight is the chief, if not the only, end of poetry", will discover, on turning to the original, that Dryden (though often self-contradictory) was here not yielding approbation but indicating a prerequisite: "for poesy only instructs as it delights." One must always gild the philosophic pill; but its end is not the sugar.

Although *Pamela* was begun as a guide to correct correspondence, it developed a sentimentality that the French Romantics hailed; after the rhapsody of Diderot, Rousseau grew mawkish in its praises, and the Channel grew salt with the subsequent tears. The sham and falsity of *Pamela's* ethical code, in turn, on equally social mission led Fielding to fiction; but fortunately Parson Adams proved too human to be sainted by the burlesque moral hero, Pamela's brother, Joseph Andrews. And while Fielding's work may give pointers to realism, no one that surveys it all, from the early plays of his harum-scarum years, through *Amelia* to the *Proposal For the Poor,* can question the sincere social impetus that animated the life-activity of this great novelist and Justice of the Peace. Though he wrote of an unruly individual, Tom Jones, he says in Tom's pages: "The provision which we have here is no other than Human Nature."

A more questionable sincerity, that of the opportunist, the grocer of literature, Defoe, in its very truckling to current prejudice indicates the demand of the time. The most horrid crimes of hanged highwaymen, the delights and profits (counted in shopkeeper detail) of the most fortunate mistress, are dwelled upon—we are solemnly assured—by no means to thrill a public that in our day gulps from the tabloids all the news that's fit to hint, and of course not at all to ward the author from the woes of penury; but wholly as lessons, as examples and warnings, for the betterment of the public, for the social good! Even the pornography of the period, in Cleland's *Fanny Hill,* works to a final reform.

Every age, of course, has heard the author's claim that his product is of value to others than himself; but there is little in common between the personal, spiritual well-being, the widening of sympathy within the individual soul, pictured (for an instance) by Shelley, in the famous passage where he asserts that poetry enlarges the imagination, so that one more readily puts oneself in the place of others, and through this understanding becomes a better man: between this, and the Augustan social consciousness contained (for another) in Dryden's blunt dictum that poetry must resemble natural truth, but it must *be* ethical. The one suggests a deep-working, personal exaltation; the other demands a lesson all may together learn.

4. *One device may serve two desires.*

EVERY age follows Nature; every age seeks the truth. What changes is not the desire but the definition. But the necessity under which some critics seem to have labored, of referring to "romantic" elements in *Clarissa Harlowe* (from which Rousseau developed the theme of *La Nouvelle Heloïse*), to "realistic" details in *Robinson Crusoe,* further suggests that, in applying these terms, incidental aspects have been taken for essential.

We expect to find that the Augustan age deals largely in general terms and abstractions; against this practice the Romantics rebelled, and sought the particular, the concrete. Thus the painter Reynolds wrote: "Perfect form is produced by leaving out particulars and retaining only general ideas"; on the margin of this observation the poet Blake pressed his pencil hard: "To generalize is to be an idiot; to particularize is the great distinction of merit." Yet this generalization of Blake's is not the only one a Romantic ventured. And Diderot demanded in poetry something outlandish, barbaric, wild; he protested that clarity weakens enthusiasm, he urged artists to be shadowy, to speak endlessly of immensity, infinity, eternity. This advice certainly opposed the earlier clarity, but hardly joined the current cry for the concrete.

Thus among the Romantics two contrary tendencies were aroused. Against Buffon and others that had sacrificed the local to the most general, losing the trees in the mass of the forest, came the cry for more color, for detailed exactitude. The minuteness of observation in Keats sets a hard example.

"Now what color", queries the farmer in *Cranford*, "are ash-buds in March?" Scarcely waiting for the "I don't know," he continues: "I knew you didn't. No more did I—an old fool that I am—till this young man comes and tells me. Black as the ash-buds in March. And I've lived all my life in the country; more shame for me not to know." The young man was Tennyson; and some see in his quest of accuracy of detail a revolt from the earlier Romantics. It is really but a continuance of their exact recordings, as in Keats. Wordsworth and Blake, however, manifest the other development, which, revolting from the previous matter-of-fact and objective attitude, exalted a personal feeling that at times became a vague emotionalism, a "cosmic" rather than a concrete expression. Exactitude or mistiness, the intimately familiar or the exotically remote: each may characterize the Romantic; none is at its core.

It is true that pompous generalization can hardly surpass the temerity of Johnson's transmogrifying of "Go to the ant, thou sluggard":

> *Turn on the prudent ant thy heedless eyes,*
> *Observe her labours, sluggard, and be wise.*
> *No stern command, no monitory voice,*
> *Prescribes her duties, nor directs her choice;*
> *Yet, timely provident, she hastes away*
> *To snatch the blessings of a plenteous day;*
> *When fruitful summer loads the teeming plain*
> *She crops the harvest and she stores the grain.*
> *How long shall sloth usurp thy useless hours,*
> *Unnerve thy vigor, and enchain thy powers?*
> *While artful shades thy downy couch enclose,*
> *And soft solicitation courts repose,*
> *Amidst the drowsy charms of dull delight*
> *Year chases year with unremitted flight,*
> *Till want now following, fraudulent and slow,*
> *Shall spring to seize thee, like an ambushed foe.*

Yet even this is no more abstract than the mystical fervencies of Blake. These range, indeed, from the creation of allegorical figures, whose descriptions are concretely detailed though their meaning remains an abstraction, to a mingling of metaphysics and moonshine incomprehensible:

> Does the eagle know what is in the pit?
> Or wilt thou go ask the Mole?
> Can wisdom be put in a silver rod?
> Or love in a golden bowl?

Here is a simple quatrain; there is less immediate understanding of such a passage (which might be culled most anywhere outside the *Songs*) as this from *Europe*:

> Enitharmon slept
> Eighteen hundred years. Man was a dream!
> The night of Nature and their harps unstrung!
> She slept in middle of her nightly song
> Eighteen hundred years, a female dream.
> Shadows of men in fleeting bands upon the winds
> Divide the heavens of Europe
> Till Albion's Angel, smitten with his own plagues, fled with his bands.
> The cloud bears hard on Albion's shore,
> Fill'd with immortal demons of futurity:
> In council gather the smitten angels of Albion;
> The cloud bears hard upon the council house, down rushing
> On the heads of Albion's angels.

And far beyond Wordsworth's philosophical stirrings pour Blake's verbal torrents, in great cascades throughout his poems, as in these lines from *Milton*:

> Within laboring, beholding without, from Particulars to Generals
> Subduing his Spectre, they builded the Looms of Generation;
> They builded great Golgonooza Times on Times, Ages on Ages.
> First Orc was Born, then the Shadowy Female: then all Los's family.

THE NEO-CLASSICAL

*At last Enitharmon brought forth Satan, Refusing Form in vain,
The Miller of Eternity made subservient to the Greater Harvest
That he may go to his own Place, Prince of the Starry Wheels
Beneath the Plow of Rintah & the Harrow of the Almighty
In the hands of Palamabron, Where the Starry Mills of Satan
Are built beneath the Earth & Waters of the Mundane Shell:
Here the Three Classes of Men take their Sexual texture, Woven;
The Sexual is Threefold, the Human is Fourfold.*

These examples should make it clear that general terms are no exclusive property of the "classical" age of modern literature. On the other hand, simplicity and directness do not depend upon "Romantic" concreteness. It is the "classical" Boileau that speaks of a sublimity "found often in the simplest words, in the very simplicity of which the sublimity resides." Racine in France and Pope in England—to mention verse only —give us, if not sublimity both, a simplicity effective as that of Wordsworth. Indeed, though both before and after Wordsworth polite folks might refer to a leg as a limb, he himself teaches us that calling a spade a spade, while it may invariably avoid circumlocution, does not infallibly produce art. Has he not written many lines like these?:

*The lamb, while from her hand he thus his supper took,
Seemed to feast with head and ears; and his tail with
　　pleasure shook.
"Drink, pretty creature, drink", she said in such a tone
That I almost received her heart into my own.*

*'Twas little Barbara Lewthwaite, a child of beauty rare!
I watched them with delight, they were a lovely pair.
Now with her empty can the Maiden turned away;
But ere ten yards were gone her footsteps did she stay...*

As the indirect may approach the inconclusive, the simple may verge upon the simpleton. At their best, they are both valid— and to be found in all ages.

[45]

TRENDS IN LITERATURE

From the Augustans I need not adduce instances of the general in diction, as this marks the predominant spirit of the time; though I shall mention Dryden's *A Song For St. Cecilia's Day*, 1687, because its theme is equally illustrative of the age's emphasis:

> *From Harmony, from heavenly harmony,*
> *This universal frame began:*
> *When nature underneath a heap*
> *Of jarring atoms lay,*
> *And could not heave her head,*
> *The tuneful voice was heard from high,*
> *"Arise, ye more than dead!"*
> *Then cold, and hot, and moist, and dry,*
> *In order to their stations leap,*
> *And Music's power obey.*
> *From harmony, from heavenly harmony,*
> *This universal frame began:*
> *From harmony to harmony*
> *Through all the compass of the notes it ran,*
> *The diapason closing full in Man.*

Yet Dryden elsewhere can be as simple as any Romantic, as in the song from *The Maiden Queen* "I feed a flame within", and in the *Song of the River Thames*:

> *Old Father Ocean calls my tide:*
> *Come away, come away,*
> *The barks upon the billows ride,*
> *The master will not stay;*
> *The merry boatswain from his side*
> *His whistle takes, to check and chide*
> *The lingering lads' delay,*
> *And all the crew aloud has cried,*
> *Come away, come away.*

Defoe comes from his customary prose, detailed as a stock-taking, to give us lines as direct as:

[46]

THE NEO-CLASSICAL

> *Whenever God erects a House of Prayer,*
> *The Devil always builds a Chapel there;*
> *And 'twill be found, upon examination,*
> *The latter has the largest congregation.*

Swift shows that he can be simple and concrete, in such poems as *On Stella's Birth-Day* and *On the Death of Dr. Swift*. Pope, too, frequently achieves a directness, and not only in the savage satires; as when he asks:

> *Is there no bright reversion in the sky*
> *For those who greatly think, or bravely die?*

or

> *O Grave! Where is thy victory?*
> *O Death! Where is thy sting?*

(though he borrows this from the *New Testament*) and as when he declares:

> *Happy the man, whose wish and care*
> *A few paternal acres bound,*
> *Content to breathe his native air*
> *In his own ground.*

or speaks of Him

> *Who sees with equal eye, as God of all,*
> *A hero perish, or a sparrow fall,*
> *Atoms or systems into ruin hurl'd,*
> *And now a bubble burst, and now a world.*

This last quotation illustrates the device of antithesis, a favorite among the Augustans for its balance of wit, and among the Romantics for its stark juxtaposition of strong contrasts.

The early nineteenth century did, of course, pay more attention to concrete particulars than the age of Pope and Johnson. Among the writers of the between-time is Thomas Gray. His notes and drawings in his copy of Linnaeus reveal his bent as a naturalist, along the trail to Darwin. His *Elegy In A*

Country Churchyard is as general in its theme as any Augustan would require, and rich in abstractions:

> Let not Ambition mock their useful toil . . .

> The Boast of heraldry, the pomp of Pow'r
> And all that beauty, all that wealth e'er gave,
> Awaits alike th' inevitable hour:
> The paths of glory lead but to the grave . . .

Within the same poem, however, are details more frequent after than before:

> Oft have we seen him at the Peep of Dawn
> Brushing with hasty steps the Dews away
> To meet the sun upon the upland Lawn;

> There at the foot of yonder nodding beech
> That wreathes its old fantastic roots so high,
> His listless length at noontide would he stretch
> And pore upon the brook that babbles by.

> There scattered oft the earliest of the year
> By hands unseen are showers of violets found;
> The redbreast loves to build and warble there,
> And little footsteps lightly print the ground . . .

The last quoted stanza was ultimately discarded by Gray; but Wordsworth knew no such reticence, as one of the *Lucy* poems will serve to indicate:

> Three years she grew in sun and shower;
> Then Nature said, "A lovelier flower
> On earth was never sown;
> This child I to myself will take,
> She shall be mine, and I will make
> A lady of my own.

> "Myself will to my darling be
> Both law and impulse: and with me

THE NEO-CLASSICAL

> *The girl, in rock and plain,*
> *In earth and heaven, in glade and bower,*
> *Shall feel an overseeing power*
> *To kindle or restrain . . ."*

For four more stanzas, Nature tells of her precious plans for the darling girl. And where is the concrete particularity in these lines of the sonnet on *Mutability*?:

> *From low to high doth dissolution climb,*
> *And sink from high and low, along a scale*
> *Of awful notes, whose concord shall not fail;*
> *A musical but melancholy chime*
> *Which they can hear who meddle not with crime,*
> *Nor avarice, nor over-anxious care . . .*

Where, in his own song *To Spring*, are the particulars Blake so loudly acclaimed?:

> *The hills tell one another, and the listening*
> *Valleys hear; all our longing eyes are turn'd*
> *Up to thy bright pavilions: issue forth*
> *And let thy holy feet visit our Clime!*
>
> *Come o'er the eastern hills, and let our winds*
> *Kiss thy perfumed garments; let us taste*
> *Thy morn and evening breath; scatter thy pearls*
> *Upon our lovesick land that mourns for thee.*

In the very midst of the classical allusions of *Endymion*, on the other hand, Keats paints a sure picture:

> *Within his car, aloft, young Bacchus stood,*
> *Trifling his ivy-dart, in dancing mood,*
> *With sidelong laughing;*
> *And little rills of crimson wine imbrued*
> *His plump white arms and shoulders, enough white*
> *For Venus' pearly bite,*
> *And near him rode Silenus on his ass,*

> *Pelted with flowers as he on did pass*
> *Tipsily quaffing.*

And when, indulging (a favorite practice of the Romantics) in one of the devices they condemned in their predecessors, Keats personifies the season of mists and mellow fruitfulness, he does not leave it a mere capitalized abstraction, but through the five senses gives it life:

> *Who hath not seen thee oft amid thy store?*
> *Sometimes whoever seeks abroad may find*
> *Thee sitting careless on a granary floor,*
> *Thy hair soft-lifted by the winnowing wind,*
> *Or on a half-reap'd furrow sound asleep,*
> *Drowsed with the fume of poppies, while thy hook*
> *Spares the next swath and all its twined flowers;*
> *And sometimes like a gleaner thou dost keep*
> *Steady thy laden head across a brook;*
> *Or by a cider-press, with patient look,*
> *Thou watchest the last oozings hours by hours.*

Not merely in each age can the simple and the abstruse, the direct and the circumlocute, be found. Within the works of the one man who has given us the most effective and straightforward poetry, at an emotional peak soaring with simplicity—Lear's recovery and reconciliation with Cordelia; Hamlet's words with his mother; Macbeth's, at news that his Lady has died; Ophelia's wanderings: from all sorts and conditions of character they crowd too full for quoting—we have also such varied indirections as Bassanio's words before borrowing:

> *'Tis not unknown to you, Antonio,*
> *How much I have disabled mine estate*
> *By something showing a more swelling port*
> *Then my faint means would grant continuance*

and the grimmer words of Othello, after the simple pathos of his grief:

> And say, besides,—that in Aleppo once,
> Where a malignant and a turban'd Turk
> Beat a Venetian, and traduc'd the state,
> I took by the throat the circumcisèd dog,
> And smote him—thus!

as he kills himself. Nay, is not even the harmonious blending of such opposites in one passage, in a single line, his frequent triumph! called by Sir Arthur Quiller-Couch, in connection with

> the sincerest, most poignant line in *As You Like It*:
> And unregarded age in corners thrown

an exquisite instance of Shakespeare's habitual stroke! with which the general idea, 'unregarded age' is no sooner presented than (as it were) he stabs the concrete into it, drawing blood: "unregarded age *in corners thrown*."

If it be objected that a botcher may quote Shakespeare to his purpose, I summon Laughter holding both his sides. For in truth the wise and concordant use of varied diction is at the command of every artist; not even Shakespeare has surpassed in their effect—though in variety and profusion of such displayed power beyond compare!—moments of the young Romantic we have already hearkened:

> *Thou was not born for death, immortal bird!*
> *No hungry generations tread thee down;*
> *The voice I hear this passing night was heard*
> *In ancient days by emperor and clown:*
> *Perhaps the self-same song that found a path*
> *Through the sad heart of Ruth, when, sick for home,*
> *She stood in tears amid the alien corn;*
> *The same that ofttimes hath*
> *Charm'd magic casements, opening on the foam*
> *Of perilous seas, in faery lands forlorn.*

A scheduled speaker, on a recent occasion, after the toastmaster's pleasing words, rose with solemn mien, and in half-audible whisper voiced hoarse regrets: "I had hoped to have the pleasure of addressing this distinguished company on the significant topic our chairman has announced, and to make my minor suggestions toward a solution of our time's most grievous problem. Unfortunately, during the late War, my left lung was affected in the manner now distressing us all . . ." and to the discomfited audience, from the hardly heard hoarseness—sudden thunder of reassurance: "BUT MY RIGHT LUNG!" . . . Too often, in considering an age, we pay most heed to the tones that have been touched by the "late war", the ailments and afflictions and conflicts of the time, to the signs of its idiosyncrasy, to its affected lung. We forget that, in the realms of gold, if not all accents are loud and clear, all are attuned to their theme. The artists of the Augustan age used the forms most expressive of their spirit; when the rebelling Romantics dubbed the Augustan diction abstract and cold, they were (beyond a legitimate protest against failures) really calling attention to the fact that common sense does not speak with the tongue of personal passion.

It might be suggested that the Augustans reasoned clearly through the use of general terms, whereas the crowding concrete particulars of the Romantics helped to conceal, at least from themselves, a vagueness of thought. Except that some of these writers deliberately set out to be vague. On the other hand, some in the same period—sometimes the same men in other mood—tried to pin the particular image with the precise concrete expression. It might be more fruitful to admit that both ages could be simple and clear when they desired; it is not the device, but the purpose for which they employed it, that marks their difference.

Critics that select a single manifestation as basically or essentially Romantic have often had to warn us that in other respects the writers exhibit the widest divergencies. That these

THE NEO-CLASSICAL

exist is quite evident; therefore, they should fit into a coherent pattern.

> *'Tis hard to say, if greater want of skill*
> *Appear in writing or in judging ill;*
> *But, of the two, less dang'rous is th' offence*
> *To tire our patience, than mislead our sense.*

Alas, often the critics combine these errors! There is room in each age for variation, for variety; it was Wordsworth's self-set task to equate poetic diction with that of prose; Hugo's, to enrich the language of verse; Coleridge's, to bring down wonder with the word.

5. *Life bows to law.*

THE Augustan era is often called the age of convention. This obedience, however, results from the emphasis on the representative, the general rule, on mankind rather than on individual men. It is important to keep in mind that this pressure is not merely, not primarily, aesthetic. Propriety, precedent, common sense, law, were the ultimate reference of the statesman, the lady of society, the scientist, the philosopher. The iron rule of determinism was finding its sway among thinkers—its wider infuence to seep upon a later time—while common sense sufficed to unite all intelligent citizens. The high priest of this faith, Samuel Johnson, neatly disposed of idealism by rapping his knuckles; the wits of the day found a choice tid-bit in the learned lexicographer's warning, to a· departing Berkeleyan, that he'd better stay, for the company might stop thinking about him, and then he'd cease to exist.

What philosophy was justifying, business banked on, politics practiced, science studied, and society observed. These forces and emphases of any period, sprung from the general conditions of the time, color all its activity, and thus find expression—bud, flower, grow rank, and fall to seed—in the arts.

All art achieves, in some way and measure, the classical harmony, the expression of unity in variety. The art of the Augustan age approaches the wire of the broomstick, not from the end of the many wisps, but along the sustaining staff of general law.

THE ROMANTIC REBELLION

THE ROMANTIC REBELLION

1. Laws invite their breaking.

GOETHE, who early wrote *The Sorrows Of Young Werther* and cried "Feeling is all", came later to deplore the fact that the English do not hearken to reason, but are of imagination all compact; he saw then that

> *Over every hilltop peace abides.*
> *Imagination, in its farthest flight,*
> *Exerts itself, but never tops the height.*
> *Yet minds that dare explore the secrets soundless,*
> *In boundless things possess a faith that's boundless.*

In Goethe indeed, as we shall see, all the pressures of the age at times are urging: from a sentimental Romanticism that produced suicide-pacts (in which he fortunately took no active part) he oversteps the border to realism, comes to observe the need of balance and, while pointing toward the symbolism ahead, moves grandly in the classical calm.

Despite Goethe's summing up of the age, and notwithstanding the long persistence of Hugo, the French look upon Romanticism as another German invasion. Mme. de Staël brought back across the border more than Voltaire and Rousseau had carried off. The reasoned defence and philosophical background of Romanticism are Germanic, Hegel describing it as the triumph of spirit over matter. We are told, at the same time, that in Germany the Romantic rebellion was mainly philosophical; in France, political; and in England, social. Which is at least a sound reminder that it was never purely aesthetical.

It is beyond the scope of this volume to present a history of European civilization, but it needs no reference to such a tome to reawaken in the reader's mind the turmoil of the world toward the dawn and in the early years of the nineteenth century. With the Renaissance had sprung an arousal of personality, a sense of individual right and power. Practice was free, though theory was binding. Those ties, however, became firm through the next hundred and fifty years, with logically convincing and physically potent rule. Long chafing in such bondage, life in a sudden rush renewed its effort to shake off all yokes. Reason? The last refuge of a barren mind! Convention, rule? Enchaining devices of city and court, far from the truth and the beauty of nature; frigid schemes of an empty heart! This is new birth: start the calendar anew! France, which carries all processes to their logical extreme, began (three centuries late) counting time for a fresh start.

In philosophy the support of this attitude grew more firm. Idealism, which Dr. Johnson had smugly snapped away, proved phoenix among the people, and spread great wing. It taught that man may create himself in the image of his dream, that destiny is mere butter when the carving hero comes, that a free will—breaking the chains Rousseau saw on every child of society—might make of the wilderness we call civilization the happy garden of Adam's innocence. The limits to human destiny were beyond the mountains of dream.

Less exaggerate than popular misconceptions, the sciences shifted with the new emphasis. Study turned from physics and mathematics, which had dealt in abstractions and universals, to geology and biology. These did double duty in the new causes; for they demand many and reiterated observations of individual phenomena; and they began to disclose alarming facts about the age of the world, and otherwise to upset tradition and supposedly predestinate law. From an eighteenth century that saw Nature as orderly and reasonable, the nineteenth century turned to a world governed by the "law of the jungle" and progressing through the "survival of the fittest."

Invention also involves an upsetting of precedent. And with the introduction of machines, young folk grew self-asser-

THE ROMANTIC REBELLION

tive enough to desert their villages, however lovely, to escape the occupation their father had accepted from a long line before him, and go to town "on their own". Young idealists died—or, worse, made fools of themselves—for freedom, ethical, social, political. In aspects beyond need or power of present telling, this was a time of emphasis upon the individual, with sublime confidence in the supreme will of an earnest and dedicate man. Men were aquiver against gravity, atug to lift themselves by their own bootstraps.

2. *Nature is behind us all.*

AMONG the signposts labeled Romanticism it is hard to choose. Many of the critical markers would lead us into blind alleys. Most of them point toward that wide word Nature: did not Rousseau almost persuade his fellows to walk on all fours! Back to nature, then, let us go.

As we start, do we not catch a familiar note in that verdant call? Have we not in our own days heard summons to the simple life, and the wayside songs of the *Wandervögel,* and rhapsodies over the innocent romps of the nudists under the sky! Did not the Augustans themselves turn for guidance to Mother Nature, for refreshing and strengthening after the blunders and perversions of the age before? And did not those predecessors likewise seek sustenance at the bosom of Mother Earth? Are not all men Antaean? Mother Cary's chickens are a ubiquitous brood.

But to the Augustans, you remind me, Nature appeared as the established order of things, discerned by Reason: nature is "common sense reduced to its principles". Let us see, then, what Nature was to the Romantic.

The Romantic took nature, you may respond, as he found it. He went forth into the fields; he lay like a country boy on sunny banks, watching through rustling leaves the drift of snow-piled clouds, and in rippling streams the flicker of sporting fish.

> *I stood tiptoe upon a little hill,*
> *The air was cooling, and so very still*
> *That the sweet buds which with a modest pride*
> *Pull droopingly, in slanting curve aside,*
> *Their scantly leav'd, and finely tapering stems,*
> *Had not yet lost those starry diadems*
> *Caught from the early sobbing of the morn.*

THE ROMANTIC REBELLION

> *The clouds were pure and white as flocks new shorn,*
> *And fresh from the clear brook; sweetly they slept*
> *On the blue fields of heaven, and then there crept*
> *A little noiseless noise among the leaves,*
> *Born of the very sigh that silence heaves:*
> *For not the faintest motion could be seen*
> *Of all the shades that slanted o'er the green.*
> *There was wide wand'ring for the greediest eye,*
> *To peer about upon variety;*
> *Far round the horizon's crystal air to skim,*
> *And trace the dwindled edgings of its brim;*
> *To picture out the quaint and curious bending*
> *Of a fresh woodland alley, never ending;*
> *Or by the bowery clefts and leafy shelves,*
> *Guess where the jaunty streams refresh themselves.*
> *I gazed awhile, and felt as light, and free*
> *As though the fanning wings of Mercury*
> *Had played upon my heels: I was light-hearted,*
> *And many pleasures to my vision started:*
> *So I straightway began to pluck a posey*
> *Of luxuries bright, milky, soft and rosy.*

He tramped over mountain passes, he lived in the Lake Country. He—I interrupt to point out that the word just mentioned is being overpassed, being forgotten (as never by the Romantic) in nature: in this pretty picture, we have said, the Romantic took nature as *he* found it. No one else's nature; his own, each Romantic's. His vision colored what he saw; nature became the background of this vision. She held out her arms to the poet:

> *The poet goes forth in the fields; he admires,*
> *He adores, he hearkens to a lyre within himself;*
> *And seeing him come the flowers, all the flowers,*
> *Those beside which the ruby's colors are pale,*
> *Those that eclipse the very peacock's tail,*
> *The little golden flowers, the flowers of blue,*

> *Assume, while shaking a welcome with their bouquets,*
> *Little intimate ways or grand coquettish airs,*
> *And familiarly, because that well becomes the beauties:*
> *Look! they say; it's our lover going by.*

Thus Hugo in France; but the English were no less drawn:

> *It was no marvel—from my very birth*
> *My soul was drunk with love—which did pervade*
> *And mingle with whate'er I saw on earth.*
> *Of objects all inanimate I made*
> *Idols, and out of wild and lonely flowers*
> *And rocks, whereby they grew, a paradise.*

Which, by the way, is not Wordsworth, but Byron.

Nature was a great reservoir from which the individual might draw simplicity, freedom, assurance of well-being, some fresh lilt of that primordial golden age from which men had draggled their hours to dross.

> *My heart leaps up when I behold*
> *A rainbow in the sky . . .*

> *Earth, Ocean, Air, beloved brotherhood!*
> *If our great Mother has imbued my soul*
> *With aught of natural piety to feel*
> *Your love, and recompense the boon with mine,*
> *If dewy morn, and odorous noon, and even,*
> *With sunset and its gorgeous ministers,*
> *And solemn midnight's tingling silentness;*
> *If autumn's hollow sighs in the sere wood,*
> *And winter robing with pure snow and crowns*
> *Of starry ice the gray grass and bare boughs;*
> *If spring's voluptuous paintings when she breathes*
> *Her first sweet kisses—have been dear to me;*
> *If no bright bird, insect, or gentle beast*
> *I consciously have injured, but still loved*
> *And cherished these my kindred; then forgive*

THE ROMANTIC REBELLION

> *This boast, beloved brethren, and withdraw*
> *No portion of your wonted favor now!*

Nature was at the service of man, benevolent, waiting, subordinate to his desire, responding to his moods, or offering gentle solace, or at least consolatory difference, from his overladen drudging with his fellows.

> *For oft, when on my couch I lie*
> *In vacant or in pensive mood,*
> *They flash upon that inward eye*
> *Which is the bliss of solitude;*
> *And then my heart with pleasure fills*
> *And dances with the daffodils.*
>
> *Thus, nature! shelter of each living thing!*
> *Universal mother! Indulgent nature! Thus,*
> *Together all of us, maternal and mystic,*
> *Seek shelter and sustenance beneath thy eternal flanks,*
> *There we are, wise ones, poets, all pell-mell,*
> *Clinging on every side to your potent breast!*

"Nature is an aeolian harp," said Novalis, "a musical instrument whose tones are keys of higher things within us ... He that is unhappy in this world, he that does not find what he is seeking, should go into Nature and live in that temple of a better world."

From nature the Romanticist sucked personal sustenance for his spirit, awing toward the rarer heights of freedom. Thus Shelley in his impassioned plea to the West Wind cried out

> *Make me thy lyre, even as the forest is:*
> *What if my leaves are falling like its own!*
> *The tumult of thy mighty harmonies*
> *Will take from both a deep, autumnal tone,*
> *Sweet thought in sadness. Be thou, Spirit fierce,*
> *My spirit! Be thou me, impetuous one!*

From nature the artist drew figures for his thoughts, symbols, hooks to draw out Leviathan from the brooding waters of his soul.

> *Flowers are lovely! Love is flower-like,*
> *Friendship is a sheltering tree.*

This choice bit is from Coleridge; but Hugo, conversely, pictures the Mexican volcano that, in disgust at their cruelty, spits lava upon the officials of the Inquisition. Equally violent though more Romantically personal, if not pathological, George Sand sets in her diary, after her break with Alfred de Musset, these overwrought words: "Farewell, blond locks, white shoulders, farewell whatever was mine and of me beloved. On warm nights I shall call your name and go embracing the trees and rocks of nature, to faint on the cold ground after my desire has been appeased." This seems almost the Romantic bravado-erotico version of the threat to go into the garden and eat worms!

Nature, thus considered, is inevitably personified. She is wrapped in a human garment which Ruskin denounces as the "pathetic fallacy", and which Francis Thompson later implicitly drapes while he derides:

> You speak and you think that she answers you. It
> is the echo of your own voice. You think you hear the
> throbbing of her heart, and it is the throbbing of your
> own. I do not believe Nature has a heart; and I suspect
> that, like many another beauty, she has been credited
> with a heart because of her face.

Rarely do the Romantics write a lyric of nature's moods and moments without a closing human application: Burns' *To a Louse* and *To a Mouse*, Wordsworth's *Skylark*:

> *Type of the wise, that soar, but never roam,*
> *True to the kindred points of heaven and home.*

Shelley's *To a Skylark* as well, in several more personal stanzas; most of the lyrics of the time are thus subjective. The poet is not always in harmony with the natural scene he summons:

THE ROMANTIC REBELLION

> *For this, for everything, we are out of tune—*

for to the Romantic the world was a screen on which, by harmonies or balanced play of contrasts, the movements of the ego were dramatized and enlarged. The French—to glance across for another moment—illustrate any of these attitudes as well as the English. Lamartine turns from a description of natural beauty with the words:

> *But to these sweet beauties my indifferent soul . . .*

Hugo laments:

> *Consider! It's in vain that here we love each other!*
> *Naught will be left us of these flowered slopes*
> *Where in our mutual fires our souls have fused!*
> *Impassive nature has already reclaimed it all.*

And if at times, in spells of utter loneliness or bleak despair, when the individual knew himself most isolate from other men, he felt drawn closely to the bosom of nature until his heart pulsed with her own and he grew one with her, it was always an individual flight into harmony, a mystic and therefore incommunicable communion:

> *. . . when first*
> *I came among these hills; when like a roe*
> *I bounded o'er the mountains, by the sides*
> *Of the deep rivers, and the lonely streams,*
> *Wherever nature led: more like a man*
> *Flying from something that he dreads, than one*
> *Who sought the thing he loved. For nature then*
> *(The coarser pleasures of my boyish days,*
> *And their glad animal movements, all gone by)*
> *To me was all in all.—I cannot paint*
> *What then I was. The sounding cataract*
> *Haunted me like a passion; the tall rock,*
> *The mountain, and the deep and gloomy wood,*
> *Their colors and their forms, were then to me*

*An appetite; a feeling and a love,
That had no need of a remoter charm,
By thought supplied, nor any interest
Unborrowed from the eye.—That time is past,
And all its aching joys are now no more,
And all its dizzy raptures. Not for this
Faint I, nor mourn nor murmur; other gifts
Have followed; for such loss, I would believe,
Abundant recompense. For I have learned
To look on nature, not as in the hour
Of thoughtless youth; but hearing oftentimes
The still, sad music of humanity,
Nor harsh nor grating, though of ample power
To chasten and subdue. And I have felt
A presence that disturbs me with the joy
Of elevated thoughts; a sense sublime
Of something far more deeply interfused,
Whose dwelling is the light of setting suns,
And the round ocean and the living air,
And the blue sky, and in the midst of man;
A motion and a spirit, that impels
All thinking things, all objects of all thought,
And rolls through all things. Therefore am I still
A lover of the meadows and the woods,
And mountains; and of all that we behold
From this green earth; of all the mighty world
Of eye, and ear,—both what they half create,
And what perceive; well pleased to recognize
In nature and the language of the sense,
The anchor of my purest thoughts, the nurse,
The guide, the guardian of my heart, and soul
Of all my moral being.*

Most of the time, however, most of the Romantics were "too much with" this unintelligible world, from the pleasures and boredom of which nature—here meaning the countryside,

THE ROMANTIC REBELLION

the absence of city and society—holds hope of freedom and quiet and peace and restoration.

The approval of nature is no less vehement in prose. Schelling, one of the German leaders of Romanticism, forced thought to turn upon the question when he declared that the essence of reality is not material things but intellectual doings. Diderot in France more directly exclaimed: "Has a man genius? he leaves the city and its inhabitants. He loves, wherever his heart inclines, to mingle his tears with the crystal of the fountains ... to stir with light foot the meadow grass; to cross, slow-paced, through fertile countrysides; to watch the work of man; to flee to the depths of the forest. He loves its secret horror ... O Nature, all that is good is harbored in your breast!" From England, let us read just the passage from Leigh Hunt selected for praise by Hazlitt:

> From previous illness and constant excitation my fancy was sickened into a kind of hypochondriachal investment and shaping of things about me. A little more, and I might have imagined the fantastic shapes which the sea is constantly interweaving out of the foam at the vessel's side, to be sea-snakes or more frightful hieroglyphics. The white clothes that hung up on the pegs in the cabin took, in the gloomy light from above, an aspect of things of meaning; and the winds and the rain together, as they ran blind and howling along the vessel's side, when I was on deck, appeared like frantic spirits of the air, chasing and shrieking after one another, and tearing each other by the hair of their heads. " The grandeur of the glooms" on the Atlantic was majestic indeed: the healthiest eye would have seen them with awe. The sun rose in the morning, at once fiery and sicklied over; a livid gleam on the water, like the reflection of lead; then the storms would recommence; and during partial clearings off, the clouds and fogs appeared standing in the sky, moulded into gigantic shapes,

like antediluvian wonders, or visitants from the zodiac, —mammoths, vaster than have yet been thought of; the first ungainly and stupendous ideas of bodies and legs, looking out on an unfinished world . . .

What a crowd of thoughts face one on entering the Mediterranean! Grand as the sensation is, in passing through the classical and romantic memories of the sea off the Western coast of the Peninsula, it is little compared to this. Countless generations of the human race, from three quarters of the world, with all the religions and the mythologies, and the genius, and the wonderful deeds, good and bad, that have occupied almost the whole attention of mankind, look you in the face from the galleries of that ocean-floor, rising one above another till the tops are lost in heaven. The water at your feet is the same water that bathes the shores of Europe, of Africa, and of Asia,—of Italy, of Greece, and the Holy Land, and the lands of chivalry and romance, and pastoral Sicily, and the Pyramids, and old Crete, and the Arabian city of Al Cairo, glittering in the magic lustre of the Thousand and One Nights. This soft air in your face comes from the grove of "Daphne by Orontes", these lucid waters, that part before you like oil, are the same from which Venus rose, pressing them out of her hair. In that quarter Vulcan fell—

Dropt from the zenith like a falling star:

and there is Circe's island and Calypso's, and the promontory of Plato, and Ulysses wandering, and Cymon and Miltiades fighting, and Regulus crossing the sea to Carthage, and

Damasco, and Morocco, and Trebisond:
And whom Biserta sent from Afric shore,
When Charlemagne with all his peerage fell,
By Fontarabia.

THE ROMANTIC REBELLION

The mind hardly separates truth from fiction in thinking of all these things, nor does it wish to do so. Fiction is truth in another shape, and gives as close embraces. You may shut a door upon a ruby, and render it of no collour: but the colour shall not be the less enchanting for that, when the sun, the poet of the world, touches it with his golden pen. What we glow at, and shed tears over, is as real as love and pity . . .

And who knows not Orlando, and all the hard blows he gave, and the harder blow than all, given him by two happy lovers; and the lovers themselves, the representatives of all the young love that ever was? I had a grudge of my own against Angelica, looking upon myself as jilted by those fine eyes which the painter has given her in the English picture; for I took her for a more sentimental person: but I excused her, seeing her beset and tormented by all those very meritorious knights, who thought they earned a right to her by hacking and hewing; and I more than pardoned her when I found that Medoro, besides being young and handsome, was a friend and a devoted follower. But what of that? They were both young and handsome; and love, at that time of life, goes upon no other merits—taking all the rest upon trust in the generosity of its wealth, and as willing to bestow a throne as a ribbon, to show the all-sufficiency of its contentment. Fair speed your sails over the lucid waters, ye lovers, on a love-like sea!—Fair speed them, yet never land; for where the poet has left you, there ought ye, as ye are, to be living for ever—for ever gliding about a summer sea, touching at its flowery islands, and reposing beneath its moon.

The natural scene inevitably summons the human association, the human emotion; the beauty is background to the story. "Scenery is fine", said Keats, "but human nature is finer—the sward is richer for the tread of a . . . nervous

[69]

English foot—the Eagle's nest is finer, for the Mountaineer has looked into it." It is not merely artless, it is less truly nature, without the *homo additus!*

Everything is in nature and therefore natural, Anatole France remarked; but we may hardly use his epigram to unify the activity of all the ages. City dwellers must absorb nature in park and picnics, in occasional week-end trips on arranged bicycle or ski trains. But such jauntings, and colonies and cults —from Fontainebleau to the dude ranch—merely emphasize the fact that communion with nature is an individual experience. The one way to enjoy nature is alone. An orchestra becomes a background as soon as one person sings. A single companion, however beloved, however silent—even though congenial as to Wordsworth the woman he calls Sister—brings humanity at once to the fore, makes the surroundings but the setting. Only when forth alone, may one banish crowding thoughts of many persons—or pervasive sense of one—or the else ubiquitous glimmer of oneself—and in pure feeling lose consciousness of the desire to feel: for it must come unsought: an act of grace, as it is beyond reason and ineffable: a mystic union, inexpressible save through the more-than-sense of art— and be at one with nature. For this communion most of us, surely most of the Romantics, are too self-conscious.

This does not prevent any man from indulging in nature-worship. Pantheistic strains, as well as mystic visions, may, of course, be found in the great nature poets. Goethe in one mood declares that only by losing oneself in the infinite does one find oneself. Schelling speaks of the World-soul, that fills the bosom of nature and of man. Such a linked harmony, akin to the later unanimism, wells in Wordsworth, a sense sublime of something far more deeply interfused; yet even to him nature remains an instrument for man's growing, a background, a place of recreation and re-creation, whence he continues to listen to the still, sad music of humanity. He seeks nature the better to hear those human strains. Man himself remains the peak and purpose of it all.

THE ROMANTIC REBELLION

In truth, although Wordsworth waxes grandiloquent about mankind, he is more closely preoccupied with his own senses and feelings. For a short period, with Godwin, the poet exalted the individual reason against the inevitable tyranny of the general will; thereafter he grew strongly opposed to "the meddling intellect". He lingered for a while in Rousseau's search of an individualistic society, with education based not on authority but on personal experience. Coleridge and Southey, his friends along the Lake, went beyond this, to dream of founding, on the far shores of the Susquehanna, a "pantisocracy" that was basically anarchic. Wordsworth's *The Prelude, or Growth of a Poet's Mind: an Autobiography,* should be read in its early impassioned version (first published in 1926) as well as in the more familiar form, recollected (and revised) in tranquillity by the aging poet. It searches through some eight thousand lines of laboriously subtle self-scrutiny. The writer of the time might not know man, he might presume to scan nature; but the proper study of the Romantic is himself.

[71]

3. Life is for conquest.

It is the consciousness of the individual self that most truly marks the Romantic. It is thus inevitable that the particular individual item that is somehow his own being should concern him most. Even when he is roused for all humanity it is, as Byron shows us, by an exaltation of the individual:

> Chillon! thy prison is a holy place,
> And thy sad floor an altar—for 'twas trod,
> Until his weary steps have left a trace
> Worn, as if thy cold pavement were a sod,
> By Bonnivard!—May none those marks efface!
> For they appeal from tyranny to God.

It is not the racial movement that the Romantic beholds, the protest of a people, but the surge of the heroes, the suffering of the martyrs. It is quite some time, as Carlyle's *Heroes and Hero-Worship* reminds us, before a mass-theory of humanity's shiftings countered the idea that the progress of mankind depends upon the achievements of great men. The Romantic would have no denying that genius, in all fields of life, leads mankind's march; within these gifted ones is concentrate our power. Beauty has in fact been pictured as the relaxing of this directive force, its turning from the battlefield and the mart: even Keats presents poetry as

> Might, half-slumbering on its own right arm

—and we know that the gentleman from Porlock broke Coleridge from his fertile dream.

It must be noted, nonetheless, that few of the great artistic products of the world have been proffered an eager people by its generals, statesmen, merchant kings, in somnolent off-hours. We have been shown the long road Coleridge really

THE ROMANTIC REBELLION

took to Xanadu, before the interrupted dream. Such a picture of the dream-starred genius is but part of the hero-image of the Romantics. Art has its own apprenticeship. The Elizabethan might echo the cry The poet is born, not made: *Poeta nascitur non fit;* but to fit him for creation, after the bird calls of mating time, no instinct will suffice. This the blithe Romantics pretended to ignore.

The more enthusiastic, of course, tried to bring individual freedom into their lives. Rousseau preached that we come into the world, not with original sin, but with original chains. Some seemed to think he was referring to matrimony; he meant all family, all social, ties. Diderot early showed the attitude:

> If I had to choose betwen Racine bad husband, bad father, false friend and sublime poet, and Racine good husband, good father, good friend and honest dullard, I'd pick the former. Of the rascal Racine, what will remain? Nothing. Of Racine the genius? The immortal works . . . I detest all those petty basenesses that show an abject soul; but I do not hate enormous crimes . . . Great and sublime actions and great crimes bear the same characteristic of energy. If one man were not capable of setting a city afire, another would not be capable of plunging into the depths to save it. If the spirit of Caesar could not have been, neither could that of Cato . . . It is only the passions, and the greatest passions, that can elevate the soul to great achievements. All that passion inspires, I forgive . . . It is they that make the scoundrel, and the genius that depicts him to the life.

Conventional behavior, with the ethical codes that confirm it, the ardent Romantics despised. Many turned their theory into practice—which, though often tempestuous, seldom reared the Romantic hero as more than a tea-potentate. The Romantic might emulate, but never equal, Attila, or the Christ.

Attila or the Christ might be the Romantic's find. He might retire to nature, from the murky battlefield of his days,

TRENDS IN LITERATURE

to nurse his wounds, to complain and find sympathy, to be healed. But like Lancelot from his nurse Elaine, he comes back to the fight. And in the immortal combat, only man's spirit can bring victory to man. To capture the world, he must conquer himself.

The war has, forever, three campaigns. Each takes its many victims.

In the first stage of his conflict, the sensitive youth in any period finds himself beaten; he drives vainly toward his goal. Family, friends, strangers—society and its ways—all limit, all distort, his individual desires. His will is clearly frustate. This is a sorry world.

Out of this *Weltschmerz* there are many pathways. Josiah Royce built youth's bafflement into his picture of religion; in the sense of one's self as opposed to the world, he saw the original sin. Alfred Adler used this defeat as the basis for his "inferiority complex". The Romantic, more personally, declared that life, thus thwarting him, is evil. In this campaign Schopenhauer, Byron, Melville, took their stand. Possibly God is not omnipotent, or if so, not all-good. Perhaps men are but driftwood on the chancy currents of void.

The true Romantic, however, will not linger in this slough, where Hardy long was cumbered. Through the gloomy depths he finds the way to a still more dazzling headland. However life's blind forces, however greed and lust, may wreak ruin of body, there is an inner kingdom of the spirit. Here manhood may salve torn flesh with balm of the ideal; nay, through the very suffering learn love, and thus arrive at godhead. Bloodied, bespattered, and befouled, the Romantic remains captain of his soul.

4. *Imagination snaps the reins.*

THE soul is a personal concern.

In the domain of art, the consequences of the emphasis upon the individual reach far in many directions. What one does, more immediately what one feels, assumes importance. Heeding as an injunction Wordsworth's remark that poetry is the spontaneous overflow of powerful emotion *recollected in tranquillity*, would keep the restless Romantics (including Wordsworth himself) most often silent. The intimate feeling, immediately expressed, is the tendency in creation, however the careful critic may poise his pen.

This Romantic spontaneity, however, as we shall see, is part of the program, more professed than practiced. Similarly, per contra, we do not wholly credit Poe's account of the mathematical creation of *The Raven*. Shelley falls upon the thorns of life and bleeds; his stumbling is recorded in a poem not only great, but intrinsically interwoven in conscious artistry. Not in a cropper does even a genius cry out the *Ode To The West Wind!*

Coleridge has wisely pictured the concordant play of reason and emotion in the artist's imagination:

> This power, first put into action by the will and understanding, and retained under their irremissive, though gentle and unnoticed, control, reveals itself in the balance or reconcilement of opposite or discordant qualities: of sameness, with difference; of the general, with the concrete; the idea with the image; the individual with the representative; the sense of novelty and freshness with old and familiar objects; a more than usual state of emotion with more than usual order; judg-

ment ever awake and steady self-possession with enthusiasm and feeling profound or vehement.

The harmonizing of opposites achieved by the artist can hardly be more succinctly expressed. Applied to the receptor as well, it becomes—under the formidable name of synaesthesis—one of the most convincing definitions of beauty. For the spectator may be roused to horror at a tragedy while he sits secure; he may pity though he make no move to succor; his mind may glow with the verbal play and intricate design of *Hamlet* while his heart pulses with the torment of the prince.

All this balance of opposed forces, however, is too central to the truth of art to restrain the rash Romantics, who hailed the imperious call of inspiration and crowded her recruiting stations. Blake in his usual emphasis proclaimed: "Knowledge of ideal beauty is not to be acquired; it is born in us." Schopenhauer, in more philosophical diction, enunciated the idea that beauty is a perception prior to any logical elaboration. Shelley remarked: "When composition begins, inspiration is already on the decline." Keats equally refuses all outward guidance, but admits a self-critical spirit: "The genius of poetry must work out its own salvation in a man; it cannot be matured by law and precept, but by sensation and watchfulness in itself."—How sure of the matter all these young men are!

Self-discipline, despite Keats' kindly words, had little scope in the Romantic scheme. It seemed too ascetic for fervor, too withdrawn for success in a clamant world. In these years began the bardolatry of him "who never altered a single line"—away with Ben Jonson and his "I would he had changed a thousand!" In this age, inspiration is lord; and imagination, his trusty seneschal, opens the gate to every self-expression. Among the Romantics was cradled the quest of originality, when difference in itself conferred distinction.

THE ROMANTIC REBELLION

5. Emotion flowers—

THE Romantic builded upon self-concern.
The more social forms of poetry, the didactic, the satiric, the dramatic, are therefore drowned in a great gushing of the lyric, the most personal of poetic types. Not only in verse, indeed, do poets make public their heart-throbs:

> Out of my own great woe
> I make my little songs—

but after Rousseau's *Confessions* they come hurrying to expose in any and every form their innermost sorrow. Not only the poets. Franz Schubert, in his *Diary* (1824), declares: "My compositions spring from my sorrows. Those that give the world the greatest delight were born of my deepest griefs."

"The heart," said Novalis, "is the key to the world." Always men put on the stylish mask. Elizabethans created imaginary Italian originals for their own works. A bit later, Samuel Daniel wrote sonnets to a non-existent lady, because it was the fashion to indite a sonnet series to one's love. Now hurry the hordes of Romantics to confess things they have done and never done. Even in the prototype of the time's unburdenings we find it hard to distinguish the "romance" from the reality: there is hardly a word of truth, to give but a single instance, in Rousseau's pretty idyll of his life as Mme. de Waren's lover at Les Charmettes. Heine wails:

> At first I thought I must despair:
> This I cannot ever bear.
> Yet I have endured till now,
> Only, do not ask me how.

and the cause of this cosmic complaint turns out to be an overtight dancing-shoe at a ball.

[77]

Lamartine says of his work: "It was not an art, it was an unburdening of my own heart, which cradled itself in its own sobs.... There is the true art: to be moved." Most, even of the Romantics, would add to their definition of art at least the expression of what has moved them. The first to see criticism as the study of expression, indeed, were the German Romantics; they first declared that art has no aim except expression, that its aim is complete when the expression is complete. With the pendulum swing, Croce came to generalize this idea into expressionism.

In all ages the poets, whatever purposes the critics acclaim, have sought expression. Dante even tried to say of Beatrice what no man had ever said of woman: the result was an intricate tapestry of divine symbol and living redemption—man's most familiar story. Milton ventured upon the expression of things unattempted yet in prose or rhyme—and reproduced another episode of the same age-old conflict. But the expression of Lamartine dipped into his *Confidences;* Vigny set down the *Journal of a Poet;* Musset, *Confessions of a Child of the Century;* Chateaubriand, *Confessions From Beyond the Tomb.* The poems of Wordsworth spring from his feelings, with a confused, personal urge toward philosophy. Shelley's work is almost always, by direct reference or allusion, brought home. The most objective of the English Romantics writes of moods

When I have fears that I may cease to be.

This much, you are by now protesting, we expect, find—nay, desire!—in every poet. While there might be some difficulty in exemplifying the trait in Davenant, shall I say, it is unquestionably a virtue whenever the poet's concern has grown larger than himself, has been fused into art. What seems most one's own, however, is that which cannot be classified, which obeys no outer law: one's intimate if not unique emotions. Reason is a unifying force. Once admitted, the force of logic cannot be withstood. Its principles are general; there is a science of ratiocination. One man's reasons may become any man's arguments. Few, however, can suffer with my agony. Debs declared that, so long as one man was in prison, he was not free. Whitman opened his heart to felons and prostitutes: "I will not deny them—for how can I deny myself?" There is also He That died on the cross. But sympathetic as others may be, and much as misery loves company, you can see my joys and my burdens, to rejoice or grieve; you can share my lot, perhaps, if you have the love and the courage; but you cannot feel my pain. Each man's consciousness, his senses, his feelings, mark his one unique claim.

Emotion, then, which is prior to reason—in the history of the race as of the individual, in power of daily impact and immediacy of concern—emotion is also the individual's most distinct reminder of his separate self. When he thinks of himself, he is likely to think of, or in accord with, his emotions. But as soon as a man thinks of his emotions, he weakens them; his energy is no longer absorbed in pure feeling; the initial rouse subsides as the examination continues. Even if one deliberately strive to steep oneself in an emotion, the full shock of the blow is soon broken into wavelets that ripple on dim shores of the spirit. Love's deepest loss may plumb the heart no farther than did the death of Rose Aylmer:

*A night of memories and sighs
I consecrate to thee.*

A Romantic, of course, could never have written those lines; for him that single night would be wailful, Stygian, everlasting. But this exaggerate eternity itself marks a diminution of the feeling, as the adverb in "I'm very pleased to meet you!" somehow lessens the sincerity. This insincere expression of emotion, the original feeling overstepped in the attempt to regain it, is the mark of the sentimental, perhaps the most frequent failing of the Romantics. They are, said Stevenson, "all for tootling on the sentimental flute."

Of all emotions, the most pervasive are the sorrowful. Joy is distinct, and instant; grief dwells upon earlier joys, and earlier sorrows. We look before and after *when* we pine for what is not. Not only in memoried effect but in concrete consequence, our woes are cumulative. Southey before Poe pointed out the special gloom of the term *never more,* which brings to mind both the golden past and the barren future.

For more reasons than that sorrow snail-like walks ever with the chambers of its past, it is the most persuasive of our feelings. Many find, in its brooding spell, a languorous inactivity more easy than the responsibilities of a vigorous life. It at once provides a not too uncomfortable retreat from life's pressure, and by its burden justifies the dreamer in his withdrawal. And even the most ardent spirit, whose desires beat pinions above the battlements of the world, finds when he must trudge its prosaic ways that in quite another sense his dreams are pinioned,

> *His mighty wings are weights to drag him low.*

The more sensitive his reaction to present stimuli, the more conscious he will be of the limitations life sets upon his will, the more afflicted by contrary forces he cannot control.

And yet, like joy, this grief cannot long perdure. Its first intensity that blots the world is soon lessened; the stricken eyes recover a vision now but dimmed as through tears. In some there even gathers a mood of almost cheerful resignation, a sweet submission that yields a milder joy. Others, more oppressed by the heavy and the weary weight, droop shoulders with an habitual melancholy. Some of the Romantics are draped in perpetual semi-mourning.

The Romantic, of course, feels himself essentially alone. But the solitary finds comfort in the savouring of sorrow. It stands like someone to whom in stillness a man may turn and offer his unspoken thought. In crowds, it nods gravely as he confides his superiority and scorn. It companions him when in the hallowed loneliness of nature he seeks the echo of his silence, discovers in nature's bosom the shadow of his mood. Read, in Shelley's *Alastor,* the long passage that begins:

THE ROMANTIC REBELLION

> *There was a poet whose untimely tomb*
> *No human hands with pious reverence reared,*
> *But the charmed eddies of autumnal winds*
> *Built o'er his mouldering bones a pyramid*
> *Of mouldering leaves in the waste wilderness . . .*

This melancholy, this sentimentality of the Romantic, on a plain of self-indulgence, is characteristically brought to nature in such a poem as Lamartine's *The Lake*, which Musset says everybody has known by heart, and has loved, from youth. The poem begins:

> *Thus always driven toward new shores,*
> *In eternal night swept onward, forever away,*
> *Can we never, on the ocean of the ages,*
> *Cast anchor for but one day? . . .*

Soon the poet hears the voice of his beloved, as on that dearest night recalled:

> *"O time! Stay your flight! And you, happy hours,*
> *Speed not on your way;*
> *Let us long savour the fleeting delights*
> *Of our happiest day!*
>
> *"Many most wretched ones pray to you here;*
> *Run for them speedily;*
> *Take, with their days, the woes that devour them—*
> *Forget the care-free . . ."*

For two more stanzas she prays time to stay its flight; then the poet interrupts:

> *Jealous time, can it be, these intoxicant moments*
> *When love pours joy on us in steady flow,*
> *Will fly far from us at the same swift pace*
> *As the days of our woe?*
>
> *What! can we not even fix their impress?*
> *What! gone forever? What! wholly lost?*

[81]

*In the ocean of time that gave them and took them
Abysmally tossed?*

*Eternity, Nothingness, Past, gloomy chasms,
What do you do with the days you devour?
Speak! Will you ever restore these sublime joys
You snatch with their hour?*

The poet then appeals, for four more stanzas, to the rocky shore of the lake, to the waters in calm and in storm, to the neighboring trees, to the breeze that shudders and goes by, to the reflected sky—to wind, reed, fragrance, all—to hold the memory of that one dear night, and somehow still to whisper: "Ils ont aimé"—they have loved!

In this famous poem we find the vagueness, the sentimentality, the melancholy, the summoning of nature to man's aid, that some have felt to be the core of the Romantic. Sophie von la Roche shed tears at the mere mention of a Negro; hearts like hers all over Europe were ready in an instant's urge to bound with joy or to bleed with sorrow. No wonder that these writers have been dubbed the school of the drowned-in-tears!

This lapse of high emotion to a moody trudge, his successors were not first to note; the Romantic himself was soon aware he was not soaring in the full surge of his first feeling. Whether one's emotion is of joy or of sorrow, there is a quick impulse of shame with the consciousness of its ebbing. Soon thereafter a man discovers that in renewal of the experience there is no return of the first fine careless rapture. How, indeed, can one renew an experience? With its allotted hour it has flown, irrevocable. A second trial is cluttered with memories; despite oneself, as in a second marriage, comparisons intrude. Repetition stales. Nothing is less endurable to the high-spirited charger, agallop through the breaches of till then untaken towers, than to feel the damp fingers of decrepitude tentatively clutch, to sense that he must in time—in no time, now—become a sorry jade plodding the dust and mire of everyman's road to

THE ROMANTIC REBELLION

town. Just as, the reins flung free, imagination may leap to mad caprice, so now the more desperately emotion demanded ever more violent incitation, by sought shock and artificial stimulus trying to recapture the momentary and elusive thrill.

6. —and goes to seed.

THIS need of constant emotional impact goaded the artist. It drove him often to mad expedients, priming and pumping his passion. Individualist to the marrow, he scorned all moral codes. The escapades of Byron, the intense unconventionalities of Shelley, the drugs of Coleridge, the opium of DeQuincey, must be multiplied among the minor aspirants of the movement. Eager to snare the secrets of art, they could copy but the cough of genius. And, in the genius, it was often enough a hiccough. When Alfred de Musset frequently failed to appear among a group of friends (if I may English the pun), to the remark "Musset absents himself too much" came the rejoinder "Musset absinthes himself too much." Among the literary "isms" we must not overlook the influence of alcoholism. But, Musset's friends went on, "God wouldn't have the heart to damn him for it."

There is something appealing, though pathetic, about these desperately earnest self-conscious young men, pinning their hearts upon their pink waistcoats for all to see—though scorning the beholders; and finding beauty, if not salvation, in excess. They had heard Blake shouting: "Exuberance is beauty; the road of excess leads to the palace of wisdom." They were all agallop up that road. Pater had not yet come to whisper that the secret of art "does but consist in the removal of surplusage." Had he then breathed, and breathed the thought, he'd have been huffed away as an Augustan fogey by the lusty Romantics.

This Romantic excess, be it exuberance or strain—spontaneous overflow or whipped urge to flagging passion—is manifest in various moods. "The desire of the moth for the star" (pretty flick of poetic fallacy!) magnifies both the moth's destination and the poet's urge. The moral of the *Ancient Mariner*, detached from the poem and taken as a lesson in life, is so vio-

THE ROMANTIC REBELLION

lently disproportionate as to be arrant nonsense. Because a bird is shot, the ship's crew must die, and the marksman spend his life telling his sorry tale. The poet protested against the moral's being too heavily pressed; but no such qualms deflected Blake, whose *Auguries of Innocence* abounds in such lines as

> *A robin redbreast in a cage*
> *Puts all heaven in a rage. . . .*
>
> *A horse misused upon the road*
> *Cries to heaven for human blood. . . .*
>
> *Kill not moth or butterfly*
> *For the Last Judgment draweth nigh.*

Blake also tells of a serpent in the chapel all of gold,

> *Vomiting his poison out*
> *On the bread and on the wine.*
> *So I turned into a sty,*
> *And laid me down among the swine.*

Florid praise of love, many periods present; but in purity and perversion, from mystic religious fervor to diabolism and drugs, few young spirits course so widely and range so far beyond measure as those that down the nineteenth century whip the steeds of Romantic indulgence till they fall.

In life or in the work of art, this emotional halt had to be cured by a deeper pricking. Delicacy, subtlety, no longer sufficed; to rouse the reader's dulled expectancy ever stronger shocks must be devised. The extravagant, the horrible, were quick to appear. (In the popular novel, they sprang before the period had grown deliberate in its rebellion.)

By such a course, the emotions came to be cultivated for themselves. Because he deems that such cultivation "sensitizes the human organism," A. N. Whitehead was led to exclaim: "It was a tremendous discovery—how to excite emotions for their own sake, apart from imperious biological necessity."

Actually, the secret is in the hands of every habitual masturbator —and the practice pervasively leaves a sense of void.

Finding that all his emotional prodding left his spirits to lag far behind the leap of his desire, the Romantic often sank through disgust to wallow in despair. "There is no more spring in my heart," exclaimed Flaubert at nineteen. "In spite of all this glamour and imaginative power," cried Lamartine, "I am the black point where things grow dark when they converge. Life is short, empty, with no interest, no tomorrow." "Pleasure cannot help me," mooned Alfred de Musset. "I find nothing but such deep disgust that I want to die. I am sad, ill-humored, tired, exhausted—sick to my stomach. Everything bores me." Alfred de Vigny said bluntly: "The greatest of all follies is hope." And along the dismal paths of opiates, many of the minor Romantics went down to poverty and suicide.

7. The hunt gallops wide.

ALL these aspects of Romanticism, however they must be sorted for description, were of course fused in the Romantics' lives and in their works. In the quest of nature's true store of simple beauty, many turned to earlier times. Percy's *Reliques of English Poetry* opened new vistas. What King George III had called "that sad stuff, Shakespeare" became the impetus to a second renaissance. All the Elizabethans were beloved in his wake. In 1775, Tyrwhitt's discovery that earlier years had sounded the final "e" restored Chaucer as a source of English beauty.

Other tongues and countries were explored as well. Bodmer went to the old Swabian for the Minnesinger and the *Nibelungenlied;* Hickes, to the Icelandic and the Anglo-Saxon. The poets hurried after the scholars, on real or pretended trails: Percy's *Runic Poetry;* Gray's *Descent of Odin;* Ossian; MacPherson. The Orient, from the *Arabian Nights* to Omar Khayyam, revealed its store of wonder. Although the excavations of ancient temples and tombs were just ahead, Shelley repeated the drama of Oedipus (*Swellfoot the Tyrant*), Keats admired a Grecian urn. Archaeology and the visual arts of earlier times attracted more than Lessing. So eager were the delvings into the nearer past, in search of each nation's earlier glimpses of glory, that some critics have described the Romantic movement as a return to the medieval. Thus Pater felt it necessary to explain:

> The essential elements of the romantic spirit are curiosity and the love of beauty; and it is only as an illustration of these qualities that it seeks the Middle Ages, because, in the overcharged atmosphere of the Middle Ages, there are unworked sources of romantic effect, of a strange beauty, to be won, by strong imagination, out of things unlikely or remote.

If you are detained by Pater's essences, note that in every artist of any period they persist; curiosity has more than nine lives. It is the nature of what is loved as beauty that varies.

But the Middle Ages saw in themselves none of the qualities Pater lists; these are all such as glow in after eyes. The Romantics, therefore, made no effort to restore the Middle Ages; in the mood of their melancholy they preferred them as ruins. The past remained a charmed era of derring-do and royal countercharge only if they left undisturbed its tombs and its crumbling memorials. But from these silent relics sounded more eerie spells; in gathering power the hallowed halls were swept with haunting wraiths of dark misdeeds. Spectres hung upon the scenes their living souls had known, until unspeakable sin was expiate, and horror piled horrendous. Walpole's *Castle of Otranto* as early as 1764 heralded the Gothic romance on Albion's isle. In Germany, ten years later, Bürger's legend of *Lenore* inaugurated a vogue; Lamb called Coleridge's attention to the English version, which reverberates in the *Ancient Mariner*, and was imitated by Sir Walter Scott. *The Mysteries of Udolpho*, *The Monk*, *Frankenstein*, and the other well-known novels, are but the survivors of a horde of ghoul-infested volumes, where empty corridors clank with ankle-bound chains, where maidens languish on the yielding brink of violation; past heroines whose shudderings make the asp seem oak, ghosts flit on errands dire until brought to book by the dauntless hero at the final shriek: all the rattling machinery of tales of terror in towered fastness and dungeon-keep grinds human bones to chill the sensation-seeking reader.

Outcries against these, and more idyllic, books, and the "novellophagists" that devoured them, pressed home not only the old objections, but new protests against the new Romantic urges. The time was quick to taste its own flavour. In several books, Hannah More repeated the main objections: The novelist's frequent use of melancholy scenes blunts the reader's sympathy for real distress. Current fiction, she cried, teaches contempt for industry, frugality, the humble and domestic re-

THE ROMANTIC REBELLION

sponsibilities. It proclaims love as the great business of life; love, which cannot be regulated or restrained, to which one must sacrifice all earthly duty. To preach obedience to one's passions' promptings is to adorn vice and promote its practice. With impulse the mainspring of action, Hannah More complained, Rousseau "exhibits a virtuous woman the victim not of temptation, but of reason——not of vice, but of sentiment—not of passion, but of conviction; and strikes at the very root of honor, by elevating a crime into a principle." William Combe would

> *— leave to misses of eighteen*
> *The raptures they from novels glean . . .*

raptures made more specific by Cowper:

> *Ye novelists, who mar what ye would mend,*
> *Sniv'ling and driv'ling folly without end . . .*
> *Ye pimps, who, under virtue's fair pretense,*
> *Steal to the closet of young innocence. . . .*

Heedless of such strictures, the blithe Romantic strutted his passionate hour before the dust.

Soon every garden in England had its carefully provided ruined tower—still to be seen in the background of many a painting of the time.

> *Oft in my waking dreams do I*
> *Live o'er again the happy hour*
> *When midway on the mount I lay,*
> *Beside the ruin'd tower.*

The mood thus recorded by Coleridge lingers for the later mischief of W. S. Gilbert:

> *There's a fascination frantic*
> *In a ruin that's Romantic;*
> *Do you think you are sufficiently decayed?*

In a similar quest of greater intensity, realism (which from our farthest venturing will shortly hale us home) after the closet skeletons dug into the sub-cellars and pits of humanity. Deeper one cannot sink a shaft save into hell; and the diabolists had their day. Villiers de L'Isle Adam's *Cruel Tales,* Borel's *Immoral Tales,* Barbey d'Aureyvilly's *Diabolic Tales;* in Germany Hoffman; American Poe; and Baudelaire's *Fleurs du Mal* ("garden of evil" where the English *fin-de-siècle* decadents loved to loll) inevitably shifted concern from the body to the soul. From adventure, outer happening, readers turned to psychology, inner response. And, by seeing the soul through the body, these men moved with their times toward a new emphasis and literary school.

To help produce the intense effects thus sought, the Romantics employed sharp contrasts and antitheses, black-and-white juxtapositions. These became a literary device widely employed, a favorite in any theme with Hugo:

> *The grave said to the rose:*
> *With the tears dawn bestows*
> *What dost thou, O flower of love?*
> *And the rose asked the grave:*
> *In your deep yawning cave*
> *What do you with the souls from above?*
>
> *The rose said: Dismal tomb,*
> *These tears in earth's womb*
> *With amber and honey I leaven.*
> *The tomb said: Dainty flower,*
> *Of each soul I devour,*
> *I fashion an angel of heaven.*

* * *

> *Some go bent beneath the burden of their woes;*
> *At happiness' feast very few are the guests.*
> *Not all of us are equally at ease.*
> *A law, that from below seems evil, unfair,*
> *Bids some rejoice, and others envy them.*

THE ROMANTIC REBELLION

*Your wing in jostling it makes nothing spill
From the jar where I quench myself, which I've
    well filled.
My soul has more of fire than you have of ash!
My heart has more of love than you, forgetfulness!*

The marvelous, the mysterious, the terrifying, must, like the melancholy, be vague. The sun and the clear winds of heaven dispel these night vapours. Precision sets the limits of reality on the supernatural. We can see the religious loom in his life when the scientist Einstein remarks: "One of the most beautiful things we can experience is the mysterious. It is the source of all true science and art. He that can no longer pause to wonder is as good as dead." A more specialized defender of the storied Romance, James Branch Cabell, observes that wonder is the gateway to the palace of art; but it was earlier observed that she is the daughter of ignorance (bitch of a horrid kennel!).

On her trail, however, the Romantic stood beside his elder brother who also had turned to nature. Beside him, but back to back. The one looked across the wild magnificence of primeval forests. Nearby was the rank overgrowth of the deserted garden, with something eerily beyond measure, wafting imprecise thoughts of eternity. Stark beauty of the noble savage (figment of a Romantic dream!), exotic beauty of decay; but beauty beyond man's limitations, not to be confined in the brittle bondage of words, to be caught only by dim suggestion, lifted on waves of emotion, in rhythms beneath and beyond language, as into the poet's, into the reader's heart. And the other turned from the shadowed hills and woodlands to gaze across sunlit fields, to see a beauty of more discernible details, in every unit of which, however minute, glimmers a fleck of nature's loveliness. Along this vista there is not an inevitability but an imperative in the words of Keats, that "what the imagination seizes as beauty must be truth." Nature is, to be sure not methodized, but particularized: the moment caught for eternity; the fleeting individual and unique landscape held in unchanging perspective. The Romantic turned a "candid camera" on nature, as on his soul.

Here again, tyros took snap-shots to excess. The realist, laying on the slab a slice of life, often no more than wallowed in mire of facts. In the Romantic, likewise, accuracy of detail—that strengthens and maintains the springy step of art—became not a means but a goal. After Hugo's *Orientales* came Gautier and the other Parnassians, grazing on the slopes, finding their "romance" in the beauty of concrete things. Leconte de Lisle would have wedded poetry and science. Others indulged in a verbal ceramics, a filigree of the picturesque. After the studied sonnets of Heredia came the long researches of Flaubert (with alas! often ephemeral result). There flourished the cult of the exact and uniquely appropriate term, *le mot juste*. Maupassant was admonished to find in every individual, then to set forth, that subtle cast of countenance, that faint flavour of his personality, which marks him from all the uncounted hosts of his fellows. From this, it was no far journey to the polished and graceful but often empty vases of the practitioners of art for art's own sake.

Beyond the forests and the fields alike, a man may find his home. Some artists lose their way in the trackless woods; some linger too lengthily culling flowers in the meadows. Yet vague immensity, far-springing from personal emotion, and minute particularity, born of an equal but more objective interest in individual things, may even together serve in the formation of the harmonious work of art.

THE ROMANTIC REBELLION

8. *Art Gives a round-trip from life.*

THE journey of the writer that seeks the picturesque soon takes him to the exotic. Here once more he finds himself beside the man that has been seeking novelty to renew the emotional thrill, that needs the unfamiliar, the remote. Here let the realist in trepidation tread: a farmer may be a "rube" in a big city; but the sleek urbanite may prove a "greenhorn" in the country. A documentary film of life in Bali will seem fantastic to a slum-dweller in Chicago; a "realistic" story of old Japan will to an Ohio villager glister with "romance." A friend of mine once tried to explain, on story-telling night in a Persian village, the elevators in a New York skyscraper. Part of the floor rising; like the magic carpet. They raised their eyebrows about as high; and the building itself!

"What do they do on the one hundred and second story?"

"Transact business."

"Oh! Business with Allah!"

Unanimously he was awarded the imaginary prize for the most imaginative story.

I must here confess a personal allure: since childhood I have longed to visit the snow-sheltered land of Tibet. It is, I suppose, my Carcassonne; the mere mention of the name flits a dream across my day. But is it the land, or myself, that is dreamy? Is it the book or the reader that spins the romance? We have here, surely, an extrinsic classification. In the lure of the unknown, the faraway, who is not spelled? Who would not often join the poet's sigh:

> *I'd like to take the first train out*
> *No matter where it's going!*

But there is a significance in the destination.

We are told that Romantic art is an art of escape, a flight from reality; and so it is. So in the same way is all art. T. S.

[93]

Eliot declares that poetry registers the author's escape from his emotion. Every work of art, by winning us to its contemplation, draws us from the other activities of life, holds us to a concern with other conflicts than our own. The story may be of everyday things, events frequent and commonplace; yet somehow the artist "makes familiar objects be as if they were not familiar." In another of his contradictory definitions, Pater pictures the Romantic as the addition of strangeness to beauty; but is not all beauty at once most intimate and strange? We see the process of shaving as a new experience through Joyce's eyes, and with Bojer we find a not unmentionable and not uninteresting detail in the changing of an infant's wet diaper. Or we may sail the seven seas, amidst waterspouts and hurricanes and desperadoes holding our staunch way, and feel the heaving deck as familiar ground. Critics here have poured salt on an ostrich's tail; their fables, not the fact, have buried its ardent eye in the sand. (The critic should ponder what is thus more elevate and exposed!) It is true that the reader is seeking to escape the drudgery of daily toil. Not life! For that, he scorns to call living. He is, rather, urging toward the wide expansion of his powers, the test and the proof of his mettle, the chance to experience and to act to the limit of his potentialities (which then will soar beyond!) that, only, deserves the name of life! All art is escape—from duller to deeper levels and modes of intensity.

Art is not, by any means, the only escape—as the lives of many of the Romantics remind us, not to mention the incests and the opiates of their stories. Sexual indulgence is more immediately stimulative of one aspect of man's nature, and equally efficacious with alcohol in drowning other urges. Some persons "go in for" solitaire. Dreaming over books, as Santayana observes, may grow a cloudy habit:

> A lovely dream is an excellent thing in itself, but it leaves the world no less a chaos and makes it by contrast seem even darker than it did. Art in the better sense is a condition of happiness for a practical and

THE ROMANTIC REBELLION

laboring creature, since without art he remains a slave; but it is one more source of unhappiness for him so long as it is not squared with his necessary labors and merely interrupts them. It then alienates him from his world without being able to carry him effectually into a better one.

Who chooses "art" as a drug, needs ever stronger doses.

But in that pilgrim's progress which we all perforce attempt, the test is not so much in the touring as in the souvenirs. Life is a one-way journey; but every opiate provides a short round-trip. We like to feel that, in contemplation of the work of art, all aspects of our being, intellect and emotions, the opposed feelings of calm and sympathetic concern, are alike intensified, poised at the peak of consciousness, readiest to function, most aware. Certain avenues of escape, however, entail what the alcoholics call a hangover. Pulp-magazine fiction and the movies, with their musical concomitant, the popular song, leave those that indulge in them dissatisfied, restless. A score of years ago, the wilder spirits of our youth might run away to become fire-through-the-holster cowboys. More recently, they might stay at home, hoping to be sawed-off-machine-gun gangsters. After seeing a "bad-man" film, the boys of one city school in grim earnest scored the mark of the "squealer," with sharp pen-knife strokes, on the brows of a dozen classmates. Less precise but more pervasive is the increasing discontent of the shopgirl that learns in the daily "true story" of the tabloids that her luckier sisters are marrying luxury. "I Found a Million Dollar Baby in a Five and Ten Cent Store" gives the sweet young clerk an early hope and a long-drawn disappointment.

Other works may more nearly produce the Aristotelian catharsis. The reader may be purged of "terror and pity" so that, these checks to reason removed, he may judge the affairs of life more fearlessly and truly. Or he may return from the book with an exhilarant springiness of spirit as after a brisk morning walk, a resilience and a readiness that quicken his response to all concerns of living. Or with pity purged, it may be, but sympathy enlivened as understanding has spread. Or just atilt with joy at the beauty he has known. Somewhere in the heart of these responses we find the pulse of beauty, recognizing all art as escape from duller to fuller, more intense and rounded, living.

What lures us to Tibet is of course not the distance but our inexperience. Keats remarks:

> *Ever let the Fancy roam,*
> *Pleasure never is at home.*

Later Baudelaire longs to—

> *Plunge to the gulf's deeps, hell or heaven—what matter!*
> *—through,*
> *In the depths of the unknown to find something new!*

And Ezra Pound cries:

> *Oh to be out of all this,*
> *This that is all I wanted*
> *— save the new.*

But surely we do not need the poets to tell us that the grass is always greener on the other side of the hill! To call this (Pater's "curiosity," Babbitt's "strangeness") Romantic is to set his pair of eyes into the definition of man. True, most men have two eyes; but so have most creatures that walk the earth or swim the seas or fly below our airplanes. What matters is not the orbs, but what they are turned on. Not the universal desire to attain the unknown, but the diverse interests that occupy one on the route, the plans one hopes to develop on arrival. In an art gallery in Milan two New York acquaintances spied one another, came enthusiastically to meet. Their faces beamed; but one spoke more quickly. What treasure-trove would he proclaim?

"Hello!" he said. "What do you think; I'm two days ahead of my schedule!"

THE ROMANTIC REBELLION

At the Antipodes, there still are mirrors.

There may be a dauntless courage (or a fear that masks its pallor in a dream) that dons a hero's beleagued boots and journeys forth to conquest, battering its way to ultimate happiness or invincible doom. Under the buffetings of fate it will stand forever unbowed, will press its footprint into the trodden stone, and leave its mark along the signposts of man's progress. Or there may be a desire to understand this dark unknown, to comprehend these mazy items and aspects of the universe, to tabulate, to measure, to survey them. The one blazes the trail of romance, the other paves the streets of realism.

9. *Realism is sibling to romance.*

FOR, in an age concerned with particulars, realism rises with romance. It refuses to set men on pedestals, to make the pleasing assumption that they are superior to other forms of being, framed in an other, and more awful, fashion. Microbes and men, massacres and martyrdoms, cabbages and kings and radiant stars, all are susceptible to our examination, dispassionate, unbiased, thoroughgoing. "Realism," says Herbert Read, "is nothing but definiteness." This too-inclusive span sets Shakespeare and Keats beside Zola and Balzac; he might at least add "literalness." The realist is willing to credit only what the senses and the intellect register and convey without the coadjutant service of blind (though radiant) faith. And if, in the examination, much that is commonplace, much that is unpleasant and sordid, is set down, the realist will not be blamed for it, having found it in life.

Whenever Romanticism flourishes, twin-born realism thus, though more hardly, thrives. Romanticism is the favorite son. It sets men above all other things, endows them with free will as with sovereign power. It therefore has the full support of all man's faith—which (like the sun) though unseeing, may give clearest light. It stands firm on the rock of all religion (which some indeed call but an offspring of Romance). To realism is left through the years but lean pickings of the bones of such reason and such science as men have tardily controlled. The opposition of Romance and realism does not inevitably involve a conflict of science and religion; at least, many scientists proclaim their religious point of view, or declare that their laws have no jurisdiction in the other realm.

It has nonetheless been remarked that in one direction the arts tend toward mathematics, in the other they aspire toward prayer. These—each accompanied by music, which may be mood or measure, heart-beat or foot-beat—are indeed the two extremes art cannot reach without self-destruction; but they mark the direction of its flow. As each of the arts has its limits —the novel is bounded by the slow-rising mountains of poetry, the table-land of history, the sea of metaphysics, and the slough of journalism; painting tends toward the limits of three-dimensional sculpture, time-spanning story, the fixing of photography, the flat flow of the cinema, and the color freedom of such devices as the Clavilux—so of course all the arts are together bound from other ranges of human functioning: on the practical plains, by craftsmanship and by action (as involved in earning a living, as urged in propaganda and pornography); and, along more contemplative borders, by pure science and by religion.

A glance at an earlier age when the individual personality was asserted, will show these two trails blazed by religious leaders. Luther emphasized the moral triumph of man, his natural capacity for good, thus prepared the pathway for Rousseau. Calvin, on the other hand, heavily stressed man's load of original sin. So great a role did he assign to God in the drama of salvation, that to many of the lusty sons of Adam it seemed futile to strive for an availant life of the spirit. These vigorous ones were thus encouraged to concentrate upon the outer world. Here, they moved to such power and control of material resources that it was evident they were in accord with the holy design. Further signs of God's grace are the assurance of these misnamed mere "captains" of industry—despite early words about a needle's eye—are the authoritative voice with which they make pronouncements in any field, and the widespread respect accorded the ethical principles underlying the terms "Business is business," *Caveat emptor, Laissez-faire*. Philosophers have justified the attitude, for later generations, both in the doctrine of pragmatism, and in the thought that out of the clash of all the individual greeds will emerge the general good. . . . The realist, however, seldom waits for this higher sanction.

It may seem, from the foregoing discussion, that realism and Romanticism, though they rise in the same period, are mutually exclusive. Actually, from opposite sides, they verge toward common ground. If nature is good, if men, as Rousseau proclaimed, are naturally good,—why, naturally they should permit no obstacle to their immediate virtue. They should obey their impulses as the soundest guide. All the agencies of restraint are therefore evil: religion, society, the state and other institutions—reason itself!—are to be cast off by the freely acting individual, obedient only to his naturally good impulsions. "Thinking man is a depraved animal," fulminates Rousseau; and Carlyle—moon-struck more directly by the German metaphysics—declares that consciousness itself is a sign of disease. A healthy body functions unaware. For the sickness of consciousness, the surrealists of our time seek a cure. The Romantic, not thus consciously combating the conscious, tolerated no hindrances to the free flow of the innocent individual urge.

Note the word *flow!* For to Rousseau the individual is naturally good because he is part of Nature; Nature is divinely good because it is the manifestation of God. All is one great, incessant flux; the only unchanging factor is the ceaseless change. Beyond this there is no abiding principle, no unity in the multiplicity of life. Reason, reflection, would tend to develop dogma, static interference with the flux. There are thus no standards, no norms of morality or truth.

"I feel, therefore I am." This is the assurance of the Romantic. Yet beyond each separate existence, through the individual self-consciousness, the personality, there is reached an agreement with those around, a *contrat social*. Without this, each speck of dust would fly a separate way. Thus bound, by mutual agreement, every item of being—grain of sand and jungle tree and sentient man—is loaded on the great pantechnicon of Nature. Each particle is still discrete; but they have promised to smile politely when they collide. And they are all coasting sturdily uphill back to Paradise . . . Rousseau's inheritors, more regardful of gravity and less confident of the destination, wobble on weary hub in lower ground.

A Shelley, a Heine, emphasizing the superiority of the individual spirit, finds analogue, in the collective stress of our time, among the humanists. Politically, the autocrat Napoleon was succeeded by the Führer of the *National Socialist* Party. Aesthetically, the spontaneous Romantic—practising what Romanticism preaches—somehow sometimes brings his personal power into a higher synthesis. Lifting himself by his own bootstraps, he achieves a self-assertion that is also universal: he wins to art. It is only when he preaches what he should practice that the Romanticist betrays himself as a horse of another stable. For Rousseau—demanding alliance with nature, bidding break the bonds of reason, proclaiming the universal flux and the beneficence and prepotency of impulse—not merely has cropped in the mangers of realism, but scarce needs the veterinarian Freud to foal surrealism. . . . It is in this sense (if I may for another moment glance ahead) that da-da and its brood have been called the *reductio ad absurdum* of Romanticism. They are, as truly, one pathway of the realist in a collective world.

10. *Sidney Carton looks at Anthony Adverse.*

"All artists know it for an axiom," Sir Arthur Quiller-Couch repeats, "that *if you are setting out to tell the incredible, nothing will serve you so well as to open with absolute realism.*" He means, perhaps, with verisimilitude. But this axiom has been observed through the ages. *The Satyricon;* the *Arabian Nights; Anthony Adverse.* The farther from daily events an author rears his hero's valor, the nearer to common ground he will set his minor figures. And the more scrupulously accurate he will provide the details. Hervey Allen—for that popular "romance" *Anthony Adverse* will help to show us the century's stride—spreads such a wealth of local color over three continents, so intimately follows the turns of the streets and the river borders, so finely discriminates the native types, that we almost fancy he must have dwelled in all these lands through the generations of the tale. Nor does he flutter at details that once would have given halt to the most thoroughgoing naturalist or his publisher; he makes no bones about it when, on Anthony's first visit to a courtyard in Cuba, "a stark naked boy, not at all embarrassed by a hearty morning erection, opened the gate." We have moved beyond an earlier self-consciousness or squeamishness, it may be; but we retain the wisdom of providing a loamy soil of actuality out of which the most luxuriant high deeds may grow. The exact observation of the poets could be as easily instanced among the "Romantic" writers of prose. Reread, of many, Scott's *Quentin Durward.* Vividness and vagueness, the far-fetched and the everyday, are concerns that have no causative connection with the basic spirit of the work of art, with its literary "school."

A comparison of *Anthony Adverse* and *A Tale of Two Cities* may make clear another aspect of the century's shifting. Dickens stands midway down the years, caught in the Victorian

[102]

compromise. A deep humanitarian spirit urged his pen; he wept over the fortunes of the folk that crowd his pages; and if—as new research inclines some to believe—it was his own lost youth he was bemoaning, his tears are but the more sincere. This aspect of his work pervades the autobiographical novels; *A Tale of Two Cities* keeps more lively vestigia of the earlier period. It has a background of historical fact—though wisely, as in most historical novels, the main figures are fictitious. Any resemblance to actual persons has nothing to do with the movements of history. The many minor characters, however, are probably drawn from actual models roundabout; what is more important, they move life-like through incidents that occur on every hand. But Sidney Carton is roused to his sacrifice by love of a woman; within his soul, this works to his personal weal. In the epilogue, the descendants of Charles and Lucie Darnay visit the scene of that sacrifice, paying tribute to the individual whose devotion made possible their continuing lives and joys. The young Anthony Adverse—we do not see young Carton— is too self-sufficient to sense any need of salvation by sacrifice. He simply enjoys life as it breaks upon him; yet, at times, vivid dreams and mystic visions sweep over him, such as Carton never had. For these are not personal moods of dissatisfaction, but vague efforts to gather life into some sort of comprehensive scheme. After his home and family are destroyed by fire, however, Anthony's lack of fulfilment drives him forth. He tries lonely vigil, but is drawn back to life. Almost like a Franciscan he cares for his fellows of a prison-chain. Peacefully he tends the sufferers in a lazar-house. Remarried, Anthony has learned that there is untruth in difference; he must be at one with people and place around. On a far corner of his wife's estate, Anthony and his new family dwell like all the village-folk, simply, part of the earth-growth. There would seem, to romantic expectancy, a shirking in the account of his death; actually, it is the peak of the hill the author has been climbing. In place of the clash of circumstance, the heroic sacrifice, there is the deliberately banal accident of a swerving ax-edge, such as might lay low any peasant. And in the epilogue, the last trace of Anthony as an individual, the little Madonna that has symbolized his unique heritage and his personal yearnings, is shattered as a "heathen idol" by the playful marksmanship of a band of pioneers, gathered from various states of the new world, seeking. Seeking in a band—for something, anything, that promises freedom, happiness. And their quest was Anthony's and is the world's. More piteously even than when Hervey Allen wrote, mankind is echoing the cry that ends the book: "Do, God! Give us *something!*" God grant it be the United Nations, and not the atom bomb!

THE ROMANTIC REBELLION

11. *Come take a journey!*

THE quest for *something,* in literature as in life, often takes man a journey. One of the best ways of launching a hero is by shipwrecking him. With the doomed vessel, Davy Jones' commodious locker tucks away the codes and conventions of his native land. He finds dubious shelter on a hostile shore; and all the rescued ones are revealed as the coatings of civilization never show them. Shakespeare sets his plots going by shipwreck in *The Comedy of Errors, Twelfth Night, The Winter's Tale, Pericles,* and *The Tempest. Robinson Crusoe* is lengthily followed by *Swiss Family Robinson* and a host. Gulliver is tempest-driven to his several coasts. Nay, from *The Odyssey* through the late Greek stories, the early Italian tales, the *Arabian Nights,* on through all countries to Stevenson, *The Admirable Crichton,* Kipling, London, and Conrad, over all the seven seas there is swift action and dramatic transfer by way of a ship storm-sunk.

More frequent still is the journey that reaches its destination. Less rousing but likely to seem more real, this too may effect a shifting of values. It may alter the traveler's circumstance and station, may bear him to lands unknown. The voyage may even lift beyond the western sun to the far worlds of what the publishers hopefully call scientifiction—or at a nearer distance equally attempt to make the miracle seem real. Some of the incredible stories of Jules Verne—*Twenty Thousand Leagues Under the Sea,* for instance—are already true. His trip around the earth has been far outspeeded. But note that, while Jules Verne sends his men into earth or sea or sky, what concerns him is just the journey, the adventures along the way. Both Cyrano de Bergerac of the age before and H. G. Wells of the period after bear us with equal speed along the sky-journey; but they dwell lengthily among the space-folk studying their ways.

TRENDS IN LITERATURE

For even in the realm of the impossible, each age attests its spirit. The medieval and early renaissance stories present a succession of disconnected adventures, each beyond reason and interesting only to the childlike; they were burlesqued in *Don Quixote* and supplanted by the more life-like picaresque tale. *Alice In Wonderland* is no more possible than the early extravagances, but its author was both a mathematician and a scion of the Victorian compromise. He knew that, while an impossible occurrence in an otherwise orderly world might seem a monstrous intrusion, with two consistent impossibilities one can draw a line to a fascinating new world. The Red Queen might believe three miracles before breakfast, but through the looking glass marches a mathematically ordered array of feigned fancies. H. G. Wells finds consistency an even greater magic; his imaginative stories observe the manner in which one impossible quality or condition pervades and transforms an otherwise normal environment. On these far-flung flights we need not linger, save to observe that even they, by the extreme of indirection, bring us home.

12. *The censor intrudes.*

I AM tempted to a digression on the censor. He is always out of place in a discussion of art; but in the light of the present thesis his basic impulsion grows clear.

My intention is not to question censorship as applied to manifestly pornographic drawings or writings—though what is obviously obscene to one time or race may seem quite inoffensive to another. The writings of Petronius, Ovid, the "divine" Aretin, Casanova de Seingalt, Restif de la Bretonne, must in English today be either surreptitiously printed or bowdlerized—which word reminds us that Shakespeare was thus expurgated in 1818. A peasant may harmlessly stoop, in a corner of a field, to perform certain physiological functions that would lead to his arrest, were he thus to squat in a city street—though, in mid-eighteenth century London, Casanova expressed surprise at beholding such activities in public, near Buckingham Palace. Along the lanes of south European villages, toward the beginning of the twentieth century, a sense of propriety if not a knowledge of sanitation was making such an act offensive. For similar reasons, the *pissoir* of European cities could not spread in America. Standards of decency in morals likewise, vary as they may through time and clime, will in any period and place mark certain items for general censure and consequent censorship. At no time could the English *Fanny Hill* or the French *Gamiani* be publicly printed. Such items, and the sincere desire to keep them out of the general hand, are not involved in the present discussion.

On quite another level stand the works of Ibsen, Whistler, Wagner, O'Neill—even Caldwell, Faulkner, Lawrence. It is not toward such a novel as *Anthony Adverse,* for all its occasional freedom, that the censor stretches eager hands—though of course there grows through Hervey Allen's book no Elinor

Glynt of the eye, no Voynitch of the gadfly of sex. But books from which these lickerishly rise are equally free from censorship—which fastens on the works, even freer from prurience, of a Zola and a Joyce.

Somehow the books that escape the censor's ire are those that pander to man's weakness or (more decently) picture his power. They show him carving his own destiny, and a competent knifesman. The wrath of the public (as roused or nursed by the censor, vigilant and usually self-appointed guardian of the god Good Taste) falls upon novels that turn from this glamorous view, to regard man as in one order with all other things. Some find it intolerable that they be deemed subject to, perhaps victims of, the inviolable laws or the inescapable drift of nature. One author was not hardy enough to continue writing novels after a title of his was travestied as *Jude the Obscene*.

On the stage, in the same fashion, it is seldom the sparkle of the Wildean or the Viennese high comedy, saturate with sex, nor yet the spangle of the chordaic revue, that draws the censor's glittering eye; but rather the presentation of some less roseate view of life; the dramas of Ibsen; *Damaged Goods; The God of Vengeance. Du Barry Was a Lady* played in cities that banned *Tobacco Road*. In these forbidden dramas some outside power, usually the inanimate grinding force of inevitable law, drives the character to the consequence of his deeds. "The wheels of the gods" turn on. But (like as the ancients hid the holy names) God may be called chance, circumstance, nature, environmental pressure, the life force. There is the rub: no longer is a special deity concerned foremost with man; all things equally bow in a common subjection. An external force commands. Gone is man's free will. Silenced, the exalting cry: "How like an angel! . . . How like a god!" Here is no rouse at which we stand astonied, nay, with which we may march trampling over time, beating with our charger's hoofs defiance to destiny, choosing the roads we travel, even when they lead to the bottomless pit—dying perhaps (for this we have not yet fashioned avoidance) at the end; but even from death wringing a twisted triumph, cheered by the ultimate call: "And what is more, you've been a man, my son!" Not this, but a driven doom.

What irks the good public, then, working through the censor, may be some unavowed, dimly felt stirring of man's pride —seizing upon religion, politics, sex, failure of a playhouse to bind the appropriate red tape about its license, as pretext. Pride in man's high destiny as the mortal-elect upon the chosen planet —masking a fear, perchance, that must not be uncovered, lest like a plucked bird we shiver in the untoward cold, poor featherless biped desolate on the crust of a hardening fragment of a mediocre flame-ball in the drift of the million million stars.

I have neither the time nor presently available volumes to pursue this notion through the history of censorship. Of course one thinks at once of Socrates. The eighteenth century French "libertines" were mainly not rakes but rebels. Cyrano de Bergerac (history's, not Rostand's) in *The States and Empires of the Sun* makes the birds that inhabit the sun sure the intruder is a man because at sight of him they are seized with "an instinctive disgust." So prompt was censorship that even later printings of the original edition of this work changed the expression; sardonically, the birds become sure he is a human because of his "effrontery in falsely maintaining he is not a man." Glancing farther back, we remember that it is for teaching man the use of fire that Prometheus earns eternal torture. Even in legend it is the realist search for understanding that is forbidden, against the romantic dream. Satan led man to eat of the fruit of the tree of knowledge. The word *Lucifer* means *bearer of light*. Andreyev pictures *Anathema* as storming the skies, to wrest the secrets of the gods. However such glimpses indicate earlier tendencies, for contemporary events this theory provides illumination.

Mrs. Mary Ware Dennet, for example, wrote a pamphlet on sane youthful growth, after which the hounds of sex leapt in full cry. For she presumes to think that there is no awful mystery of life, surging like a flood tide into the breasts of good citizens-to-be, there (especially if they are female!) to be stemmed by innate sense of decency. Rather, she sees it all as a natural process, neither mysterious and glamorous, nor yet abominable and of the foul fiend; a process knowledge of which might help toward a sound unfoldment. To the censor-mind, sex is apparently either sacred or satanic. We may laugh at it; we may love it—even hate it; but we must not study it. For it is God-given; not amenable to nature's law.

In France, the novel picturing post-war debauchery among liberated women and the newly rich, *La Garçonne,* was attacked only after it was widely discussed abroad as typifying French moral degeneration, at a time when France wanted the good will of the world. Nor did the Legion of Honor, in striking from its rolls the author, Victor Margueritte, forget that he had also written *Au Bord du Gouffre,* an unsparing study of the causes of the First World War. Many novels sexually more outspoken than *La Garçonne* were freely published—*L'Art d'aimer* and *La Toison d'or* of Jean de Gourmont, for example—and freely sold; but these had neither political repercussions nor effort to make an honest study of the contemporary scene. In them, man moves in an erotic preoccupation remote from all other earthly concerns; therefore those concerned in mundane things leave such books alone.

Again the censors roused when Bertrand Russell was appointed to the faculty of the College of the City of New York. It may be that, initially, his appointment was inadvisable. It may be, furthermore, that political and pacifistic complications urged Russell from his native land. It may even be that the opinions of Russell, as quoted from his books in the decision voiding the appointment, are erroneous. But what roused the clergy to make outcry is that Russell has attempted a scientific study of "sacred" things, of marriage and the problems of sex. Thereupon a judge calls him obscene. His appointment, declares the learned justice, "is an insult to the people of the City of New York" and "is, in effect, establishing a chair of indecency." Weigh just this point: Among the passages from

THE ROMANTIC REBELLION

Russell's books, the court quotes: "The peculiar importance attached, at the present, to adultery, is quite irrational." Later, the decision presses home: "Section 100 of the Penal Law makes adultery a criminal offence . . . consider the vast amount of money that the taxpayers are assessed each year to enforce these provisions of the law. . . . Considering Dr. Russell's principles with reference to the Penal Law of the State of New York, it appears that not only would the morals of the students be undermined, but his doctrines would tend to bring them, and in some cases their parents and guardians, in conflict with the Penal Law, and accordingly this court intervenes . . ." The only ground for divorce in New York is adultery, which, as the judge truly emphasizes, is a criminal offence. Yet on Manhattan Island, in five years before the Bertrand Russell decision (1935-1939), there were 6770 divorces—and three indictments for adultery, all dismissed! Here was the world's major crime wave! Or is there more than coincidence in the fact that while Love is blind, Justice is blindfold?

The attitude is pervasive of all living; we see it at its apogee in the fields of art. The *Decameron* and the *Droll Stories* won freedom before the sober scientific studies of marital relationship. Magazines proffering "snappy" or "spicy" stories flourish; the pin-up girls of the "Silk Stocking Parade" can be bought at the public stands. The frail suggestion of the nude *September Morn,* the more florid smile of many a magazine-cover trollop, with frank flesh between tight garter-top and sheer step-in, achieve a wide and uninterrupted sale: thump go the statues out of Radio City. They have, it is true, returned; but had they curved into form a godliness of stature, a majesty of bearing, to give substance to man's self-esteem, they might have been bare as a pilgarlick's pate, and never tottered. Rodin's *Balzac,* Epstein's *Adam,* similarly shocked because they set no incense before the altar of human pride.

Those interested in maintaining their political power or religious domination may sometimes discern a threat in art, and move through censorship to its obliteration. Even here, of course, their conduct is rooted in soil of man's lust for power or sense of higher destination—which must be held secure, even against fact. But sex censorship is less directly explicable, for sex-play is in some measure the modern *circenses* (and the Pan!). It is a sop to Cerberus, to cram the maws of the monster *Masse-Mensch* who might otherwise devour his proper master, the "self-made" man that through his own endeavors has risen to the top. The number of burlesque houses increased during the depression. During the critical days of the blitzkrieg in England, London first let down the bars to allow the bare routine called the strip-tease. With the upturn of business, burlesque licenses in New York were not extended; but at higher cost purveyors renewed the nudity, with night-club "fan" dances, the "bubble" dance, the "dove" dance, and gay girlies taking a bath in wine.

For such reasons, it becomes apparent that the objection's core does not lie in the sex, however human in its erotic implications, but—however honest in its natural exposition—in the "debasing" of man to the level of other animals. There is the gesture not of outraged morality but of offended pride. The overcovered raw of a fear is prodded, and the proud flesh squirms.

For is not man truly other than the lilies of the field, that toil not, neither do they spin? Is he not, sconced in his towers of steel, truly higher than the creatures of the valley and the down, which he bends to his service, harnesses to his will, holds to his law—while he admits for himself no law save his own, based on the love and law of his Father in heaven, who has set man over all created things, has set man free? And if free will is no more than a dream, man wills that the dream be undisturbed.

"Romance," the London Times takes occasion to say, on the death of the man that forty years before wrote *The Prisoner of Zenda,* "Romance survives all the realisms." Which means that, faced with two possible but incompatible views of life, the majority of men, by a natural and unwitting choice, do not pause to test them but accept at once that view which presents man in the better light. The New York Herald-Tribune columnist, a week later, remarks that "the romantic is a neurotic who dramatizes his life." But, sitting for his portrait, most any man would take the pose that reveals him at his best; why be more careless before eternity? Only a comparative few, in life or in art, resent this "glossing over"; only a few feel that that is but semblance of beauty which does not look all around, and deep within, for truth. Romance is the assumption of the self satisfying pose; realism, the refusal to pose at all, the insistence on being taken as imbedded in one's surroundings. In either case, the value of the portrait depends upon the artist not as sitter but as wielder of the brush.

13. *Fear leads us far.*

THE fear that turns the censor howling against realism finds cover and proud parade of courage in romance. Dabblers in the alchemy of the soul wrap fear in the cocoon of many pupal theories. Against Freud's libido is erected Adler's sense of inferiority, which comes when the infant first feels his dependence, and never leaves the man. The behaviorist notes that of the four first responses of the new-born child—to stroking, to squeezing, to dropping, and to loud, sudden noise—cooing love and bristling anger together but halve the total impressions with huddling fear.

Further cause of fear, more concordant with the present point, is indicated by the French thinker, Alain. Looking at primitive man, he observes that those speculators that give primacy to sex or to economics overlook sleep. For food, or a mate, man fought his fellows; he exercised and he displayed his strength, his sense of power, his pride. While these quests encourage rivalry, they enjoy company; eating delights in, and love demands, a companion. These are social urges; but they need no bolstering of society. But sleep holds a man apart. One-third of his life, early man was shrunken helpless in slumber. He was at any one's mercy, hence afraid; therefore he formed groups, set guards, built walls. But while he slept his fears found him again, in dreams; magnified, hence requiring greater powers to dispel them. Society and religion were thus fostered by sleep, by the fears that rise when man feels himself alone.

In the adult today, at any rate, fear is both a cause and a consequence of isolation. A lonely man is always a little afraid. Conversely, when a man draws back in fear, he is pricked aware of his essential loneliness. Few punishments are more dreaded than solitary confinement. Shelley's *Alastor* (as

Peacock, who gave it the title, insists we shall not forget) treats the spirit of solitude as a spirit of evil. From this, perhaps, springs the Romantic spread-eagling love for humanity; as Adler would have us see, in conquering heroes, men desperately struggling to master themselves. By extension from the individual need rise the social consciousness and the humanitarian concern that mark the mid-century in its growth toward our day.

Beyond the emphasis on the individual that promotes and is again pointed by the awakening of fear, furthermore, the Romantic deliberately waves aside man's chief recourse against the world's dark terrors. When he abrogates the rule of reason, a man in his greater hours may stand open to the promptings of inspiration, the surge of his genius; but in lengthening spells he will lie exposed to the unchecked whispers and discordant cries of an imagination that, as the *Book of Wisdom* observes, may set all nature out of harmony:

> *Whether there were a whistling sound,*
> *Or a melodious noise of birds among the spreading*
>   *branches,*
> *Or a measured fall of water running violently,*
> *Or a hoarse crashing of rocks hurled down,*
> *Or the swift course of animals bounding along unseen,*
> *Or the voice of wild beasts harshly roaring,*
> *Or an echo rebounding from the hollows of the mountains,*
> *All these things paralyzed them with terror.*

The abandonment of reason brings, not madness first, but fear.

The bulwarks of sanity against fear, once reason has been relinquished, are faith and love. Faith, in the ordered creeds, requires self-subjection, bowing to an interpretation and therefore to a will imposed. The individual Romantic (whose atavars roused the Reformation) preferred the prouder, more isolate way of a personal belief, which left him still with but his own resources. Shelley, expelled from the university for his essay on atheism, was profoundly religious; but he must, even toward the kingdom of heaven, find his own path. The one sustenance that came to the Romantic from without, even brought an outer source of strength into intimate union with his inmost self, was love, "a going out of our nature, and the identification of ourselves with the beautiful which exists in thought, action, or person, not our own." Beyond all restraint the Romantic leapt into love.

THE ROMANTIC REBELLION

14. *Enter: woman, and love.*

THE "romance" is always a love story. And "Romantic love," sprung with the violets all new when the ash-buds were black in England's Helicon, has risen out of the early Renaissance to the most frequent theme of modern fiction. The great works of world literature deal with more fundamental concerns, however a woman may determine their movement, as in *Medea, The Divine Comedy, Macbeth.* In them, the love story may appear as an episode: Paolo and Francesca, or Heaven Well Lost For Love. They are reared, however, upon life's basic drives: man's firm nobility in the face of wrathful gods; his far coursing to break down the uncrossed barriers of the world —the barriers, early, of space and hostile hordes, but always the walls of ignorance and of predestined fate; the long discovery that "character is fate"—and still against that doom the maintenance of man's high dignity, and man's ideals. But the romance is always a love story.

The development of love as a theme for art is intricately bound with the evolution of woman's status. The Greek and the Roman erected the double standard. For their play the courtesans prepared their lives; to them might be dedicated "love" poems—verses of bodily love, frank movements toward sexual fulfilment. In the background waited the daughters of citizens, with whom marriages were arranged, for the continuance and elevation of one's family and the well-being of the land. In the dark ages, save for the few who won exemption through marriage to Jesus, women were little more than chattel. The trace of that peonage still occasionally surprises an American when a foreign couple of peasant stock boards a train, the woman carrying the bundles; if there is but one empty seat, into it plumps the man. The same attitude lingers in the German saying that woman is meant for "kitchen, children, church."

The increasing leisure of lordly ways under the feudal system, however, gave milady both time to while away and wiles wherewith to charm it. Under the sun of her gracious smile grew the Provençal ceremonial of the page's, the knight's, adoration, and blossomed the troubadour songs. In the society drawn to its consummate expression in Dante's *Comedy,* and spun to the most exquisite weaving of the threads of love and virtue in *The Faerie Queene,* the Christian romance held the beloved lady as earth's fair copy of her in heaven whose bosom gave suck to the infant Saviour.

For a time the lusty Renaissance disregarded this symbol. I may be pardoned if I draw from the past my first published poem, to fancy the young Renaissance dramatist addressing a suave romancer of today. Quoth Kit Marlowe (among other things) to James Branch Cabell:

Man's love of woman is the least of life—
Like food, perhaps, but no more imminent;
Man builds his world on lust of gold or power.
Fashion a harem where a king may loll,
Anthony, Heliogabalus,
And the people writhes—but let the king grow wroth,
Let him sweep conquering over continents,
Alexander, Caesar, or our own great king,
And patriots run to die to clear his way.

But the readers of *Euphues* were women. The gentlemen of the time had their romances to live. They strove for fortune on the Spanish Main; they carved careers on a dozen challenging fronts; they died on the scaffold. At home, in the meantime, even the shrewd and active Elizabeth had time to be amused. Are we not told that she called for a play showing Falstaff in love—romanticizing that most earth-bound of mortals! The ladies of the court, with little else (save occasional spying and intrigue, with which this could pleasantly intertwine) to occupy their fancy, had time to harp on their heart-strings. The fact that their Queen was unmarried helped to keep the theme forward in their thoughts, as favorites moved their gallant way to London Tower. The feminine preoccupation with courtly etiquette, sweet sentiment and dalliance gay, spun the threads for the psychological novel, which turns from bold adventure forth, to emotions, soul-states, inner responses to the world's events.

Euripides long ago made Medea cry:

> Men say we women lead a sheltered life
> At home, while they face death amid the spears.
> The fools! I had rather stand in battle line
> Thrice, than bear a child.

The demand that woman be allowed to stand in line with man, and fight life's battles by his side, is not given voice, however, for many centuries. It breaks out as a lone cry in the dramas of Nicholas Rowe, *Jane Shore*, and *The Fair Penitent*, which in 1703 protests:

> How hard is the condition of our sex,
> Thro' ev'ry state of life the slaves of man.
> In all the dear delightful days of youth
> A rigid father dictates to our wills
> And deals out pleasure with a scanty hand;
> To his, the tyrant husband's reign succeeds;
> Proud with opinion of superior reason,
> He holds domestic business and devotion
> All we are capable to know, and shuts us,
> Like cloistered idiots, from the world's acquaintance
> And all the joys of freedom. Wherefore are we
> Born with high souls, but to assert ourselves,
> Shake off this vile obedience they exact,
> And claim an equal empire o'er the world!

It does not announce a lasting "woman's movement" until it speaks through Ibsen's *A Doll's House* in 1879. For the long centuries between, women did not desire independence; they were content to rule. Softer ways to dominance were sweeter; the men were bound in the silken chains of sentiment. In 1667, while Racine's greatest success, *Andromaque*, attained but twenty-seven performances, eighty were given of Thomas Corneille's *Timocrate*: in this popular success the hero, in love with the princess whose citadel his troops are besieging, goes out every night to repair the daily damage his army has inflicted.

The salons of France not merely were adorned, but—what is less important though more significant—were controlled, by women. Their smiles and frowns established literary taste through long years of Academy intrigue. *Les amis* of Conrart, meeting from 1629 to 1634, with the support of Cardinal Richelieu founded the French Academy; but the election of a new member, or the acceptance of a new word into the language, was argued as potently by *les amies*. More than one salon was known, for its generation, as the ante-chamber of the Academy.

The literary women of the period stand out almost beyond the men. Mme. de Sevigné was "the queen of letter writers." Mlle. de Scudéry seemed "the marvel of the grand century"; she had "taken all that's good of the ancients, and bettered it." Loyal subjects at her salon included the Academy's secretary, its law-giver Boileau, and such of the lesser members as could gain admittance. Beyond the contemporary praise extends the work of Mme. de la Fayette, who inspired Rochefoucauld. The "tenderness" Racine set as the center-stone in passion's coronet is magnified in Mlle. de Scudéry's *Clélie* until it underlies a rolling blossomed countryside, laid out and its topography mapped in minute detail: The Land of the Tender. Mme. de la Fayette, (if she wrote *La Princesse de Clèves*) waters that soil with virtuous tears, so that it proves doubly rich, and spreads fertile ground for English *Pamela*.

Women have not often had such open control of the literary world; but they have never since ceased to be a determining factor. They provide the majority of the readers, and an increasing proportion of the creators in all fields of art. Julien Benda in our day bitterly complains that the whole of modern aesthetics is designed for the women. The literary qualities now dominant, he asserts, are those women chiefly manifest: absence of general ideas, worship of the concrete; an intuitive grasp at the world; a solo of sentiment; interest absorbed in the self, in the gossipy, in the most intimate, in the incommunicable. While we may not agree that these characteristics are necessarily feminine, we should note that they are all qualities we have associated with the Romantic.

In poetry and in fiction, more than in other art fields, women are showing a competence that challenges that of the men. Both as writers and as readers, they are drawn to the novel because it provides—Chesterton sees the same linkage as Benda—"a hearty and exhausting overhauling of that part of human existence which has always been the woman's province, or rather kingdom: the play of personalities in private."

Doubtless we may suspect that in the life of every age, however absent in its literature, there were youth-found sweets in love. We may track them, boisterous in the free vein of Ovid and Apuleius—with the charming interlude of Cupid and Psyche; tumbling later in Boccaccio and his fellows. We may dwell upon their idyllic aspect in the Greek romances of the fourth century, Longus' drawn story of Daphnis and Chloe, Heliodorus' of Theagenes and Chariclea, and the rest. Chaucer was far from unaware of women's ways, as he lets peep now and again, witness *The Nonne Preestes Tale*:

> *For also siker* In principio,
> Mulier est hominis confusio;
> *Madame, the sentence of this Latin is —*
> *Woman is mannes joy and al his blis.*

But it remained for the Elizabethans—for Shakespeare—to lay bare the deeps, and the tragic consequences, of the passion of love; to explore and linger over and play upon romance's most ecstatic experience, the sublime mystery of wooing.

In *Love's Labour's Lost* Shakespeare sets the theory of Romantic love:

*For when would you, my liege, or you, or you,
In leaden contemplation have found out
Such fiery numbers as the prompting eyes
Of beauty's tutors have enrich'd you with?
Other slow arts entirely keep the brain;
And therefore, finding barren practicers,
Scarce show a harvest of their heavy toil:
But love, first learned in a lady's eyes,
Lives not alone immured in the brain;
But, with the motion of all elements,
Courses as swift as thought in every power,
And gives to every power a double power,
Above their functions and their offices.*

In *The Taming of the Shrew* the playwright rollicks through a post-espousal wooing; but in *The Tempest* smiles indeed

Who ever loved that loved not at first sight!

and in *As You Like It* romps merrily through an enchanted courtship. Love fortifies Brutus and Macbeth, with different motives, to similar ends; as its excesses move Gertrude, and its deficiency (in Ophelia) leaves no way to mend Hamlet. And in *Troilus and Cressida, Romeo and Juliet, Anthony and Cleopatra,* and *Othello,* Shakespeare has for all time demonstrated that the greatest art can rise from the portrayal of the deep-striking aberrations of the passion of love.

In the artificial comedy that came with the Stuart line, there is something of a return to the ancient attitude: arranged marriages, and schemed affairs. But here, even the ladies are courtesans. The lovemaking, however, is less personal than in the age before; more abstract, a game as much as a passion. Occasionally, under the coquetry of her trifling, as slipper-toe beneath brocaded gown, a Millamant lets peep the more winsome responsiveness of a maiden in love. With the nineteenth century, in freshet flood love springs anew, washing muddy sediment toward the underground sea of Freud. It has lost,

THE ROMANTIC REBELLION

in large measure, the symbolism of the early Elizabethans; love has come down to earth. Love's charms are intertwined with nature's beauty. And it finds as many moods as a moonbeam maiden. From the simple troth of *The Lady of the Lake* it ranges to the heaven-held languishment of *The Blessed Damosel* and the rapturous rue of Swinburne. In music it swoons in the ecstasy of Wagner. In the novel, love climbs to the perfervid all-inclusiveness of Richard Feverel: "It is all that is worth living for in the world: lead whither it will I follow it: it is worship, religion, life."

Many causes have thus combined to make courtship and the tangled skeins of passion chief task for the unraveling of play or novel. We have already traced the Romantic emphasis upon the individual; the discrediting of reason with consequent backflood of fear and bulkhead of love. And the growth of leisure, of time to read and to fancy. We might normally expect that the woman, with her burden of continuance, would have her mind set on practical matters and provident schemes. Among many primitive tribes, as among the bees, the luxuries of adornment and of art are left to the dreamer, often the drone, that is the male. Man, however, differs from other animals in two pertinent respects. He may store, separately, far more than his personal needs require. And partly as a consequence of this gleaned power, he has created a new type within the species: the *gentle*man. At this point the practical shrewdness of his mate may be discerned; for she has (Eve-like) ribbed him into the creation of the lady. Gradually insinuated into the gentlemanly code are assumptions that the lady must be guarded in effortless security, her pampered ease and displayed extravagance a proof of his lordly prowess. The lady became the earthly blossom of Our Lady; then man's worship made her an idyll, an idol, idle. The Romantic pattern was complete.

More frequent among women than the cigarettes of today were the smelling-salts of a hundred years ago, to revive the sensitive damsel or dame when a mouse or a murmur of unexpected tidings upset the even tenor of her delicate days. Whenever a family rises above the stark line of mere subsistence, the woman reaches out to a leisure and an adornment that in other animals mark the male, but that man in his blind vanity accepts as a sign of and tribute to his own masculine power. The basis of such subservience is, of course, an exaltation of love, of what a man will do—"should do"—for his beloved.

In our day of the new freedom for women, there has been some lessening of the men's respect. Perhaps, as observation in the subway rush-hour indicates, below the taxicab level the gentleman hardly penetrated, or soon became extinct. But the woman, while eager to take advantage of all the privileges of her more independent movement through the days, is reluctant to relinquish any of the prizes of the old sheltered state. The modern girl wants to be at once a hustler and a queen. Watch any automobile intersection on a Sunday, and you will see how far the females carry the maxim "Ladies first"! In the meantime, it has carried them far indeed. Yet in their far circumference they hold the Romantic core. Lin Yutang observes that the position of the American woman today is colored by "the romanticism of Madame de Staël, expansive, humanitarian, cosmopolitan, and emotional." She claims the rank of reason, yet would wield emotion's power.

Another provocation to the theme of love is the desire for novelty. Jaded emotions seeking fresh stimuli; creators that must conform to patent and copyright law; the fickle fair in quest of new diversion: all prize originality. Of the emotions, love has the widest range, and provides the readiest self-deception. Throb a thousand beats on the single drum of sex, and the ready heart will fashion as many songs. The popular author in *Beggars on Horseback* wrote his sixteenth best seller by dictating his fifteenth. Change the names; at once the reader can build herself into another life. Excess of fear, or of anger, may have dire consequences; their deficiency—unless the rash exploits of stunt-fliers, and the mad careers of a Tamburlaine, a Napoleon, a Hitler, be sprung of too little fear—their lack brings no such disastrous damming as inability to love. Love may be baffled by frustration, through rivals or hostile circumstances or just its absence in the beloved. It may be warped through perversion. It may (since the fig-leaf made woman a secret and a sin) fall upon the unworthy, as in bestowal upon one that drags the lover down. *Of Human Bondage* proffers example. Through these clogged channels love may burst into excess, which may burn in quickly fired jealous rage, or scorch in grievous lust. The milder moods of love show variance too; its ardent yet tender courtship, its fresh pleasaunce of flowered dalliant way, its springs of hope and wells of deep devotion and autumns of falling leaf to dolour and despair. For a myriad causes, love is dear to the Romantics, and the mainspring of romance.

15. *Foremost is form.*

THE lyric pulse-reading of the Romantic, his concern with his pangs and his passions, has led critics as divergent as Pater and Croce to declare that the Romantic approaches art along the highway of matter; the classic, along the avenue of form. The inner tumult without which there is no art occupies the one, the outward representation without which there is no art concerns the other. Nor is there much doubt, insofar as manner and matter are separable, that what a man feels and thinks lies at the heart of genius. The message is the man. The personality dictates the procedure.

One finds it a bit hard, however, to picture even the most classical artist scurrying about for subject-matter. Milton weighed many stories; when he decided upon the fall of man, he almost caught it in a drama; but he was never at a loss as to what he wanted to say. He sought the framework, the best (and he took the best known) plot by means of which to express his conception of life's ultimate problems and man's destiny. "Truth is simple and gives little trouble," said Goethe. And indeed to each of us our own point of view is an unconscious background of life; like breathing, just quietly there until challenged. Then perhaps defying definition: Goethe added that truth is beyond intellectual formulation, can be made manifest and humanly coherent only as poetry.

What a man has to say is fundamental—but by him taken for granted, like the sun, like healthy digestion. But the "inner tumult" demands organization; this ordering is the basis of all art. Conceivably, a barren mind might cast about for subjects, might question: "What can I write about?" But even in casual conversation a speaker is often irked by the inability of others to see what to him is as plain as the nose on their face; because it is rooted in his basic and unquestioned attitude—but not in theirs. To a fertile artist in any age, a fortiori, the problem is: How shall I make these lunkheads understand? How make them see how wise (good, powerful) I am? How convince them of the validity of my thesis, of my being? How—more personally—can I work these tumbling fragments of life into a whole? How make this growing shape mean what I must have it mean? Sound as my soul hears it?

St. Nicholas brought three children alive out of a pot when they had already been boiled down into soup; but the creation of the children was prior to his miracle. The sum total of an artist's being at the moment of the work is what he has to say, no matter of what he is talking; his problem is to bring himself out of the soup. He must crystallize his personality, with all its quirks and humors and inconsistencies, its logic and earnest desire for truth and dogmatic impulsive rouse out of feeling; he must distill his spirit, in the medium of his story, into an essence the receptor will deem worth the holding. How works the alembic art? Through the expression, through the form.

One must not hence conclude that form is the more important aspect of a work of art. It is merely the easier to tinker with. There are works in which the pains lavished upon form but the more fully reveal a banal or trivial substance. Indeed, the better the form—the more persuasive the orator, the more seductive the poet—of an evil spirit, the more dangerous the resultant work.

Actually, of course, the artist is contained in the work as a whole, form and substance being one. What we isolate as form, as well as what we distinguish as substance, is determined by the nature of the artist. Insofar as they are separable, however, a man's substance kindles at the creative moment beyond his control; he can in some measure monkey with "the mechanics of form." To that extent, he also alters, mars or mends, the substance.

The themes of literature are perennial; it is the form that shifts. As Dryden says:

In general, the employment of a poet is like that of a curious gunsmith, or watchmaker: the iron or silver is not his own; but they are the least part of that which gives the value: the price lies wholly in the workmanship.

How many have told fair Helen's tale? The continent paid the English Chaucer a high compliment in calling him "the great translator." Every great actress must play Juliet, Lady Macbeth, or Phèdre, Camille. When an artist has grown beyond apprenticeship, he reaches out, not to new stories from beyond the stars, but to an old, familiar theme. This is no sign of approaching sterility, no drive of the writer's itch persisting when inspiration flags: too many names crowd to attest the fact, from Shakespeare the sublime adapter through Milton and Pope to Shaw and Robinson and Masefield, in English alone. It is an indifference to the tyro's vaunted difference. It is a fulness of self-knowledge, that needs no prop of external novelty of story; the originality is within. Thus the great artist is drawn to themes that have always been test of genius, and draws upon his own resources to achieve the work. A hundred daubers may work with Rembrandt's model; *it is not the sitter, but himself, that Rembrandt paints.*

Every sonnet contains fourteen iambic pentameter lines of ordered rhyming. Every sonnet, nevertheless—as every poem in heroic couplets, every work of art—has its unique form. It is built, within the frame, of shaded harmonious movements of sound, sense, and suggestion, of pause and rhythmic continuance and suspended then satisfied expectancy. Through these it manifests the many qualities—discordant, but here caught into intricate and finely balanced, enduring and delightful equipoise—that *are* the artist. It has been said that every work of art is an autograph. Read not in dates and outward facts but in spirit and rounded being, every work of art is an autobiograph.

A plot can be discerned without much imagination; a story lends itself to summary. For this reason, partly out of school-day practice, even critics tend to emphasize the story aspect of a work. What this presents is, however, largely accidental, at most incidental. For this, nonetheless, is neglected the true substance of the work, which is the artist himself, gathered—through and during the process of creation—into form. *It is in this sense, not as plot, that substance and form are inseparable.* Information can be transferred; novelty ceases to be new: these things are outside the man; the style is the man himself. *Le style, c'est l'homme même.* The inner tumult and the outward order thus balance like all the polarities that through the artist's counterpoising are the constant themes of art. They form a hyperbola: two opposite movements, two impulsions apart, yet doubly bound together, and truly one.

The Romantic preached obedience to impulse, to the spontaneous urge. Having suspected him of a more personal self-consciousness, we may, despite his precept, look for attention to form. Yielding to emotion's drive should carry the personality plump into the work; yet we observe that these men who despised the middle class went out of their way to shock it. They could not merely scorn it, but must make it feel their scorn. Which tells the psychologist a different story.

Gray, for his *Elegy,* by but a twelvemonth scanted the injunction of Horace to let one's words lie gestate nine years— "for what cometh forth from the mouth goeth not back therein." The most effervescent of the Romantics, Blake, worked on some of his poems (*Vola* was never finished) as long as a decade. The poets might print in haste; they revised at leisure. Blake's well known quatrain;

> *He who bends to himself a joy*
> *Does the winged life destroy;*
> *But he who kisses the joy as it flies*
> *Lives in Eternity's sun rise—*

originally read "He who binds to himself a joy . . ." We know that Keats strove lengthily to achieve the "spontaneous" line: "A thing of beauty is a joy forever." Coleridge in *The Ancient*

Mariner wrote "the furrow followed free," changed it when a sailor showed him that furrows do not "follow" but "flow off," then rescinded the change for the sake of the poetry. The standard editions of direct Wordsworth and rapt Shelley note revised readings. Carefree Byron wrote to John Murray:

> With regard to what you say of retouching the *Juans* and the *Hints,* it is all very well; but I can't *furbish.* I am like the tyger (in poesy), if I miss my first spring, I must go growling back to my Jungle. There is no second. I can't correct; I can't, and I won't. Nobody ever succeeds in it, great or small. . . . You must take my things as they happen to be: if they are not likely to suit, reduce their *estimate* then accordingly. I would rather give them away than hack and hew them. I don't say that you are not right: I merely assert that I cannot better them. I must either "make a spoon, or spoil a horn." And there's an end.

But there's not an end, in Byron's poesy! Probably he was here writing for his public. For in private Byron went over his work constantly. On the margins of his own copies of his printed poems are many emendatory notes; on one occasion he avowed that he was going over his work "to make some additions and alterations to render it more worthy of public perusal."

In such fine phrases as Wordsworth's "recollected in tranquility," as "write with fury and correct with phlegm," there is a false cleavage. Revision is not likely to improve a work of art unless the first mood be recaptured for the second thought. And even in the initial urge, in the most spontaneous dictation of an inspired spirit, reason plays a swift part in the fully responsive personality of the artist—and usually beyond this a more deliberative judgment exercises a measure of creative control. No distinction between literary schools can be drawn along this line; every artist quiets that inner tumult in the press of form.

16. *Freud's finger probes.*

It was too much to expect to complete this picture without Freud. F. L. Lucas brings psychanalytical batteries to bear, in *The Decline and Fall of the Romantic Ideal*, which drops dive-bombs of wit and charges with eighty-ton tanks of implacable analysis. Can we hold our judgment free?

Although Mr. Lucas carries the standards of Freud, he proffers an "Aristotelian" definition: "Romantic literature is a dream-picture of life; providing sustenance and fulfilment for impulses cramped by society or reality." We may see in this merely a heavy-toned restatement of the thought that literature is escape. But Mr. Lucas insists that we probe more deeply; the essence of the Romantic, he repeats, is the liberation of the less conscious levels of the mind. To make this precise, he sets the inner man in a Freudian triangle:

1. *reality-principle* = the world = reality, facts, the sense of what is.
2. *super-ego* = the ideal = society, the sense of what is fitting, what ought to be.
3. *id* = the instinctive, the animal (level of imagination and passion) = the sense of what one wants to be.

If the first of these dominates, realism results; from the second springs classicism; the third gives birth to romanticism.

Mr. Lucas thus fits for his authors a Procrustean bed. They twist strangely to lie in it. He must intertwine realism and romance, present a whole "society" grown romantic, declare that the opposition is "not simply Emotion versus Reason, though it often is." What more the conflict may involve, he does not make clear; nor indeed does he (despite his summoning of psychology) seek beneath the combat for its cause. The dream is to him so basic that he never questions why, more than others, the Romantics dreamed.

Thus Lucas sets as a characteristic of the Romantics' "dream" what is really its cause, what drives them to this indulgence in their feelings and their fancies: their "lonely egotism . . . an exaggerated ego which in the Romantic often grows as bloated as an ant-queen among her crawling subjects." He avers that, of all their loosened passions, chief is their "passion for themselves."

Precisely! And it is this concentration on themselves that leads in their writings and their lives to ever greater quest of stimulation, of sensation, that induces artificial aids to reverie and to feeling, that lures them toward narcissism, sadism, masochism, incest (in book and bed) and all the other horrors of the Freudian museum.

The respect that the name of Freud too widely evokes leads me to point out further flaws in Mr. Lucas' analysis. He applies freely to the works what he finds in the lives. It is in letters and diaries that we read such remarks as "I *am* Emma Bovary," which Mr. Lucas quotes; Flaubert took long pains to make his book objective. Byron's scorn of revision is also adduced, without mention of the fact that this was but pretense. One curious betrayal of the "analytical" mind: we are told that the medieval man didn't lay a frog's tongue on his mistress' heart while she slept, to make her confess her secrets, because he believed it would work, there was no need to test it. I can imagine a man refraining, in fear of what might be revealed; but Mr. Lucas apparently has no idea but that the intent in applying the magic charm could be only to test its efficacy, not to discover the secrets!

It is strange, in this volume analyzing the "dream-picture" of the Romantics, to find no mention of the two Freudian types of dream, the anxiety-boding, and the wish-fulfilment. Perhaps too many of the Romantic works would fall outside these classes. Shelley's cry to the West Wind: "Be thou me, impetuous one!" springs from a surge of revolt; more often there is a "dreamy" melancholy not in the mood of a dream. Laziness is diffused rebellion; but sloth of the will hardly tends to the triumph. Not

THE ROMANTIC REBELLION

even all the instances offered by Mr. Lucas accord with his basic theory. When Tannhauser warmed with a pagan love on the Venusberg, it seemed a sin too horrible for absolution—Shades of libido! in what dreams is love thus damned? Rather, these Romantics are like Jurgen's grandfather, who deemed what he did important enough to deserve eternal chastizing.

While Mr. Lucas' definition speaks of "impulses cramped by society or reality," his discussion is limited to the writings, as though they were an isolate phase of man's being. He does comment, it is true, on the Romantic writers, mainly on their intoxicant or erotic excesses; he even permits himself a Romantic relaxation: railing at Hitler and Mussolini and "our present civilization of scientific chimpanzees." But economics, politics, science, all the interrelationships of one's being, as an individual but in society, are neglected in this Freudian picture.

We tend, finally, to replace the old triangulation—the good, the true, the beautiful; intellect, emotion, will; the world, the flesh, and the devil—with more resolved oppositions along the principle of polarity. But Mr. Lucas has a new desperate strangulation: the *id,* the *super-ego,* the *reality-principle,* each in a corner with its hands around another's neck. It might be more widely fruitful to consider that his organic, lawful "society," with a sense of what is fit, must balance into equilibrium the pressure of the unique individual in each of us; while the "third point" of his triangle is a different antithesis, as that same individual deems himself one with the world of facts in all its laws and interlockings, or a being with diviner springs and goals. Such, at any rate, is the thesis of the present volume.

The earnest adolescent—permit the probe a minute more! —finding his desires checked by an indifferent world, may move in any of several directions. He may grow cynically to "make the best of it" by turning the world's weapons against itself, seeking his own advancement. The path of American industry is crowded with "robber barons." He may, after his "season in hell," go off as did Rimbaud to organize and lead caravan trains. If he be resentful or bold, he may kick back at the world, in socialism or in satire. Less courageously, he may accept the invitation of one of a dozen flowery lanes of soft retreat. (Save that such "escape"—but for actual or moral suicide—is usually temporary; on return, the world seems harsher still, requires more desperate remedies, more distant or more wondrous journeying.) The "introvert" pathway moves back toward childhood, toward the irresponsibility of the infant, with varying degrees of mystical or physiological relinquishment of reason, toward the soothing "dark mother" of D. H. Lawrence, and the warm haven of the womb. The "extrovert" roadways range more widely across the earth, after Stevenson and Gauguin to the orient seas, the "paradise" of Bali and the flower-decked dancing maidens of the sunkissed sandy shores. "Wish-fulfilment," less colorful imaginations seek in fabulous changes nearer home: the sentimental twists of the O. Henry endings grow tinged with happy gold; though also thence rise the glamorous kingdoms like Graustark or spread the invigorating regions of Poictesme where anything is rather more than likely to happen. Sturdier spirits may even venture to *Erewhon*, again by backward path hoping to find the remedy for human ills. They seek everyman's Utopia, the beautiful place that is no place.

On all these journeyings, however, one must not confuse the beatific goal, or the magic carpet of dream that transports one there, with the impulse that urges one forth, with the absorption in one's own feelings, with the preoccupation that implicitly assumes that one's feelings, one's troubles and sad burdens and desires, overweigh the onward imminence of all the world besides. It is this self-concern, this egocentric vision and evaluation, that seems to me the initial impetus toward the far-stretching fields and the multiform deeds and devices commonly called Romantic. And that is why most of us have a ruddy core of Romance!

17. Goethe gathers all.

As parallel lines in space, so down the vista of time even divergent ways may seem to meet. The many aspects of a period take shape along a single perspective. Its variety may coalesce in the work of a single man. Dante gathered into one great store what the Middle Ages had harvested for the feast of the Renaissance. The conflicting forces of the early nineteenth century, the germane and the germinating emphasis, all strive within the multiplex work of Johann Wolfgang von Goethe.

The early novel, *The Sorrows of Young Werther,* is almost maudlin in its emotional preoccupation; Thackeray's burlesque shows how near to silly is its sentiment. The final *Faust* moves through the tremendous range of its driving energy to a humanitarian close. Along the way, we may note some of the stages.

There is the lament of the Romantic, whose will is frustrate in life:

> The longer I live, the more it grieves me to see man, who occupies his supreme place for the very purpose of imposing his will upon nature, and freeing himself and his from an outrageous necessity—to see him taken up with some false notion, and doing the very opposite of what he wants to do.

The humane ideals of justice and the passion for freedom expressed in *Götz von Berlichingen* helped form the manly aspects of the Storm and Stress movement. *Werther,* despite its thesis that the world belongs to the strong in will (which led Goethe to regard Napoleon as a force for order) was responsible for a long series of sentimental episodes and of suicides in fiction and in life. It was in this period that the first sketch of *Faust* was written, the *Urfaust,* from which is retained the piteous tragedy of Gretchen.

Goethe meanwhile went to Weimar. Here he began the genuine contributions to science, as a forerunner of Darwin, that mark his study of comparative morphology and plant metamorphoses. The shifting concerns are reflected in *Wilhelm Meister's Apprenticeship*. When the influence of this work on the form and spirit of the contemporary novel began to wane, the ever imitated Goethe gave his followers a new impetus in *Elective Affinities,* which traced experiences not externally but in the soul.

As a realist, Goethe took his stand in nature and experience:

> Nature does not confound herself with any error, she herself cannot do other than always act rightly, unconcerned with what may be the result.

Man must therefore observe "the natural laws that rule his own nature and that, for all his freedom, he cannot alter in the least." Yet beyond this bondage, the author of *Faust* perceives a higher freedom, in the union of the opposing elements through love. Not the paired love of the Romantic: this he has subsumed; nor yet the conventional social impulse of the Augustan: this in him grows soul-deep and mankind-wide; but a creative interaction of man upon man, a sense that what each does is important for all, that in the beginning was the *deed*. Goethe declares:

> All happenings are symbols: while presenting themselves as complete they hint at something beyond. To recognize this requires at once the highest audacity and the deepest humility.

It was easier for the coming generation. Goethe showed the scars of his fight. But in his mighty flow, he spread from the freshet-spates of spring romanticism to the broader stream, with cited banks, of the impulsions of the mid-century. It is a fitting symbol of his life's import, that his last words were "More light!"

SYMBOLISM

SYMBOLISM

1. *Self puts on a social mask.*

As the nineteenth century moved on its massive way, certain of its early manifestations revealed unlooked-for ends. The individualism of Napoleon waned on St. Helena; although in America the same spirit suited the pioneer days of the surge across the land of opportunity, and (with the approving adjective *rugged*) found advocates as recent as Herbert Hoover. Many a mode thus outlives its time: even from the sown teeth of its senescence may spring to second growth.

More than the unions that divided the strength of Europe, the Holy Alliance, the Triple Entente, indicated that there were disadvantages in isolation. The legal codes of most lands, throughout the early years of the industrial revolution, encouraged individual enterprise; but two avenues of social betterment were soon paved. The inevitable hardships wrought upon the workers tended to unite them, first in sporadic upheavals such as the machine-wrecking riots, then in the more organic Unions. At the same time, those that were extracting from the new order a larger share of worldly goods woke to some sense of duty to their less fortunate fellows. Both protest and charity were organized. Cynical materialism was complemented by the labor movement and Marxism on the one hand (with recent offshoot of a "benevolent despotism" in Soviet Russia); and on the other hand by humanitarianism, spreading from free loan associations and united charity drives to the return of a portion of the spoils in the shape of free libraries and educational and scientific Foundations (with recent offshoot of a "benevolent despotism" in Fascist Italy and a zealous paternalism of relief and alphabetical jobs in the "new deal" United States of America).

Before dwelling upon the continuance of these movements in our own time, however, we may observe the earlier signs of the gathering conflict. There battled in various lands the desire to expand in personal, or at most in national, glory—reckoned now in trade figures; and the more generous wish to hurt no one else in the process. Futile dream! Thus England stretched forth until the sun could never set on her flag; she freed her slaves; but the Boers, the great hosts of India, the Chinese that had to buy British opium, and the recalcitrant Irish knew rather Justice' blinders than her scales. And the United States, which freed its slaves in bloodier wise to sorrier living, promulgated the Monroe Doctrine, sent missionaries and garments sewn by pious old maids to the benighted heathen, and at the same time took Texas most questionably from Mexico, by bold chicanery let the Pacific through Panama (an enterprise of great benefit to mankind, incidentally driving out yellow fever), broke Spain's tyranny in several lands, earning from the Filipinos a not unmixed blessing, and developing in a nearer island a steady degeneration, recently described as *The Crime of Cuba*.

Once more I neither can nor need trace the manysided developments of the period. Social conscience battled with individual greed. Onmarching science was pitted against alarmed religion. Rationalism prodded at implicit faith; free will defied determinism. Schooling and suffrage spread almost as fast as poverty and slums; smiling pretense put gloves on the grimy hands of grim fact.

The sense that he was spreading his country's power overlarded any pricks of conscience in the imperial tradesman; they never troubled the south-bound carpet-bagger. Smugness was seldom cured as in *A Christmas Carol*. Now it was that the Englishman discovered the prescription revealed by Bernard Shaw, for attaining an illicit end: persuade yourself, first, that the thing is unpleasant, even obnoxious but, second, that it is your duty. For, according to the gentleman's code, as worded by a Victorian shaver of sham:

Duty, duty must be done,
The rule applies to everyone.

SYMBOLISM

*And painful though that duty be,
To shirk the task were fiddle-dee-dee!*

In England, the expansion occurred during the reign of a queen; but alas! this time not a virgin, and emphatically not amused. It was a period of conflicting, confused standards; therefore the orthodox code was dogmatically set down. Victorian morality spread its control over British art, from the laureate Tennyson's justification of the age to the length of the skirts of a Gilbert and Sullivan chorus. But its idealism was out of touch with the practical world, as its optimism was unwarranted by the world of the spirit. The famous faculty of the British for muddling through worked from the Romantic egotism to a Victorian compromise.

2. *The Victorians muddle through.*

IN the novels of Dickens, the adventures of the individual, which provide the thrills, are wrung to social ends, which bring the tears. Often the very names—Scrooge, Stryver, Dotheboys Hall—make immediate play upon the emotions. In other words, a type or a general condition is being presented, full blown; not the gradual development of an individual growth. Dickens' types, indeed, at times are caricatures. Cruikshank and Daumier are his analogues in art; in poetry, his nearest neighbor is the author of *The Song of a Shirt* and *The Bridge of Sighs*.

And during the years 1830-1865 the land might well have been called Dickens' England. The moral vacillation of the period finds parallel in his confusion, equally ready to decry, for humanity's sake, all that left things alone and, for freedom's sake, all that sought to improve them.

Among the many factors that were coming to bind the land, not the least were the strong steel bands that made "the right little isle" a much more "tight little isle". And the police that the railroads required, as an individualist nation gradually learned the practices of State control. Through these years, the Englishman was on his way from the unlimited and rowdy license of the eighteenth-century commoner to the docility of the twentieth-century citizen who cannot cross the road until the administration gives him the green signal.

Amid the heaving brews of this agglomerate age, Thackeray looked beneath the conventions, disclosing the greed, the snobbery and affectation, the times had bred. Even in his novels that do not touch on contemporary life, the shift in emphasis is evident. The madcap Barry Lyndon becomes the author's mouthpiece, for such general observations as "The commencement of mankind is, I think, the period of our ex-

SYMBOLISM

tremest selfishness." In the name of poetic justice Thackeray scanted history in his revision of Scott's *Ivanhoe,* to have the hero marry not the pretty Saxon doll but the active and sterling Jewess. The "overture" of *The Newcomes,* giving "the moral before the fable," protests:

> It does not follow that all men are honest because they are poor; and I have known some who were friendly and generous although they had plenty of money. There are some great landlords who do not grind down their tenants; there are actually bishops who are not hypocrites; there are liberal men even among the Whigs, and the Radicals themselves are not all Aristocrats at heart.

Likewise Gilbert:

> *Hearts just as pure and fair*
> *May beat in Belgrave Square*
> *As in the lowly air*
> *Of Seven Dials.*

This drives at an excess of the realists; the Romantics are similarly reminded of proportion, as in Thackeray's well-known burlesque of Goethe's *Werther*:

> *Charlotte, having seen his body*
> *Borne before her on a shutter,*
> *Like a well-conducted person*
> *Went on cutting bread and butter.*

"It is to the middle-class," Thackeray declared in his study of George III, "that we must look for the safety of England."

The novels of George Eliot are illustrations of the working of moral law.

As time wells toward the swift communication of our day, from nation to nation forces are more quickly felt and speedily interactive; yet in the days when Dickens presented the English conflict, more sombre tones to the north voiced in their stories the same opposition of individual freedom and the social good. Earlier, the revolutionary forces aflame in Byron (1788-1824) found echo in Pushkin (1799-1837). Dickens' novels appeared from 1838 to 1866; in the latter year Dostoievsky wrote *Crime and Punishment*, Tolstoi completed *War and Peace*. The first of these great novels is an almost schematic presentation of the progress from personal judgment to social sympathy to love which is God. One of Tolstoi's parables is entitled *Where Love Is, There God Is Also;* his masterpiece is a transcendant example of such optimism as marked Victorian England, such humanitarian hope as urged Ruskin and Morris. Tolstoi's man of promise was the unspoiled moujik; and the peasants of Turgenev's earlier work (*A Sportsman's Sketches*, 1852),—before the bitter novels written in exile—are better than their masters. Gogol, whose *Dead Souls* appeared in 1842, is equalled by the *Encyclopaedia Britannica* to "Dickens at his best." One might, with little exaggeration, declare that the constant theme of the great Russian writers marks the transmutation of downtrodden individuals. Either they attain a spiritual release such as Henley acclaims in *Invictus*:—

> *My head is bloody, but unbowed* . . .
> *I am the captain of my soul.*

—or they share a distant glimpse of social redemption.

Zola's first writing appeared in 1864; his Rougon-Macquart series, begun in 1871, grew in power with *L'Assommoir* 1878, *Nana* 1880, *Germinal* 1885, *La Terre* 1888. While he was crashing through symbols with the weight of his social sympathy, and the French symbolists were more consciously struggling with the problem of the one and the many, Ibsen of Norway (though he dwelt in Germany from 1868 to 1891) was leaping on symbols to the heart of the fray—with *A Doll's House, The Wild Duck, Pillars of Society,* a button-maker, a floating crutch—the same soul-searing struggle of the individual to find adjustment in a warped world.

The concern with social values is also strong in the two

SYMBOLISM

poets that, with Dickens and Thackeray for the novel, come to mind at the word *Victorian*. Although Tennyson tells us that the allegory in the *Idylls of the King* is not insistent, its outline is clear. Gareth, for instance, the upright middle-class young man, eager to make his name in the world, is scorned by Lynette (public opinion); he must force his way to recognition and repute. The successive battles of the world bravely waged, death itself is as a puny child. It is significant that Tennyson not only makes a change at the end of *Gareth and Lynette,* but in the poem calls our attention to it. He tells us that in the earlier version Gareth wedded Lyonors, whom he reached beyond the encounter with death (his reward in heaven or, if you wish, post-mortem glory); whereas Tennyson mates his hero with Lynette, thus according him success and fame while still alive.

The optimism of this Idyll is counterbalanced by the passing of Arthur: the world is not ready for perfection. Just as Arthur is to come again, however, so above the wave of despair that rolls through *In Memoriam* one feels the reassuring trade-wind of faith:

> *I would the great world grew like thee*
> *Who grewest not alone in power*
> *And knowledge, but by year and hour*
> *In reverence and charity. . . .*
>
> *Are God and Nature then at strife,*
> *That Nature lends such evil dreams?*
> *So careful of the type she seems,*
> *So careless of the single life. . . .*
>
> *I stretch lame hands of faith, and grope,*
> *And gather dust and chaff, and call*
> *To what I feel is Lord of all,*
> *And faintly trust the larger hope . . .*
>
> *Man, her last work, who seem'd so fair,*
> *Such splendid purpose in his eyes,*
> *Who roll'd the psalm to wintry skies,*
> *Who built him fanes of fruitless prayer,*

[145]

*Who trusted God was love indeed
And love Creation's final law—
Though Nature, red in tooth and claw
With ravine, shriek'd against his creed—*

*No more? A monster then, a dream,
A discord. Dragons of the prime,
That tare each other in their slime,
Were mellow music match'd with him.*

*O life as futile, then, as frail!
O for thy voice to soothe and bless!
What hope of answer, or redress?
Behind the veil, behind the veil. . . .*

*I trust I have not wasted breath,
I think we are not wholly brain,
Magnetic mockeries; not in vain,
Like Paul with beast, I fought with Death.*

*Not only cunning casts in clay:
Let Science prove we are, and then
What matters Science unto men,
At least to me? I would not stay.*

*Let him, the wiser man who springs
Hereafter, up from childhood shape
His action like the greater ape,
But I was born to other things.*

*Love is and was my Lord and King,
And in his presence I attend
To hear the tidings of my friend,
Which every hour his couriers bring.*

*Love is and was my King and Lord,
And will be, tho' as yet I keep
Within his court on earth, and sleep
Encompass'd by his faithful guard,*

SYMBOLISM

> *And hear at times a sentinel*
> *Who moves about from place to place*
> *And whispers to the worlds of space,*
> *In the deep night, that all is well.*
>
> *And all is well, tho' faith and form*
> *Be sundered in the night of fear;*
> *Well roars the storm to those that hear*
> *A deeper voice across the storm*
>
> *Proclaiming social truth shall spread* . . . .

These moods of alternate hope and hopelessness, of individual loss but the general gain, recur throughout the poetry of Tennyson. They are less frequent in Browning, who prefers the sermon to the sigh. The simple optimism of

> *God's in His heaven,*
> *All's right with the world*

is, of course, Pippa's rather than the poet's; yet the songs that well from her personal moods rise to the general welfare. But stick your thumb into Browning at random; you're almost sure to plum a lesson, such as this (or most anything else) from *Fifine At the Fair*:

That's the first o' the truths found: all things, slow
Or quick i' the passage, come at last to that, you know!
Each has a false outside, whereby a truth is forced
To issue from within: truth, falsehood, are divorced
By the excepted eye, at the rare season, for
The happy moment. Life means—learning to abhor
The false, and love the true, truth measured snatch by snatch,
Waifs counted at their worth. And when with strays they match
I' the particolored world,—when, under foul, shines fair,
And truth, displayed i' the point, flashes forth everywhere
I' the circle, manifest to soul, though hid from sense,
And no obstruction more affects this confidence,—
When faith is ripe for sight,—why, reasonably, then,
Comes the great clearing-up. Wait threescore years and ten!

Browning more than Tennyson, however, reached beyond the age's compromise toward a rounded synthesis. He beheld, if he did not always achieve, the aesthetic union:

> *Art hangs out for sign*
> *There's finer entertainment underneath;*
> *Learn how they ministrate to Life and Death—*
> *Those incommensurably marvellous*
> *Contrivances which furnish forth the House*
> *Where the Soul has sway.*

and again:

> *"Sordello, wake!*
> *God has conceded two sights to a man—*
> *One, of men's whole work, time's completed plan,*
> *The other, of the minute's work, man's first*
> *Step to the plan's completeness."*

and again:

> *Art—wherein man nowise speaks to man,*
> *Only to mankind—Art may tell a truth*
> *Obliquely, do the thing shall breed the thought,*
> *Nor wrong the thought, missing the mediate word.*
> *So you may paint your picture, twice show truth,*
> *Beyond mere imagery on the wall—*
> *So, note by note, bring music from your mind,*
> *So write a book shall mean beyond the facts,*
> *Suffice the eye and save the soul besides.*

and again and again

SYMBOLISM

3. *The century eases onward.*

THE Englishman through the midyears of the century most nobly bore the white man's burden. Wherever his duty called him as the Empire grew, however, not only when April brought the chaffinch, or May scattered pear-tree blossoms on the clover, did he sigh

O to be in England!

The spirit of England accompanied him and sustained him, in deepest India, in darkest Africa: a national pride and a humanitarianism that were the lacquered compromise over greed and misery. Polishing these two surface virtues made them mirrors; what lay beneath was comfortably concealed. The surge of Empire is celebrated in a series of works that culminate in the bugle calls of *England-über-alles* Kipling. The impulse to help their fellow men developed the combination of aesthetics, ethics, and practical craftsmanship of the creators of Ruskin pottery and the Morris chair. To these men their poetry, their type-fonts, their ironwork, were equal ways of bringing beauty to serve the general good.

In the United States, the same ethical concern had less practical consequence. The American Transcendentalists, as the name implies, framed another effort to reach beyond the separate items of existence to their common essence. It was a curiously unreal blending. The New Englander lived in a world of isolated facts, self-sufficing farms and villages; Yankee individualism is proverbial. And these insistently disparate spirits had to find a social cohesive, an Over-Soul. For rugged individualism, as preached in Emerson's essay on *Self-Reliance*, on the material level leads to the multi-millionaire; it must be emphasized that its ethical drive whips toward the saint. Practically, it views the rest of the world as source of income then

[149]

subject for philanthropy. On moral grounds, therefore, these writers must be impractical.

Emerson thus had to reenforce his individual urge with a social aim. Concrete phenomena he saw all around; first he set on one plane the achievements of nature and of man:

> *Knows't thou what wove yon woodbird's nest*
> *Of leaves, and feathers from her breast?*
> *Or how the fish outbuilt her shell*
> *Painting with morn each annual cell? . . .*
> *Earth proudly wears the Parthenon,*
> *As the best gem upon her zone . . .*
> *O'er England's abbeys bends the sky,*
> *As on its friends, with kindred eye;*
> *For, out of Thought's interior sphere*
> *These wonders rose to upper air;*
> *And Nature gladly gave them place,*
> *Adopted them into her race,*
> *And granted them an equal date*
> *With Andes and with Ararat.*

There was one more step to take. For the ultimate binding—with an innocence that makes the United States (a fortiori, California) the happy hunting ground of religious outcroppings—Emerson turned to the Orient. He calls *Brahma* his poem that celebrates the fusion of all things in a central unity:

> *If the red slayer thinks he slays,*
> *Or if the slain think he is slain,*
> *They know not well the subtle ways*
> *I keep, and pass, and turn again . . .*
> *They reckon ill who leave me out;*
> *When me they fly, I am the wings;*
> *I am the doubter and the doubt;*
> *I am the song the Brahmin sings.*

The confusion of these seekers for social ends to their individualist urgings is indicated in the fact that, despite Emerson's re-

SYMBOLISM

peated unifying declarations, best remembered is his statement that there is one law for man and another for thing.

Save for anti-slavery agitation that was so high-minded it quite overlooked the realities of the situation, the lives of the transcendentalists produced, outside their writings, little more than the aborted socialism of Brook Farm. It was when she went to Europe that Margaret Fuller became both an active worker (superintendent of the military hospital at Rome during the siege of 1849) and a cosmopolitan personality. While these New Englanders were building their communal castles in the air, Ruskin was striving to interweave art and life, Taine was writing a history to demonstrate the interdependence of the environment and the work, Mazzini was seeking a human brotherhood, and Nietzsche was elaborating the moral code of the superman. Everywhere the age was urging from individual to collective concerns.

In England, less extreme attempts to balance the opposed forces of the period found their mild voices. The nearest approach to order lay in the work of Landor and of Arnold. In the former, the absence of fire may result less from a deliberate withholding of the spark than from weak hands at the bellows:

> I strove with none, for none was worth my strife.
> Nature I loved and, next to Nature, Art:
> I warmed both hands before the fire of life;
> It sinks, and I am ready to depart.

The greater intensity of Arnold was fortified by his prose writings, and by his position in the educational world. He could appreciate that

> *the loftiest hill*
> *That to the stars uncrowns his majesty,*
> *Planting his steadfast footsteps in the sea,*
> *Making the heaven of heavens his dwelling-place,*
> *Spares but the cloudy border of his base*
> *To the foil'd searching of mortality —*

[151]

but he brought back from Greece no more fervent message (not a gained harmony, but again a compromise) than the rebuke and admonition:

> *But thou, because thou hear'st*
> *Men scoff at Heaven and Fate;*
> *Because the gods thou fear'st*
> *Fail to make blest thy state,*
> *Tremblest, and wilt not dare to trust the joys there are.*
>
> *I say, Fear not! life still*
> *Leaves human effort scope.*
> *But, since life teems with ill,*
> *Nurse no extravagant hope.*
> *Because thou must not dream, thou need'st not then despair.*

Arnold seems rather to exclaim at than to experience—"Listen, Eugenia!"—

> *Eternal passion,*
> *Eternal pain!*

Every compromise will seem sordid to bolder spirits; the Victorian facing-both-ways closed eyes to much that was ugly and mean. The efforts at revolt, however, turned away from the age. They sought a beauty out of time. Rossetti defined the goal of the Pre-Raphaelites as "realism, emotional but extremely minute"; but over the gold bar of heaven all they could discern was a distant dream-garden. In its quiet walks, amid the twinkling lights of angels, humanity stepped lightly in beauty's quest. Later—but following the French, to whom they summon us—Pater, Swinburne, Wilde, Francis Thompson and more, in varying measure retreated to anodynes dictated by personal needs but drawn to general application.

In mild-mannered continuance of the time's trend, Pater even sets the general opinion as a test of the highest art: "the classic comes to us out of the cool and quiet of other times, as the measure of what a long experience has shown will at least

SYMBOLISM

never displease us." The positive tone of the Romantics has softened here, almost to an apology. While Thompson sees the source of all creation in the sun, the father of the gods, he sets God as prime mover; he trusts the "Hound of Heaven" to track mankind to godliness. Swinburne, on the contrary, turns back to Proserpina from the conquest of the Galilean; he seeks unity in a timeless first principle that "set the shadow call'd God in your skies to give light." His *Hertha* is an anticipation of D. H. Lawrence's Dark Mother, an all-embracing source and sustenance:

>I am that which began;
>Out of me the years roll;
>Out of me God and man;
>I am equal and whole;

God changes, and man, and the form of them bodily; I am the soul.

>First life on my sources
>First drifted and swam;
>Out of me are the forces
>That save it or damn;

Out of me man and woman, and wild-beast and bird: before God was, I am.

>Beside or above me
>Naught is there to go;
>Love or unlove me,
>Unknow me or know,

I am that which unloves me and loves; I am stricken, and I am the blow.

>But what thing dost thou now,
>Looking Godward, to cry
>"I am I, thou art thou,
>I am low, thou art high"?

I am thou, whom thou seekest to find him; find thou but thyself, thou art I . .

[153]

> *For truth only is living,*
> *Truth only is whole,*
> *And the love of his giving*
> *Man's polestar and pole;*
> *Man, pulse of my centre, and fruit of my body, and seed of*
> *my soul.*
>
> *One birth of my bosom;*
> *One beam of mine eye;*
> *One topmost blossom*
> *That scales the sky;*
> *Man, equal and one with me, man that is made of me, man*
> *that is I.*

Swinburne's poetry is a heady wine that all hebetic spirits since feel that they must imbibe. Often they fling the cup aside for a flagon of Whitman. Many thereafter judge it by the lees. But the muscatel of Swinburne was pressed of a choice vintage. Baudelaire (to whose memory one of Swinburne's greatest poems is inscribed) had in anticipation characterized pure poetry. In it, he says, is created "a suggestive magic containing at once the subject and the object, the world outside the artist and the artist himself." For what in the Victorian was confusion and compromise, in the more logical and lucid atmosphere of France grew as a conscious program.

SYMBOLISM

4. *France takes direction.*

By diverse convergent ways the Continent swept back from the Romantic extreme. Both romance and the tardier realism lingered; but, while they persisted, their successor arrived. Cabell has tried to dismiss realism by declaring that it assumes that our mileposts are as worthy of consideration as our goal, and that the particular post we are now passing reveals an eternal verity. But of course that is precisely the function of the sign post! If only we can read . . .

Such literacy leads us to symbolism. For on the swing from the particular to the universal, the pendulum must move through the moments of their blend. The English humanitarian emphasis colored political theory, industrial policy, and the social mores; it muddied art with didactic concerns. *Uncle Tom's Cabin* remains somewhere now playing, to remind us that in the United States a similar literary infiltration ensued. The Americans do everything on a large scale and—unless it is material—a generation after; hence we more nearly approach our own day for the wild-eyed exposures of the rampant muck-raker. But neither the planless bungling that somehow blunders into the future, nor the megaphonic blustering that lets the chips fall where they may (and plays a leathery game of poker!) so frequently characterizes France as an ability to read a logical sequence into the course of events. The French may do a worse thing, but they will have a better reason. The harmony toward which the Germans were yearning was heralded by Baudelaire.

Influences from various lands aided the French in their development. The social sympathy of England was reenforced by the Russian chorus. The positivism of Comte was countered by the progress of Renan toward intellectual idealism. For Renan moved from his original aristocratic program—the chosen few in power, but bound by equal obligations to the masses—to a belief that "Caliban" may at length develop self-control. In religion he broke from the established creeds—which William Mallock from England vigorously defended, while vehemently attacking the radical economic theories Marx and Engels hatched in the library of the British Museum. Wagner was calling for an art that should move *ab exterioribus ad interiora, ab interioribus ad superiora*: from without, inward; from within, upward. Goethe, and Browning, viewed the work of art as a sign-post for an inner journeying. Heine declared: "In matters of art I am a supernaturalist."

These beacons were blent by Baudelaire: "In certain almost supernatural states of the soul, the very depth of life is revealed in the spectacle, ordinary as it may be, beneath one's eyes. It becomes a symbol."

Here is the birth of symbolism. Symbols, of course, are as old as man. Language itself is a symbol; and every art is another tongue; and every artist proffers but his coined token. But now we are told that every sensible phenomenon may yield the central core of all philosophy. Mallarmé, most deliberate of the school, strove to make every phrase "a plastic image, the expression of a thought, the stir of a feeling, and the draught of a philosophy." Object and essence, the view and the vision: here is a blending indeed!

Passing thoughts of the Romantics, as we may expect, pointed in the direction their successors took. Tieck says of one of his poems: "To be sure, there is no logical connection of ideas in it, but nonetheless it moves on as our thoughts shape themselves . . . Why should the story make up the content of a poem?" Diderot observed another human trait:

> A single physical quality can conduct the mind that dwells on it to an infinity of diverse things. Take a color, for instance yellow: gold is yellow, silk is yellow, corn is yellow, bile is yellow, straw is yellow. To how many other threads does not this thread corre-

spond? The madman does not notice the change. He holds a wisp of yellow straw in his hand, and cries that he has caught a ray of sunlight.

Remembering Shakespeare's linkage of the lunatic, the lover, and the poet, Sainte-Beuve seized upon this passage; from it spread the xanthic rays of his famous poem *Rayons jaunes*. Tieck's arrow flies toward the "stream of consciousness" technique; Sainte-Beuve's sheaf is emptied toward the far-ranging analogies of Proust.

Baudelaire goes farther. He says this is neither the phantasmagoria of the madman nor the vagrant pattern of the dream, but vision—all things "having always been expressed through such reciprocal analogies from the day when God declared the world a complex and indivisible whole."

> *Nature is a temple whose living spires*
> *Send mingled words at times upon the air;*
> *Man journeys through a wood of symbols there*
> *That kindle as he goes with friendly fires.*
>
> *As long-drawn echoes in a far-off bond*
> *Blend in a deep and shadowed unity,*
> *Vast as the night and as vast clarity,*
> *Color and sound and fragrance correspond.*

The neo-classicists, it is true, had recalled the remark, "poetry is like painting." To refute this, Lessing wrote *Laocoon*. Then the Romantics declared, "architecture is frozen music." These are, however, mere simile and metaphor; they did not call, nor indeed make room, for any changes in artistic practice. The newer emphasis is both more inclusive and more manifest in the works. The figure becomes a theory, and sprouts a school. Not only literature, but painting, sculpture, music, the dance, go to class. The arts came to be conceived, in both methods and aims, as essentially one.

5. Baudelaire builds time's bridge.

BAUDELAIRE gathers into one strong potion all the spirits spuming in the age.

The attitude of critics toward Baudelaire has ranged from abomination and the contempt of silence to adulation and the encomium of volumes. The torture of his days has been wrung through reams of explanation. His influence has been lengthily, even laboriously, traced. He has been linked with Poe not merely through their natural associations of spirit but in the comment that his moods are too limited for him to be a great poet. It is true that his collected works—poetry, poems in prose, critical essays, translations—fill fewer volumes by far than are bulked by the novels, plays, and poems of the author that declared the age would be known by his name; but Hugo was, one may say, the heat given off by the light of the period; Baudelaire was the fulcrum on which the epoch turned. On him the many conflicting forces of the time most heavily pressed: whirlwinds of atoms, electrons sparked from their orbits within his withstanding spirit: the century moved!

In France the Catholic faith raised firmer bulwarks against atheistical science than were built in Anglican England. Rationalism, however, is native to Parisian soil; and perhaps priestly submission on the catechistical points yields elsewhere greater freedom. Baudelaire pointed the way, in every direction. His *Litany To Satan* scorches with blasphemy—though his vaunted Black Mass was probably never celebrated. Skeptical rationalism peeps in the remark: "When Jesus Christ said 'Blessed are they that hunger, for they shall be filled', Jesus Christ was gambling on probabilities." Deliberately he overlooked the otherworldly implications of Jesus' words. A deeper need, on the other hand, is manifest in the statement that "Even if God did not exist, religion would still be holy and divine." And there was a yearning, almost an anguished, piety, in Baudelaire's prayer to his father and to Edgar Allan Poe to kneel as his intercessors before the throne of Heaven.

After Baudelaire, we hear in many tongues the confident chorus of Catholic poets, reverent always, but often boonfellow with their God. They call Him the Hound of Heaven, the World's Miser (Who will not let a swallow fall unobserved). Having known Him so much longer than their Protestant half-brothers, they need not be formal; they can sit with crossed legs in His presence.

But equally after Baudelaire we find the many sacrilegious moods. The poet felt that the complement of every deep piety is a fierce blasphemy, out of a need so urgent that it is truly (as discord in a symphony) but one more tone in the great hymn to Heaven. From Huysmans, who carries us a Dantean journey, the tone dissipates to the bland mockery of Anatole France, the suave condescension of James Branch Cabell, the impish glee of the American versifier who serves titbits from the lives of the saints to gourmetic unbelievers. Whether or not all these writers own Baudelaire's influence, they have been lifted by the lever his force balanced. The impulses of the age, meeting in him, have severally after him urged to their wide expression.

All the Romantic regard for nature finds voice in Baudelaire. He uses her as a fountainhead of imagery. One of his best known sonnets compares the poet with the albatross: of all birds when on earth most ungainly, most out-of-place; but, when it soars, effortless, inimitable, serene. The poet knows the languor of nights of the moon:

> *The moon more indolently dreams tonight*
> *Than a fair woman on her couch at rest*
> *Caressing, with a hand distraught and light,*
> *Before she sleeps, the contour of her breast.*

The romantic melancholy wans toward despair:

*You are a sky of autumn, pale and rose;
But all the sea of sadness in my blood
Surges, and ebbing, leaves my lips morose,
Salt with the memory of the bitter mud.*

And the tone deepens:

*In vain my reason tried to cross the bar,
The whirling storm but drove her back again;
And my soul tossed and tossed, an outworn wreck,
Mastless, upon a monstrous, shoreless sea.*

Beyond the Romantics, the paths to nature took two courses. Discarding the usefulness to man, the goodness, of natural things, came a purely pagan delight in their beauty. This attains its apogee in Swinburne; but it is vinous in Mallarmé, and it empurpurates the orthodoxy of Francis Thompson. This wild joy in nature wooed the spirit of Baudelaire, seeking him forth from his abodes of gloom. And the drop from such free joy as would exult an unchained spirit, the nose-dive to earth of reality, to the ugliness of man's ways, spatters over his work a blasphemy against Pan, a mockery of ball lightning, or a blow-torch hate:

*When the low, heavy sky presses like a lid
On the groaning spirit, prey to long vexations,
And when, sweeping the full circle of the horizon,
It pours us a black day sadder than our nights,*

*When the earth is changed into a sodden dungeon,
Where the black bat hope, with timid wing,
Beats, flying off, beats dead against the wall,
Banging his head upon the rotten ceiling;*

*When the rain, spreading out its lengthy trailers,
Mimics the bars of an enormous jail,
And a mute host of horrid spiders comes
To stretch their webs in the hollows of our brains;*

[160]

SYMBOLISM

> *Suddenly bells start forth in a great fury*
> *And lance a frightful howling at the sky,*
> *Like wandering spirits without any homeland*
> *Who, stubbornly persisting, will complain.*
>
> *And long hearses, without drums or music,*
> *Move slowly in my soul; and conquered hope*
> *Weeps, and cruel, despotic anguish*
> *On my bowed skull sets firmly its black flag.*

It lures him to Lesbos, land of warm and languorous nights; it reaches out in the swan exultant for rain; it urges him to hold away from life,

> *plunged deep in the pleasure still*
> *Of summoning the springtime with my will,*
> *Drawing the sun out of my heart, and there*
> *With burning thoughts making a summer air.*

For against the Romantic conception of nature as the source of good came in full reverse the feeling that in her soil spreads the root of man's evil. "Nature is the limit set to man." Not only are natural things non-moral, free from our ethical codes, indifferent to our fate; they are from a human point of view immoral; they set in motion forces against which we strive in vain. They press labor upon our bodies; they lay unrighteousness upon our souls. From nature man may wrest at most a chancy spell of joy. And they are after all *The Flowers of Evil* that Baudelaire has culled. He knows that the most fertile of "natural" soils is the dung-heap. (This, in the mind of Jean Richepin, is the one justification of the middle class.) And Baudelaire advances in counter-attack:

> The greater number of errors relative to the beautiful date from the eighteenth century's false conceptions of morality. Nature was regarded in those times as the base, source, and type of all possible good and beauty ... If, however, we consent to refer simply to the visible facts, we see that nature teaches

nothing, or almost nothing. That is to say, she forces man to sleep, drink, eat, and protect himself, well or ill, against the hostilities of the atmosphere. It is she also who moves him to kill and eat or imprison and torture his kind; for, as soon as we leave the region of necessities and needs to enter that of luxuries and pleasures, we see that Nature is no better than a counsellor to crime . . . Religion commands us to nourish our poor and infirm parents; Nature (the voice of our own interest) commands us to do away with them. Pass in review, analyze, all that is natural, all the actions and desires of the natural man, and you will find nothing but what is horrible. All beautiful and noble things are the result of calculation. Crime, the taste for which the human animal absorbs before birth, is originally natural. Virtue, on the contrary, is artificial, supernatural, since there has been a necessity in all ages and among all nations for gods and prophets to teach virtue to humanity; since man alone would have been unable to discover it. Evil is done without effort, naturally and by fatality; good is always the product of an art.

Here too, Baudelaire blazed a trail. In that quaint volume *The Novel and The Modern World,* David Daiches declares that "the slogan 'art for art's sake' is a way of distinguishing a belief in the worthlessness of art which, if expressed bluntly, would be too discouraging for the artist." Baudelaire's ax chipped nearer the line of truth. Remy de Gourmont leaps back to Aristotle, reenforcing the poet with the thinker. For if art is an "idealizing imitation" of life, showing us what we ought to do, then it follows that life should be guided by art. Widely promulgated, in every period, is the theory of art for life's sake. This is precisely what lies under the thought of Oscar Wilde, pressed into his epigram that life strives to be art. Pater advocated the cultivating of living as a fine art. Thus the proponents of art for art's sake are merely suggesting a more direct advance upon the goals of life itself. We should be indulging quite harmlessly in the widespread practice of taking the appetizer for the main course (paralleled physically every time one uses a contraceptive) if we were to advance the notion that spiritually one could do many things worse than living life for art's sake. This is, manifestly, remote from any sense of the worthlessness of art. It may spring, per contra, from a sense of the worthlessness of many other aspects of being; in any event, the advocates of this attitude would subject the cruelty and chaos of natural things to a considered, fashioned order.

As the most fundamental characteristic of the Romantics was the direct presentation of the personal feeling, we must expect their successors' subjectivity to be accompanied by a deliberate attempt to remove any signs of the artist's emotion. To the Romantic, a poem is a heart-cry, or a tear. Even with Gautier, it is nearer to an itemized account; and many today consider that a work of art should be modeled upon a stock-taking or a laboratory experiment. Again the symbolist bridges the chasm between the instant emotion and the ultimate calm. The ego and things, man and nature, were, in the Romantic, opposed; in the Parnassian, severed—and the ego withdrawn; in the symbolist, fused. Mallarmé arrives at this unity through the force of a rigorous logic; Baudelaire forges it in the white heat of passion. Suffering, soul-wringing anguish marked the life of Baudelaire, as his diaries deeply attest. His normal state was akin to the chaos of madness; it was only when he was inspired (as Plato would say, possessed) that his spirit through the pressure grew clear and radiant as diamond. Then the torture of his days, the wind from the wing of imbecility, the knell of a wretched doom, were chaliced in loving attention and crystallized in deathless form.

The Romantic wept for his own sorrow. The Pharaohs more wisely erected the pyramids to a service that would begin when their emotions ended. The multi-millionaire builds a mausoleum to his beloved, or more fruitfully endows (or bequeathes) a hospital in fond memory, or fellowships to foster research. Such poets as Baudelaire at once express and conquer their feelings by converting them into chaste monuments, firm against the gnawing teeth of time. Out of his torture at the ugliness of life, Baudelaire, by a syntony of genius that critics but strive to explain, produced an intense yet graven beauty. The emotion is buried beneath the image it evoked. The work is at once quiet and most disquieting. Like the nymphs, who though constantly deflowered are ever virgin, such poems drive so searingly through passion that they burn clear and dispassionate in themselves, though retinent ever of some quality of the flame. It is not without significance that Baudelaire calls the largest group of his poems *Spleen and Ideal*.

SYMBOLISM

6. *The Senses make sense.*

ANOTHER linkage in Baudelaire that after him broke into divergent schools was the bond of sound and sense. One road leads direct to Swinburne, whose love of the euphonic possibilities of language reaches the height of the ridiculous in *Nephelidia,* that superb self-parody:

> From the depth of the dreamy decline of the dawn through
>   a notable nimbus of nebulous moonshine . . .
> Made meek as a mother whose bosom-beats bound with the
>   bliss-bringing milk of a balm-breathing baby,
> As they grope through the graveyard of creeds, under skies
>   growing green at a groan for the grimness of God.

In our day, this path has come to a dead end. First Gertrude Stein reversed the usual poetic process, by employing sense merely as an overtone to sound. Then Hugo Blümner and others tried the purest type of pure poetry, patterns of sound syllables that only by accident achieve any sense at all.

Along the other path, heralded by Whitman, we reach those that, like lyric Frost or childlike Kreymborg, attempt to approximate their rhythm to the spoken tongue. Take care of the sense, and the sounds will take care of themselves.

This division comes down the years after Baudelaire. In himself, sound, sense, and suggestion are so intimately joined, theirs is a chemical union. All poetry is untranslatable, but none more fully than his justifies the Italian proverb: *Traduttore, traditore*: translator, traitor. In his critical writings, furthermore, Baudelaire was one of the first to recognize and to hail the new artists that in other fields, in music and in painting, were moving with the age toward a wider synthesis. As the unifying emphasis began to be felt, in keen comments he elaborated the thought condensed in the closing line of his best known sonnet:

Color and sound and fragrance correspond.

He returns in various moods to this commingling of the senses:

> *Too exquisite the harmony*
> *That governs all her body fair,*
> *For impotent analysis*
> *To note the many concords there.*
>
> *O mystic metamorphosis!*
> *My senses into one sense melt.*
> *Her breath makes music,*
> *And her voice makes fragrance.*

Such phrases were not intended as mere figures of speech. They found actuality in the practice of the artists of the time. Sculpture sought to impart movement to the stone. Painting strove to tell stories, to sweep into action; music, to tell stories and paint scenes.

The most obvious, although the most mechanical, of these endeavors played upon the associations of color and sound. The sonnet of Rimbaud—

> *A black, E white, I red, U green, O blue,*
> *Vowels:—*

was followed by the schematization of René Ghil, which linked (in other order) colors and musical instruments with vowel and consonantal sounds. "Symbolism will rule the future," commented the young Anatole France, "if the nervous condition that produced it becomes general. Unfortunately, M. Ghil says O is blue, and M. Rimbaud says O is red. And these exquisite invalids argue under the indulgent eye of M. Mallarmé." Perhaps deliberately, Anatole France mixed the colors. Naturally, such scoffing gave a spurt to a fashion that was about to fade of its own sterility.

While some contented themselves with announcing the linkage of visible and audible tones, others tried to weave them into works of art. Mechanical attempts drenched an auditori-

SYMBOLISM

um with color while the orchestra played, as with Scriabine's *Fire Music*. John Gould Fletcher, in equally literal linking, pursues the color green through

> E, parakeets of emerald shrieking perverse in the trees,
> Iridescent and restless chameleons tremulous in the breeze
> Peace on the leaves, peace on the sea-green sea.

More subtle are the efforts of Oscar Wilde's *Symphony in Yellow*, and of Walter de la Mare's *Silver*, which evokes a soft landscape in rhythmic repetition:

> Slowly, silently, now the moon
> Walks the night in her silver shoon;
> This way, and that, she peers and sees
> Silver fruit upon silver trees;
> One by one the casements catch
> Her beams beneath the silvery thatch;
> Couched in his kennel, like a log,
> With paws of silver sleeps the dog;
> From their shadowy cote the white breasts peep
> Of doves in a silver-feathered sleep;
> A harvest mouse goes scampering by,
> With silver claws, and a silver eye;
> And moveless fish in the water gleam,
> By silver reeds in a silver stream.

Many other sensations are interlocked or interchanged, in the works of the time. In *A Rebours*, Huysmans' decadent hero — hero as well to the generation — savours symphonies of perfume, and sips études of blended drinks. "A 'singing' picture of Claude Lorrain or Watteau," says Spengler, "does not really address itself to the bodily eye, any more than the space-straining music since Bach addresses itself to the bodily ear." In a New York exhibition of the Independent Artists, a painting of a woodsman strove for motion with six pairs of arms, from high up, ax overhead, to down, with the ax imbedded. These should of course be seen successively, as the blow travels. Take a look at Rodin's *John the Baptist*. In great stride, the saint has both feet flat on the ground. Such a pose would be unnatural; but it is not a pose: with the flick of your eye from leg to leg, the man has taken his step!

Music that otherwise might still be simply music, with the aid of title and program note struts boldly forth into design and story. *First Symphony* and *Etude* 34 give place to *The Sorcerer's Apprentice, Garden in the Rain, At Dawning, L'Apresmidi d'un faune, Scheherezade, Tyl Eulenspiegel*. Earlier numbered pieces are rechristened by ductile minds. Mozart's last symphony has been crowned the *Jupiter;* what Beethoven called *Piano Sonata in C sharp minor* we refer to as *The Moonlight Sonata;* his *Grand concerto for piano and orchestra composed for and dedicated to His Imperial Highness Rudolph Archduke of Austria (in E flat major, No. 5) opus* 73 was properly shortened, but descriptively dubbed *The Emperor Concerto*. These new titles are seldom accompanied by stories; but even the specifically "program" music is often anything but specific. Thus Pitts Sanborn, in his notes for the New York Philharmonic Society, of Sibelius' symphonic fantasia *Pohjola's Daughter,* says that the opening theme may be the sliding of the hero's sleigh or the shuff of the maiden's weaving. What is significant here is not the failure or success, but the effort to blend the methods and appeals of the arts.

In this process we may discern, and I ask you to keep constantly in mind, that there is no precise point at which all phases of an emphasis die, and its opposite rears in full triumph. Literature — using the same words as the business of life — responds more immediately to life's promptings than do the fine arts. In the works under discussion, certain elements observed in the Romantic may persist. The definiteness of a story, for example, as opposed to the abstract, merely mood-evoking, appeal of neo-classical music and dance.

Jules Romains, perhaps led by such survivals, makes the suggestion that in every age one of the arts other than literature is particularly equipped to satisfy and to interpret the dominant tendency of the time. Then literature, of all arts most responsive to human needs, seeking to render similar satisfaction, seems to imitate this other art. Thus, in the middle of the last century, painting; thereafter, music; today, the cinema. Romains, however, is viewing a reciprocal process from one end only; painting and music have equally striven to be story. All the arts in unison move with man's marching.

In every age drawing toward an emphasis upon universals, it will be felt that all the senses convey one basic message to the spirit of man. There will follow efforts to blend the sense appeals. In the eighteenth century, Castel in France developed a color-harpsichord, forerunner of the efforts to match color scales and musical tones today. In England, Dryden and his fellows tried to capture in their verse effects of painting and music. A favorite minor form of the period was the *impresa;* with two lines and three syllables, this expressed a general idea through a device and a motto, "since it was then held that ideas must not merely be incarnated in words, but grasped by all the senses at once."

In the poetry of the symbolists, words and music were one. Baudelaire announced the intimate union: "Poetry joins music by a prosody whose roots plunge deeper into the human soul than any classical theory indicates." Looking back on the great symbolist period (1885-1895, during which decade the partial bibliography of Remy de Gourmont lists one hundred and thirty magazines of the school), Valéry goes so far as to say: "What has been baptized symbolism is, very simply, the determination of several groups of poets (otherwise enemies) to recapture their endowment from music. We are nourished on music, and our literary heads dream only of winning from language the same effects as pure sounds produce on the nervous system."

Valéry's literary head put the matter very simply indeed. What the symbolist hearkens is the music of the spheres. He seeks to express the eternal and essential analogy "between a moment of the continuance of the ego and a moment of the continuance of things." Ruskin might characterize this as pathetic fallacy; but it is an apotheosis of such a linking of man and nature as Ruskin describes. Here is no mere external harmony of mood, no metaphor, no leaf dancing as often as it can because it soon must fall. Build what system of metaphors you will, the symbolist overtops them.

The Romantic counterbalances man and nature:

> *Brother, of those two strange, unheard voices,*
> *Endlessly rising, endlessly dying away,*
> *That the Eternal hearkens throughout eternity,*
> *One whispers Nature! the other, Humanity!*

When they unite, they have joined in battle. The Romantic asks

> *why the good Lord, Who alone reads His book,*
> *Endlessly mingles in a fatal match*
> *The song of nature and humanity's cry?*

But the symbolist not only sees them as one, but — as an alkaline metal and a lethal gas unite to create the very salt of life — in their union leads thought on from meaning to higher meaning.

Such a journey, alas, soon takes us beyond mere human understanding. For the symbolist stands between two eras, trying to draw their impulsions into one. As the world, however, has not yet run down, the pendulum does not stop at midswing.

Symbolism set for itself the impossible task of making universal the fusion established only — and always uniquely — in each several work of art. Life has not the time to examine every object, every act, and extract its symbol.

Paul Elmer More allows only the first two degrees of symbols to literature. Simplest is the significative: "rally round the flag", in which the symbol is but a conventional sign. Next is the metaphoric "pure as a lily", wherein the sign is strengthened by a natural association. Then the commemorative: "to bear a cross", which to the first two references adds the memory

SYMBOLISM

of a literal application. Finally, the sacramental: "to eat of the bread," which bears all the other values, and in addition actually identifies the symbol and the thing symbolized. The last two degrees, More would restrict to religion. But the symbolist knows that higher unity: every poet lifts water and proffers wine of His blood.

A rose, beyond its virtue as a flower, may be a metaphor to express the beauty of the poet's beloved; it may be a token from her, thus carry the light of her love to irradiate his heart; it may grow from that personal love to a wider sharing, as sign of love itself; and it may spread its petals with the ineffable glory of the presence of God, as in the last great circle of Dante's paradise. The symbolist — not in preaching but in poetry — could move that far with any human action, with a chance flower in the crannied wall, or with a grain of dust.

7. *Mind and heart reach out.*

MOST critics wear blinders. They see clearly along the line of their bias; everything they behold, indeed, must fit within that point of view. Therefore this critic states once more that, within the rouse of symbolism, two different avenues lead to the same goal. The period is animated by those that (through reason and science) equate man and nature, and those that in separate exaltation elevate mankind. In the symbolist, realist and Romanticist tormentedly conjoin.

I have said that Baudelaire attained the sense of unity through the searing of passion, while Mallarmé recognized it through the colder processes of thought. This being a French movement, behind each of these poets lurks a philosopher.

By way of rationalism, the all-inclusive search of the age was advanced by Hegel. Out of life's oppositions he weaves not a trinity but a triad: thesis, antithesis, and the higher synthesis. Light, for example, has its opposite, dark; but their blended resolution, color, alone is within the usable range of vision. It is this harmonizing union which Mallarmé, an avowed disciple of Berkeley and Hegel, sets as the goal of his questing. In a period of unfixed standards and changing ideas of truth, what validity should be given aught external, save in the blend whereby it snares the soul? "There is no reason for our regarding any existing object, save as it represents our inner state: the ensemble of mutual characteristics within our soul sanctifies the symbol."

The outer event is the only possible manifestation of the inner impetus, yet from this takes its whole justification. The object frames the idea. For this reason the object, the expression, does not have to be explained. Nay, attempts at explanation will befuddle the mind. The clarity of logic reveals, however precisely, but the naked body; the soul is still undiscovered within.

SYMBOLISM

Hence, in the writings of the symbolist, figures may be stripped of their literal half. Much of the difficulty many readers find with recent poetry springs from this suppression of the reference in the metaphor. When Hugo says:

> *The fleece of the sinister sheep of the sea*

the mention of *the sea* helps you convert *the fleece* into the white-caps of the "herd" of rounding billows. But when Mallarmé exclaims:

> *The flesh is sad, alas, and I've read all the books.*
> *To flee! to flee down there! I sense that birds are drunk*
> *To be amidst the foam and skies unknown!*

you must sense that the birds are awing with the desires they embody. Still more abstrusely in the first lines of the *Seaside Cemetery* by Mallarmé's greatest disciple, Valéry:

> *This tranquil roof, where pigeons walk,*
> *Vibrates between the pines, between the tombs—*

you must discern in *the roof* and *the pigeons,* the distant sea and its boats with their dipping sails.

The difficulty, for the reader, becomes greater still when the poet finds an image that seems a full capture of his soul-state. The impressionist painters climbed the same path, but the public is less insistent on discovering what a canvas means— being less insistent on looking at a canvas. But when poets sought the sonorities that would scientifically reproduce their sensibility at the given moment, even the hardiest reader might be left gasping in the lurch. Some of the symbolist poetry is beyond current comprehension.

After his early Romantic days, Victor Hugo embraced a humanitarian ideal, but in *Fraternité* (1877) indicated its shift from an individual concern to a social concepton:

> *One day, I saw an unknown woman stand.*
> *She seemed to have descended from the skies;*

TRENDS IN LITERATURE

Wings graced her back, and heaven was in her eyes,
Honey her mouth; and with a gentle hand
The tired voyager, the drooping head,
She guided to a pathway through life's shade.
The human race with her was unafraid;
She seemed to whisper: Ye might be misled.
Behind her softened monsters I could see,
Suave lions, penitent tigers, kissed her wing,
Quiet; saved Nimrod, Nero in tears. At times
She was so good she witless seemed to be.
I bowed in worship, as at service chimes . . .
She read my thought, and smiled me into shame;
You think me Pity: Justice is my name.

In the symbolist, the earlier realism was carried by the concerns of the age—in science, philosophy, politics, social economy, industry—to a rationalist, intellectual point of view. The synthesis was sought through the formal processes of mental action. Thus if the poet perceived a logical relationship between an idea and an object, he set down the image and let the reader leap for the idea. Too often, lacking the agility of the poet's mind, the reader plumped into the mire of misunderstanding. Getting up, wiping the mud away, he might refuse another trial.

These over-intellectualized references called for at least a familiar frame, and the poetic forms of these writers are orthodox and simple. Given a usual pattern of the verse, such as Mallarmé and his followers, including Valéry, always provide, the reader is free to deal with other more intricate aspects. These he finds aplenty, to challenge his understanding, even in Mallarmé's best known works; they pervade the poet's less enucleate allia of thought:

> *All pride smokes with dusk,*
> *Torch in a smothered flare*
> *Nor can the immortal puff*
> *Delay its drift from there!*

SYMBOLISM

> *The heritor's old room*
> *Where the rich trophies pall*
> *Would not be even warmed*
> *If it stole along the hall.*
>
> *Essential dreads of the past*
> *Clutching as with claws*
> *The tomb of disavowal,*
>
> *Under heavy marble outcast*
> *No other fire draws*
> *Than the lightning-capped corbel.*

After many years of scientific study during which he put poetry aside, Valéry wrote his *Introduction to the Method of Leonardo da Vinci,* and declared that

> *The universe is but a flaw*
> *In the purity of non-being.*

The sinuate music and acroamatic thought of Mallarmé's *L'Après-midi d'un faune* and *Hérodiade* are matched in the classical verse and elucubrate ideas of Valéry's *Narcisse* and *Jeune Parque.*

For the works of these earnest poets, Anatole France posed as apologist: "Doubtless humanity is tired of understanding; words have had meaning for quite some time!"

A less mocking and more lucid explanation is offered by Rodin. The merging of nature and man these poets were seeking to imprison in the texture, rather than the text, of their poems, the sculptor was vainly trying to bring out of his marble. His figures persisted in remaining but partly formed, within the half-hewn block, and he cried:

> Don't you see? Only in ages when men know what life is all about, can they produce a fully defined plastic art. When the Greeks gave their gods human behavior, what more natural than to give them human form, bodies that you can walk all around, as

you can a man or woman down here? In the same way, if you were a thirteenth-century Christian, you would give your stone saints the full relief that testifies an assured faith. So, if you were a monarchic artist, you'd show your courtiers enamoured of elegance; as you'd picture citizens roused in patriotism, in Napoleon's time. But how can you expect my forms, in this time of uncertainty, of groping toward new goals, not to stay caught in the substance that submerges them? This marble from which the bodies do not wholly rise in round relief, is the unknown quantity from which I cannot clear my figures. I should be insincere if I declared, in my own troubled state, that I can go freely around them.

By less intellectual, more intuitive pathways as well, man was striving to go all around his ideas, to see them whole and as one whole.

Instinctive art
Must fumble for the whole; once fixing on a part
However poor, surpass the fragment, and aspire
To reconstruct thereby the ultimate entire.

As the scientist rebuilds the mastodon from an eye-socket and a knuckle, the visionary from a wisp and a wish-bone gives us the cosmos. Rimbaud (anticipating the surrealists) declared that the poet must make himself a visionary through a "reasoned derangement of the senses."

The philosopher of this mystic vision is Bergson. Not by reason but with images, with figured words, he brings his brood into the very fields where the rational Hegelians have been grazing. The true road to knowledge, this guide assures us, is intuition, which "by the sympathetic communication it establishes between each of us and all other living things, will guide us into the proper domain of life, which is reciprocal interpenetration, indefinitely continuous creation." This is true, he continues, because

SYMBOLISM

the intuition of our continuance, far from leaving us suspended in the void, as pure analysis would do, sets us in contact with an unbroken spread of continuances, which we should follow, either up or down. In both cases, by a more and more violent effort, we can expand indefinitely; in both cases, we transcend ourselves. If downward, we move upon a continuance more and more dispersed, of which the palpitations, more rapid than our own, dividing our simple sensation, dilute its quality through the quantity: its limit being pure homogeneity, pure repetition, by which we define materiality. Moving in the opposite direction, we approach a continuance that stretches out, draws closer, grows more and more intense: its limit being eternity. Not now the conceptual eternity, which is an eternity of death, but an eternity of life. Eternity living and consequently still moving, wherein our own continuance is rediscovered as vibrations in light; eternity, the concretion of all continuance, as materiality is of all dispersion.

This discussion is vague enough to seem foretaste of the symbolist obscurity; but Bergson moves still farther on the path:

No image can replace the intuition of continuance. But many diverse images, drawn from quite different orders of things, may by the convergence of their action direct the consciousness to the precise point where there is a certain intuition to seize. Selecting images as disparate as possible may prevent one or another of them from usurping the place of the intuition it is charged to summon . . . Making them all demand of our spirit, despite their different aspects, the same type of attention and about the same degree of tension, will little by little accustom the consciousness to a particular and well-defined predisposition, precisely that which it should assume to appear to itself, unveiled.

[177]

The intuitive moves by feeling rather than reason. Hence he is likely to move with violence. After Baudelaire, Samain walks equably in Bergson's pathway; but Rimbaud rushes to his *Season in Hell*—Rimbaud whom the pious Claudel today (one of the many recently hailing this intense poetic figure) calls "a mystic in the raw."

The Romantic and the realist moved, in one direction—"down", Bergson would say!—to excess of the detailed, in pretty picturesque or ugly grossness; this in the symbolist vaulted with far-fetched figure. In the other direction, the tendency toward excess of the vague, exaggerated emotional states or cries of liberty or social love, strained for an intuitive grasp of the great harmony. By way of piety or blasphemy, through bland humanitarianism or emetic concern with human misery, it sped until again what were stressed were not the ways of correction but the cruelty and the horror. Laforgue's *Complaint of the Lad With Heart-Disease*, Corbière's *Rhapsody of the Deaf-Mute*, are pity and irony on the way to decadence.

On this emotional journey the ideas are more recognizable. The quest for a synthesis may therefore safely range in the realm of form. From Baudelaire's *Poems In Prose*, which painted such pictures, Gustave Kahn, pioneer and pamphleteer of *vers libre*, has traced the development of free verse. Whitman in the United States, it may be remembered, spoke of his own efforts as freeing poetry from the prison of verse form:

> In my opinion the time has arrived to essentially break down the barriers of form between prose and poetry. I say the latter is henceforth to win and maintain its character regardless of rhyme, and the measurement-rules of iambic, spondee, dactyl, etc., and that even if rhyme and those measurements continue to furnish mediums for inferior writers and themes, the truest and greatest POETRY can never again, in the English language, be express'd in arbitrary and rhyming metre, any more than the greatest eloquence, or the truest power and passion. While admitting that

SYMBOLISM

the venerable and heavenly forms of chiming versification have in their time play'd great and fitting parts—that the pensive complaint, the ballads, wars, amours, legends of Europe, etc., have, many of them, been inimitably render'd in rhyming verse—that there have been very illustrious poets whose shapes the mantle of such verse has beautifully envelopt—and though the mantle has fallen, with perhaps added beauty, on some of our own age—it is, notwithstanding, certain to me, that the day of such conventional rhyme is ended. In America, at any rate, and as a medium of highest esthetic practical or spiritual expression, present or future, it palpably fails, and must fail, to serve. The Muse of the Prairies, of California, Canada, Texas, and of the peaks of Colorado, dismissing the literary, as well as social, etiquette of over-sea feudalism and caste, joyfully enlarging, adapting itself to comprehend the size of the whole people, with the free play, emotions, pride, passions, experiences, that belong to them, body and soul—to the general globe, and all its relations in astronomy, as the savans portray them to us—to the modern, the busy nineteenth century, with steamships, railroads, factories, electric telegraphs, cylinder presses—to the thought of the solidarity of nations, the brotherhood and sisterhood of the entire earth—farms, factories, foundries, workshops, mines, or on shipboard, or on lakes and rivers—resumes that other medium of expression, more flexible, more eligible—soars to the freer, vast, diviner heaven of prose.

Amy Lowell has experimented with what she calls polyphonic prose, paragraphs using the devices of verse without meter. A student of rhythms describes free verse as an alternation between moments of prose and snatches of poetry, a jumping back and forth from one side of the fence to the other. But however successful and however derided, free verse is an ef-

[179]

fort to widen the scope of poetry and intensify its appeal, by drawing into its flow rhythms of prose, by blending the effects of the two arts of language.

Not only in art was language thus unified; for commerce or for international brotherhood, universal languages were sought: Esperanto, Volapuk, more recently Basic English, lingual attempts at world unity until peoples were joined in the World Wars.

Behind language, thought itself toward the turn of the century was drawn from successive centerings to the notion of a single stream of consciousness. William James described this; his brother Henry began to present it in fiction. The best known attempt at this interior monologue, in Joyce's *Ulysses,* had, as Joyce himself pointed out, a rich forerunner in *The Laurels Are Felled,* by Edouard Dujardin, which was written at the height of the symbolist movement.

Either through thought, and the Hegelian synthesis, or through a mystic vision and the Bergsonian intuitive flash, the symbolist sought to express the union between the constant multiplicity of events and the multiplex constancy of their meaning. He rides the pendulum at mid-swing.

"Rimbaud and Mallarmé," declared Gide, "have become Adam and Eve. The apple was offered by Cézanne. And we shall always bear the burden of this original sin." Baudelaire plucked his posies in the midmost of the garden.

Symbolism was seeking an impossible fusion; two irreconcilable compulsions were tugging it apart. It was—striving to set all things at one with one another—inevitably at odds with itself. It was foredoomedly shortlived. And it was the common source of the impulsions of today, springing from its significant release in two main courses, in the unifying emphases of our age.

SYMBOLISM

8. George Sand shows the pattern.

WITH more brazen though less orchestral tones, "George Sand" responded to her age (1804-1876) as Goethe earlier (1749-1832) had led and echoed his. Romanticism burst upon France as the century's third decade rounded to the fourth; just then Aurore Dudevant came to Paris to wear her sailor hat and man's attire beside Gautier's pink waistcoat, and to tell the story of her early love in a novel signed George Sand (the lover was Sandeau). That early love of liberty and love burned in her endlessly: Alfred de Musset, Flaubert, Liszt, Chopin, are but the better known of those she scorched as her passion for the expression of her passion bore her from country to country, bed to bed, book to book. Her many-paged diary, her voluminous letters, her innumerable novels, all told her story. *Indiana,* her first, and *Valentine,* are best of this early drive for freedom. "Love is the key," she said, that unlocks every door, and every law.

In the famous letter to Chopin's friend, in which she justifies her intention of taking the musician, George writes: "I have no preconceived ideas, no habits, and I believe no false principles, either of license or of restraint. I have always trusted my instincts, which have always been noble." Whereupon she swept Chopin away to Mallorca.

But in the core of this Romantic passion-rose already coiled the canker-worm. The pursuit of passion is a doomed journey; the wayside blossoms George culled were dusty, and soon drooped. In her novel *Valentine,* the hero is Benedict; patterned after the once bright, hopeful boys, he has drained the cup: "Boredom, this terrible evil that is the curse of the present generation, had taken hold of Benedict's destiny in the flower of his youth; like a cloud it covered up his future. It had killed the best faculty of his age: the power to hope!" A letter to Sainte-Beuve more directly shows George's struggle: "Don't you know that I cannot live without pain? It excites and whips along my jaded nerves. From its convulsions I derive the strength to struggle and to curse. Those that hope to die in a coma know nothing of death's voluptuousness."

Through her personal vitality rebounding from the self-concern that brought her to the brood of death and the half-savour of suicide, George Sand moved, as the 1830's neared their end, with a more embracing love, toward humankind. Her life was as intense as ever, but her associates had likewise changed. Her beloved Liszt, for example, had written a challenge to the doctrine of *noblesse oblige* in his *Génie oblige,* which declared that the aim of art is to manifest and to promote human progress. Liszt looked upon his own career as a social mission; in 1837 he gave a concert for the Lyon strikers. In this period, with a sincerity that made it her best novel, George Sand wrote *Mauprat,* a picture within a sensual man, last of a lawless line, of the gradual growth and triumph of the spirit. Her *Letters to Marcie,* of the same years, proclaim: "Whatever harnesses the instincts, fortifies the will, and leads human emotions into regulated channels, helps to establish God's kingdom on earth, which is none other than the supremacy of love and truth."

This linking of art and life was not unaccompanied by other signs, more purely aesthetic, of the transitional age. E. T. A. Hoffman, who suggested the identity of color, smell, and sound Baudelaire later hailed, was a favorite of Liszt and Sand and their circle. They frequently quoted Hoffmann's Kapellmeister Kreisler, playing with such ideas as "I saw inside the stone. Its red veins opened like dark carnations whose fragrance rose visibly in high singing rays." But the impulse toward this wider embracing found more fruitful outlet in their practical work.

Through the following decade, George roused more constantly, more consciously, in the people's cause. With the followers of Saint-Simon, especially her intimates Michel de

SYMBOLISM

Bourges and Lamennais, she aspired to become a leader and a teacher. The artist must make his symbols reveal the divine truth, and waken the people to love and justice. Declaring that in the old days she had been a victim of megalomania, George gave more and more time, in books and public actions, to socialist propaganda. The Revolution of 1848 was a breaking wave of the ideas she helped foster; she took an active part in its course; and in the subsequent reaction only the Emperor's admiration of her early books preserved her to write more. In 1849 her play *Claudie* first brought the proletarian and the peasant seriously upon the stage. Her life continued its quest of a synthesis she never quite achieved, of her individual desires and the social needs. More widely she now exclaimed: "Yes, love is the key to the enigma of the universe!"

In 1863 George Sand wrote a novel, and in 1864 produced a play—*Mademoiselle la Quintinie*; *Le Marquis de Villemer*—the reception of which proved she was as popular as ever, even though these were both round attacks upon clerical abuse of the people. In 1864 she also wrote: "Universal suffrage has its rights today and tomorrow, even if we have more dictatorships . . . Learn to judge things from a higher level." In 1867 her novel *Cadio* studied the effects of the Revolution on the common man. After 1870, the struggle between the Republic and the Commune involved her fierce attachment. Her most serious quarrel with her friend Flaubert was roused by his statement that the masses are always stupid, that one must hate the world. "You tell me," she cried, "that the public has always been savage, the priest hypocritical, the bourgeois cowardly, the soldier a brigand, and the peasant an ass? You tell me that you have known this since you were young, and that maturity has taught you nothing else? Then you have never been young. Ah, we are very different indeed, for I have never ceased to be young, if to be young means to love."

In her last years, symbolism, the growth toward the universe within each separate part, had deepest hold on her. "I

TRENDS IN LITERATURE

am not dreaming when, standing before a towering mass of rock, I feel that these mighty bones of the earth are mine, and that the calmness of my mind shares their apparent death and dramatic immobility . . . I think of the hidden work going on in their molecules and I incline to attribute to them an existence similar to our own. I, too, am a stone which time disintegrates." The pebbles and the earth of her "disintegration" form the soil seeded with our time.

SYMBOLISM

9. *America strikes up the band.*

THE French symbolists did not seek that their poems be understood. Beyond the image the reader's mind should flash to a comprehensive idea; thus only can he comprehend. The poem is one flow, from word to wisdom. Explanations muddy the stream.

"A poem should not mean, but be." After the symbolists, others have moved to meaningless syllables in current patterns of sound. The English-speaking peoples incline to regard these esoteric experiments as on the lunatic fringe; at best, alien. Gertrude Stein and James Joyce settled as expatriates in Paris. T. S. Eliot supplied notes to *The Waste Land*; Hart Crane in letters and elsewhere told his intent. We like our non-sense to be nonsense, and our nonsense is unparalleled. In our serious endeavors, we turn from the Joycean deep-Liffey diving, with ever muddier haul; we remember Shakespeare's success with Leviathan, as we would

> *Read the rounded verse and understand it:*
> *Not merely hook our fish, but—Heavens!—land it.*

It takes the logic of a theory to go to its extreme.

While England muddled, and France cut figures, America just growed. The rough and ready United States bulked its way into time. Here, then, we may expect the least self-conscious, the most direct, expression of the age's movement toward the universal. In literature, this came through Walt Whitman.

The French initiators, aristocratic in mood, were aware of their significance; they supplied manifestoes and traced their own path. The democratic Whitman was in one sense fully Self-conscious: he took his body in proclaimed detail as paean-worth. But his utterances are not commentaries, they are battle-

[185]

cries. He puts into words the silent scorn of the pioneers for classical themes:

> *Come Muse, migrate from Greece and Ionia.*
> *Cross out, please, those immensely overpaid accounts,*
> *That matter of Troy and Achilles' wrath, and Aeneas',*
>   *Odysseus' wanderings;*
> *Placard "Removed" and "To Let" on the rocks of*
>   *your snowy Parnassus—*

Sweeping these aside (along with the barriers between poetry and prose) he finds "the clue to the past" in

> *Democracy—the purport and aim of all the past.*

No longer "Arms and the man", but

> *One's Self I sing, a simple, separate Person;*
> *Yet utter the word Democratic, the word En-masse.*

> The poetry of the future aims at free expression of emotion, and to arouse and initiate, more than to define or finish. Like all modern tendencies, it has direct or indirect reference continually to the reader, to you or me, to the eternal identity of everything, the mighty ego.

This sense of brotherhood immanent in Whitman crosses all barriers: "Walt Whitman am I, a Kosmos."
He links the limits of time. He reaches back:

> *I raise the Present on the Past.*
> *(As some perennial tree, out of its roots, the present on the past.)*
> *With time and space I him dilate—and fuse the*
>   *immortal laws.*

He touches forward:

> *. . . outlining what is yet to be,*
> *I project the history of the future.*

SYMBOLISM

He fuses body and spirit:

> *Was somebody asking to see the Soul?*
> *See! your own shape and countenance—persons, substances,*
>   *beasts, the trees, running rivers, the rocks and sands.*

Then he flatly declares:

> *Objects gross and the unseen soul are one.*

He welcomes all things:

> *I behold the picturesque giant and love him—and I do*
>   *not stop there,*
> *I go with the team also . . .*
> *I am of old and young, of the foolish as much as the wise,*
> *Regardless of others, ever regardful of others,*
> *Maternal as well as paternal, a child as well as a man . . .*
> *Endless unfolding of words of ages!*
> *And mine a word of the modern—the word* En-masse . . .
> *All truths wait in all things.*

Every page of the *Leaves of Grass* is rich with embracings, whether we read *A Noiseless, Patient Spider*, or *Salut au Monde* or *Crossing Brooklyn Ferry*, or *A Woman Waits For Me*: "she contains all, nothing is lacking . . . In you I wrap a thousand onward years."

At one moment, as in his answer when "A child said *What is the grass?* fetching it to me with full hands", Whitman roves through many diverse figures (as Bergson advises); at another, as when he elaborates on the cry "Sex is all", he sails with a fresh inland breeze over the sea where later D. H. Lawrence sinks in dark, mystic brooding. Those that feel, in his *Calamus*, too physical a celebration of comradeship, should reread from it the poem beginning:

> *And now, gentlemen,*
> *A word I give to remain in your memories and minds,*
> *As base, and finale too, for all metaphysics . . .*

to its enunciation of that base in fullest love:

> *The dear love of man for his comrade, the attraction
> of friend to friend,
> Of the well-married husband and wife—and of
> children and parents,
> Of city for city, and land for land.*

In Whitman, the *Answerer* is abroad, who

> *resolves all tongues into his own, and bestows it upon
> men, and any man translates, and any man
> translates himself also;
> One part does not counteract another part—he is the
> joiner, he sees how they join.*

Finally—though I could pertinently reprint his volumes — Whitman sees the poet as the unifying force between the ego and the world without:

> *When the full-grown Poet came,
> Out spake pleas'd* NATURE *(the round impassive
> Globe, with all its shows of Day and Night)
> saying,* He is mine;
> *But out spake too the* SOUL *of man, proud, jealous
> and unreconciled,* Nay, he is mine alone;
> *—Then the full-grown Poet stood between the Two,
> and took each by the hand;
> And today and ever so stands, as Blender, Uniter,
> tightly holding hands,
> Which he will never release untl he reconciles the Two,
> And wholly and joyously blends them* . . .

> The peculiar glory of our land, I have come to see, or expect to see, not in their geographical or republican greatness, nor wealth nor products, nor military nor naval power, nor special, eminent names in any department, to shine with, or outshine, foreign special names in similar departments—but more and

more in a vaster, saner, more surrounding Comradeship, uniting closer and closer not only the American States, but all nations, and all humanity. That, O poets! is it not a theme worth chanting, worth striving for? Why not fix your verses henceforth to the gauge of the rounded globe? the whole race? Perhaps the most illustrious culmination of the modern may thus prove to be a signal of joyous, more exalted bards of adhesiveness, identically one in soul, but contributed by every nation, each after its distinctive kind. Let us, audacious, start it. Let the diplomats, as ever, still deeply plan, seeking advantage, proposing treaties between governments, and to bind them, on paper; what I seek is different, simpler. I would inaugurate from America, for this purpose, new formulas —international poems.

Out of the manifold conflicting forces of America, at a time when the Union itself was in bloody struggle to survive, out of the wide land where the rugged individualism of the pioneer was opening new areas and developing new sources of energy in a continuous growth that industry, also, was bending to individual control and individual ends; while regional fiction was extending its fields, and the emergence of national types in the drama reflected the general attention to local differences, to Yankee, Hoosier, Kentuckian, comic Negro, comic Irishman, comic Jew; carpet-bagger, miner, promoter, greenhorn, cowboy—to all the diversity and counter-urging oppositions in the land, the voice that is unanimously recognized as most significant and most prophetic is that of Walt Whitman, singer of brotherhood, of harmony, of union. Even in the farthest reaches of individual enterprise, the distant call of a common cause is heard.

MONITORY INTERLUDE

MONTORY INTERLUDE

MONITORY INTERLUDE

IF you have consented at least to try on my blinders, you observe that as we approach our own day the unity increases. The pendulum that was at mid-swing with the Victorians and the Symbolists bears upward into the period of the universal. Our age is one of emphasis upon society, the needs of which the individual must fill. Whatever lip-service may be paid to freedom, in every sphere we stress law, union, unity, pervasive traits, central essences, cooperative organizations, the collective state.

But before we seek to read the new lines the pendulum-tip traces on time's chart, let us pause to observe that it does not rise unclogged.

Every point of view, once initiated, persists. Neither time's change nor logic's denial can stop its course.

Thus in our social epoch, there are continual reminders of the era of the individual. What we think of them depends upon our own stand in the age. We may despise them as laggards of a time outworn. We may hail them as heralding the new day yet to come. Or we may more calmly deem them sages persisting in a chosen path despite the shiftings of the hour.

Stevenson was a stout defender of romance—though to it he opposed:

> the haunting and spectral unreality of realistic books ... In each, we miss the personal poetry, the enchanted atmosphere, that rainbow of fancy that clothes what is naked and seems to ennoble what is base; in each, life falls dead like dough, instead of soaring away like a balloon into the colours of the sunset; each is true, each inconceivable; for no man lives the external truth, among salts and acids, but in the warm, phantasmagoric chamber of his brain, with the painted windows and storied walls.

TRENDS IN LITERATURE

Stevenson, however, and partly for this reason, is a children's author. His stories are read before late adolescence brings the clustering of ideals and social impulses that quicken our youth with the spirit of the time. The great body of romantic survivals lies rather in what we might call vestigia. Our grownup children seek playgrounds of the fancy. Yesterday they strolled with Beverly through Graustark, with Alice in old Vincennes; today they swing with the swift lovers of "true-story" and "confessions" magazines, or dash into the future with Buck Rogers and Superman.

In poetry, a childlike quality may hold its charm. The life and work of Verlaine, for example, lingered in the romantic mood. "Symbolism?" he queried; "I don't get you. Must be a German word, eh? What do you make of it? Anyway, the devil with it! When I suffer, when I'm happy, or when I weep, I know darn well that's not a symbol!" The soul of a child held Verlaine from sophisticate meanderings. He felt the child's need of caresses, which led him to sin, even to perversion, but without perversity. For his child-soul sustained him in candour. He dwelled in the realm of immediate feelings. In his art is the Romantic's direct response to life's sensations:

> *The heavy thrall*
> *Of the sobbing call*
> *Of the fall*
> *Weighs, nor departs,*
> *Like my heart's*
> *Pall.*
>
> *Overcome*
> *And dumb*
> *As the hours creep*
> *I see the haze*
> *Of olden days*
> *And weep.*
>
> *And I go away*
> *The wind's prey,*

MONITORY INTERLUDE

> *In barren, brief*
> *Whirl hither and yon*
> *Like a wan*
> *Dead leaf.*

Scheduled to lecture at Oxford, Verlaine arrived late, patch on's eye, arm in a sling, limping; he began by declaring a man cannot be a poet until he has *lived*.

Samuel Butler—to choose an opposite instance—was ignored in his own day, and brought to popularity by Bernard Shaw, who hailed him as heralding the age to come. Butler carried the iconoclastic spirit into his writings, but the laborers of England had put the same spirit into grim practice. They sought to wreck the machines that had put them out of jobs; in Butler's utopian *Erewhon*— read it backwards—every invention less than two centuries old is cast aside. By the time the author was rediscovered, his thoughts were literary commonplace. From diatribe and satire they had come to motivate the drama. *The Machine-Stormers* tells the literal story. *R. U. R.* shows the machine triumphant, as a mechanical contrivance (for which the play supplies the name, *robot*) replaces man.

Gerard Manly Hopkins, whose poetry remained in manuscript during his life, is another who, both in form and feeling, pointed toward the age aborning. His "sprung rhythms", his unconventional punctuation, anticipate the experiments of his editor Robert Bridges and of e e cummings. At the same time his basic piety embowers the eternal sense of the deeper unity of God: beyond

> *All things counter, original, spare, strange;*
> *Whatever is fickle, freckled (who knows how?)*
> *With swift, slow; sweet, sour; adazzle, dim;*
> *He fathers-forth whose beauty is past change:*
>   *Praise Him.*

Realism is less likely to lag behind the generations. It comes more consciously; it sees man intimately bound with things about hm. And it seeks no escape from these binding forces. The very titles of many outstanding novels show that they share a larger vision. Zola's greatest works are grouped about a family. Balzac offers, for cosmic laughter, the human comedy. Maugham is concerned with the fact of human bondage. Dreiser sets down the career, not of Barry Lyndon nor of John Halifax, Gentleman, but of The Genius, The Financier; the dark impulses of our civilization bring on, not poor Clyde Griffith's fall, but An American Tragedy.

Even where the title seems more personal, the social sense prevails. Galsworthy's *Forsyte Saga* "keeps a stiff upper lip" for the upper middle class. Clemence Dane's *Broome Stages* shows many pronouncedly individual members of a family held together by a core of genius. Despite disruptive seduction and disintegrating deaths, Mazo de la Roche's chronicle of the Whiteoaks keeps the family intact in Jalna. G. B. Stern's Matriarch maintains her unifying rule. Hugh Walpole's account of the Herries runs more romantically with the rebels and the rogues: yet even here it is social conscience stronger than their personal desires that in the final volume severs Benjie and Vanessa, and brings the ultimate tragedy upon their illegitimate child.

For there is, in all these books, however romantic-seeming, a basic change. The recent growth has moved beyond Balzac and Zola, who sought to cover their broad canvas with many individual portraits. Jules Romains, in the preface to his monumental *Men of Good Will,* calls the earlier two outmoded. True, the fashion of our time has passed them by; but they can safely bide. That fashion we may linger with later; at the moment I wish to indicate the change even in what some still call romantic writing. The "romance" of Cabell's essays is markedly akin to Shaw's "life-force"; their difference is as of the rapier and the broadsword. Each posits a basic, universal

MONITORY INTERLUDE

impulsion. There is a deliberate bringing down to earth in the inclusiveness of Cabell. His Jurgen is that catch-all of modern life, that gatherer of the odds and especially the ends of failure: a pawnbroker. While in his dream-Poictesme anything is rather more than likely to happen, it is in his earthly brokerage that he makes ends meet. And it is *The Cream of the Jest* indeed that the magic charm that transports us to the ideal world turns out to be in truth the sesame to everywoman's renewal: the top of a cold cream jar! A broken one, at that. In this way does Cabell jar us back to the contemporary waste land.

But in truth his Jurgen—to front him with longer-lived fellows—is no more of a man than Gulliver, than Don Quixote, than Christian. These are all individual not in that they are uniquely complex, like rounded, living beings; but in that they are uniquely simple, one quality dressed as a man—not particular at all, but universal. They embody a single but general trait.

We have glanced at *Anthony Adverse* already; let us view it in this light. For Henry Seidel Canby calls the book "a picaresque romance modernized only by a frank and vivid realism of detail." (If Dr. Canby thinks that quality distinctively contemporary, he should reread the picaresque tales!) The author himself knew better, before the book, in it, and after. As motto to the work is prefixed a sentence from Sir Thomas Browne:

> There is something in us that can be without us, and will be after us, though indeed it hath no history of what it was before us, and cannot tell how it entered into us.

Anthony himself is troubled with doubts about his place in the scheme of things:

> Something must control both life and reality, he saw, vision and fact, man and nature. To that something he felt akin as if some portion of it were in him.

Yet *he* was also in nature; yet the material world lay without!

This perplexity grows to assurance, as a flower of light blossoms in his mystic vision:

> The light was in him now. He understood one day, as he lay on the beach timelessly gazing into the water of the cove where the light seemed to concentrate, that he was like and one with the rocks and the trees and the plants about; one with the creatures that moved only a little, down there on the sand-floor under the water . . . "Let there be light". Instantly a flower of light bloomed furiously in the void. It was a day stream beautiful beyond expression that spread outward in all ways at once, a sphere that instantaneously pre-empted all of space and yet was forever spreading. Where it was not was nothing. Where it reached was light. All things with bodies were part of it and existed only in this flower of light. To watch the shifting of its endless petals of things from stars to seashells was to peep at time. To see the whole flower itself ever expanding through the nothing of darkness was to see all of time and to see it as one flash. For though the flower existed for eternity, that which looked at it as from a great distance and apart from it saw it as one outgoing flash. Instantaneously everything from the beginning to the end had happened.

And the author has later declared that the theme of *Anthony Adverse* is

> that it is impossible to make a business of life; to conduct it on a basis of things, and that, if final satisfaction is to be attained, the physical world and the body must be subdued to the higher values discernible to the heart, the intellect, and the spirit of man.

MONITORY INTERLUDE

While all these books are marked with the stamp of our age, it must not be thought that all tokens of other times are (like Erewhon's machines) stored in the museums. They may still be found at the libraries marked "One week only: not renewable." Every impulse, once it has rippled on the waters of life, back even from the farthest shores of forgetfulness is somehow swelled again.

POLITICAL PREAMBLING

POLITICAL PREAMBLING

A. The Hope of Democracy

DEMOCRACY is the pathway of progress.

Mankind moves in a low spiral; impatient spirits try to leap the loops. Hence democracy is often damned—but never doomed. Meanwhile the headstrong plunge into the abyss.

A hundred and fifty years ago, as we have seen, men stressed their powers and rights as individual beings. Considered in relation to other men, this attitude tends toward two extremes. One of these is anarchy; the other, tyranny. The anarch takes as his motto what Rabelais set for the monks of Theleme: Do what you will. Practically, this meant that he did as he pleased, and did not trouble himself with the feelings of others. They might do the same. The tyrant's motto is even simpler: Do what I will.

In either case it is the personal will that counts. The tyrant exalts his own will, despotically; the anarch equates every will, to be exercised separately. Politically, of course, the anarch builds no party; his followers are personal but unconjoined. Forgotten droves of young Englishmen misbehaved like Byron and Shelley; but such are slaves; the anarch walks alone. The tyrant (if successful) builds an industry or an empire; his following also is personal, but bound together by loyalty—as we see in the cohorts of Napoleon. It was love for "the little corporal" that held them fast even in disaster, even after death, even through the puny days of the eaglet they fledged in his father's memory.

Practically, the anarch is a tyrant in his circle. For though he declares that everyone may follow his own desires, most of us do not, while the anarch does. We are all familiar with minor instances where the individual desire runs counter to that of the group. The family has planned a picnic; then father, who has to drive the car, decides it is an ideal day for his golf. Happily, in most groups such disappointments are fairly well spaced, and rise from both parties; with the anarch, they occur constantly, and all on one side. If he resolves to leave his wife, willy-nilly she must live without him. The logical place for such a man to dwell is in the lonely woods. Usually he prefers more occupied spaces. Practically, therefore, the anarch is a miniature despot. Those around him find their ways troubled, their feelings hurt, their world shaken, by his actions heedless of aught save his own will. Those that do not move out of his way, or with his whim, are as liable to breakage as any that stand in a tyrant's path.

Thus extremes meet. But we need not meet the extremes. Never are the end-points the only alternatives; seldom are they the wisest.

Men exist in states. In a period that emphasizes the individual, the state is cursed. To the Romantic generation, *Leviathan* was not a biblical fish too great to be hauled on a hook, nor yet an ocean liner, but Hobbes' picture of the Moloch state, feeding on its own citizens. Herbert Spencer leaned over, with the weight of his scientific prestige, to declare that all dependence on the state is slavery.

Nonetheless, men abide in states. Sleep, if no other need, would set guards, would band men together. To this necessity the anarch responds by pretending it doesn't exist. The tyrant again is simpler; he subsumes the opposition. He says "I am the state." But America found democracy, which says The people are the state.

Democracy began in the United States at a time when individualism was rampant through the world. And a rugged individualism admirably suited our pioneer days. Then the industrial revolution, sweeping new concerns over Europe, brought wider problems to our broadening land. Capitalism is the attempt, on an individualistic basis, to cope with the complexities of large-scale production. Individual initiative called for collective carrying through.

Gradually, through a century and a half, our democracy has been shaping its course to meet these changing conditions. The early Bill of Rights ensured the basic individual essentials of justice and fair-dealing. Since then, by amendments and interpretations and laws, at the time the Victorian was muddling through, we adjusted ourselves to the collective emphasis, within the framework of democracy.

It should be noted that communism (with a small *c*) is not a political principle but a way of life. The first fire companies were privately owned. Crassus made his fortune in Roman real estate by going to the owners of burning buildings—it may even be that he set them ablaze!—and offering to buy them. If the owners accepted his absurdly low figure, he called his extinguishers; if they refused, he let the buildings burn. Now you and I and our fellow-citizens own not only the fire hydrants but the lampposts—but we cannot each come claim his own and carry it away. Such common ownership is a manifest means of democracy.

Some persons today complain that government ownership is a dump for individualistic failures. The post-office, water, electricity, railroads (for the federal charge), subways (for the city) are urged upon the public when they become private burdens. Never are the new enterprises, the now thriving 'bus traffic, air transportation, radio, given into government hands. While in a few cases this complaint may be true, it still is groundless. For by its teaching, one that believes in government ownership need only wait, all will be grist; and one that does not, may take comfort in the constant growth of new fields of human endeavor. In the meantime we may note that the common ownership of public utilities, and the private inauguration of new enterprises, both accord with the principles of democratic living.

Today the emphasis has swung full tilt. Individual importance is submerged in the collective. Stressing the state forces us to consider our relation to other men. It also tends toward two extremes. One of these is Communism; the other, Fascism. The Communist (capital *C* this time, please!) declares that the State belongs to the people; therefore they must work to keep it sound, to deserve its care. The Fascist says that the State exists to keep the people sound; therefore, they must work to belong to it, to deserve its care. In Soviet Russian practice, what was called the temporary "dictatorship of the proletariat", until the people learn self-rule, lapsed to a dictatorship of the leader—precisely as in the Fascist State. Again, extremes have met.

But time has turned the spiral. The collective emphasis of our age is clear in the way we handle our Fuehrers: we convert them into systems. Communism and Fascism become Leninism and Hitlerism. Even offshoots are swollen into further claims of new world orders, and Stalinism and Trotzkyism are scorned by the Hatestonites.—Did anyone in the Little Corporal's day hear talk of Napoleonism?

Men have spoken of a Shelleyan idea, a Byronesque attitude; thus they pointed back to the individual. I have mentioned the intense individual devotion that held men to Napoleon. The people followed Hitler for what he promised for the race. It was the dream and not the man to which these folk were loyal. This was made clear in the fate of the man dubbed "The American Fuehrer," the leader of the German-American Bund, Fritz Kuhn. When Kuhn was indicted for misuse of the Bund funds—not after a Bund outcry but against Bund protests, by the public prosecutor—the defense attorney explained to his clients that, in the state of public opinion, a conviction in the lower court was almost certain; but equally certain was a reversal on appeal. The Bund provided funds for the trial, and stood solidly with the leader. He was convicted. Membership in the Bund did not decrease; but Kuhn lodged in prison unvisited by his former associates, who did not even trouble to raise funds for further trial. For half a century, Napoleon's cause was sustained by those that loved Napoleon; Fascism

POLITICAL PREAMBLING

here is being furthered by those that have forgotten Kuhn. The hero has been supplanted by the herd.

In our age again, despite the very practical meeting of the extremes, their theories are opposed. Communism represents, within the collective emphasis, the extreme of the development traced by those that see man and nature as a continuum, all bound by the same physical and chemical laws. Hence the immediate attacks on religion by Soviet Russia. Fascism is the extreme outgrowth, within the collective emphasis, of those that believe in mankind's free will and assertive power. Hence the return of the battling Nordic gods in Germany. A Freudian Marxism to the north stands against the claims of the superman and the super-race.

The outcry is heard, especially among wistful liberals that see themselves "perforce" as fellow-travelers, that one must choose. Either Communism or Fascism: which will you have? Our answer is: Neither, thank you; but democracy.

Once again, extremes are not alternatives. They may end, indeed, by counterbalancing one another, until from their death-struggle history resumes its onward march, democratically around time's spiral.

Many otherwise intelligent persons have meanwhile been caught between the jaws of this delusion of choice. Among them is T. S. Eliot, whom some consider the acme (others, the acne) of modern thought. Eliot declares: "Everyone who believes in principles rather than compromise will be driven in spite of himself into extremity, either of Toryism or of Communism." Which will you have, poor fish, the frying pan or the firing squad?

What a fetching way of advocating one's desire! Are there any compromisers in our midst? Out with the base fellows! Such language proves effective with those that take color of feeling, instead of thought. Professor Morris Raphael Cohen refused to read *The Daily Worker* because he did not wish to be bored from within; but here we are, all compromised, unless at once we impale ourselves upon either end of the pole!

—As much as the automobile is compromised for rolling along the street, instead of on either sidewalk! "Principle" and "compromise" are here balanced like good and evil; yet surely to follow the golden mean is no mean principle—though it does mean compromise. All life involves, nay demands, "compromise." This should be as clear to T. S. Eliot as that he cannot avoid some degree of evil, or of stupidity, or of darkness at night. I rather believe he prefers the dark at sleeping time. His remark is as absurd as to say that, unless he believes in compromise, a man that wants a bath will be driven in spite of himself to take it either scalding or freezing.—Unfortunately there are many, like T. S. Eliot, that think they can keep out of hot water only by sitting on a lonely iceberg. We prefer to temper the shower to our taste.

The confusion that rises with our age's emphasis on the collective is further illustrated in a recent advertisement:

"TECHNOCRACY
    Is opposed to the conscription of labor alone as
        Fascist legislation.
    Is opposed to the conscription of capital alone as
        Communist legislation.
    Total Conscription of Men, Machines, Material, and
        Money is neither Fascist nor Communist. It is
        the *American* Way."

If you don't approve of highwaymen, and you don't approve of gangsters, set them to working together, and you will have the ideal state! Fortunately, amid the two sets of polar opposites, anarchy-tyranny and Fascism-Communism, "the American way", democracy, remains the middle path.

The Communist says, The State will lead the people. The Fascist leader says, I will guide the State for the people. The democrat continues to remark, The people are the state. He may, in deference to present-day emphasis, reverse the remark, and allow: The State is the people. This means that through our years the condition of the great masses will be of most con-

POLITICAL PREAMBLING

cern, until with another turn of the spiral there will be still greater individual opportunity for all. For democracy is poised and geared to the endless see-saw shifting of power, as the individual will and the collective urgings teeter on the boards of time.

Democracy contains the instruments for concordant growth in either direction. The New Deal, the recent decisions of the Supreme Court, the breakdown of the precedent against a third term, many other measures of the Franklin D. Roosevelt administration—which led its enemies to call it paternal, if not totalitarian—indicate the direction in which the United States can democratically move, during years of collective emphasis. Its protection of the rights of the individual, on the other hand, has ample illustration in our history; the structure of our government has the same readiness, when time comes again.

For come it will. Already the signals are glowing in the sky. Robert E. Sherwood, in the apostolic anger of his play *There Shall Be No Night,* declares that, really, the individual is just becoming conscious. Gone, he says, is the glory of war. Men fight in grim resignation, because they must. But out of such mood, tomorrow, they will ask: Why must we? Then the totalitarian states are doomed.

This is of course a wishful picture, but it holds a truth. For the excesses of every period prepare its oversetting. In the midst of the collective urge, which sends countless men to self-immolation: which totalitarian state had not thousands of "volunteers" for the suicide squads?—some individuals withhold. And the epoch to come takes birth for its distant triumph.

That day, despite Sherwood, is far down the century. In the meantime, once again, many find the path along the spiral too slow. Democracy believes that certain things—tolerance, justice, to name but two—are more important than 100% efficiency. The individual deserves respect; the organization demands production. In an age of emphasis upon the state, therefore, neatness, despatch, in material things—a Five Year Plan or a program of conquest, announced in advance and ruthlessly carried through—seem to many persons in all lands, caught in the urges of the times, items of significance and high merit.

It is easy to abuse our enemies; it is better to understand them. But in the midst of battle, who can take thought? Especially hard is it to understand those of one's own land that fight in the opposite forces. Yet "traitor" is not the word to describe all that within recently liberated lands abetted the advancing foe. In every country today, the collective emphasis rings a rising undertone of persuasion. In a hundred ways—in science, work, social life, the needs of the home—every one is pressed upon by unifying forces. The basic unity, the law, the state, is assumed as naturally and properly dominant. Such is, I repeat, the tenor of our age. It is natural, then, that the more impatient or dissatisfied should be drawn to one of the extremes. Not only enemy agents, but such impatient ones, eager for the millennium in their own time, within the neighbor lands helped prepare the way for Hitler and for Stalin.

The United States cannot escape such spirits. They make increasing efforts, as the pendulum widens its wing. They prophesize the approaching mass era with increasing assurance. Yet democracy is in little danger here. Stupidity may hamper its development or limit its range. Greed may abet the efforts of the impatient. But force cannot drive us from our freedom. And our government is too plastic, too fertile in adjustments to our needs, for any extreme attitude long to thrive. Extremes are rigid, and can only break; from middle ground one can advance in both directions.

The history of our international relations is made up of adaptations to world change. We have formed and formulated policies and treaties—the outstanding example is of course the Monroe Doctrine; we have waged wars, bought and freed countries — Cuba, the Philippines — without any permanent damage to our democracy. We have withheld from a League of Nations, and become a prime force in the United Nations Organization. As long as we are secure against physical domination, we may stand assured. In any battle of ideas, in any long-range test of human happiness, democracy will survive.

B. The Dilemma of Democracy

These words of democracy, though they could have been written before the Hiroshima blast, are more than pre-atomic bombast. All rule is at best an approximation to the ideal, until such time as mankind is capable of truly democratic living. Democracy, that form of human organization which allows fullest individual freedom in social harmony, is the goal of all good government.

The very approach of democracy to the ultimate ideals, however, sets it at a practical disadvantage in any conflict with less advanced systems, in this uneven world. Listening to the voice of the people, permitting the publication and wide expression of various points of view, with official deliberation and debate, of necessity slows action. The country that must convene and convince its senate, before any declaration of war, is less able to plot, and to set date for action, than a country wherein the decision is that of a single man.

There was a time when all the world accepted slavery. President Lincoln declared that this nation could not exist half slave and half free. It was a long and bitter war that won the land for freedom. Other countries more wisely found ways of abolishing slavery without fighting.

Now radios, airplanes, atomic bombs, emphasize that we are living in "one world". One world, as one nation, cannot continue to exist half slave, half free. Freedom must ultimately come, throughout the world. Yet seldom do the masters of their own accord lay down their whips. Herein lies the danger of still more fierce, of almost annihilating, conflict.

The present situation—possession by the United States of the atomic bomb—gives this country the power to set upon the world a greater pattern of freedom. Ironically, its very democracy forbids—yes, prevents—it from taking any such steps. There is a self-contradiction in enforcing freedom. More ironically still, democracy must stand almost helplessly by while totalitarian governments press their own form upon their neighbors.

Even further: it is all but impossible for us to go to war, without first an overt act of another nation. For various reasons —of which a genuine love of peace is not the least—it is hard to picture our Senate voting us into war, until acts of war have roused our citizens, and fired us with righteous indignation. We will not enter upon a conflict as part of a long-range scheme of expansion; nor are we likely to be persuaded that we must strike—Now!—to anticipate and prevent such aggressive desires elsewhere being ripened.

An astute and absolute ruler in another land may profit by these reluctancies. Scientists declare that Russia should have atomic bombs within five years. Economists tell us that Russia "must have peace" for a decade. (Demosthenes warned the Athenians against Macedon for twelve years, before Philip of Macedon—meanwhile seizing neighbor lands—openly struck against them.) For Russia to have peace that long, all she need do is refrain from the overt act. Ignoring requests and agreements beyond the brink of affront; by devious devices or direct veto delaying action she does not want; meanwhile gathering her material resources within, and increasing her prestige and power abroad: who shall challenge such behavior? When the enemy chooses to strike, then must democracy rouse in self-defence.

Then will the world lie in ashes, and desolation abide in the homes of men. If man is wiped from the earth, democracy will die with him. Yet if some hardy few survive, to scratch a primitive pathway into the future—as after the ice-age, after the flood, so after the great bombing will they trace anew the inevitable path of men, toward the fullest freedom of the individual in social harmony, we call democracy.

Let us hope that the world can find freedom without such war!

For further examination of the trend of our times, in fields other than art—in science, education, psychology, etc.—readers may turn to the section OTHER FIELDS.

TWAIN TURMOIL OF TODAY

1. *Words bear, and bare, the trend.*

THE symbolists declared that each symbol drew in the universe. Our time, continuing this intension, examines the symbols, and erects them into systems. From the mistiest realms of the psyche to the most lucid range of stellar physics—where clarity chimes with beauty in balanced law—that omnium gatherum, the symbol, is supreme. We may therefore expect to find evidence of this in connection with man's chief symbols, his current coin of expression, words.

At first glance, it may seem that the worth of words has been waning. Science has been slipping away from linguistic forms. In every field where accuracy is increasing, speech is dwindling in importance. Signs, formulae, non-verbal symbols, baffle any lay reader that turns the pages of a study in advanced physics or the higher mathematics. Science has, moreover, shifted its basic concepts in this direction. It has moved from a literal acceptance of its accomplishments, the "copy theory" of the last century, toward the notion that our scientific conquests gain for us only symbolical representation of the actual universe. Philosophy, likewise, has in two ways been challenging the value of language. In the first place, it seriously questions whether what Anatole France calls "the cry of the beasts of the forest or the mountains, complicated and corrupted by arrogant anthropoids", intended for practical, functional ends, can serve to grasp and to present the metaphysical mysteries of the world. In the second place, it swings the chop-axe of logic to strike the reality out of our speech: to name a thing, it avers, is at once to turn it into a fiction, a fixed abstraction that belies the concrete fluidity of life.

According to the emphatic school of logical positivism, the utterances of metaphysics are neither true nor false: they are meaningless. Even at the other extreme, in the common-sense realm of everyday goings on, the same scepticism is wide. (It was long ago pointed out that scepticism is always, ultimately, scepticism of the word.) Surveyors of the social scene complain that everywhere the word has become substitute for thought. Labels and slogans sway mankind, whether it be to buy a particular cigarette or to embrace an especial ideology. "Everything", we are told, is propaganda.

And more minute observers of objects and events call our attention to the fact that speech gives us but the flimsiest outline of any actual situation or thing. Not only is the word *horse* quite different from the image we summon on hearing that sound or seeing those letters—and that mental image, again, quite other than the creature itself—but the lengthiest description would leave most of the creature and our relationships with it perforce untold: the feel of the stroking along the sleek back; the nuzzling of the muzzle in the hand; the trembling of the nostrils, so different when it sniffs from when it whinnies; the smell of the cleanly stall: these are beyond the capture of words. Korzybski declares that after every sentence stretches a long *etc.* Life is "unspeakable". To find reality we must burst the shell of words.

In every field the fragments of shell are flying.

But as we examine the new chicks that peck their way around, we come upon the eternal paradox of life, recaught in language. The destruction manages somehow to recreate. The analysis follows its pattern to a new synthesis. The word must be decried, disrupted, denied—because the word is essential.

The scientist that, impatient at its insufficiency, would do away with the word must admit that the non-linguistic symbols of the sciences must finally be reducible, and be reduced, to words. In truth, says Carnap, the logic of science—its assurance of validity—is naught other than the syntax of its language. From such recognitions rise the more rational examinations of the problems of language, of words and of meaning—widespread today as never before. But the claims of the word-handlers extend much farther. The propagandist, who has a way with the word, sweeps along. And propaganda analysis, the first effort to break down word patterns, to break through word disguises, to discern the play of intention, finds complementary force as suggested by "the best selling book of nonfiction of our era": *How To Win Friends and Influence People*. And as the general semantics of Korzybski (in *Science and Sanity*, and the journal *ETC*) maintains that human ailments, from schizophrenzy to international war, result from the misunderstanding and the misuse of words, he and his disciples have erected a system of cure in every field, on the basis of the proper, "non-Aristotelian" use of language. He is what James Joyce would call a *panaseer*.

The experiments of James Joyce in the creation of new verbal syntheses are but the extreme of a pervasive trend. It might of course, be averred that e e cummings, in such poems as:—

! blac
k
agains
t
(whi)
te sky
? t
rees whic
h fr
om droppe
d
,
le
af
a:;go
e
s wh
IrlI
n
.g

is breaking down words; but it would be more in accord with aesthetic courtesy, as well as contemporary concern, to suggest that he is seeking to elevate syllables, even letters, into units of poetic significance. He finds in a letter the sibilation of a line; he sweeps a syllable like a significance across the page. We might picture e e cummings at home upon an asterisk, as the Spanish poet Pedro Salinas sings his joy at dwelling within the pronouns!

We may, in truth, trace in such writings the binding efforts of the age. As the sculptor and the painter seek to suggest the movement of their forms, so the writer tries to enable his reader to grasp at one time things that occur, or are observed, together.

The problem of description has always perplexed the artist whose medium is language. While the eye with one glance can take in many details, words in utterance come to the ear singly, in succession; even on the page an idea is glimpsed but a bit at a time.

Scarcely any authors have tried to overcome this drag in the written presentation of things seen simultaneously. The attempt to do so has complicated poems of e e cummings, who by eccentric use of capitals and spacing, and by other devices —as in the following lines—has striven to make idea and action coetaneous:

```
                                                          l oo k —
                pigeons fly ingand
   whee(   : are ,   SpRIN, k, LiNg    an   in - stant
           with sunLight
   then) l —
   ing all go BlacK wh - eel - ing
```

The unusual spacing and capitalization set the emphasis, and even try to suggest the fact, as of sprinkling. The words in parenthesis describe what happens while the pigeons are wheeling, and for that reason the word *wheeling* is divided to include them.—Such poetry, obviously, is addressed not to the ear but to the considerate mind.

The more usual practice is Joycean. James Joyce telescopes, rearranges, combines, like a German philologist riding a nightmare; but his technique is equally and more widely at work in the columnist and through the folkways. The gossip-monger that speaks of a couple seeking a divorce in Reno, Nevada, as *Renovating* their household, is making a palpable double play. But the folk itself assists when, the *A* type of limp (non-rigid dirigible) balloon having failed, the successful *B* type limp is christened the *Blimp*. Who gave currency to the *Wacs* and the *Waves*? Who whisper at the *Gestapo,* shudder at the *Gaypayoo* (*G P U*) ? There is a synthetic spirit in the times that combines, builds letters or syllables of successive words into new names. Advertising made conscious use of it early, as in *Nabisco* (*Na*tional *Bi*scuit *Co*mpany), *Socony* (*S*tandard *O*il *C*ompany *o*f *N*ew *Y*ork), and other devices to catch the public memory and fancy. It ranges from medicine (*sulfanilamide*: *sulf*uric, *anil*inc, *am*monia, *-ide*) to implements of warfare (*radar*: *ra*dio *d*irecting *a*nd *r*ange-finding). It is an immediately recognizable feature of our day.

The separate individuation of the word no longer contents, no longer suffices, our age. The quest of a greater unity, which in international affairs produced the War and may dictate the peace, which has given fresh impetus to the search for a universal tongue—Basic English; Interglossa—in literature as upon the lips of farmer and clerk has stirred a new animation within the very word. Hegel declared that language is the actuality of culture; at least, it is a weather-vane of the spirit of man.

2. *The single mind emerges—*

CRITICISM is a temporal task; with our age it too has swung into the collective emphasis. Whether questioning its own function or considering literary works, the mass-man sits on the scales. As practiced and proclaimed by such writers as V. F. Calverton and Michael Gold, criticism becomes a sociological survey of literature, which at times seems to evaluate a work wholly in terms of the author's political principles. Morris U. Schappes, in Calverton's *The Modern Monthly,* quotes T. S. Eliot to justify such an attack upon T. S. Eliot:

> It is the present political-economic situation that makes the *kind* of criticism I have written necessary. Without confusing valid categories, criticism should now concern itself, not exclusively but with emphasis, with laying bare the hidden class-alliances, class confusions, and class-hypocrisies of our men of letters. To bewail the need is weakness; to control and use it, intelligence. Only in a unified, classless order will internal criticism of detail be significant; at present, one can write such criticism only by winking the eye when pressed by more urgent business. Criticism must now be hostile, fundamental. Anything else is out of tune with the age; hence, in the larger sense, without relevance, almost without meaning. "If it be objected that this is a prejudice of the case, I can only reply that one must criticize from some point of view and that it is better to know what one's point of view is." (*Selected Essays,* p. 96) First things must come first.

In an editorial of *The Saturday Review of Literature,* the cause of this social attitude is sought:

> It is a noteworthy fact that as interest in economic and international problems has grown, preoccupation

with problems of personality has diminished . . . Part of this flagging of interest is due no doubt to the fact that the sensational value of Freudianism and psychoanalysis has been exhausted, and that fashion no longer demands babbling of "complexes" and "inhibitions". But more than this is the fact that the world has become so chaotic, the moment so confusing, that the problems of the individual, at least so far as they are spiritual and not practical, have become less dramatic and less charged with importance for himself than the composite fate of society.

This shift of emphasis is not merely recorded, but praised, in another issue of the same periodical:

It is an excellent thing that so many of the newer novels are getting away from the extreme thinness of material so common a few years ago,—when often a single character, and that not a profound one, was considered enough to make a book,—and are offering the reader a wider range of view. But though this is a worthier undertaking, it is by the same token a much more difficult one, and the difficulty sometimes becomes all too plain in the author's attempt to fit his diversified matter into a unified pattern.

A leading article in *The New York Times Book Review* goes even further, regretting that Sholom Asch, in *Three Cities,* has restricted himself to the narrower, to "infinitely the lesser", the individual point of view.

Asch's passionate idealism gives to his book a great quality. It gives it nobility. Conquered by its sincerity, its integrity, its disinterestedness, no thoughtful reader will find in Asch a political bias, a mere taking of sides, or a protest against systems in themselves; his protest is too obviously against all that is not humane in all humanity. Yet in this book Asch is a historian no less than a novelist and philosopher; and it is something of a pity that he has used his history, after recreating it so superbly, for infinitely the lesser of two ends. For he has not used it to show its effect upon great masses of men; he has not used it, in other words, to create a great social novel. He has used it to show its effect upon an individual, a Zachary Mirkin, in a sense a Sholom Asch. For all its scope, *Three Cities* is strongly, overwhelmingly, individualistic in tone. . . . The point involved has nothing to do with the merits of Soviet Russia; the point is that Mirkin's kind of individualism, set up against those Moscow days, has no point. For Mirkin himself, a weak-willed idealist, is neither a fit hero nor a fit symbol for a book so teeming in social history, in human action both good and bad, in world life, as this one. His disillusionment is implicit in his very idealism, since he cannot ever come into contact with life without suffering and dismay. Though the two are ceaselessly identified, Mirkin's humanitarianism and Asch's are very different things; the first is founded on weakness and hypersensitiveness; the second, on a noble and passionate sense of right. Because that sense of right is so passionate it sweeps over and beyond the weakling Mirkin, breathes life into the novel, and saves the day. . . . Fortunately, though Asch's own conception of his book is delimited by its individualistic slant and further delimited by the inadequacy of Mirkin as an individualist—fortunately, so large and so densely packed and illuminating is its canvas, it presents an almost unsurpassed picture of three centers of life. So much is there that we may deduce from it more than the author's philosophy allows. A novel like this enlarges one's knowledge, takes one a little farther along the road of human experience.

It happens that the *Times* reviewer, in his regret, has failed to see how the book really supports him, sustains the universal quest that marks his desire, as it marks our time. "The point is that Mirkin's kind of individualism, set up against those Moscow days, has no point." To Mirkin a Communist protests:

> "But, Comrade, what is a man? A sausage-skin that can be stuffed with anything. The essential point is, whom does the man serve? The man himself is nothing—yesterday he was one thing, today he's another. The main question is simply, Whom does he serve?"
>
> "No, a man isn't just a sausage-skin. A man represents an absolute value in himself. He is sacred, he is an end to himself!" cried Mirkin.
>
> "What! Are you an anarchist?"

And in the three cities where Mirkin's days center, we discover that his individualism is an inadequate weapon in the collective world of today. Those around him that have retained the olden ways still preserve a unity, their salvation, in submission to the divine will; those that, becoming articulate, have lost the speech of their fathers, still seek a union with a will higher than the personal. In the wide vista of *Three Cities*, through the Russian Revolution, it is the invalidity of the personal view, the need of some broader vision, that rises through the study of Sholom Asch.

So great has been the surge of fictional sociological studies, in truth, that some reviewers have drawn back. It is just a few years later that another first page article in *The New York Times Book Review* declares: "There is enough social significance in our fiction, not to say in real life, to entitle us to a vacation now and then." And in the same issue, an advertisement recommends a book as just the volume for you "when you feel that, for the moment at least, you don't want another novel of social significance." Both comments show, by their reservations, that there is still potency in the cry of the Union maids to their lovers in the *Labor Stage* revue *Pins and Needles*:

> *Sing me a song of social significance,*
> *All other themes are taboo!*

Brief indications will suffice to show that, in many arts and many lands, it is the social that has significance: unity not the unit is the goal. Thomas Craven approves of the statement, in *Art and the Artists* by Otto Rank, that "a new art must spring from a social basis and a collective ideology, and not from the deposits of the cultural forms of the past."

The theatre, in all its aspects, makes manifest the change. Writing for the American "revolutionary" dramatist of *Scenery, the Visual Machine,* Mordecai Gorelik, himself a better designer than his words may indicate, declares in *New Theatre*:

> I take it for granted that the revolutionary designer consciously identifies himself, as a worker, with the revolutionary vanguard of the working class. This implies that the designer must have a Marxist viewpoint, and one which is neither vague nor entirely theoretical; it must be the result of a close study of the revolutionary theory, tested in practical action within revolutionary organizations.

Thus is the background of a play socially set. From Revolutionary Russia likewise comes the style of design called essentialism, used in the New York production of Sidney Howard's *Yellow Jack*. The earlier constructivism, which also flourished especially in Soviet Russia, partly because it was inexpensive, employed bare walls, arches, stairways, platforms at various levels, to suggest the essence of space. This type of setting met the general requirements of a localized scene, while it permitted swift changing, or—better still, in the age's impulse—allowed all the various points of action to be seen on the stage at once. On the house beneath the tree in O'Neill's *Desire Under the Elms,* the front wall is movable, permitting four rooms to be hidden or visible, alternately or together, as the action impels. Increasingly on the experimental stage, as in the 1937 productions of the Mercury Theatre: *Julius Caesar, The Shoemakers' Holiday,* settings lost their local precision, became simple, general. In *The Cradle Will Rock,* the actors sat on plain chairs, in a line on the stage, until they stepped forward as their parts summoned them. The Broadway success and Pulitzer Prize play *Our Town* was presented without scenery.

Some of these plays have been influenced by a mode known as the Epic theatre, developed about 1920 by two graduates of da-da, Bertholt Brecht and Erwin Piscator. Drawing its name from Aristotle's statement that epic has a wider range than tragedy, this school expands in all directions. Scenically, it introduces various levels of action, stairs, treadmills, motion pictures, caricatures, loud speakers, parades down the aisle; actors amid the audience, spectators on the stage. In theme, it strives to draw the world into every drama, to present a scientific image of life. Although the sympathies of its directors have been proletarian, the Epic theatre is advanced not as propaganda but as a "tribunal" to investigate facts, so that all may learn. Thus, Piscator's production of Gorky's *Lower Depths* had as its object to explain the concept *rabble;* all necessary changes to produce that end were effected. Into his New York production of *King Lear,* Piscator introduced words of today's refugees showing their plight; he ended with a speech from *Troilus and Cressida* that pointed a more hopeful conclusion. The director in this wise becomes almost a new playwright; indeed, Piscator has dramatized that novel of wide canvas, Tolstoi's *War and Peace.* He tells us that this wider utilization of the theatre dawned in him while "digging in" at Ypres when "English and German corpses lay stinking" after the first release of poison gas: he determined that his theatre would not retreat from life. In America, the *March of Time* motion picture and the *Living Newspaper* are further endeavors to bring life alive onto the stage, to emphasize not the individuals of the dramatic action but the social background, the universal forces, that determine man's ways.

The same tendency toward a wider embracing is manifest in the persons of the theatre. In an article entitled *The Theatre: A State Concern,* the French monthly *La Revue Mondiale,* protesting that "the theatrical state has become a mushroom patch of syndicates", and advocating a central control, gives "an incomplete and haphazard list" of pre-Hitler organizations in France, comprising twenty-eight societies, unions, and associations wherein individuals interested in the theatre have combined for cooperative effort. Whether of professional theatre folk or of audience groups, the growth in Great Britain and the United States has been greater still. Here, the stage-hands have one of the strongest of all unions; but, from press agents and box-office treasurers through actors and playwrights and producers to critics and audiences of theatre, motion pictures, and radio, every aspect of the public arts is represented by an organized group.

The play's the thing in which to catch the conscience of the hour. Look just at Maxwell Anderson's *Valley Forge.* Earlier histories show Washington, by the force of his personality and iron will, holding together his starved and frozen rag-wrapped men. The play pictures a discouraged general, suing for peace, reproached by the rank and file (the proletariat!) of his ragged forces, and through their determination (mass-pressure!) brought to a new resolve. The past presents but a mirror to sequent ages!

No different is the movement of other literary forms. Writing of *The Twentieth Century Novel,* though a bit early in its growth, Joseph Warren Beach traces the shift from individual morality and psychology to general situation. The novel today, he thinks, is less often entertainment than social document. "The entire book production of recent years," André Berge asserts, "though quite individual, even individualistic, is the manifestation of a single, collective soul." In a literal sense, also, this has measure of truth. At no time have there been more popularizing works, books that collect everything for everybody: *The A B C of Atoms; The Outline of History; The Outline of Knowledge*. And never before have there been so many co-operative books, from literary anthologies to elaborate surveys of social periods, wherein experts and specialists pool their erudition and understanding, to work out the jig-saw puzzle of the time, writing of all things knowable, and more.

Edith Wharton, in an attack upon the Faulkner-Caldwell brood, declares that

> The experiments of the new novelists, and the comments of their docile interpreters, have proved, in spite of both, that any lasting creative work must be based upon some sort of constructive system; the creator must have a conviction to guide him. The conviction of the new group is that there should be none; but this, too, is a system.

Despite Miss Wharton, the da-da-ists are perhaps the only artists that have made a system of denial; those she has in mind rather seek to tear down the present system that they may erect their own. The critics along this path look at our history through the curved mirrors of their desire. Donald Davidson, for example, attacks the collective values of industrial America, but by insisting on its sectional unity; in *We Take Our Stand* the group that once issued the magazine *Fugitive* flees from an all-embracing materialism to an agrarian hope. On the same journey, Henry S. Canby declares that, after the destructive pictures of our industrial society, as in Sinclair Lewis and many more, there is an increasingly calm dismissal of the material world for truer values: "The country (or is it the soul?) wins."

Most writers do not thus easily abandon the material world. Less concerned with a soul the existence of which they doubt, they seek to reshape the body of this age. They begin by reinterpreting it to fit their hope. Thus Granville Hicks, in *The Great Tradition*, emphasizes certain strains in Emerson and others, builds his climax by declaring that even Whitman "in later years was not unaware of the wisdom of curbing the individual for the collective good. . . . This is the great tradition of American literature." This is, of course, by no means the dominant note in our country's writings; but it may well seem the "great" one to the man that declares:

> For decades the existence of the frontier gave meaning to the doctrine of self-reliant individualism; but the passing of the years has shown that America is no exception and that, here as elsewhere, the only clue to the tangled web of life in the last century is the Marxian analysis.

John Middleton Murry goes even farther than Hicks, to declare that unless the artist feels himself spiritually secure, in a society that is an organic unity, he cannot truly create. Just how he finds such a society around Shakespeare, around Dante and Goethe who fought their environment most of their lives and were at times in exile, Murry does not reveal. His brand of Communism, moreover, is strangely though widely collective; as he defines it, it owes "as much to Blake and to Jesus, to Shakespeare, and . . . to Keats . . . as to Marx."

The fullest effort to weave into our concept of literature the ideal of a collective impulse is probably that of Henry Hazlitt, in *The Anatomy of Criticism*. Here is advanced the postulate of the social mind. The notion had earlier appeared in the field some call social "science". Literal-minded men accept figures of speech as real. B. M. Anderson, in *Social Value*, and especially C. H. Cooley in *Social Organization: a study of the Larger Mind*, advance the claim that all our minds are one organic whole. There is a group mind, a national mind, a cultural mind, a world mind. Individual minds—so-called—are like instruments in an orchestra; what matters is the collective music.

No one would think it necessary or reasonable to divide the music into two kinds, that made by the whole, and that of the particular instruments, and no more are there two kinds of mind, the social mind and the individual mind. The view that all mind acts together in a vital whole from which that of the individual is never wholly separate, flows naturally from our growing knowledge of heredity and suggestion, which makes it increasingly clear that every thought we have is linked with the thought of our ancestors and associates, and through them with that of society at large. . . . Whether, like the orchestra, it gives forth harmony may be a matter of dispute, but that its sound, pleasing or otherwise, is the expression of a vital cooperation, cannot well be denied.

The author of this pretty figure of the orchestra seems never to have heard of a solo recital.

Choosing a different analogy, J. D. Unwin in *Hopousia* declares that considering individuals is like observing electrons, in whose realm anarchy seems to reign; whereas the behavior of the organism, of the society, is determined. "In social science the unit is not the individual but the society." A. W. Small adds that the individual is a confusing and discredited hypothesis. A. Rapoport similarly attacks "the illusion that this 'self', the 'ego', the 'I', was capable of independent existence;" and Trigant Burrow, taking it for granted that the "social substance, I" is an evil, says we have a biological urge toward a more inclusive, more *organismic* mode of feeling, which he presents as Phylobiology.

Hazlitt enlarges such pictures. Just as it was long ago recognized that a dog's conscience is in the eye of his master, so it is recognized now, Hazlitt declares, that "a man's conscience is in the eye of society, and has been formed by unconsciously watching that eye." This recognition lies, of course, with those that see eye to eye with Hazlitt. Others may suspect a logical slip in that jump from the literal eye of the master to the figurative eye of society, which we "unconsciously" watch. Is it not this individual mind, plus that one, and that and that, which grow into the fiction of the social mind? It seems an odd reversal, to have the monster creating Frankenstein! Yet precisely such is the looseness of popular thought, which speaks of Frankenstein when it means the monster, and tells the plot of a motion picture naming the stars instead of the characters. Thus Hazlitt is merely conforming to the "social mind". Again, if, as he avers, "the individual critic applies the social standards of his time and thinks he is applying his own", why are there such varied critical opinions? Even when critics agree, they often base the same conclusion on different premises. Either this social mind is confusingly multiplex, or there are many conflicting social minds. In either case, the term has lost its value.

Following his fiction nonetheless, Hazlitt reaches an interesting conclusion. He chides you, intelligent reader of the twentieth century, with the thought that were you living in the thirteenth you would be sharing an unshaken belief in hell. We may allow that, through an age when one orthodoxy holds a race or a civilization, in that regard the fiction of a social mind has cogency as a convenient label— but brings danger, as is evident from Hazlitt's own rushing down the centuries to apply it to so disjointed a period as our own. Does the social mind today make one a Catholic, a Christian Scientist—pick from the thousand creeds—an atheist, or a Nordic Pagan? But Hazlitt, having drawn his convincing illustration from the solid and assured thirteenth century, brushes religion aside:

> Our immediate concern is with social aesthetic and literary values, and my contention, in brief, is this: that these values are *objective* so far as the individual is concerned, just as economic values are; but that they are *subjective* for society as a whole, and beyond this *social subjectivity* it is impossible for us to pierce,

The very possibility of such a statement proves the thesis wrong. For Hazlitt would have had to pierce that subjectivity to recognize the fact; and if it can be seen and studied, it may be overcome. As a matter of fact, however, Hazlitt has but coined a new phrase for a well-known condition. Shaw has declared that men will attain true judgment of values if they can live, say, three hundred years. Even before reading the preface to *Back to Methusaleh*, Chesterton emphasized that the only way to avoid the constant conflict of successive generations is to teach men to stretch their minds and inhabit a larger period of time. Hazlitt's *social subjectivity* of values means merely that many of us are still provincial in time. We regard, if no longer our city's, our age's ideas as ultimates. But the man of culture has broadened not only across the continents but along the years. He does not insist that the hour's guide-post is the eternal pillar of truth. By tracing the oscillant flow of thought through the years (as this volume partially marks) he has learned more sensitively to feel the pulse of other ages in our own. Hazlitt's presentation of the principle of social determinism in aesthetics, while another outcropping of the time's emphasis, not only would convert a figure of speech into a basic reality, but points its own denial.

Philosophers as well as sociologists leap into this communal stew. Out of the boiling waters of the world their isms grow collective. Thus Samuel Johnson's friend would no longer cease to exist if he dropped out of Johnson's mind; today the hypothesis holds that if we all stopped thinking of it, the universe itself would cease to be. A collective idealism of this sort grows from the notion of a collective consciousness. Fortunately, there are so many persons that always one or another must be thinking of the world; otherwise, we should have to assign a vigil-guard, as at the tomb of the Unknown Soldier, to keep the thought of the universe alive! I do not mean, in these glancing words, to dispose of the conception; but merely to note how even the philosopher fits his theories to the times.

Popular imagination does no less. Even the "cosmogonic

intention" revealed by astrology marks the change! For the world, we are told, is emerging from two centuries dominated by Pisces to enter a similar period under the influence of Aquarius, which means a shift of emphasis from the individual soul to the general condition of the masses. It must be consoling to know that the heavens in their courses reflect our human ways!

There is no doubt that the urge of a period exercises both strong and subtle power. Even those that oppose it show strains of its impelling. One of the four books of Robert Bridges' *The Testament of Beauty* is devoted to the celebration of Selfhood. This is, of course, an exaltation of the individual ego. Bridges tells the story of Brasidas, who caught a mouse, but when the creature in its fight for freedom bit him, he recognized its love of liberty and released it. Thus in the poet's very presentation of the urge in each of us toward the individual, unique expression of personality, he pictures a universal tendency, as fundamental in the unreflecting rodent as with the furtherance of reason in man. It is not the unique expression, but its ubiquitous immanence, that throughout he emphasizes.

Among many such instances in fiction, let us look at one from the novel *The Brave and The Blind,* by Michael Blankfort, a picture of the Spanish revolution, defending democracy—which is based on the idea that all men are created free and equal, but different. The one man in the Franco fortress expected to vote for surrender to the Loyalists thinks in these terms: "I have always stood up for the rights of the single human being against the clammy syndicate of the army. The right of an individual to flaunt the bee-hive." Yet when two individuals within that fortress fall in love, and Blankfort tries to express the depth of Dolores' feeling, he dips right into that bee-hive for the honey. All differences drown in a syrup of collective rhetoric. From the paragraph let a sample suffice:

> On the tidal sweep of her boundless blood were carried all the discovered and the undiscovered joys

that had ever been tasted or would ever be. With her
lips, all women kissed, and with her hands, all women
touched the miracle of their beloved.

Thus persuasively the collective emphasis of our age works upon even its rebels!

Those that swim with the tide may equally be swirled in the currents. One of the stoutest swimmers is V. F. Calverton, who spread through many pages of several magazines and books his challenge to all individuals. In *The Liberation of American Literature* he sees the "petty bourgeois individualist" supplanted by the "proletarian collectivist". He too finds early strength in Emerson and Whitman, while he declares of our first Nobel prizeman: "Lewis' failure is not that he has not 'gone' proletarian, but that he has not adopted the social point of view, which is essentially the Marxian point of view."

The artist is by nature a rebel; it is the critic that would have him conform. And of course the politician. Thus the group authority upon which Calverton hazily insists would press the creative energies of nations into a singly directed channel. Modern German literature (says Arthur Eloesser in a book of that name) was, like the others arts, being organized for the purpose of the State. Voicing a plea for the maintenance of spiritual values in the coming socialized commonwealth, Thomas Mann, in *Past Masters,* attacks the protracted opposition of culture and civilization. He urges "an alliance, a compact between the conservative culture-idea and revolutionary social thought, an understanding between Greece and Moscow"; yet he moves toward this union within national bounds:

> Cosmopolitanism must be sought through Germanness. The great German writers have been cosmopolitan by being more German: Goethe, Lichtenberg, Schopenhauer—there is no help for it; these are European prose, in the original German.

In his study of Zola, who declared that "the only hope lies

in the people", Henri Barbusse widens the remark to declare that "the only hope lies in the international proletariat and its organization."

Italy has manifesto'd several literary movements. First Bontempelli led the *Novecentismo* in an international surge toward the "supercitizen". Then he joined with Bardi in the *Quadrante,* which stressed architecture and the cinema, and proclaimed the creation of "the art of the Mussolini era." This Fascist group listed itself as "against aestheticism (decay of the classical spirit), against psychologism (decay of the romantic spirit) . . . antilyrical, antimetric, antistylistic . . . against orientalism . . . overcoming the 'advance guard' spirit." It sought a collective art, to make clear "the expressive center of our lives", the central rhythm of existence. It aimed at the basic unity of man and the recapture of the Mediterranean.

Equally linked with the State are the literary aims of the Soviets. Over the door of the Kharkov world conference on Communist literature, in 1930, hung as motto a message from Stalin: "Proletarian literature should be national in form and socialist in content." This criterion had been earlier set by the R A P P (Union of Proletarian Writers), which declared: "Every proletarian artist must be a dialectic materialist. The method of creative art is the method of dialectic materialism." When, after nine years' exercise, the monopoly of this Union was wiped out by official ukase, in 1932, it was because its work had been thoroughly done. "There are no longer any fellow-travelers, but (apart from isolated outsiders) only a great united front of Soviet writers, willing to participate creatively in the work of the socialist cultural revolution."

The foremost Soviet poet, Vladimir Mayakovski, wrote specific instructions for the composition of a work:

> What, then, are the necessary conditions for getting one's poetic work started?
>
> 1) The existence of a social task that can be accomplished only through poetic work. There must be a social command.

2) An exact knowledge of or at least a feeling for the aspirations of the group you represent, toward this social task.
3) The material, words.
4) Means of production (Pencil, food, etc.)
5) The habit of elaborating words.

For instance, the social task is to write the words for a song to be sung by the Red Guards, who are going to defend Petrograd. The purpose is to defeat Yudenich. The material is words from the common speech of soldiers. The tool is a pencil point. The form, a rhymed chastuchka. The result:

> *I got a jacket and some socks*
> *From a girl friend of mine.*
> *Yudenich is running from Petrograd*
> *As though soaked in turpentine.*

What in Russia many see as a nightmare is, in many other minds throughout the world, still a sweet anticipant dream. The path of progress through education to ultimate control by the ballot puts Utopia too far away. To impatient youth, it seems impotent apathy. You can hardly blame a young man for wanting a world he won't have to wait for his great-great-great-grandson's children to enjoy. He is thus an easy prey to panaceas. The poets, eternal pioneers of the spirit, already view the dawn on far horizons. In the introductory essay *Toward Revolutionary Poetry* in his volume of verse *Comrade: Mister*, Isidore Schneider sets the aim:

> Individualism has become more and more a malady. Growing cancerously upon our economic processes, it has become such a monstrosity that society disintegrates beneath it . . . As a consequence love poetry has fallen into morbid eroticism, and the regard for nature into the contemplation of a wasteland. The world cries for a new social cohesion, and poets for a new theme.

Here again the machine age turns the logical trick of having the cart pull the horse (automobile logic!). Our economic processes have grown out of individualism. *The Deserted Village* is not a poem of our period; equally, the eroticism Schneider bewails ran amuck in every time.

In the social flow of our age, however—Schneider is to this extent in line, if not correct—individualism is more and more deemed a malady. It is set at the basis of all tragedy by Maud Bodkin, who thrusts the needle of Jung's psychanalytic eye into art:

> The form of tragedy—the character of its essential theme—reflects the conflict within the nature of any self-conscious individual between the assertion of his separate individuality and his craving for oneness with the group—family or community—of which he is a part. The sense of guilt which haunts the child whose emerging self-will drives him into collision with his parents echoes that guilt which shadowed the early individuals who broke the bonds of tribal feeling and custom; and the personal and racial memories combine in our participation in the tragic hero's arrogance and fall.

How much that increases one's understanding of Romeo, Hamlet, Macbeth!

Feeling "guilt" too strong a word, Adler found the term inferiority. Josiah Royce, linking the same notion with the Christian forms, speaks of this ego-sense as the original sin. Such champions of the herd have apparently not reflected that it is this very sin—eating the fruit of the tree of knowledge—this individual ego, that differentiates from the ant and the bee the creature we know as man.

Our herded age, nonetheless, follows the bellwether. To escape from this guilt, declares Archibald MacLeish, the poet must celebrate "that which has happened always to all men, not the particular incidents of particular lives." William Rose

Benèt comments: "The point that Mr. MacLeish is making is that the industrialism of our society has ended individualism, whether we know it or not." Benèt demurs, indicating individualistic work even in MacLeish's collection, but Eda Lou Walton agrees with MacLeish. She feels definitely that the most significant work is produced by the poets that "in this new anthology treat of mankind rather than of themselves, or, if of themselves, only as a mirror of mankind. Hart Crane, the leader of such an attitude, is here, MacKnight Black and Lynn Riggs—all impersonal in their approach to their material." Of this "leader", she elsewhere states:

> Hart Crane, seeking to integrate a disorganized world of ideas and actions, has pointed to new emotional values in a world of anonymous creation, a world in which the creative instincts of men may have outlet in the building of an industrial nation, a world in which not the single engineer or a single poet, but many unknown men may construct bridges and poetic hymns.

Miss Walton feels that the poet must join to his intellectual powers a passionate faith, a faith in some centripetal unity; she sees the present hope for poetry in the Russian Communists, or in the young English that "have accepted, intellectually, at least, a new creed, that of Communism." Meanwhile, in his introduction to *New Country,* the anthology of these English poets, Michael Roberts protests that "the real statesmen and artists are in danger of having only the disconnected individuality of lost sheep;" he sounds the call for a sense of collective purpose. Again the bell to the herd is heeded. Stephen Spender —of many—may illustrate the response:

> *Not palaces, and earl's crown*
> *Where the mind dwells, intrigues, rests;*
> *The architectural gold-leaved flower*
> *From people ordered like a single mind,*
> *I build.*

The representative art of today expresses the wide impulse in the direction of a people ordered like a single mind. Carl G. Jung declares ("Psychology and Poetry", *Transition,* vol. 19-20) that the poet "is the collective man, the carrier and former of the unconsciously active soul of mankind."

3. — and subdivides.

AGAIN in our generation eyes look two ways. The collective mind may be seen as binding, or as bound. In politics, as we have observed, these views end in Fascism and Communism. But they equally divide the workers in every field, including that of our present concern, **the arts**.

The heir of the romantic, transferring his devotion from the hero to the race, looks upon mankind as the unique species for whom, and through whose intelligence and moral force, the universe will be led to its highest manifestation. The scion of the realist, in similarly widened view, still questions the notion of progress, finds in all men a core of sameness that is one with the essence of the animal, the physical, world, and seeks the universals, of substance, energy, and law, that catch reality in a single whirling span.

Each of these visions widens through many works.

4. Romanticism turns social.

MANY still see in the world today the Emersonian opposition of law for man and law for thing. To most of these, the present chaos is the consequence of a spiritual collapse. Mankind has lost the power to believe. Except to believe in power. Man has lost faith, has swept overboard the notion that "there is an immortal essence presiding like a king over his appetites." Caliban has come down with a club upon Ariel. So believe those that have kept faith in their world-view.

This view beholds, in life, three levels of experience; in man, three levels of conduct: the animal, the human, the divine. Each of these has its proper sphere and value. Today, however, even the heavens are filled with the engines of violence. The munitions factory is more regarded than the church. Mankind lacks humanity; the animal rears with bloody paws over the divine.

Somewhat as the will functions—like a walking-beam—moving and maintaining the rhythmic interplay of the intellect and the emotions, manifest only through their ordering, so must the *human* work, and reveal itself, in the balance seldom and but precariously maintained between the animal and the divine.

One is led, along the lines of this vision, to use religious terms, although some maintain that God is not essential to the attitude. Many scientists, however (as we have seen) call upon His aid; and more among the artists. Ludwig Lewisohn vehemently dismisses any evasion. T. S. Eliot again cries extremes:

> There is no avoiding that dilemma: you must be either a naturalist or a supernaturalist. If you remove from the word "human" all that the belief in the supernatural has given to man, you can view him finally as no more than an extremely clever, adaptable, and mischievous little animal.

At this juncture, shall man, monkeylike, climb the principle of polarity, and perch somewhere between the angel and the beast?

What makes, if not religion, some set code essential to this point of view, is its postulate of a controlling will. If anything other than purely personal inclination is to choose among man's desires and ideals, it must be something larger than and outside of the individual will—which does not create but functions in accord with the wider law. Conceivably, in a wholly known universe, such an ethics might be drawn from a social application of economics, psychology, and biology. But through the eternity until man's intellect has plumbed nature's final dark, the only sure standards are such as men hold divinely given, received in faith, the cherished possession of the common conscience of mankind. Science may lead through nature, to truth; it is *con*science that points to good, which is God.

To such a conclusion a rigorous logic drives those that take this pathway. Not all writers are ready, however, to take spur of reason backward (they deem it) to deity. Most, in truth, lack the urge or the power to carry through the intellectual analysis. They content themselves, like most other busy folk, with the assumption of a standard of values, a norm of human conduct, without permitting the question of its origin to obtrude. "Every decent man" knows what, in such and such circumstances, ought to be done, and has the will to do it. Such an assumption, of course, links a writer closely with his readers.

The concept of a controlling will, of a *frein vital* or inner check, has been mocked by many opponents as purely negative. Such persons are prone also to speak scornfully of a book that promises heaven to such as refrain from certain acts or attitudes on earth. The word "prohibition" is in ill repute. We stiffen our chins when some one tells us "Thou shalt not!"; many reject this, even as a self-command. All these are purely emotive response to an emphasis. *Negative* is a term of basic significance only in mathematical relationships. In electricity it is an arbitrary term; in dispute, its use is shocking. Is a truth positive and a lie negative? We are told that the hardest word in the language to pronounce has but two letters: N-O. The act of refraining often requires more "positive" power than the acquiescent deed. The next time you are charged with having a "negative attitude", change your "I will not do it" to the strong affirmative: "I will resist such imposition with all the power of my body and soul!"

What to resist is not found by following the advertisers' slogan: Obey that impulse! Conscience, then control, trace mankind's path. The necessity for an "artificial" betterment is emphasized by Baudelaire in his earlier quoted essay *On Cosmetics;* it is applied to the present concern by Gorham B. Munson:

> The point is that *naturally* we are not self-controlled. Only by effort and training do we acquire, first, self-knowledge, and second, self-mastery based on self-knowledge. In this way there *is* a discontinuity between Man and Nature. Nature takes care of eagles, but she leaves man to discover his own essence and to live in accordance with it.

Munson has slipped along his polarity; here is a question of degree. Many animals are born blind; many are not naturally self-controlled. Its parents teach the eagle; nor is it entirely our parents' fault that we learn too little from them. But the point is sharper than some of the minds that press it. The infant is taught the distinction between good and evil; the adult, in any situation, at once knows. He may not follow the right; he may cast about for evasion or excuse; but in almost any situation, at once he knows.

Based upon this common sense of what is right, is the doctrine of each individual's responsibility for his own conduct. No mute Milton, this view declares, remains inglorious; if he be a Milton, he may be blind but he cannot be mute, or long unheard. No "victims of society" may toss the burden of their sins upon an oppressive world. The humanitarian had shifted the blame for conduct and fortune from men to social and natural forces and laws. The humanist proclaims the free choice of the individual, rooted in the common knowledge of the greater good. Many today, it is true, have abandoned affirmation of such freedom. But "Why not", asks Irving Babbit quoting Walter Lippmann:

> Why not affirm it first of all as a psychological fact, one of the immediate data of consciousness, a perception so primordial that, compared with it, the deterministic denials of man's moral freedom are only a metaphysical dream?

Humanity is, by all that look through such eyes, seen as apart from and higher than nature, endowed with free will but subject to rule of common conscience, properly exercising its will in accordance with universal standards for the highest development of all mankind.

It will have to come to the minds of those that have kept in touch with literary controversy, that the attitude here presented provided a fireworks display of charge and counter-charges, through the otherwise drab years of 1930 and 1931. But neither can the many defenders of humanism arrogate to themselves the sole application of their term, nor can the derisive more deny it when it properly falls upon themselves. Humanism in its essence holds the faith of the majority of our time. Before noting its manifestations in literature, however, let us observe the characteristics of its complementary point of view. As humanism is romanticism turned social, what is the offspring of realism in a collective age?

5. Realism rips the skin.

MODERN science, exponents of which are this morning hurriedly building rafts of the spirit, until last night floated complacently on the shifting waves of material-force. "The method we term scientific", declared John Dewey, "forms for the modern man the sole dependable means of disclosing the realities of existence. It is the sole authentic mode of revelation." Bergen Evans declares that doubt is the basis of thought; that man has a moral obligation to be sceptical; that man, in being asked to believe without evidence, is being asked to abdicate his integrity. "Any man who for one moment abandons or suspends the questioning spirit has for that moment betrayed humanity." Freud, discussing religion in *The Future of an Illusion* and more generally with the group that contributes an *Outline of Psycho-Analysis* to *The Modern Library,* affirms that science is the only source of truth. A strict determinism is the basis of this creed. These men make short shift of conscience. When a philosopher, a popularizer, and a pioneer precede him where he wishes to go, why should the artist withhold?

Frederick Pierce, in *Understanding Our Children,* takes the attitude back to the womb. He warns the parents of today:

> There is another tradition which has probably done more than any other one thing to retard and hamper the development of really sound methods in the parental education of children during the first few years of life. I mean the tradition that human beings are born with a conscience. The most thorough research has failed to show anything whatever which can properly be called conscience, or a moral sense, in the infant child. Thousands of years of ethical and herd co-operative training in the heredity have certainly

conditioned the human mind so that it very quickly acquires a moral sense if it is properly taught; but we have no evidence whatever of an inherent sense of good and bad in the infant mind.

Seeking, as they do, herd cooperation, such men strive to penetrate the personality, the unique garment of individuality, to reach the race-stuff, to discern the primal laws that determine our every action. D. H. Lawrence has made the attitude most clear:

> I don't care so much what the woman *feels*, in the ordinary usage of the word. That presumes an *ego* to feel with. I care only about what the woman *is*—inhumanly, physiologically, materially—according to the use of the word . . . You musn't look in my novel for the old stable ego of the character. There is another ego, according to whose action the individual is unrecognizable, and passes through, as it were, allotropic states which it needs a deeper sense than any we've been used to exercise, to discover are states of the same single radically-unchanged element. (Like as diamond and coal are the same pure single element of carbon. The ordinary novel would trace the history of the diamond—but I say "Diamond, what! This is carbon!" And my diamond might be coal or soot, and my theme is carbon.)

Commenting on these words, Aldous Huxley declares that "most of us are more interested in diamonds and coal than in undifferentiated carbon, however vividly described." These words give any writer pause; for they show how easy it is for a reader, in this case an editor and supposed interpreter, wearing blinders of his own convictions, to misunderstand. Lawrence means that beneath the individual differences described—"my diamond might be coal or soot"—we should discern the basic unity. Huxley's point, nonetheless, is well taken. A mere realism would set even a king in the animal world; the romantic goose-girl won her monarch by assigning him to the kingdom of heaven. So always will humanism, exalting mankind, be by most men preferred to a materialistic conception that chains them in nature's iron bonds.

A fresh concern with things of the spirit is welcomed in the English novel by Hugh Walpole, who declares that the books of Charles Morgan, reawakening to this mood, insist that "man does not live by bread alone, a doctrine that has been absent from the more intellectual novel for nearly twenty years." But Walpole is unduly impressed with the renascence, for realism had no such fell grip. Not only are its implications too unwelcome, but too perplexing grow its consequences in art. For if, as an art teacher once observed: "Your personality, miss, interests only your mamma!"—if the artist in a collective age seeks beyond the individual to the essence, beyond the human to the universal, the results are likely to be, at the least, puzzling, are likely to seem, at the best, bizarre. Mr. Zero, in Elmer Rice's *The Adding Machine,* summoned by his Boss on the twenty-fifth anniversary of his employment, expects an increase in wages, and—is fired! What is the essence of one's reaction to such a shock? Dizziness; a sudden consciousness that the earth is rapidly spinning: and that part of the stage on which Mr. Zero is standing at once begins rapidly to revolve. Brancusi, in his famous statue the *Golden Bird*, seeks to capture "the nucleus of flight", the essence of upward impulse, without excrescence of crest or claw; the result is an uptilted dirigibloid of bronze, for which the United States customs officials tried to collect duty as metal in bulk.

Ultraism—the quest, beyond the individual and the external, of the essence: I select the least firmly attached of the several available *isms* of our day—ultraism seeks the collective *all* of an equated universe. Rejecting man as a self-determining entity, it not only dismisses the appeal of personality, but invalidates all codes of value. The humanitarian who is a determinist must find a mechanical substitute for self-control, must discover in social forces checks upon individual greeds. Hence the curious theories of the blind leading the blind: through the clash of individual selfishnesses comes universal good. Those less concerned or less sentimental, but still unable to face a valueless world, will lapse into what Lewisohn calls "the gray and almost pathological despair of Joseph Wood Krutch", will halt, with Cabell, in the unbuilded home of the half-ways, or will, after Faulkner and Hemingway or Mencken and Nathan —searing or wise-cracking—"go hard-boiled." Thorny is the unbeaten path, for him that without guide of faith would walk ahead.

The humanist, beneath the pressure of science and the emphasis of the age, has had to admit the weighty influence of natural forces, but always as obstacles or temptations, never determinants. The ultraist tells us that the personality of the artist disappears as his work takes form, that the poet is no more than a catalytic agent in the production of the poem, that the task of the creative worker is the artistic rendering of otherness, for "this something not ourselves is yet a something lodged within us; this quintessence of otherness is yet the quintessence of our proper being." Ultraism seeks to isolate the essence that is at once fundamentally each of us and us all.

6. Art looks beyond.

AMONG the English-speaking peoples, ultraism has taken no strong hold. Its manifestations are fullest in the work of those that have been long resident in France. For—in addition to the natural hostility toward an attitude that equates mollusc and man—the English have never been so wholly won to the sweet clarity of reason as their French neighbors, who will venture with the intellect's searchlights into incomprehensible realms, but in these farthest reaches will accept no other guide. Through the mouth of a Frenchman, Humbert Wolfe expresses the contrast:

> You said a little earlier, almost eloquently: "At its highest moment verse trembles on the edge of thought, and we peer, awe-stricken, over the tall battlements of life." Well, we French take the view that beyond thought is chaos, and we do not wish to peer over the battlements of life, because there would be nothing to see. We will carry thought to the ends of the earth, but where thought ends there the earth ends. Perhaps this difference is, indeed, fundamental. We have heard much over here of your poetry of the Celtic twilight. I have read in the essays of your W. B. Yeats these phrases: "I see, indeed, in the arts of every country these faint outlines and faint energies ... which I call the autumn of the body." We French would call it the winter of the mind.

Both seasons may yield strange fruit.

The first wide sweep of ultraism over the literary field, finding fullest outlet in the drama, was the fashion called expressionism. "A copy of the universe", says Rebecca West, "is not what is required of art: one of the damned thing is ample."

TWAIN TURMOIL OF TODAY

The requisite is indicated by Kasimir Edschmid: "The world is here, it would be absurd to reproduce it. The chief task of art is to penetrate the world before our eyes, to seek out its intrinsic essence, and to create it anew." Oskar Pfister likewise declares: "The expressionist wants to reproduce the intrinsic meaning of things, their soul-substance." Galsworthy, intending to mock, completed the definition when he characterized these artists as "expressing the inside of a phenomenon without depicting its outside." Some of the insides are strangely remote from aught in the usually visible world; but if physics tells us the chair we are now comfortably sitting upon is really no more than myriad swirls of tiny forces, of what fantastic shapes may the mental world well be composed! There is more recognizable dressing of a man in his essentials when (in *Beggars On Horseback*) the business-man with his golf bag has a telephone attached, and a ticker service, while the gossipy matron walks about with a rocking-chair fixed upon her buttocks.

Although the French caught up, played with, sought rational sanction for such ideas, their source and serious promulgation was in more mystic Germany. The manifesto of expressionism, which bade the artist seek within himself to discover the universe, was issued in 1911 by Otto zur Linde. Discarding the conscious quest came the originators of da-da, Tristan Tzara and Francis Picabia, in 1916. Their platform consisted of one knot-holed plank: Seek not, and ye shall find. Save that every young French writer and painter, and many artists from abroad, now well known, took bath of da-da, the school might better be left unconsidered. Its practitioners uttered the warning: "Understand da-da, and you are not a da-da-ist!" While one might be content to remain outside the ranks, even there one finds no assured comprehension. In truth, the name of the movement places it at the inchoate start of intellectual activity, *ma-ma* being the first emotional cry of the awakening infant, *da-da* (so a male might say!) marking its first approach to reason. All after the invention of the name may be considered **anticlimax.**

TRENDS IN LITERATURE

Even in the aberrations of these writers, the binding urge of the times may be discerned. These are the opening lines of Picabia's *Ninie*:

> *Perfumes, flowers, love, dancing, music,*
> *Sleeping beneath the fair star,*
> *The nude Aphrodite,*
> *A child that's beginning to walk,*
> *The Spartan*
> *Biting his lower lip;*
> *The cithern's sound:*
> *I am the man who's inventing the new cement.*

Allowing full play to inspiration, da-da leveled all values, and by association linked all things. The French, however, could not be long content with this unjustified relinquishing of reason. The French intellect, reasserting itself, soon gave logical basis for its own abandonment. The surrealists championed the cause that the da-da-ists had merely espoused. Their work has been called a splitting-up of the naturalistic document; it has been compared to slow-motion in the cinema. In his *Manifesto of Surrealism,* in 1920, André Breton is more enlightening. It is in the unconscious, he declares, that humanity thinks. Consciousness is a protective cloak. Reason is a device for justifying our desires. Doff these cloaks, and you have naked mind, the prime thought-stuff of the race: it is in the unconscious that the individual uncovers his essential, universal self. Surrealism is thus the effort—following Freud, though later some contorted it toward Marx—to allow to gush, or more deliberately to pump up, from the unconscious, the impulsions and the impressions there concealed. Out pours the truth from the bottom of the well of human consciousness. The basic man uncloaked, unchoked, by reason; the essential, spontaneous I. This, any Freudian will tell, is not merely essence but universal essence, basic Man: plumb to the primal urges and needs of all our kind. And the works of surrealism are not works of art; they are the dictation of this unconscious thought, in the complete absence of any control by reason, beyond all concern for morality or aesthetics.

Any artist will tell you that his happiest finds seem to well up—unsummoned, or after a long and vain petition to the Muse—from unfathomed, subliminal depths. Inspiration, however arduously wooed, comes with sudden and as it were spontaneous spurt, then with imperious call. It is the voice of humanity rising through the individual. Thus every great man builds better than he knows. The Renaissance, also, cried that the artist must let the pen go as the spirit moves it.

Yet you have observed that all that glitters is not in the golden realm. Inspiration should carry over to the beholder. The lunatic, as well as the lover and the poet, is of imagination all compact. Though we may quote the madman against the surrealist, however, we cannot gainsay him until we have solved the mystery of genius. But genius still slips from our grasp, even as the creature Breton names as title of his sample of surrealism, supplied with the Manifesto: *Soluble Fish.*

The surrealist will welcome the madman. He is really interested in living, not in art: "There is no surrealist art; there are only proposed means." Katherine S. Dreier withdrew her work from the 1937 show at the New York Museum of Modern Art, because exhibits from insane asylum inmates were included. But the natural surrealist act was their inclusion. It follows the third method by which these men seek to obliterate individuality.

Inspiration may suffice the constant genius; but most genius is inconstant as the moon, the patron deity of lunatics and lovers. André Breton therefore suggests elementary assistance for the beginning surrealist. Start with whatever comes to mind; write rapidly until hesitation shows that reason is trying to intervene; then regain automatic activity by starting anew, your first word commencing with a letter that popped into your mind before you started.

Since that naive approach, surrealist methods have developed considerably. Three sorts of ego-annihilating devices stand out. Some strive in cooperative or vicarious activity, as when four work at the one canvas, or Max Ernst and Hans Arp drop in and sign one another's works at random. In Soviet Russia, Kuprianov, Krylov and Nicolai Sokolov have for twenty years been painting together works that they sign with the collective name Kukryniksi. (A picture of the three appears in the *U.S.S. R. Information Bulletin* of July 30, 1947, on the occasion of their winning a Stalin Prize for their joint work. *See Other Fields,* Section 3.)

Others rely upon outside forces. The "laws of chance" are invoked when Kurt Schwitters builds his figures of bits of string, glass, match-ends and other material picked up on a walk. Marcel Duchamp (best known for his *Nude Descending The Stairs,* the intricate lines of which defy discerning either female figure or stairway) created *Three Standard Stops* by holding three one-meter threads in succession one meter above a blank canvas, letting them drop, and varnishing the curves they lay in after falling. Mechanical motion, such as the whirling of a gyroscope, may also be the basis of a design; even better is the spinning of a top, in that it combines mechanical principles and the working of chance. In the enforced externality of the graphic and the plastic arts, the surrealists—by *collages*: combinations of newspaper cuttings, strips of metal, bits of cloth; and by *frottages*: patterns formed by smudging the grained surface of stone or wood, taking their pattern as police take fingerprints—seek a spontaneous capture of the superreal, the essential, irrational but interrelational harmony of all things. Added to this is often a sardonic humor, "black bile", which laughs irrationally at life's incongruities, and is an extension of the bohemian's desire to shock the philistine.

Their favorite path is the third one: within. There, they abandon reflection for the reflex. Through interior automatic processes they seek the level of dreams, of the submental man. Beyond dreams they journey—with the psychanalyst but for another end—amid hallucinations and hysteria. Through automatic writing and "induced paranoia", not merely the easily attained delirium tremens of the drunkard but all manifestations of mania, they seek below and beyond reason for the universal soul. One of the most characteristic acts of this school was the crashing plunge of Salvador Dali from his bath-tub through the plate glass window of Bonwit Teller's department store onto Fifth Avenue. Unreason and chance, and levity in the onlookers, were admirably blent with the inscrutable and universal urge of gravity!

Yet there may be more than the mere vagary of temperamental spirits, more than the charlatan's quest of the public eye, more even than wide dissatisfaction with the results of conscious human endeavor—what a mess our supposedly thoughtful ones have made of the world!—to lend sanction to the surrealist attempt to slough the skin-game of reason. There are psychologists that suggest that awareness and reason mark only our moments of indecision. When the body wavers among possible acts, the impulses side-tracked in the brain stir round and round as mind. Thought is the sign, perhaps the result, of an impediment to the deed. And by a wide-scale "compensation" for this continual hesitance, we elevate our weakness as our pride. We glory in that reason which differentiates us from the unhesitant animals. One of the greatest triumphs of the laboratory is the recent success in rendering a mouse neurotic. Its aberration is our norm. At least, so frequently does irresolution cloud us into consciousness, into that oscillation before the act which we call reason, that most elaborately we have erected it as our guide. Many proclaim it is our surest star; some beneath it read the human horoscope to declare that the goal of man's endeavor is not action but contemplation.

From this erring anthropocentric self-esteem, the surrealist would rescue us. If his early efforts seem less than reasonable, we should observe, first, that any assault upon an established and gratifying conception is likely to seem violent and, secondly, that he challenges the very reason by which we judge him. It is neither reasonable, nor equitable, nor valid for truth-finding, to allow deciding voice to the very item that is being questioned.

The surrealists, save that they deny and discard reason, might draw further assurance from the inability of logic to acquaint us with any true mode of ultimate knowledge. Where does reason bring us, after all? One can fully know, declares one group of thinkers, only that which is apart from oneself, that which one can observe from without and all around. Otherwise—and often even then—one becomes entangled in the invisible yet ubiquitous snares of the subjective. A biophysicist I know, conducting experiments on vision, rests over an hour in a totally dark room before starting observations, so as to exclude all prior images his retina or brain-path may be holding. Yet it is through his own eyes he must look. And what if he—or the artist—be color-blind? Try telling an author he has no sense of humor! Boldly accepting this inevitability, a larger group declares that subject and object are inextricably interwoven: the more one learns about oneself, the more one knows of the universe. This attitude is of course more in accord with the unifying tendency of our age; yet the truth is that, despite either assumption, man remains with the uncomfortable feeling that he but gropes and stumbles through the dark.

Just as the Christian metaphysics tries to solve the problem of Providence, of the impassable gap between the finite and the infinite, by the concept of a divine human, so it seeks to resolve this dichotomy of knowledge, the separation of the ego from the rest of the world, by the mystery wherethrough one "loses oneself to find oneself." It is not opposition to this, as Benjamin DeCasseres seems to think, but further indication of man's unappeasable need, to object to this "withdrawal from ourselves", and to cry: "The more I grow, the more I *find* myself. I find my I everywhere . . . God is an inflated I." He might as shrewdly have said "I am a deflated God." DeCasseres (with his host) has turned upside down man's universe-measuring yardstick labeled "And God created man in

His own image; in the image of God created He him." We must all seek to decipher a reality outside ourselves—at any rate, an appearance outside ourselves—by means of exploratory apparatus confined within.

Shall we, then, declare that emotions, hindering reason, handicap our search? This is the trail from Plato through T. S. Eliot, who maintains that even the poet does not express emotion, but escapes from it. Or shall we try to utilize emotion in the quest? This path proceeds from Aristotle as far as those that deny the validity of reason: "Gefühl ist alles"—on to those that in the binding impulse of our day declare that consciousness itself is an emotion, that thinking is merely a glaciated form of feeling, that feeling is our surest, indeed our only, way of knowing. While there are, DeCasseres insists, "laws of those secret correspondences that knit all things into a diaphanous whole", we must beware lest we "lose the wisdom of the rutting earth and substitute the perception of secret relations for instinctive participation in the secret relations themselves."—The surrealist believes that we have lost the wisdom of the rutting earth; he seeks the renewal of a direct, instinctive participation in the basic currents of being.

Further support for surrealist ideas comes from other sources. Charles Fort in *The Book of the Damned* declares that the truth-finding method is guess; the world-embracing doctrine, irrelativity. The easily extreme DeCasseres does not stop there:

> Whatever I arrive at by the route of reason always seems to me to be untrue. I secretly doubt anything that can be proved. . . . The profoundest thinkers and the greatest poets all agree that "life is a dream." That is precisely, also, what it seems to everyone after passing a certain age (the revelation varies with experience and temperament). "We are such stuff as dreams are made on" is literally true. Now

the main characteristic of dreams is incoherence, nonsense, incongruity, timelessness, grotesquerie. These are the characteristics of life.

It matters little, to a man that brushes reason aside, that another hundred characteristics of life could easily be summoned, all of which are lacking in the dream. Yet Fort, however eccentric (in the scientific sense) he may think he is—and however eccentric, in the common sense, his followers may show themselves to be—moves as do the surrealists in harmony with the age: we are pressed, he declares, in an automatic design. We on earth are all merely parts of a larger organism in whose life we function (and as void of free will) as a cell in our own body. We are the atoms of God. Again, *a Fortiori,* DeCasseres swallows the camel:

> *"Freedom" is another form of necessity.* For absolute surrender and absolute disobedience are to me now one and the same thing. Thy will be done! or My will be done! it is all alike.

The most literal of the determinists, the most surreal of the surrealists, could say no more. But the surrealists' link with Freud, and Charles Fort, causes me to note the fortuity that made the Latin stem *fort* signify both *chance* and *power*: the underlying *for*ces that drive us are, etymologically at least, akin to *fort*une's whirl. The scientists tell us that power, man's *fort*ress against *fort*uity, is in the electron linked with the "laws of chance".

If we may, for these considerations, grant some scope to surrealist theory, it must be admitted that to the inquiring and most open minds its products are puzzling and weird. Yet again we must withhold judgment. Perhaps we have not yet learned the technique of probing the infra-mental regions of the spirit. This groping by way of sought dreams and induced hysteria may be no more than the first stab at a process Freud has but brought to our attention, not helped us to learn. It may be, on the other hand, that we really are like that inside; the subrational self, freed from logic's binding, may in all of us play such fantastic romps. (Similarly, we may too summarily discredit spiritualism because most of the summoned "spirits" confine their activity to such silly pranks as tipping tables, and ask questions that to our mundane ignorance seem either trivial or absurd.) Although, furthermore, the surrealists claim to be reaching fundamental, universal impulses, they may, actually, be revealing no such general forces but merely the personalities and idiosyncrasies of the particular surrealists. And inasmuch as few well-organized minds would be tempted long to discard reason, it may be assumed that most of the sincere surrealists have no great measure of mentality. Hence, perhaps, the vagaries of their products. For all these reasons, one is forced to conclude, it is unfair to impugn the validity of the idea and the effort of surrealism on the basis of the works thus far set forth. Yet the movement may properly be described as an aberration or extreme of the nature-and-man-merging mass-impetus of our time.

The ultraist view is not always linked with denial of reason. The belief that everything is determined brings in its train the notion that mental stir is equally automatic; but few persons that hail the engine examine the contents of the cars behind. Christianity faces the problem and suggests a solution; but Christianity is not among the impedimenta on the train of materialistic determinism. Thus comfortably in the parlor-car (though all other trippers must show their tickets) reason rolls unchallenged along the tracks of science. And by its methods a more controlled approach may be made to art.

It is along the roadway of the intelligence that Paul Valéry journeys. He is concerned less with meaning than with form, less with emotional than with intellectual evocation, as though the poem were a formula. His forerunner Mallarmé, on the quest of pure beauty, had "mummified" some of his own works; compare *The Whipped Clown* of 1864, beginning:

> For her eyes—to swim in those lakes, whose piers
> Are planted with fair lids the blue morn pierces,
> I, Muse, your clown, have leapt the window
> And fled our hovel where your oil lamp smokes . . .

with the same poem, of 1887:

> Eyes, lakes with my simple rapture to be born anew
> Other than the mountebank who with the stroke conjured up
> As a pen the ignoble soot of the oil lamps,
> I have bored a window through the canvas wall.

Valéry, in later editions of two of his best-known poems, *Palme* and *Cimitière marin,* altered the sequence of the stanzas; and in the second stanza of *Palme* deliberately reversed the meaning by replacing *avec* (with) by *sans* (without). Nor does the modern poet always wait for revision to take such liberties. Valéry uses words in new senses; in strange orders. They become algebraic symbols; through them he endeavors to set beauty in equations. Some day the equations may be solved.

Nonetheless, like T. S. Eliot, Valéry is no trickster. Neither man doffs cap to mediocrity. Both turn by complex involutions toward the core of the universe, whether (as Eliot) withdrawing from The Waste Land he sees today or (as Valéry) advancing toward the cold range of the galactic whorls of finite yet boundless space.

As the poetry of Claudel stems from and re-echoes with religion, so this deliberate structure draws poetry to the mother of all science. Mathematics and prayer, indeed, might serve as a loose phrasing of the extremes toward which the movements of our time are urging, in their efforts to distil the essence of life, to attain the ultimate universals. Those that believe reason sets the pointers along the way, move toward general principles, formalized or formularized methods, and ultimate abstractions evolved along the convolutions of the brain. Bertrand Russell declares that what reason cannot tell him, man cannot know. Those that, dogmatically or with reasoned arguments, deny the validity of reason as a guide, or as the sole guide, seek truth along the paths of faith or intuition or instinct (terms are vaguer and more pliant, along the Cismentian slopes!), for the pull into the essence of things trusting the tugs of the viscera. D. H. Lawrence patted his solar plexus as he exclaimed: I can believe only what hits me *here!*

Some may be inclined to smile when they hear that one critic recognized great works because they gave him gooseflesh, that another had to stop shaving himself because poetry came into his mind, his hand trembled, and his face was gashed. But the likelihood of such occurrences goes deeper than any intellectual scoffing. We find it, for example, rooted in our language growth, which continues in spite of science's disposal. We no longer make frequent reference to *the bowels of compassion; splenetic* and *bilious* are obsolescent; but *phlegmatic* and *melancholy* survive. Recent slang was urging everybody to *Have a heart;* and every other popular song still connects that organ with the amorous impulses. Now that *pluck,* a century ago prize-fighters' slang for *courage,* has advanced into accepted usage, street urchins in emphasis plunge right back into the viscera and admiringly exclaim: "That guy's got *guts!"*

But what might have been dismissed, a score of years ago, as folk-psychology lapsing into figure of speech, has again found scientific sanction. Even more than physics twistingly admits the alchemist's claims, physiology confirms the people's. Not merely the alligator folk-tale but bitter war experience reminds us that literally one's bowels are loosed with fear. If there is truth in the currently orthodox James-Lange theory, that the bodily stir produces the emotion—since most persons are swayed rather by their feelings than by their thoughts, we are not far from a scientific rehabilitation of this reliance upon somatic promptings. Those that in the name of reason smile at this hearkening to the visceral urge, are in truth, then, less moved by reason than they pleasantly deem. Their sense of superiority is wholly unreasonable.

The poet is naturally in the forefront of this vision. Yeats entunes it:

> *He that sings a lasting song*
> *Sings in a marrow bone.*

An American elaborates:

> *Only when bodies*
> *Have shut out mind*
> *Can they learn the calm*
> *Motion of dream.*
>
> *Would we could know*
> *The way men moved*
> *When thought was only*
> *A great dark love*
> *And blood lay calm*
> *In a depthless dream.*

This is not a prescription for surrealist work, but the yearning of a "proletarian" poet. Similarly the *flux* of D. H. Lawrence, his Dark Mother like this "great dark love", was borne by Messrs. Auden, Spender, and Day Lewis wistfully toward Communism. Such radicals, however, when they declare that the impulses of the abdomen are as trustworthy as the deliberations of the brain, should pursue their own logic. Alas, having discarded it, they do not see that they must lend equal sanction to Puritan conscience and Nazi Blutgefühl. . . . Yet the recoil to reason leads us no more positive way.

From all this ratiocination, which leads to reason's removal, some find it a relief to turn to purely formal patterns. Abandoning the quest of a pantology, Hugo Blümner and his fellows are content to seek the essence of their art, a "pure poetry" that grows through organic structures of meaningless sound:

> *Oiai laéla oia ssisalu*
> *Ensúdio trésa súdio mischnumi*

TWAIN TURMOIL OF TODAY

Ia lon stúaz
Broor schatt
Ua sésa masuó túlú
Ua sésa maschiató toro. . .

One might more readily mock these deviators from sense if they had never shown comprehensible merit. But just as the abstract art of Picasso gains respect from his excellent work in the recognizable forms, so when the German translator of Ibsen, and author of lovely lyrics, Christian Morgenstern, drops verbal bombs producing explosions of the language, we must not merely run for shelter, but examine the debris—as in *Das Grosse Lalulà* of his *Gallows Songs*. Explosions in the firmament may flower with new worlds.

Sometimes, to these constructions of sound (analogous to the color-patterns that flow from Wilfred's *Clavilux*, that marvelous trajector of symphonies of rhythmic light) the poet adds overtones of meaning—reversing the usual poetic practice of fortifying the meaning with overtones of sound. This method renders irritatingly incomprehensible to many the writings of Gertrude Stein. One must, of course, remember Miss Stein's experiments in "automatic writing" at Harvard; and the fact that she is "fond of writing the letter m" takes us Through the Looking Glass. Yet her work, however it may be related to the echolalia of the insane, is recognizable as creating forms wherein meaning is but the grace-note to sound. Her opera, *Four Saints in Three Acts,* beautifully produced in 1934 with music by Virgil Thompson, and performed as an oratorio in 1941, begins with these lines:

To know to know to love her so.
Four saints prepare for saints
It makes well fish.
Four saints it makes well fish,
Four saints prepare for saints it makes it well well
  fish it makes it well fish prepare for saints.
In narrative prepare for saints.

Prepare for saints.
Two saints.
Four saints.
Two saints prepare for saints it two saints prepare for saints in prepare for saints.
At least.
In finally,
Very well if not to have and miner.
A saint is one to be for two when three and you make five and two and cover.
A at most.
Saint saint a saint.
What happened today, a narrative.

Through the apparently meaningless movement of sound in this opera—not to be judged by the phrases that here and there thrust out a tongue of sense—may be traced an aura of significance to which the sound of the words and the music flows. All the comprehensible allusions to St. Teresa in Act I are to childhood, its sanctity unaware yet implicit: "one, two, three, four, five, six, seven, all good children go to heaven." The Second Act meanings are a fluency around "How many saints (doors, windows) are there in it?" while on the backdrop of the enacted opera we see a House of God such as St. Teresa (and as Ignatius Loyola) builded. In the succeeding scene, the working followers of Ignatius, after a final earthly lure (spelled by the dancers), demand his authority, and are inducted into the Jesuit order. The funeral procession, in a magnificent choral, intones the words "dead, lead, wed, said", obvious as rhymes, but significant as implicit transcendencies: heavy as lead, but led to light; wed no more on earth save to the worms, but wed above to Jesus; said—alas unavailingly how many times, yet once and for eternity. Then the saints are reassembled to tell why they went away to stay: united in heaven, and conjoined as an influence (alas how little felt!) on earth. This cloud-cathedral of suggestion, with its spires and its gargoyles, may be discerned beyond the word-design. But it should be held in mind that one must expect no more elaborate structure of meaning than the usual work has traceable pattern of sound.

A complete brief poem (which a sceptic might feel lets peep the secret of Miss Stein's method) is

CONSCIENCE

Racket is a noise. Noise is a poise. Boys with the b
  spelled like a p is poise. Boys is poise.
And then I read the men. Men say. Leave me and be
  gay.
Men say tenderness today. Men say go away.
And leave me.
A potato field and the promised land. It is a very
  pleasant burning smell.
Armandine Armandine yesterday noon. Armandine
  Armandine what is the tune.
Devotion. What is devotion. He is devoted to that.
  She is devout. And an opening. An opening is
  covered by Caesars.
Sharp wire. Do sharpen wire. Devotion. Devotion is
  determined by design.
When this you see remember me.
I do mean to replace crockery with furniture. I do
  mean to organize victory. I do mean to say grace.
I am not a bar tender.
Automatically but not silently.
Little fool little stool little fool for me. Little stool little
  fool little stool for me. And what is a stool. That
  was the elegant name for a cow. Little stool little
  fool little stool for me. Little fool little stool for
  me.
Let us let us conscience.
Let us conscientiously renounce the sense of reticence.

TRENDS IN LITERATURE

Words are so closely bound with meaning that their separation, if possible, seems strange. The arts that work with palpable media may more profitably extract the formal essence. Most writers try to keep within the limits of sense, even on the quest of an all-embracing universal. The stretching out to a wider inclusion is evident even in the verbal reco-ordinations of the "revolution of the word" proclaimed by Eugene Jolas and illustrated by many writers in the pages of his magazine *Transition*. They seek to use the word as "an instrument of percussion not precision", to spread "the panaroma of all flores of speech." Thus *viterberation* packs the double violence of a quarrel. *Mielodorous is thy bel chant* brings taste and smell to fort the other sense. *Joepeter* at once summons and dethrones the gods. James Joyce, most prominent of the experimenters with the word, enlarges the associations: "We may come, touch and go, from atoms to ifs, but we are presurely destined to be odds without ends": *atoms to ifs* not only bodies forth Adam and Eve, but in its little span comprehends man's growth from primordial matter to metaphysical speculation. There is equal condensation when he puts "all space in a notshall".

Such word play seems the game of a nimble punster, a linguist who delights in mental gymnastics and verbal acrobatics beyond his readers' recapture. He is really, however, a hunter with words his lure, seeking to snare the snark that is the universe. But what if his take be a Boojum!—We must remember that even Browning left his own generation agape.

At least, excessive though the experimenters may be, they indicate the opportunities, and explore the boundaries, for sequent artists.

A verbal inclusion easier to understand is that which reaches out to many tongues, creating, at least in diction, international poems. The last six lines of *The Waste Land* use five languages. To follow Ezra Pound's *Cantos,* one must have tags of Greek, Latin, Late Latin, Provençal, Old French, French, Spanish, Italian, English—early, late, correct and in various corruptions—business abbreviations here and abroad, and obscenity.

Far beyond such verbal extension, this sense of an underlying unity in all things may pervade a volume. It does so almost mechanically in Robert M. Coates' *Yesterday's Burden*: Henderson is now a man about town, now a Bowery tramp; ever he grows more generalized, until the author declares:

> He was a young man, like any other young man in the city: I saw him only occasionally and as if at random, and even then it was as if a different Henderson presented himself to me at each meeting. Even then it was as if the city had come between.
>
> And then, at last, the city surrounded him, made itself a part of him as he of it and (blending together: losing himself as if one by one,) and (but even more subtly changing: like a crowd that has not yet compacted itself, but splitting apart, dividing and subdividing. He) as if dispersing, as if lost in very multiplicity, even as I approached. He like a crowd and himself lost in the crowd, and, vanishing, finally, before my eyes.
>
> I never saw him again.

Of Franz Werfel's novel, *The Forty Days of Musa Dagh*—and the remark is applicable to all his work—William Saroyan says: "His perception sinks deeply to qualities in man that do not end when men die, but go on forever in the living."

Ernest Hemingway calls his 1940 novel *For Whom The Bell Tolls*. The title is drawn from a sermon by John Donne:

> No man is an Iland, entire of it selfe; every man is a peece of the Continent, a part of the maine; if a Clod bee washed away by the Sea, Europe is the lesse, as well as if a Mannor of thy friends or of thine owne were; any man's death diminishes me, because I am involved in Mankinde; And therefore never send to know for whom the bell tolls; It tolls for thee."

Bernard Gilbert, whose writings are little known in the United States, but whose *Bly Market* (the "moving picture" of the series) is one of the soundest ventures in the new forms of the novel, conceives his *Old England* as a work in twelve volumes showing different aspects of the same scene over the same period, building in as many modes a single picture, capturing the universe in a country town. James Joyce in the lengthy *Ulysses* joins the glittering past with the jittery present, all in a Dublin day. In a double page advertisement, the publishers of *Ulysses* emphasize its theme as "the dominance of circumstance over mind". Its unifying forces are manifest. In his *Finnegans Wake* Joyce streams still more inclusively across the world. Two gossiping washerwomen bend to their task on opposite banks of the River Liffey near its source; as they talk, the stream widens between them, until they bind the continents in their local chat. "In America they call me the Missus Liffey." Joyce's basic purpose, as several analyses point out, is to uncover the essential identity that underlies the variety of external phenomena.

A remark of his own puts the case succinctly. Reminding us that *Odysseus,* when he hid his identity from the Cyclops, called himself *Odys* (No-Man): so, Joyce continues, when the artist withholds any iota of himself from his work, it is inevitably the *Zeus,* the god in him, that is sloughed, and no man that remains. The artist has the choice of Ibsen's Brand: all, or nothing.

This desire for all-inclusiveness troubles the artist. André Gide strives for it in his novel *The Counterfeiters,* by inventing an author who is writing a book of the same name. Hear that character speak:

"My novel has no subject. Yes, I know; what I'm saying sounds stupid. Let's put it, if you prefer, that it will not have a subject. 'A slice of life', says the naturalist school. The great fault of that school is to cut the slice always in the same direction: that of time, lengthwise. Why not in width? or in depth? And I'd rather not cut at all. Understand me: I'd like to have everything get into this novel. No scissor-snips to cut off its substance, here rather than there. For over a year that I've been working on it, nothing's occurred to me that I haven't poured right in, that I haven't wanted to use in it: what I see, what I know, all that my life and others' lives teach me. . . ."

"My poor friend, you'll make your readers die of boredom."

"Not at all. To obtain my effect, I'm inventing a novelist-hero; and the subject of the book, if you insist, is precisely the conflict between what reality offers and what he makes of it."

Not content with this triple creation, Gide also published his *Journal for "The Counterfeiters"*, the story of the days through which he wrote the book.

The multiplex life-work of Marcel Proust, *A la recherche du temps perdu* (*In Search of Times Gone By*), presents a wide pattern of achieved unity and revealed essence. The world of aristocratic society, most widely limned, is intricately interwoven with the bourgeois world of Marcel's childhood, with the peasant and small-shop world of the Guermantes' cook, with the world of Albertine and her *jeunes filles en fleurs,* with several other worlds, until out of the many distinct social groupings and levels of life there rises a sense of the interdependence, the unity of all living. Within the growth of an individual we may discern several stages, to those about apparently detached, independent, as life carries the person into different associations and activities, but gathering for the reader into a continuously unfolding personality, dynamic but unified. Just as complete knowledge of anyone is denied us in life, Proust affords us constant glimpses that alter our impression of a character, building ever a more rounded picture, nearer to though always short of completeness, allowing for life's surprises yet establishing the unity of a person growing through the days. Still on the quest of understanding, and aware that one man's green is another man's gray, Proust is seldom satisfied with the direct presentation of an incident: he stops to consider it psychologically, to analyze its causes, human motives and seemingly fortuitous bindings; he drapes it in Homeric simile, draws memoried association in its train, speculates upon its likely influence, its possible offshoots of action or misconception; he repeats his tale in various guises and lays on it patina of long consideration, until from his manysided patient returning we rise—with a gathered sense of long familiarity, or of the inevitable movement of a natural force we now first wittingly watch, or of the opening of a dusty door into the depths of the human spirit—to a rich but single impression. And always in Proust we behold the action, the person, the situation, the object, gradually peeled of its exterior characteristics until its essence has been laid bare. As the author himself declares, in *Le temps retrouvé*, he is searching through actions and speech, through the very manner of the speech, for the character, and within the character for its revealment of the "psychological generalization", of the characteristics common to all human beings; the qualities shared, universal. The essential unity, and the single essence, of all diversified things.

Other writers, not venturing so wide a scope, seek unity through the vision of a single eye. Ellen Glasgow states that "in *Barren Ground,* a long novel, I felt from the moment Dorinda entered the book that there could be but one point of view. From the first page to the last, no scene or episode or human figure appears outside her field of vision or imagination." This presentation of the whole story through the eyes of one character is more frequent in the theatre, where it has been given the name of monodrama. This often seems much like the usual play, as in Arthur Richman's *Theatre Guild* play *Ambush,* whereof the muddling clerk whose vision colors the drama is twin to us all. It may move, however, through the distorted minds of emotion-tossed figures. In Meinhard and Bernauer's *Johannes Kreisler,* the devices of expressionism lend an eerie power to the vision; as when Kreisler's enemies stand before him in the dark, he swishes away their bodies, and the decapitate heads in a grisly green light still leer at him. Kaiser's *From Morn To Midnight* follows an absconding bank clerk through the turbulent hours from temptation to final penalty. However normal or eccentric the eye through which we look, the device is another quest of embracing unity.

The fullest union of all things, in art, is sought through the life-work of Jules Romains, founder of the school of unanimism. It finds its philosophical sanction in Bergson's theory of creative evolution:

> With this doctrine we feel ourselves no longer isolated in humanity, and humanity no longer isolated in the nature that it dominates. As the smallest grain of dust is bound up with our entire solar system . . . so all organized beings, from the humblest to the highest, from the first beginnings of life to the time in which we are, and in all places at all times, do but evidence a single impulsion. . . The whole of humanity, in space and in time, is one immense army.

This unity echoes in the poetry of Romains:

> *The air I breathe is fresh with spirit-savour.*
> *Men are ideas that a mind sends forth.*
> *From them to me all flows, yet is internal;*
> *Cheek to cheek we lie across the distance,*
> *Space in communion binds us in one thought.*

He sought to capture it in his first novel *Somebody's Death,* in 1911, and in his other books. The quest led him to his researches in the field of extra-sensory perception, the psychic phases of which have been expanded in the United States, especially in the *E S P* work at Duke University. At last, in his continuing master-work, *Men of Good Will,* he feels ready for a complex and comprehensive view of life, showing its organic multiplicity, the ceaseless linking and interdependence of all living.

In the preface to this lengthy novel, Romains discusses earlier endeavors to survey a wide social scene. An author might produce a series of separate novels, so ordered and with such recurrence of characters as to give a composite picture of a whole society. Not such adventure books as *The Three Musketeers* and its sequels, but Balzac's *Comédie humaine,* Zola's *Rougon-Macquart* series. These, Romains feels, did not, in their own time, convey any sense of underlying unity; their approach is too individual in our day to be revived. A novelist may, on the other hand, write a long book, or a series, given unity through the person of a single hero, whose adventures carry him up and down the social levels, so that out of his contacts and conflicts the whole of society emerges. *Les Miserables, Jean-Christophe, A la recherche du temps perdu,* employ this method; with the individual replaced by a family, *The Forsyte Saga,* and *Buddenbrooks.* But in such works, either society is scanted, or the hero becomes a pretext, a clothes-pole for hanging the wash of events. Romains considers this binding of the story around a central personage an anachronism, a literary hangover from the time of individual emphasis. He points out that his early efforts at a form more worthy of our collective age have been widely seconded, notably in Russia and in America, and that they have influenced the cinema as well. He then asks the readers to make no hasty judgments, on reading the first volume of *Men of Good Will.* They will discover that this general picture of society traces several apparently disconnected stories, and presents persons that are never seen again, "meteors that burn to dust, or aperiodic comets of the human firmament. A full pathos of dispersion, of disappearance, with which life abounds, but which the books almost always refuse, preoccupied as they are, in the name of the olden rules, with beginning and ending the game with the same cards." In life, as in the cluster before an attractive show-window, the persons come and go, the crowd is unchanging. The American public heeded Romains' plea by making one volume of the book, that called *Verdun,* a best seller.

Unanimism has by now won wide recognition, having gained entrance into the novels of H. G. Wells. It has, by some, been limited to a concern with mankind. Romains himself remarked that if spirit may be treated as matter, we may contrariwise treat matter as spirit. This is doubtless the thought of the pious Claudel when he declares:

> Truly, blue knows orange; truly the hand, its shadow on the wall; truly and really, an angle of a triangle knows the two others precisely as Isaac knew Rebecca.

It is the same spirit we may discern in George Edward Woodberry, unanimist before the term was used:

> *Although I transmigrate from friend to friend*
> *Yet do I own an undivided soul;*
> *From form to form created things must roll,*
> *And of their transformation is no end;*
> *But in my substance do I never bend;*
> *Still unity my being doth control,*
> *And still I give myself entire and whole*
> *In all my loves, and with my object blend.*

With most in this mood, however, the embracing is universal. Ezra Pound begins a poem:

> *I stood still and was a tree amid the wood.*

Count Hermann Keyserling states, in more emphatic prose:

> I can deny what this world is today just as little as I can deny my personal condition. . . . Even the transient gesture of every individual continues to be effective through aeons of time. Thus, no one may or can sever himself from the whole.

This inevitable identity of the individual with his surroundings is made the basis of one of the time's most credited theories of beauty. Anything is beautiful, according to the doctrine of Einfühlung, or empathy, that draws us into its being. Thus Souriau says "We have only one way of imagining things from the inside, and that is, putting ourselves inside them." Bergson declares that the spectator must become actor. Lotze asserts that we accomplish the feat: "We project ourselves into the forms of a tree, identifying our life with that of the slender shoots that swell and stretch forth, feeling in our souls the delight of the branches that drop and poise delicately in mid-air." Leaping ahead from this charming pathetic fallacy, Irwin Edman announces this union "most notable and obvious in sculpture. We feel ourselves poised in movement and in rest with the discus thrower, and our own muscles grow tight with the tensions of some of the figures, tortured and muscular, of Michelangelo." Münsterberg carries on: "If the energies we feel in the lines are external projections of our own energies, we understand the psychological reasons why certain combinations of lines please us." And Vernon Lee puts it across: "When this attribution of our modes of life to visible shapes and this revival of past experience is such as to be favorable to our existence and in so far pleasurable, we welcome the form thus animated by ourselves as beautiful." Thus the subway-crushed salesgirl becomes the movie's heroine!

Identification with the Wild West hero is easier than to obey Shelley's imperative—Be thou me, impetuous one!—to the west wind. Nor is anyone likely to admit becoming, let us say, the chief figure in Gray's *On a Favorite Cat, Drowned In a Tub of Gold Fishes*. Even on the stage, despite frequent assertions to the contrary for public delight, the actor thinks his way into his role, does not identify himself with his character. Most persons, telling their friends the plot of a motion picture, use the names of the players, as though the events were happening to those that take the roles; but—as a star of both stage and screen, Ann Harding, responded when I put the question: "The theory of 'living the part' won't stand any sort of test. How in Heaven's name are you going to 'live' Hamlet eight times a week? How about Camille? Do the exponents of that doctrine *actually die* twice on Wednesdays and Saturdays?" Everyone that has attempted performance will recognize the aptness of Lynn Fontanne's description: "the ability to keep the temperature of your head at zero while your heart is at ninety-nine in the shade."

The plight of the empathetic beholder is more piteous still. He must die, not only with Hamlet, but with Polonius, Ophelia, Laertes, Gertrude, the guilty king—yet still survive in Fortinbras. Except perhaps before monodrama, he must be all men, all things, and all together. Within an insult's hurling, Antonio to thrust and Shylock to receive. Or perhaps just Shakespeare. That blending would be prime! The simplest answer to the claim of empathy is that it is a figure of speech: a pious wish, but a pure fiction. We cannot identify ourselves with others, any more than the bottom of a stick can climb up and merge with the top. Turn it upside down, you have merely transferred the terms of the equation. The only way to make ends meet is, as I have said, to chop them asunder. This destroys them but doubles your problem. Somehow, along the unbroken stick, rhythms may throb from pole to pole. Without becoming our surroundings, we may feel with them, understand them. But our age, on reason's Icarian wings, in the urge of a universal embracing, is not content with Love thy neighbor; it says Thou art thy neighbor, too! Alack how often even self-love builds to hate!

7. *Reason runs awry.*

REASON is the rampart of our age. A few voices cry against it, denounce its despotic reign. A. E. Housman, in *The Nature of Poetry,* declares that the intellect is not the fount of poetry, may actually hinder its production, cannot even be trusted to recognize it when produced. Eda Lou Walton launches similar attack:

> Look at the imagery of these poets. . . . If the word "mind" appears once in recent poetry, it appears fifty thousand times. Mind, brain, skull, passion of the mind, stone of thought, ivory of the brain, jewel of the brain, and similar images are constant. . . . The word or image of the "heart" has almost disappeared from poetry. "What matter if the heart live on?" If it does live on, it becomes a nagging kind of contradiction, an ancient hunger which the mind cannot quite neglect. The heart, the emotions, are really lost to most modern poets. Human feelings are known to be momentary only, without ultimate value. Human beings are mere ants which appear and disappear under the microscope. First their bodies disappear (their hearts within the flesh), then only their spinning heads are left, detached and mechanical as some scientific invention. "The mind that lives on print becomes too savage." Finally it freezes up altogether. And so throughout most modern poetry, conceptual language is the language used. Physical imagery in any pure form is gone. As scenery for the translation of emotions, it is no longer useful. A new language for the mind, the only thing that most of these modern poets have left to talk about, has been invented. Poetry

is burdened with abstract, ideational, pseudo-scientific phrases and images.
All this is a kind of death in the desert.

Perhaps we should pause to note the far-wanderings of those that, with or without its bright parade, thus reject the mind.

A little reason is a dangerous thing;
Think deep, or waste not the psychotic spring.

The rabble-rouser, always reliant on the quick flare of passion, soars to his heights in such an age as ours, which finds arguments against the validity of reason. The witling can quote logic to his purpose. And the demagogue becomes the dictator.

The interlinking of the arts and life, and the confusion regarding the place of reason in the world today, are nowhere better shown than in the attempts of the artist to look at politics. Three plays (coincidentally, each by a member of the Playwrights' Producing Company, and produced in logical sequence) illustrate the process. In Robert E. Sherwood's *There Shall Be No Night*, the leading character, a Finnish doctor, speaks via radio to America. He declares that the world has gone mad, has been attacked by a pandemic insanity. This madness is defined in Elmer Rice's drama, *Flight To The West*. A Jew has impulsively leapt between a revolver and a Nazi: the liberal nearby asks the German whether this courageous and generous deed has not softened his heart. The Nazi laughs scornfully:

> His action was entirely unmotivated — it was nothing more than a muscular reflex. If he had had a moment for thought, he would have taken good care not to intervene.

The German calls himself a scientist and a realist, not allowing his conclusions to be disturbed by "personal and irrelevant accidents". From their talk, the liberal is roused to his awakening, the spiritual climax of the drama. Extolling the "generosity, tolerance, self-sacrifice, brotherliness" that the Nazi has put aside, he declares that

> rationality carried to its ruthless logical extreme becomes madness, because man is a living and growing organism and not a machine, and in all the important things of life, a sane man is irrational.

This sense that our best impulses spring not from the head but from the heart is carried into everyday life in S. N. Behrman's *The Talley Method*. Dr. Talley is called a Fascist by the "understanding" poetess in the play, and we are expected to agree. The good doctor's crime is that, although intelligence and application have made him a demon in the duodenum, he cannot cope with his children. It doesn't matter to Behrman that the seemingly arbitrary and inconsiderate acts of the doctor are *irrational*, are the *emotional* consequences of his unfamiliarity with the proper course, of his well-meaning but embarrassed groping. It doesn't matter to Behrman that the "Talley method", the application of reason and cold thought—which helps keep the duodenum clear—is the avenue of equal success with the family, when applied by the sound teacher, social worker, and psychiatrist. Nor does it matter to him that the "intuition" of the loving mother is often the cause of the evils the psychiatrist later has to try to cure. In his own play, the coming of the "understanding" poetess into Dr. Talley's life is the direct cause of a suicide, of the daughter's leaving the house forever, and of the son's loss of independence and weak lapse into submission to his father's will. Having created this mess, she calls Dr. Talley a Fascist, and flounces out of his life, promising to reconsider her decision if he awakens. Behrman seems to admire the lady; the audience applauds. We are supposed to recognize the superiority of warm feeling to mere mind.

Such a pseudological triumph of emotion over reason marks the muddle of our would-be intellectuals, who indeed think with their desires. Elmer Rice's liberal is doubly in the dark. He assumes that the Nazis are logical. But no one that proclaims the superiority of a race, that boasts of a pure racial strain, that claims the prepotency of *Blutgefühl,* rests upon reason. What the Nazis have done is to erect a logical structure upon an irrational premise. All is correct, save the initial assumption. Like most persons, only more unanimously, they have twisted reason to defend their emotion's drive. This has given them a pseudo-realism, which they flaunt as scientific and true. Those with as little reason may be taken in. Instead of attacking their false premises, then seeking sound bases for the erection of a logical system, Rice's liberal—with many throughout the world—seeks to dynamite the whole structure. (I refer, of course, to intellectual dynamite.) Because he is confused, because he cannot think his way to a solution, he abandons reason volte-face, and hails another guide. Feeling once more sits on her pedestal. The liberal's new panacea is the old destroyer. He has rejected his only instrument. He is at one with Hitler. What he needs, alas, is not less but richer reason!

In spite of the plausible plea for love and kindness, these are the obverse of the coins of cruelty and hate—too easily we toss them heads or tails! Passion needs no justification; it awaits no logical support; it springs. Thought is its one control. It is by reason man rises from the brute.

A score of years ago—one the ages' round—it was being crudely argued that, since no person can present the whole truth, since therefore objective impartiality is impossible, it is the duty of the artist openly to take sides—and of course he must side with the striker against the paid police! It is no more sensible to say—though currently proposed—that, since truth is beyond our grasp, reason therefore always insecure, we should rest our decisions upon some deeper, cosmic urge, of love, or faith, or somatic feeling. To argue in this way, to turn reason upon itself, is no more feasible than for the well-known snake to swallow its tail. At most, it can but shed its skin.

Not understanding these aberrations when they appear in art, the layman laughs. He cries that Dali is daft, perhaps applauds his "clowning". But Dali-words are more dangerous;

he cannot grasp their meaning, but catches within himself an echo of their mood. The belittling of reason is likely to please those that have little. Such persons also have little humility; they read, therefore assume that they can judge—hence, the power of propaganda. "I have a right to my opinion" is a frequent phrase, grasped as a final crutch when arguments have stumbled. But no one has a "right" to an opinion unless he has the appropriate material for its forming.

"The cleverest ruse of the devil is to persuade us he doesn't exist." The shrewdest play of emotion is to strut in reason's garb. But, despite proverb, the devil can only garble Scripture —can persuade only those already lost. Those that use reason to deny reason's force would, if they succeeded, merely refute themselves. The cogency of their arguments would prove the power of reason. Nonetheless from all sides today the claims of other criteria are urged; and a greater host take not the time to argue. Thus, instead of a pseudo-realism, the muddled many present a political surrealism. Reason (like freedom) has always a slippery hold.

The logician is not the only one, however, that stands firm against such pleas for feeling. Why should I not write love poems, says the young poet of today, since it's my trade to make poems; do they ask of an architect, before he's commissioned to build a station, that he shall feel like riding on the train?

"The end of the enjoyment of poetry," Eliot expresses the view, "is a pure contemplation from which all the accidents of personal emotion are removed." This is achieved largely by the labor of the intelligence. Reason can point the way out of the waste land, if it cannot light the torch; surely the feelings have proved no more certain guide. Yet reason, which at first blush seems to set us above the beast, in its exercise tends to reduce man from the headline part of the chosen creature to the unstarred role of the present product of one evolutionary chain.

It would be thoughtless, however, to assume that all poets whose technique is "radical" are speaking in ultraistic mood.

TWAIN TURMOIL OF TODAY

The examples of Mallarmé and Valéry should incline us rather to believe that when a poet's theme is difficult, in itself or because it is new, he is likely to couch it in a familiar form. This must be borne in mind when reading our modernist versifiers, in such anthologies as Alfred Kreymborg's *Others* series, or in their single volumes, or in tendentious magazines; and perhaps Miss Walton has, in some measure, mistaken a deliberate intellectualization of treatment, a fashionable concealment of emotion, for the lack of feeling or faith. It is true that Robinson Jeffers calls to the ocean that

> *The tides are in our veins, we still mirror the stars,*
>   *life is your child, but there is in me*
> *Older and harder than life and more impartial, the*
>   *eye that watched before there was an ocean. . .*
> *Before there was any water there were tides of fire,*
>   *both our tones flow from the older fountain.*

Maxwell Bodenheim, though he bows to the public by *Returning to Emotion*, explains his inspiration in the foreword to *The Sardonic Arm*: "The lurking emphasis behind life separates into little, curious divisions of sound." He also sets man in his place:

> *The contours of a rose*
> *Bribing the quiet madness of evening*
> *With cunning promises of red,*
> *Are more important than your sweating love*
> *And the rushing dreads of your market-places.*

But the inspirer and leader of the aesthetically radical poets of our time but covers with show of learning a social satire as simple as that of Sinclair Lewis. In an early poem, before he had found his distinctive disguise, Ezra Pound directly bade his songs:

> *Speak against unconscious oppression,*
> *Speak against the tyranny of the unimaginative,*
> *Speak against bonds . . .*

> *Be eager to find new evils and new good,*
> *Be against all forms of oppression.*

Drawing later on Provençal lore, and in his *Draft of XXX Cantos* on ancient, medieval and contemporary deeds, as he gathered a following Pound accumulated erudition, which he would not waste. *Canto VIII* begins:

> *These fragments you have shelved (shored).*
> *"Slut!" "Bitch!" Truth and Calliope*
> *Slanging each other sous le lauriers:*
> *That Alessandro was negroid. And Malatesta*
> *Sigismund:*
> > *Frater tamquam*
> *Et compater carissime: tergo*
> > *. . . hanni de*
> > *. . . dicis*
> > *. . . entia*
> *Equivalent to:*
> > *Giohanni of the Medici,*
> > *Florence.*
> *Letter received, and in the matter of our Messire Gianozio,*
> *One from him also, sent on in form and with all due dispatch,*
> *Having added your wishes and memoranda.*

Canto XIX, after some letters from the year 1454, ends:

> *That's what they found in the post-bag*
> *And some more of it to the effect that*
> > *he "lived and ruled"*
> *"et amava perdutamente Ixotta degli Atti"*
> > *"ne fu degna"*
> > > *"constans in proposito*
> *"Placuit oculis principis*
> *"pulchra aspectu"*
> *"populo grata" (Italiaeque decus)*

TWAIN TURMOIL OF TODAY

> "and built a temple so full of pagan works"
>   i.e. Sigismund
> and in the style "Past ruin'd Latium"
> The filagree hiding the gothic,
>   with a touch of rhetoric in the whole
> And the old sarcophagi,
>   such as lie, smothered in grass, by San Vitale.

Dip anywhere, and you net like pawn. Cantos XIV and XV are a hog-wallow travesty of the Inferno—in what Pound's disciples call "the greatest poem of our time Pound's *Cantos*."

The *Objectivists Anthology* of 1932 is dedicated to this Canto-concocter, "still for the poets of our time the most important." To that collection, with the comment "You can note that it belongs to the best and most active period of jazz; before the new neo sentimentalism set in", Pound sent the piece of in-inverted sentimentalism beginning:

> Gentle Jheezus sleek and wild
> Found disciples tall an' hairy
> Flirting with his red hot Mary
>   Now hot momma Magdelene
> Is doing front page fer the screen
>   Mit der yittischer Charleston Pband
> Mit
> deryiddischercharles
>   tonband. ----

and — surely the master was not hoaxing his disciples! these

WORDS FOR ROUNDEL IN DOUBLE CANON
(maestoso e triste)

> O bury 'em down
>   in blooms—
>   buree
> Where the gravy tastes like the soup,
> O bury 'em down in Blooms—
>   buree

[281]

TRENDS IN LITERATURE

> Where the soup tastes like
> last night's
>   gra-
>   vee
> O bury 'em down in Bloomsburee
> Where the damp dank rot
> Is never forgot
> O bury 'em down
> In Bloomsburee
> Where the soup tastes like
>   last night's gravee
> O bury
> 'em down
> In Blooms-
> buree
> Where the gra-
> vy tastes
> Like the
> Soup.

Without seeking to impugn Pound's sincerity in his *Magnum opus*, we may be permitted to aver that his disciples' panegyrics recall the Gilbertian lines:

> *The meaning doesn't matter if it's only idle chatter of a transcendental kind.*
>   *And everyone will say,*
>   *As you walk your mystic way,*
> "*If this young man expresses himself in terms too deep for me,*
> *Why what a singularly deep young man this deep young man must be!*"

Except that Ezra Pound was old enough, though no better, even before his Italian years.

  The ultraist mood more truly pervades the work of the outstanding recent American poet in the traditional modes. About the meaning of Edwin Arlington Robinson there can be little doubt. His poems are cold with calculation; his analysis,

[282]

TWAIN TURMOIL OF TODAY

an intellectual autopsy. In much of his work the thought does not hide within figures. We hear a "man from Stratford":

> *It's all Nothing.*
> *It's all a world where bugs and emperors*
> *Go singularly back to the same dust,*
> *Each in his time; and the old ordered stars*
> *That sang together, Ben, will sing the same*
> *Old stave tomorrow;* . . .

The Man Against the Sky looks over a world that has lost faith without gaining knowledge, and concludes:

> *All comes to Nought,—*
> *If there be nothing after Now,*
> *And we be nothing anyhow,*
> *And we know that,—why live?*
> *'Twere sure but weaklings' vain distress*
> *To suffer dungeons where so many doors*
> *Will open on the cold eternal shores*
> *That look sheer down*
> *To the dark tideless floods of Nothingness*
> *Where all who know may drown.*

In the "modern miracle play" of Eugene O'Neill, "the dark warm womb of Nothingness" is the temptation held out by the demon Hate.

Even Robinson's early cry for the restoration of the spirit, his well known sonnet against the "little sonnet-men", yearns only for a flare of beauty. It is out of tune with our time both in the cry of immortality and in the stamp of individuality: "his name forever more". These anachronisms perhaps explain (since he chose not to drown in Nothingness) why Robinson lingered in the past, giving olden tales new psychological kinks and twistings. But the voice calls to Lancelot:

> *You are not free.*
> *You have come to the world's end, and it is best*
> *You are not free. Where the Light falls, death falls;*
> *And in the darkness comes the Light.*

Merlin is as darkly cheerless.

Though the beast in man again beats him down, O'Neill's Lazarus has returned from the grave with an ecstatic message: "There is no death, no fear, no loneliness! There is only God's Eternal Laughter! His Laughter flows into the lonely heart!" Robinson has no consolation for lonely hearts; his Lazarus comes back, to meet Mary's questions—

> *Is Nothing, Lazarus, all you have for me?*
> *Was Nothing all you found where you have been?—*

with a gloomy "I do not know . . . I do not know."

After nine pages of argumentative soliloquy (contrast it with Browning's painters' monologues!) Robinson's Rembrandt bids himself grow reconciled:

> *If at the first*
> *Of your long turning, which may still be longer*
> *Than even your faith has measured it, you sigh*
> *For distant welcome that may not be seen,*
> *Or wayside shouting that will not be heard,*
> *You may as well accommodate your greatness*
> *To the convenience of an easy ditch*
> *And, anchored there with all your widowed gold,*
> *Forget your darkness in the dark, and hear*
> *No longer the cold wash of Holland scorn.*

Robinson's occasional returns to our time are no more humanly hopeful. His Christmas message for 1929 rings out the cheerful word that

> *Only the God that you have made*
> *Has mocked you in the sky.*

The dialogue between Dionysus and Demos pictures the two as endlessly disputing life's command, with Demos now in the ascendency, and the world grown grey at his breath:

> *Punctual, accurate, tame and uniform,*
> *And equal. Then romance and love and art*

> And ecstasy will be remembrances
> Of man's young weakness on his way to reason.

What lies beyond?

> The rest would be an overflow to tell,
> Surely;—and you may slowly have inferred
> That you may not be here a thousand years.

Robinson was esteemed, despite his themes, because his packed phrases, his psychological emphasis and analysis, his leveling of man with all else, are attuned to the age; he will lapse from regard because through (or despite) his vision he does not rise, nor let rise, in exaltation some breath of beauty and joy. Dunsany jimmies *The Glittering Gate* of heaven, to find no human prospect, yet still the "blooming great stars"; Robinson's empty eyes cloud with the fore-fog of despair.

When he does not use words, man is less tangled in the consequences of his beliefs. In other arts, therefore, it is less disturbing to move on the quest of the universal and the absolute. Their implications force no immediate involvements. Music, therefore, never really at home in program compositions, moves from story-telling and landscape painting back to moods and abstractions.

With the rise of the middle class, literacy without culture, wealth without wisdom, leisure without pleasure, came a host of predigested foods: "the five-foot shelf"; *The A B C of the Atom*; relativity explained in the movies; program music. Eager ignorance gulped capsules of condensed culture, below the lorgnettes of plumed pretense. Now the wind blows from other shores. But at first the old technique, sincere or satiric, is made to carry the new themes. Note how long it is taking the automobile to develop from horse-coach models to intrinsic automotive designs. Thus in music *Skyscraper, Tabloid, Pacific 231, L'Histoire d'un soldat, An American In Paris, Les Courses,* use "program" titles to express the machine civilization. Then, in search of the spirit beneath the manifestations, new forms were found for our new time. The first dancers permitted by the Soviet government to perform abroad surprised us with no novelty, but with gymnastic ballet; so, audiences discover once more music that is merely music. Increasingly such titles as *The Sunken Cathedral* and *Station W G Z B X* are supplanted by *Klavierconcert, Opus* 36, *No.* 1; and *Quartet for Strings, Opus* 30. The six concerts of contemporary chamber music given in New York, in 1934, by the Roth Quartet, consisted entirely of merely numbered works. At the concert the League of Composers gave in honor of Arnold Schoenberg on his arrival in America, all his works were listed under such titles; and the *String Quartet With Voice, Opus* 10 presents for singing a poem by Stefan George that ends:

I am but a spark of the heaven's fire,
An intonation of the heaven's voice.

This trend in abstract titles continued through the eighteenth festival (first in the United States) of *The International Society for Contemporary Music,* which was heard for twelve days on March, 1941, in concert halls and on the air. And it remains.

Belatedly looking about, Curt J. Ducasse (in *Art, The Critics, and You,* 1944) spanks along its way the departing tendency. He declares that calling, for example, Severini's painting *Hiéroglyphe dynamique du Bal Tabarin* by the less suggestive title *Composition dynamique* would leave the beholder unbound by initial wonderings, free to observe the nonrepresentative form. The hunt for that nude descending the staircase doubtless led many from more pertinent concerns. It may, however, be suggested that those that content themselves with seeking the incidents of its story through the notes of "program music" or the patterns of a picture, would probably be unable to follow the more formal aspects of the work: they might be allowed their little fun. Meanwhile, in the surge of our time, the specific fades into the more general movement.

Music and dance, being untrammeled by verbal habits, may help clarify the tendency inaccurately pointed in the remark that poetry moves toward mathematics or toward prayer. For all three of these arts began in religion; all three move from ritual on two continuous pathways. They are laughing and lyric (and spontaneously romantic or humanist) with joy; or placid and plastic (and meditatively realist or ultraist) through wisdom. The dancing of Isadora Duncan illustrates both movements: At the peak of her early career, that unforgettable ecstasy when, like released Ariels in their joyous bound, she and the Isadorables commanded all hearts to leap with the instant beauty of their *Marche Militaire*. And the serene triumph of her later growth, when in pattern of pure fluid beauty, nay in almost motionless hold, she stood alone and swung the doors of eternity ajar. None after Euclid may have "looked on beauty bare"; but in such a spell the dance, and music, for a sublime moment lift her magic veil.

Less complicated by meaning, music and the dance belong in the realm of the abstract, inducing "soul-states" not telling particular stories. Program music, except for the mimicking of specific sounds, would be beyond interpretation as a tale, without the explanatory notes provided. The lyrical grace of ballet is one relic of pure dance; although, of course, ritual movements are constantly brought to us from many lands, in authentic form (as by La Meri), or modified by native artists (like Uday Shan-Kar) or by our own (like Ruth St. Denis). The story ballet is a drawing into the dance of other olden forms, the commedia dell' arte, the masque, the pantomime. In our age, music and the dance return to the abstract—but still many try to tell tales. *The Green Table* of the Joos Ballet, the comic work of Trudi Schoop, the satiric or descriptive skits of Agnes de Mille and Angna Enters, all are hybrid. This does not imply that they are inferior; opera, theatre, are also mongrel arts. Many dog lovers will tell you there's more fun with a mixed-breed pup than with a thoroughbred. But these forms in dance and music were at their apogee in the days when Baudelaire hailed the intermingling of sensuous appeals, rather than the later time when the quest of the universal became more generalized.

Many composers and choreographers, of course, (like artists in other fields, like subscribers to party programs) move without clear understanding of what whips them on. They are confounded by our contemporary confusions; they mix unwittingly—often with a social cement—shreds of outworn devices and inchoate fragments of the new. William Saroyan's ballet *The Great American Goof* well illustrates this muddling mixture. (Saroyan's produced plays—*My Heart's In the Highlands*; *Love's Old Sweet Song*; *The Time Of Your Life*; *The Beautiful People*—in varying degrees of whimsicality present the humanist hope for a world in which the fellowhood of simple men will lead mankind to good. Amid the urgings toward that time to come, "the great American goof" blunders through his ballet.) Such an inner discordance, when added to the cacophonies that seek to capture the essence of our noisy and violent age, explains why many persons wish to stop their ears and close their eyes to modern music and dancing.

Martha Graham, a leading exponent of the modern dance, calls one of her patterns *Frontier*. Seek and ye shall find: the awkwardness yet the indomitable will, the parched life yet the inexpugnable yearning, the endurance that is not submission but patience rooted in faith that a different day will dawn: here is an American pioneer wife, or one who faces the timeless frontiers of the spirit. Yet there would have been equal trove with the title *November*, or *Rainfall*. Much more effective are the movements, whether of Isadora Duncan's, or Martha Graham's own, or Mary Wigman's, that in "elevation" seek to raise the dancer, not the masses, that give us turns not Revolutions! that are concerned only with beauty's pattern in the dance. The dance, like music, can adapt its flow to any age's mood. But when the new language of the modern dance is jargonized by these that through it would hasten or hail the new Utopia—though the etymology and grammar of that language neither these choreographers nor these performers know—and with a strain and awkwardness more appropriate to our disjointed times than to the fluid medium in which they would hurry the coming day—it is little wonder that the ballet attracts increasing devotees of the dance, who adopt as their proud title *balletomane*.

In the field of popular dancing, that pelvic pressure has relaxed which a few years ago joined a couple in the embracing emphasis of our age; in its stead has come—more rapidly paced for our flying though far from soaring spirits—a recurrence of barn dances, a succession of new forms (e.g. The Big Apple; The Conga) or of heavier beats that call for group action, that swing the entire dance floor in one emotional sway. Somehow even the dancing couples are drawn into a larger symphony.

In painting and in sculpture, the quest of the universal, and the rift between the humanists and the ultraists, are equally striking. A visit to any modern gallery, a fortiori a survey of the annual *Independents'* exhibit, and the paintings cry this forth from their canvas. Consider first the principles of dynamic symmetry, as now developed and taught at many an art school. Worked out by Jay Hambidge and others as a sort of grammar of Greek art, then utilized by commercial artists as a convenient way of dividing their advertising space between copy and illustration, dynamic symmetry has grown to a method of establishing the essence of inevitably right proportion. A landscape as seen, its exponents point out, is an accidental arrangement; the whole composition, distances and details, is formed by chance. Within the healthy individual, however, one may view the whole: the unit—tree, rooster, man—reveals a basic and eternal harmony of nature. Take, then, a living thing, a bush, a rabbit, a woman: forget its superficial, individual characteristics, determine its essential character. Set down its basic form, in angles, curves, lines of emphasis. Before you now, in a geometry of relationships, you have one of nature's true patterns, a dynamic symmetry. And after this pattern, along its high spots and centerings and pointing lines, you can draw landscapes, abstractions, portraits, whatsoever you will, assured of the rightness of the proportions, the essential eurhythmy of the design.

This quest of an essence beneath the surface portraiture seems to Sheldon Cheney the pervasive aspect of all modern art, Maillol, Lehmbruck, and Epstein in sculpture, Sullivan and Wright in architecture, Craig and Appia in the theatre, Duncan and Wigman in the dance, "even while broad enough to embrace the varied contributions of the Post-Impressionists, Fauves, Cubists, Functionalists, Purists, etc." Not only pervasive, but enriching:

> Implicit in the attempt to achieve a revealing bit of the creative formal order, the abstract architecture in the canvas, there is a universal-mystic significance. An intensely creative abstract work of art, affording an enjoyment that may border upon rapture, links with the mystic's search for personal identification with the rhythm at the heart of the universe, with the consciousness of dynamic order and harmonious progression of the cosmos, beyond time and space . . . Knowing something of the mystic's conception of the structure and meaning of all that is, we find our faculties better able to identify, and enjoy, the echo of universal-eternal architecture in creative art.

This formal meaning is the only valid significance in sculpture, to R. H. Wilenski, who in *The Meaning of Modern Sculpture* declares that such artists as Brancusi, Zadkine, Epstein, Gaudier, Leon Underwood, Barbara Hepworth, Richard Bedford, Henry Moore and Maurice Lambert have organized formal energy into symbols for the universal analogy of form.

Clive Bell, in *Art*, earlier argued that all works of art, to be included within that term, must have some thing in common: this is "significant form". But similarly, all things that produce death—automobile crash, swallowed poison, bomb from an airplane, slip and fall—should have a common quality. They have: they all are lethal. This is manifestly definition by consequence; not by prior similarity, of which there is none. Thus Bell's term is no more than a label. The old witchcraft won power over a thing by naming it; apparently onomagic still holds potent sway. Nor did it ever occur to Clive Bell to explain of what this form is significant!

Reproducing an ovoid Tang statue, Wilenski comments:

> From the modern sculptor's standpoint this Tang statue is essential sculpture in that it has the meaning of a permanent universal form—the egg; and the linear treatment of the drapery is approximated to painted decoration on the form. The modern sculptors are not concerned with the other meanings which this statue may have had a thousand years ago. From their standpoint those other meanings are of no service because they regard them (a) as nonsculptural and (b) as dead; whereas the meaning of the statue's form is still alive.

This would be a quest of the essence in its ultimate material manifestation: form for form's sake, the cubicity of the cube. It grows dangerously near, however, to a reversal of Galsworthy's description, showing the outside with the innards left out. The form is of value to us because we know the content. How an egg would collapse in our estimation if we suddenly spied a hole through which it had been sucked dry! An empty shell! Wilenski's error is revealed in his saying that the sculpture *has* the meaning. It *holds* the meaning. It is not the oviform that is symbolic, but the seed of all life that it contains. Again the principle of polarity reminds us: form and content are distinct though inseparable. Wilenski's blunder is to ignore the distinction; ultraism's saving grace is their inextricable hold. The tortoise time has clamped its jaws. Thus in the Tang figure we perceive the essence of Buddha, the serene contemplation that is the Oriental ideal. Thus in Brancusi's *Golden Bird* we behold not the mere cigarroid metal but the essence of upward impulse, the naked urge to fly. Thus beneath the ultraist structures we may discern the fundamental rhythms, harmonies, forces, that join all things of a class, all classes, all things, in common origin and end.

TRENDS IN LITERATURE

In music, we may not all have attuned our ears to the new language of the modernists; but we long ago freed ourselves from a range limited to sounds of events in nature. In sculpture and painting, however, with few exceptions down the ages we have wanted a resemblance on the canvas, in the statue, to things seen around. And the law court, the seed catalogue, have so accustomed us to linking words and meaning that it has never dawned upon many that in art other linkages may serve.

8. God faces both ways.

F̲EW persons are born linguists; most others trouble to learn only such tongues as are thrust upon them. The majority, therefore, continue to look upon the ultraist works as freaks. It is likely that their chief permanent effect, as with *Ulysses*, will be to open to the less experimental artist new devices and elements of form. Their eccentricity rouses a critical storm; in the after-calm, somewhere the rainbow shines. The work itself has meanwhile been roundly damned. Commenting on Wilenski's list of sculptors, Frank Jewett Mather, Jr. in his *Modern Painting* emphatically declares that if the hope of the art lies in such men, then the case of sculpture is desperate indeed. Of the ultraist program, Mather observes:

> Against this austere, not to say pedantic, oversimplification of a really delicate and complicated matter, let me set the old humanistic and commonsense argument, that style is generally a byproduct of an endeavor for something else—truthful representation of something lovingly and admiringly observed, desire to communicate a choice experience to a fit spectator— in short, that the great artist, while naturally studious of the technical problems of his craft, is equally concerned with experiences which he shares widely with his fellows, and finally that the great artist normally proceeds from the particular to the universal, and rarely if ever from one kind of universal to another—Mr. Wilenski's program. What we actually have in the heterogeneous modern sculptors selected for praise by Mr. Wilenski is so many sorts of mannerism. Save for Epstein, who is great, or nearly so, only when he is offending all Mr. Wilenski's formulas, we have merely the parading of virtual no-

bodies—at best of eccentric talents—to illustrate a set of hard principles which they by no means consistently follow.

Such, however justified in any particular case, is the constant cry raised against those that have blazed new paths on beauty's quest, by crickets (as Sancho Panza calls them) unwilling to acknowledge or unable to understand the serious purpose of the adventurers. There is some justice in the general protestation. Along these uncharted ways troop the professional rebels, men who, without comprehending the new, proclaim it because it's agin the old. Here struts the self-parader in preened exhibit. Here, in novelty's guise, beckon the playboy and the charlatan. What foolhardy judge will pronounce this spurious, this sincere? A greatly praised painting was made by the swish of a donkey's tail. A canvas hung upside down won a coveted prize. *Spectra*, a volume of verse by Morgan and Knish, launching a poetic school, was confessed a hoax by Witter Bynner and Arthur Davison Ficke. The distrust that rises from failure to understand is multiplied by the deeper though less formulated uneasiness roused by an attitude that calmly wipes away man's assumption of supremacy. Such facts, fancies, and feelings rouse, in the majority of those at all concerned with art, a righteous sense that these ultraists are at best queer fellows. They may be tolerated, of course, in the confraternity of the artist, but on condition that they be not taken seriously. The serious avenues of man's expression today are reserved for the humanist. Walking the known ways, he shows seldom the mountebank, though often the mediocre. Genius makes its own paths, even on trodden roads. But in the battle that is eternally waged within the soul of man, the humanist is on the side of the angels.

Some persons that delight in bludgeoning the humanists are their close kin. Many a disease germ is cousin-german of the bacterium that devours it. The late popularity of H. L. Mencken, the early vogue of Burton Rascoe, the réclame of Alexander Woollcott, indicate that these were spokesmen of a group, whose opinions and attitudes they partly formed and vigorously expressed and emphatically elevated. The humanists, sometimes more suavely, do the same; save that they represent another, a longer established, body of opinion. Paul Elmer More speaks for what in England would be the aristocracy; the three just named made vocal the newly arrived middle class, whereof the culture and breeding have not kept pace with the prosperity and comfort. Those that cannot picture themselves as imposing, try imposition. Lacking grace, they strut their insolence. Their open condescension betrays their secret envy. Not only in collected *Americana* and other writings is this attitude exposed; it has become a way of living in certain theatrical and cinematic circles. The celebrity in the play *The Man Who Came To Dinner* flings indiscriminate indignities; he calls his faithful nurse "Miss Bedpan"; through an evening of continuous insults the audience roars with laughter, each wishing that he could thus floor his acquaintances.

It has been remarked that a gentleman is equally at ease with a monarch and a tramp. Mencken, in his anthology of "booboisie" stupidities, and elsewhere, spends a deal of time exposing to laughter those that have not risen to his literate level; Rascoe, especially in *Titans of Literature*, from a lower station shoots at greater targets. Mencken at least has a bludgeon in his style, a broadsword in his language; the expression of Rascoe is worthy of his thought:

> Meredith, anxious to forget that his father was a tailor, wrote a book about dukes and duchesses and about a brilliant aristocracy which had no more relation to the facts of that aristocracy than a *chanson de geste* had to the exploits of a feudal plunderer; and he endowed that aristocracy with a wit and intellectuality in conversation which is to be found only among intellectual Jews—which is to say Jews without money . . . Henry James' idea of culture was that of a prim and not too bright finishing-school girl, and he never got out of it. Nevertheless he did have a cer-

tain undefined, unapprehended groping toward form; he said a few things with a certain hesitant grace; and in *Daisy Miller* and *What Maisie Knew* he wrote two novels almost as profound as *Gentlemen Prefer Blondes* by Anita Loos . . . His highbrow fame rests upon a critical acceptance of the pompous and pathetic social values he placed upon himself . . . "The *Divine Comedy* is like a forest of truth", writes Henry Dwight Sedgwick in his *Dante,* "in which a thousand men climb a thousand trees, and each man, as he mounts nearer toward heaven, fondly believes that he has chosen the poet's tree of life." The innocent incongruity of that image is the comical one presented to me by all the commentators on Dante who seek to perpetuate the fallacy that Dante is still worth reading. I see Matthew Arnold shinning up one tree, Macaulay up another, Carlyle up another, George Saintsbury up still another and so on and so on, no less than a thousand of them up a thousand trees, all jabbering about the ineffable beauties of a dreary catalogue of names and vices and about the "grand style" of a poem that, by any sensible standards whatever, is no more worthy of admiration than a carved replica of the Battleship Maine assembled inside of a bottle.

A thousand critics do not give him pause; he borrows assurance from less literate laughter.

Such writers as Mencken and Rascoe are aptly called iconclasts, image-breakers; the poet being an image-maker. But for the cruder group that delights in their display, that takes courage in their claim of superiority, such writers (as the humanists for their group) enact the role of "conscience": mentor and judge and sentencing voice. The humanist might say they are on the side of the devil. Both angels and devil presuppose God.

9. *Value arises.*

THE many currents in the ocean of print today, angels might fear to tread. No living man can walk these waves; fortunately, no thorough charting of that turbulent sea is here required. Any lesser survey, I am aware, in such a book as this, leaves the author open to the easy charge that he has proved his point by bringing forward only such works as press it. Thus, for an instance, Bernard deVoto on that ground attacks Mary Austin, William A. Orton, V. F. Calverton, Ludwig Lewisohn, and Lewis Mumford:

> By ignoring all parts of the past, all sections of the country and all Americans that contradict his thesis Mr. Mumford easily satisfied the requirements of his Golden Day. But it is the Golden Day of Mr. Mumford, not of America . . .

There can be no adequate answer to such a charge, save by the reader. From him the author must hope for unprejudiced perusal, with a mind receptive but questioning. He must watch that the quoted works be representative, and accurately aligned; he must check the adduced examples with others of his own summoning, allowing the author in unfamiliar fields the credit earned where he can best appraise the facts and figures; he must balance the author's conclusions on the scales of reason. Recognizing the difficulty and the obligation, let us glance at those great groups, and great writers, that in today's collective emphasis lay chief stress on man.

The writers most obviously concerned with the soul of man, with humanity's progress toward its ideals, are those whose work rests upon a basis of religion. The ultraist would explain this by saying that religion is the deification of man's fear. The dread of annihilation is soothed away by the erection

TRENDS IN LITERATURE

of an omnipotent deity pledged to man's immortal and blessed continuance. A typical ultraist attitude toward God colors the concluding poem in Isidore Schneider's *The Temptation of Anthony*:

> *Thus on the sky we read His mountain script*
> *and say "God" too. And let a storm parade*
> *to drumming trees and windblare and we're made*
> *Believers. The Unknown that we have gript*
> *And lost is our surviving mastodon.*
> *When weariness bends back our limbs and fear,*
> *Its jackal, turns the hunt on us, we rear*
> *And look to God, and to His covert run.*

Feeling such doubt and questioning in the world, Thornton Wilder made his novel *The Bridge of San Luis Rey*—a bestseller of its season—an explicit search for God's handiwork in the apparently accidental collapse of a bridge. Definitely, too, such writers as Maurras, Massis, Maritain and the other neo-Thomists, in France, assert the Catholic point of view. Jacques Rivière founded the *Nouvelle revue française*, in 1912, as an organ of the renaissance of the classical, the assured, values. In England that enthusiastic convert, G. K. Chesterton, and Hilaire Belloc, and lately C. S. Lewis, have been but the leaders of a large body that, in writing and in living, have reawakened the Christian way. T. S. Eliot has recoiled from the cul-de-sac of suicide to the refreshing arms of the church. Through reason's guidance or emotional need, or following the bright finger of faith, many more have worn a beaten track home to God.

The Broadway theatrical season of 1938-1939 showed a banner harvest of plays in which religion was the theme or the foundation of the drama. The Pulitzer Prize play, *Our Town*, with its last act beyond the grave. *Shadow and Substance*, voted the best play from abroad, a direct treatment of religious attitudes. *Murder In The Cathedral*—not a mystery play, but the story of Thomas à Becket; *Many Mansions*; *Father Malachy's Miracle*; *On Borrowed Time*; *Susan and God*. Religion

TWAIN TURMOIL OF TODAY

shines in homely piety through *The American Way* and *American Landscape*. It surges in the revival scenes of *Mamba's Daughters* and the Federal Theatre production *The Big Blow*. It smiles in the musical comedy *I Married An Angel*. It soars, direct and triumphant, in *The White Steed*. Judgment Day gives sentence in the final scene of the revived *Outward Bound*. And what a surprise awaits the spectator that judges only by the title, when he sees *Here Come the Clowns!*

The American theatre has indeed moved in this mood. Elmer Rice continuously studies the conflict of values in society. Though he does not directly center them upon religion, more often than most of his contemporaries he indicates (as in *Counsellor-at-Law*, in *Left Bank*, in *Two On An Island*) the good that can rise in the midst of the current evil. Philip Barry more searchingly examines, in successive dramas, one after another of the conflicts inherent in the social order, the sirens—of habit, conventions, wealth, love—that seduce man from his ideals. Then in *The Joyous Season* Barry points the way to triumph through faith. And in *Here Come the Clowns* he again strikes to the heart of the religious problem, symbolizing the conflict of God and the devil in the world today.

These two dramatists exhibit a coherence, a power of synthesis, lacking in their more prominent fellow-playwright, who soared to alas, temporary grace from earlier despair. Eugene O'Neill, although his constructive skill scantily bears him through a full-length drama (in compensation wherefor he writes much longer plays) and although he lacks that without which all is as a dull sounding in a void: poetry—has nonetheless, by constant and fearless experimentation, by a keen potency in analysis, and by an intensity of social (not personal) passion, achieved powerful symbols, though they reach out to inclusions beyond their grasp, and social studies that are also, though perfervid, moving dramas. It is the very extent of his embracing desire that in one way limits Eugene O'Neill. The Hairy Ape knows where he belongs; he is *steel*, he is *power*: "Everyting else dat makes de woild move, somep'n makes it

[299]

move. It can't move witout somep'n else, see? Den yuh get down to me." But he yearns toward that part of the world which excludes him, which he has but glimpsed; and it is only in death that there, "perhaps, the Hairy Ape at last belongs." In this existence of ours, which is a *Strange Interlude* between two long draughts of darkness, Nina Leeds is a more mathematically inclusive figure; we see the one woman joined in every possible relationship with the opposite sex: ideal dream-lover, father, husband, flesh-and-blood lover, boon companion, son. *Mourning Becomes Electra*, like a conscientious syntagmatist, rings all the changes on the Oedipus-complex, the Freudian incest impulse: while Mrs. Mannon is thus drawn only to her son, Lavinia is stung with desire of her father and her brother, Orin is avid for his mother and his sister. Here is inclusiveness indeed; yet from the fall of the house of Mannon ideals upsurge. In *Dynamo* the idealistic impulse leads the earnest son of the minister to build his hopes, which rest on science and mechanical advancement, into a rapt religion. That such an electrified creed proves insufficient, disastrous, marks O'Neill's advance, intense, almost grim (however heavy-footed) into the realm of the spirit. Here, in his "modern miracle play", *Days Without End,* he comes to God.

In this play John Loving, having lost his faith, careens through the substitutes of socialism, anarchism, Communism, the creeds of the Orient, Lao Tze, Buddha, to return and declare that man must build new goals on the recognition of a mechanistic world whirling toward nothingness. The promise of redemption that the love of a woman brings to him, he wrings to its tortured denial. His other self with the weapons of reason opposes faith; it stalks John as an ever-present ghastly masked figure, bearing rationalism as another mask over hate and fear. As the ultraist pictures faith as the tower raised by fear, so atheism is here shown as the trench dug by hate. And either point of view sees reason as the betrayer, wrung from its proper use to be the tool of hate and fear. By reason alone, the play indicates, man dies; through faith, he may be born again. Out of his anguish John cries: "There must be faith—somewhere." And when, before the cross that once had seemed a mockery, John's love is renewed as his faith is restored, the current of love sweeps over and saves his dying wife. His other self sinks vanquished, and John brings Lazarus to mind with the exultation of his final words: "Life laughs with love." Then, in *Ah, Wilderness*, O'Neill seemed, after the long nightmare, like a weary but waking Launfal, to find warmth, love, peace, God, at home.

There must be a deeply felt re-emphasis on religion if it shines from Hollywood. In the film *Brother Orchid* (1940) the gangster hero is in quest of "class". He finds it nowhere in the haunts of the wealthy, in the world outside; but it waits for him in the quiet monastery where, by precept and example, godly ways work weal in him. And, after a brief excursion into his former world, to right a wrong, the one-time gangster returns to the monastic warmth of God's abiding love. In swift upsurge of warm public welcome, there followed the three excellent Catholic films, *Going My Way, The Song of Bernadette,* and *The Keys of the Kingdom,* steeped in firm faith and universal love.

Without the pointed pathway to a specific creed, many other works induce the same religious turning. Franz Werfel's *The Pure In Heart* urges against material disintegration of our times the ages' religious holdings. Less explicitly such books as Charles Morgan's *The Fountain,* as *The Good Earth* of Pearl Buck, rest on a sense of unquestioned spiritual values. Myriads, here unnamed, and of course most motion pictures, through these years keep burning such candles of faith.

In poetry, the love of humankind slips here and there into a humanization of man's friends among the beasts. Vachel Lindsay, in addition to his better known rhythmic bellowings: "Are you washed in the blood of the Lamb?" has written *Dirge For a Righteous Kitten, The Sun Says Its Prayers, The Old Horse In the City.* The pious mood of these is even deeper in the French poet Francis Jammes, whose *Prayer to Go to Heaven with the Asses* is an innocent picture of humility, in a gallery of faith.

Lindsay is, says Ludwig Lewisohn, the mystic poet of American Fundamentalism. There is a tone truly fundamental (though not merely American) in the poet's cry upon the youth of his day:

Not that they starve, but starve so dreamlessly,
Not that they sow, but that they seldom reap,
Not that they serve, but have no gods to serve,
Not that they die, but that they die like sheep.

From this point of view, the basic quality in poetry is a passionate belief. So great is the urge toward such a renascence of faith that what is of importance, says Lewisohn,

> What is of importance to the point of laughter, to the point of tears, is the proof offered by Vachel Lindsay that the poet must believe—even if he believes nonsense. And that again throws a lurid light upon the tragic difficulties of the poets who have minds and cannot believe. But any belief is evidently, from the point of view of sheer poetry, better than no belief, since it releases vision and music and the eternal child in the heart of man.

Lewisohn might pause to reflect that the object of one's loyalty or one's belief is of some slight importance. What one puts faith in may prove to be far worse than "nonsense". Many followers of Hitler were doubtless swayed by a very passionate belief! We may question whether what has been released in their hearts is what we like to picture as the eternal child!

This need of belief, nonetheless, has led others than Lewisohn to hail its appearance, despite the quality of the ideas believed. Eda Lou Walton, we have seen, cried approval of the English poets that leapt from the waste land into Communism. Similarly she declares that Horace Gregory marks a turning-point in American poetry because he believes and can therefore "fuse deeply felt personal experience with social criticism." One might question whether social criticism is this basic a part of poetry's realm, and wonder whether Miss Walton remembers Lowell, Whitman, Amy Lowell, and the majority more. For this "turning back to belief" merely brings the comparatively few rebels into line with the long tradition that—despite radical forms and ultraist neighbors—has never deviated from the credent way. This majority is manifest in the advanced Harriet Monroe's anthology, *The New Poetry,* as well as in *Modern American and British Poetry* gathered by the more catholic Louis Untermeyer. Even the figs gathered from thistles by the glamorous young Edna St. Vincent Millay were seeded with ideals:

> My candle burns at both ends,
> It will not last the night;
> But ah! my foes and oh! my friends,
> It gives a lovely light.

In her *Renascence* the upsurge of the spirit is explicit:

> I know the path that tells Thy way
> Through the cool eve of every day;
> God, I can push the grass apart
> And lay my finger on Thy heart!
> The world stands out on either side
> No wider than the heart is wide;
> Above the world is stretched the sky—
> No higher than the soul is high.
> The heart can push the sea and land
> Farther away on either hand;
> The soul can split the sky in two
> And let the face of God shine through.

The most prominent of French Catholic poets of today, Paul Claudel, reasserts the doctrine that art is the guide to the better life. The "idealized imitation" of Aristotle, the thought of Oscar Wilde that life copies art, are blent in his emphatic cry:

> As if art were not the negation of life! As if poetry were not the negation of life! Men formulate as a dogma the doctrine that art ought to imitate life. Art has as its end the realization of that for which life gives us but preliminary sketches. Life is an album to thumb, a collection of subjects for inspiration; raw material, not model.

Equally moving toward universal values and high human ideals are many that avow no specific religious belief. They may move by the lonelier leapings of mystic vision or personal inspiration or poetic transport. One of the earliest works of the poetic leader of the Irish renaissance, William Butler Yeats, is a dialogue between Anashuya and Vijaya; the Orient is not far from the Celtic fairyland with which he covers the Platonic core of the movement. He has said:

> Often at evening when a boy
> Would I carry to a friend—
> Hoping more substantial joy
> Did a nobler mind command—
> Not such as are in Newton's metaphor,
> But actual shells of Rosses' level shore.
> Greater glory in the sun,
> An evening chill upon the air,
> Bid imagination run
> Much on the Great Questioner;
> What He can question; what, if questioned, I
> Can with fitting confidence reply.

Many indeed of the Europeans—Herman Hesse; Franz Kafka, in his allegorical novels; Romain Rolland—draw from the Orient their doctrine of healing and wholeness. In *Die Nachtwache*, by Waldemar Bonsels, the "nightwatch" is the unresting, unconscious stir of daily existence out of which only exceptional men can emerge, and these as by grace, by a something beyond and above them. This grace is a social product, an embracing power of love; and in the novel (note the names) it is the ideal woman Christa that leads Paul to salvation.

Romain Rolland in all his writings manifests his conviction that a social intention is necessary in art as in life. *Jean-Christophe* draws to its close with a sense of all-embracing emotion:

> Now all is one heart. The smile of the day and the night entwined. Harmony, the august marriage of love and hate.

And the novel ends with St. Christophe's struggle across the raging stream with a child on his back:

> "Here we are! How heavy thou wert! Child, who art thou?"
> "I am the day soon to be born."

In Rolland's next novel, *L'Ame enchantée*, the picture of a society through an individual, which worked in *Jean-Christophe* toward a Utopia of honest living, has been wrung by the war into a broader view of the evils of society, especially as erected upon the four corner-stones of the bourgeois world: conventional morality; the family; capitalist politics; and poverty. Rolland shows Annette, in her apparent compromise, genuinely serving a higher end; those around typify other responses, but "Marc rejected with fury all the movements of his generation, all the incoherence, frivolity, selfishness, cynicism; all the masks and lies of servility and impotence." The strain of the struggle tears him; but in the delirium of his fever he is found by Assia, a Russian whom suffering has led (like the chief figures of *Crime and Punishment*) to a new faith. Stripped of his ideals, shorn of hope, gelded of curiosity, Marc is brought back to life by this woman, whom we grow to recognize as the symbol of the enlightened cooperation of mankind, shedding upon the darkness of a moribund age the dawn-glow of the new society to follow.

Beyond the mystics we may view the misty, those whose assumption of standards and values is left in the unclarified background of common acceptance. Standards imply a knowledge of what is best; ideals presuppose a recognition of man's true goal. Many writers, without bending to the authority of faith (which, in this clouded universe, can alone light the way to these certainties) take some values for granted as universally human. They may in most respects follow the determinism that underlies Freud and Marx; yet in the movement of their works they endow mankind with a collective sense of direction and with free will to choose the way. Thus, an editorial in *The Thinker* states that the author of *An American Tragedy* "would object strenuously to being classed with the Humanists, though Mr. Dreiser has spent a lifetime searching for values that even the orthodox must desire to place in his scale." Nor is there any doubt that such books as *The Genius* and *The Financier* attempt to indicate general conditions arising out of a social state, and in their sympathy and indignation press ideals.

At this point, however, a basic distinction must again be pressed. It is the humanist that "would object strenuously to being classed" with Mr. Dreiser. For his title indicates that this is not Clyde Griffith's but "an American" tragedy; the poor lad doesn't even know whether he is really guilty of murder or not; his conscience has dissolved into a squshy ooze of vacillation; and the reader is left to pity him, as a sorry victim of the forces of society, an example of what "life can do to a man." Clear away the slums and you clean the slum-dwellers' souls. Similarly, in Elmer Rice's *The Adding Machine,* blundering Mr. Zero, the befuddled man of today, tries to tell the jury what thoughts were in his mind before he murdered his Boss, gropingly himself seeking the causes, assuming that if they understand, they must pardon. To know all is to pardon all.— This identifying of explanation with excuse the humanists unflinchingly reject. Men of the highest spiritual integrity, contributors to human betterment in all fields, have grown out of the slums. Chicago produced both Scar-Face Capone and Carl Sandburg. The environment cannot be blamed for the blackguards; nor indeed are the majority of slum-dwellers foul with sin. On the other hand, the homes of the rich have produced full quota of self-seeking, sadistic, syncopating wastrels and destroyers. The contrariwise likelihoods have so often been the subject of satire that the humanitarians should by now have been laughed out of court, did they not deem the subject too serious for laughter. What matters, the humanist contends (rather, is content with affirming, as self-evident) is the individual soul-quality. Firm on a recognition of right and wrong that in its fundamental assurance is common to all, stands the individual, responsible for himself (to himself as well, but that is a lengthy story) in the selection of his course, in the deeds by which he makes his quality a factor in the life around. For in the current of our days we may be driven, but we need not drift; we may be overwhelmed in the swirl of resistless forces, but we need not choose to drown. Natural laws, as they summon each man to ultimate death, may sentence him to earlier defeat; but he may hold his head high if through the days of driven doom he has upraised, intrepid, the banner of human idealism, the integrity of a spirit attuned to mankind's lofty goals, the torch of the journey that has led his species up from the beast to the estate of man. Thus, in a collective age, the romantic vision of man as victor is transfused to humanism, that sees mankind upholding the human standard.

Many, to be sure, find less that is worth while, in living. Not trusting reason, and not finding faith, they lapse through fear into despair. This journey marks the personal failure of Eugene O'Neill, as recorded in *The Iceman Cometh*. Despite his agonized quest, faith did not hold. Returning, after a silence of twelve years, to the theme of his one, early short story and to the scene of his own slum days, O'Neill brings the iceman Death to a New York lower West Side saloon in 1912, amid a group of derelicts kept alive only in the stupor of drink and pipe-dreams.

What led to individual despair and suicide among the Romantics, however, our age has generalized into a universal urge. Freud, in *Beyond the Pleasure Principle*, presents as fundamental in everyone a drive of inertia toward death. A century and a half ago, the lemmings were adduced as an argument for Special Creation, as they were thought to be rained from heaven. Today, their legendary march to drown themselves in the ocean is frequently related—thrice in four months, in America's sophisticate magazine, *The New Yorker*—to give courage of companionship to the rootless ones in our time, as though there were a "lost generation" in nature. Like the men created in Freud's image, the lemmings are endowed with a "death instinct". John Masefield has likewise generalized the theme of Philip Barry's *The Petrified Forest*: in *The Lemmings* he too takes the animals as a symbol of the way in which we all "press Westward, in search, to death, to nothingness".

Nothingness seems the terminal of those that deny reason and lack faith. For with the failure of faith they slough also hope and charity.

Some do not yield without a bitter struggle. A number of writers picture a grim tug-of-war between mankind and inexorable natural laws. To his novel *Karl and the Twentieth Century,* Rudolph Brunngraber prefixes the words:

> "Politics are destiny." (Napoleon at the beginning of the nineteenth century.)
> "Economics are destiny." (Walter Rathenau in the twentieth century.)

He sees a world wherein the individual does not matter; but out of the general bitterness and gathering despair, the youth turn and cry *Heil Hitler!* as they would hail any promise of a saviour. Economic forces drive implacably to desperate ends. In the heart of such writing, however, whether in propaganda or in what calls itself art, snuggles the vision of a working-class solidarity than can, as it gathers self-consciousness, will to pit itself against these forces and by opposing bend them. From Hauptmann's *The Weavers* through Toller's *Masse-Mensch* and the plays of John Howard Lawson, this vision stirs. In the novels and tracts, including the universal history, of H. G. Wells, it becomes a prophecy if not a religion. Blent cynicism and science are brought to its support in the plays and prefaces of Bernard Shaw. In particular, Shaw's *Back To Methusaleh* envisages a world sprung to the ideal on the wings of the applied principle of the inheritance of acquired characteristics; there is a racial recognition, a basic gathering certainty of mankind, that only through individuals living long enough to grow really mature—say three or four hundred years—can mankind learn, and achieve, humanity's true ideals: the recognition forms the racial will, which brings the fact.

In this country, Sinclair Lewis, Upton Sinclair, and others before and after, less frequently builded Utopias than burnt bonfires to light Main Streets and Robot Highways, indicating their desire by what they detest. John Dos Passos, in *Forty-Second Parallel* and in 1919, is one that moves beyond a mere social sympathy and lashing of evils to a revolutionary zeal; and Waldo Frank, especially through *City Block* (as Lewis Mumford says) "expresses in aesthetic form those elemental

[308]

solidarities and interpenetrations which must serve as the substratum for a Communist political program." The stories of Sherwood Anderson, more sensitively than the wider canvases of Dreiser, convey the wonder of the individual as to his place in this collective world of ours, and (as in *Marching Men*) the gathering hope and confidence of the uniting workers. Then Sherwood Anderson returned to blend with the life of the countryside, to become one with the flow of America, which his last book, *Home Town,* attempts to depict. And Carl Sandburg paused in his work on the life of Lincoln to produce a volume entitled "The People, Yes!"

In all these writers, the ideals rest either upon religion or upon a less definite but equally firm faith in man's ultimate power for good. For most, that faith is unquestioned. Reason is rigorous. Its path is lined with pitfalls. Few have the patience to test, the skill and the endurance to traverse, that stony pathway.

Paul Valéry drives his essays and poems with the force of the intellect. "If I must write," he declares, "I had infinitely rather write a feeble thing thoroughly conscious and with entire lucidity of mind, than give birth to the most beautiful masterpiece by grace of a trance or of something outside of myself."

Valéry's compatriot, André Gide, in his essays and novels emphasizes his concern with those actions that are impelled from the viscera: somatic impulses, beneath and beyond reason, stir in the individual the universal command. Yet in the works of Gide as of Valéry an active intelligence moves; the humanist emphasis on values of course does not require absence of thought. The novels of Galsworthy, with painstaking concealment of the author's pains, present their wide survey of society; nor does the deep sympathy that pervades *Of Human Bondage* weaken Maugham's understanding. Not for long would such men move from the tang and tasks of earth:

*It's when I'm weary of considerations,
And life is too much like a pathless wood*

*Where your face burns and tickles with the cobwebs
Broken across it, and one eye is weeping
From a twig's having lashed it open,
I'd like to get away from earth a while
And then come back to it and begin over.
May no fate wilfully misunderstand me
And half grant what I wish and snatch me away
Not to return. Earth's the right place for love:
I don't know where it's likely to go better.
I'd like to go by climbing a high birch tree,
And climb black branches up a snow-white trunk
Toward heaven, till the tree could bear no more,
But dipped its top and set me down again.*

It is from the blending of the two qualities of understanding and sympathy—questioning and faith—that art must rise; as in all periods, whatever the initiatory impulse, the works make manifest. The humanist may move either emotionally or intellectually, to his presentation of values in humanity's climb. If it seems that most of our writers are thus ranged with the humanists, now as in any age most men will naturally stress the human role in the world. The essence of humanism, I repeat, is an emphasis on the collective, not the individual but society, mankind—this indeed characterizes all our day; and beyond this an insistence on man's difference from other creatures, in that he is equipped with a soul, or a conscience, a sense of values, a knowledge of good and evil: with this, through the collective will, man may determine the direction of his days. Such a point of view will naturally be in favor. The thoughtless hold it without knowing. Those that build on faith make it their cornerstone. Already the vast majority are enlisted. They are reenforced by many that build with bricks of reason. From this last group, almost exclusively, the ultraists are drawn.

One of the new-sprung activities of our day is "propaganda analysis". It seems to rest on the assumption that Americans are amoebas, to be pressed into the shape of the shrewdest and most potent propaganda. Everything that is presented to us must therefore be analyzed, to detect the tricks of the purveyor. Once his wiles have been exposed, we are immune. The tendency of such a drive is to equate all propagandists, hence all ideas, all values. The ultraist, along his different pathway, does the same. To substitute nature's law for human will, with a future inevitably determined by the past, is to render all conduct indifferent, to make morality meaningless, to reduce human plans to empty mouthings. Perhaps reason tells that they are. If so, most persons will reject that end of reason. Thought is a tool; we'll use it when it serves.

Most persons feel that they have a right, in looking at the world, to form their own opinions. Democracy rests on the assumption that such opinions are valid in the main. I. A. Richards, limiting his range, says that "to set up as a critic is to set up as judge of values." The same prerogative is really taken by all that live.

Values may be sought by the intellect, but must win the emotions. Understanding, and love. The eternal truth, and the everlasting mercy—burgeoning from

> ... *the winds that blew,*
> *The rain that makes things new,*
> *The earth that hides things old,*
> *And blessings manifold.*
>
> *O lovely lily clean,*
> *O lily springing green,*
> *O lily bursting white,*
> *Dear lily of delight,*
> *Spring in my heart agen*
> *That I may flower to men.*

Here we stand.

THUS flow the four great streams toward the classical garden.

When events order, realism exhibits the victims; romanticism displays the heroes. When the essence reigns, humanism sets anthropocentric, therefore moral, standards; ultraism seeks the bared core of all things. The romantic and the humanist, concerned with man, tend to link the beautiful with the good; the realist and the ultraist, intent on the wide range of actuality, bind rather the beautiful with the true. Whatever the alliance of those that give theory voice, the work of art creates the trinity. For always these are turbulent stormings, with spindrift wake of beauty, it may be, but clouded from the concordant calm, the harmonious sun, of the clear-skied classical work. True art arises in any period, from either point of view approaching the center, suggesting the universal within the individual, or out of the abstract and the general leading us to ourselves. It is this ultimate union of the one and the many, this precarious capture of the ever-shifting harmony of the ego and the world, that gives the work of art its permanent hold upon the human mind and the human heart.

ART ABIDES

Art abides.

HERE were our task done, save that humanity seeks ever in terms of values. Having pictured the generations bound, as in tidal flow, between individual concern and emphasis on the collective good, one is drawn to question which is the flood and which the ebb of that eternally restless sea of life, what flotsam and jetsam the tides carry, what strands they cover or expose. Should a man hold firmly, even unto death, to the integrity of his individual will; or should he be ever ready to recognize a higher good, to subordinate his desires for the betterment of mankind, to die, if need be, for God and country, for the State?

Inquiry might be checked by the thought that every age will assume the attitude most suited to its quality. In pioneering days, for example, the rugged individualism that drove men forth built our mighty land; but in the industrial age that has succeeded the era of conquest, cooperative endeavor is essential, not only to manufactories and trade, but also to humanity's well-being. Such a consideration, however, may be no more than a post facto reading of inevitability into history's pages. Surely there was the cooperation at least of bountiful hospitality, among the far-scattered pioneers; surely the early communities survived through no single-handed efforts; and perhaps a fuller measure of collective enterprise would have brought sooner, or richer, or more widespread harvest. Nor are there today lacking, in every field (Robert Frost is one distinguished spokesman), the defenders of the emphasis on the individual. While one need not engage in the frequent though futile game of speculating as to what the world would now be like had Grouchy been on time at Waterloo, one should equally refrain from the easy error of assuming that, because a series of events has culminated in a particular climax, has been marked by a certain mood, that ending and that attitude are the only, or even the most appropriate, possible products of the earlier happenings. It is (again futilely) quite arguable that the first four years of reconstruction after the Civil War would have left this land more wholesomely developed, had Lincoln lived to guide them: individualism and the pioneer, human betterment and the cooperative commonwealth need not be inseparable connotations. We must learn to apply, in our consideration of oft-linked terms, what Remy de Gourmont has aptly called the dissociation of ideas.

To consider the past with such a dichotometric eye would be an academic exercise, or at best a dramatic game of "If I could do it over"—with the likely repetitive results pictured in Barrie's *Dear Brutus*. Such a gaze looks down no dusty halls, however, but deep into the dark abysms of man's progress, when it turns upon our present courseway to the future. The choice among the political philosophies a man will make today —to mention but one aspect of required action—will depend largely upon the emphasis he lays on the individual or the collective good.

Here again, unfortunately, inquiry beats upon a wall. This barrier, moreover, seems unbreachable, and never by us to be climbed; for to the scaling must be summoned wings that can outstrip time. In order to determine whether the good of one ought to be sacrificed when necessary, for the good of all, we must first know what is the highest good. To recognize this *summum bonum,* we must have at least a glimpse of man's ultimate destination. This future haven and earthly heaven we can chart only with the implements of science—unless we move with the pen of faith. Though we hazard what we hope are increasingly close approximations, complete scientific apprehension of the universe is still far off. The recently applied wonders of electricity, the unimaginable powers released (so far for destruction only) within the atom, the newly discovered roles of allergy and sulfanilamide and vitamins—to say nothing of the conflicting theories drawn from the self-same facts—warn

ART ABIDES

us against building, upon man's present knowledge of the universe, any more than tentative system of human politics, ethics, and ideals. The pen of faith, on the other hand, while no longer tipped to a goose-quill, has been too prone to spatter, and spatter blood. Nor is there any sound method—neither longevity, nor appeal, nor number of adherents—of ascertaining the comparative values of diverse conflicting faiths, and of the ethical codes pronounced by their gods and their sages. It has not been established, save by the tender reasons of the heart, that the pity of which the Greeks wished to be purged, and which curls at the core of Christianity and of our social system, promotes man's well-being more than the stern Spartan virtue, or the ruthless drive of the Nietzschean superman. The means by which man must move ahead are not yet matters of fact; they remain questions of policy. Such questions are unanswerable in scientific terms, until at least three preliminary researches, into the actuality of free will, into the physico-chemical roots of biology, and into the biological background of ethics, have been successfully carried through.

On the unlighted road into the years ahead, man must in the meantime make faltering advance. We are faced, proponents of programs are fond of reminding us, not with a theory but with a fact; while we question and quibble, cast about and pendulate beyond all certainty, life pokes us impolitely in the rump. Prodded, we leap. Where do we land? Many things combine to determine. The personality; the conditioning environment. Is one but the consequence and sign of the other? Is a person swept in concord with, or rebellion against, the age? The argument is endless, and here irrelevant. What is presently pertinent is that the individualistic and the collective attitudes can summon equally cogent, and equally inconclusive, arguments. A man (because of his background or his temperament or their interaction) first embraces one of these attitudes, and only secondly calls forth invincible array of persuasory collocutions. *Sum, ergo cogito.* He believes because he is. Hence it comes that political and sociological discussions are often heated and always unconvincing, leaving each disputant to wonder whether the other can possibly be sincere, can possibly be blind to what is as plain as a barn wall beside him. Hence, also, the frequent resort to force.

Yet all agree upon the goal. Beyond the darkness of the nearer journey shines the beacon of the desired end. All parties, all creeds, join in the enunciation of the one ideal. The dilemma is very simply resolved: as recently by a veterinarian with an actual bull, its two horns are patted together and made to grow as one. The human ideal, so obviously as to shame utterance, is the maximum of individual freedom with the maximum of social good.

This ideal will be achieved when the dream of anarchism comes true. Man will live without laws; no monitory Thou-shalt-not will be brought down to enjoin restraint. Everyone will do just as he pleases—but will be pleased to do what will allow everyone else equal freedom.

All other forms of government are admittedly make-shift stop-gaps, to render living in society possible until the realization of that dream. Democracy hopes to train man for self-government; this implies self-imposed law, obedience to which is freely given. Socialism announces that on the firm substructure of social equity the individual spirit will erect ever greater monuments of human freedom. Communism protests that the dictatorship of the proletariat is a temporary regime, to be deposed as soon as practical by the rule of one ubiquitous working class, whereunder all will be free for the spirit's ripening. Fascism likewise "faces the facts" with an imposed leader, because the people are not yet fit to govern themselves. Until the happy day of human perfection, indeed, a good argument might be made for government by a benevolent despot. If we make the trite discovery that the benevolent are seldom despots, nor despots often benevolent, we may think of aristocracy, rule by the best. Even then, we must be certain we can recognize and secure the best. A literacy test, for example, makes the explicit false assumption that ability to read has a positive relation to intelligence, and the implicit false assumption that intelligence is allied with desire for the general good. And beyond all the rulers, however chosen and however good, range the many minor posts that must be filled by the not so good, in the pyramid of bureaucracy. And still there lurks in the mind the benevolent mother that told her children not to go into the water until they know how to swim. Democracy, as the process of learning to swim in the water, can also find staunch defenders; but in the press, without a teacher or a helping hand, a goodly number are pushed under or sink, and drown.

In life, then, the ideal combination slumps to a compromise. Sometimes with greater sacrifice of individual liberties, sometimes with a weakening of the collective ties, always the truce of living relinquishes good at both ends. Always each individual must yield part of himself, nor gain the broad communion. Save by grace: within the folds of religion there are those that by giving all have gained all, themselves and the Lord besides. But these saintly ones seem apart from the earthly urge of society. While it might prove humanity's salvation to walk their hallowed way, they have constantly, to win such freedom, renounced the world—the world which is the present if not the only battleground of mortal striving. In the practical stir of human affairs, the best most men can hope for is a neighboring of the golden mean.

Though this may always glister, too often it is mean. Once compromise is accepted as inevitable, it veers toward justification of the immediate desire and the most available means. While the sincere bigot may feel that the end justifies the means, the compromiser begins to shrug his shoulders at the ideals. The downright, the robustious, of all ages, have naturally scorned the middle course.

Many words, and with measure of reason, have nonetheless been spoken for compromise. If men were to live a wholly individualistic life, they would be as the herdless beasts in the trackless forests, huddling in single families perhaps, or joined but in the mating season; while if the race were bound in a thoroughgoing collectivism, it would be even as the swarm in the ant-hill, with serried ranks of specialized robots. We owe our more adaptable growth to the fact that our history has been traced along varying degrees of the compromise.

The basic evils in our lives we come upon, or we tend to justify, by the extremes. It was in the name of individual liberty that there were preached the world's enslavements; save when they were demanded for the sake of the country and its gods. Individualism brings in its train *laissez-faire,* and the practice that might makes right. In the name of the collective good, dictators and minorities not only in our day have imposed their wills upon the multitudes.

In each age, one of the twain attitudes finds fuller expression, in science, industry, politics, ethics, art. To it, all the ills of the time are attributed by those that in ameliorative ardor burn for the other extreme. The sensitive young Romantic was overburdened with the world; he stumbled, fell upon the thorns of life, and bled; then he sought balm for his wounds in a disregard of all social and conventional restrictions, trampling heedless over hearts and bodies on his anarchic questing. The sensitive young Communist beholds the great captains of industry grinding human bones, not, as the ogres of old, for bread, but for the gilt frosting on the cake of their content, which they may nibble and then crumb into philanthropies; being individually helpless in this collective world, out of his ailment the young zealot prescribes for humanity—and if you don't relish the medicine, he'll hold your nose and pour it down your throat—all, as once the Grand Inquisitor, that you too may be of the community of the saved. Each, despising the middle course, taking note of only the antithetical element in the compromise, bolsters his hopes with the promised panacea of the other extreme. Dimly beyond that he senses, he proclaims, the ultimate ideal: after the dictatorship, the fuller freedom. But now we must fight, he cries, for the extirpation of the evil. Thus men constantly act as though the individual and the col-

ART ABIDES

lective are mutually exclusive, irreconcilable. The new interpretations of religion, and the green psychologies, pay homage to this irreducible polarity.

Compromise, to many, bears undertone of weakness; recall T. S. Eliot's dismissal of its path. In an effort to escape the term, some prefer to speak of our days as a field of tension, wherein our deeds take shape from the opposed tuggings, as iron filings form a pattern from the positive and the negative pull of a magnetic field. Life is electric! This figure, however, though it may sound more pleasant, in the scientific tone of today, actually reduces men even more, to the impotent subjects of external powers. And, picturing our position as determined by the comparative strength of competing forces, it has merely set in an image the same unescapable compromise.

Whencesoever the theories twine, in all the tangles of daily life we must walk the middle way. Our days hold to the mean; in attempting to fortify man through a union of his two concerns, they achieve only that compromise, abandoning now more of the individual savor, now more of the essential core, but always sacrificing something of both, always (under varying degrees of protest) accepting living at a loss.

Save only in art.

It is the glory and the mystery of art that there alone, thus far of man's most striving, the irreconcilable ends are fused and glow with strange concordant power. Conflicting passions are harmonious grown; reason and emotion are together roused; the one and the many, the individual and the universal, are revealed, not opposite, not side by side, not intertwined, but blent in a chemical, a spiritual, union where each by yielding itself is reborn, itself and something more—where the breathed-on water is wine, and the tasted wine is blood of God—in the precarious capture, the exhilarant harmony, of the work of art. Hence wells the eternal power of the work of art, that in it man finds, or feels, this union of his two primal impulses, this leap to the elsewhere unattainable ideal, wherein both human emphases—individual freedom and collective concern—gain equal potency and fulness, and soar to tense yet quiet beauty. In all the wide ranges of human activity and intercourse, this is the condition of full and final achievement; within the present grasp or glimpse of human limitations, realized only in the compassless realms of art.

OTHER FIELDS

Our Conglomerative Age

BEYOND Victorian compromise and Symbolist fusion, our age stresses the social, the national, the universal, the essence not the individual, not the many facets but the single core. As always, and in every field, this attitude takes color according as man is regarded as one with all other things, or is held as a being apart. Here are examined some of these manifestations in other fields, **as well as art.**

OTHER FIELDS

1. *We take the plunge.*

AT the start of this century, the Ariel-minded sought to lift man on the wings of his ideals. An all-embracing brotherhood was to work with a universal language through international ideals to world peace. In the meantime the Caliban-conscious, the practical men of affairs and the diplomats, for the sake of their nations wove secret alliances about the throats of the trusting. They knew that words of the war to end war, to make the world safe for democracy, were pretty pictures to snare the idealist, who (like Caesar) never did ill thing save for good cause. Thus the fourteen fine conditions of peace set by Woodrow Wilson were like diamond points pressed against amoebas. With single-minded wariness, the diplomats gave way only to bulge and bulk all around; they held by yielding and flowing back as pressure waxed and wanned. Thus World War I gave us the shell of a World Court. And broken faiths, and a sense that the idea of progress is a poisoned lollypop.

The young men that had shouldered arms marched home defeated. The aftermath of war is a spiritual retreat. Some of the soldiers, in a romantic self-concern, brooded over the horrors of the conflict and its deadening consequences. In memoirs and other books of the War they poured forth true incidents beyond the shivery shocks of jaded or morbidly sadistic imaginations. Modern scientific warfare is beyond exaggeration. Others of the war generation, left somehow alive, felt that they were living "on borrowed time." Their high hopes had been shell-shocked; their idealism, gassed. The optimism of an H. G. Wells seemed the echoless cry of a happy lunatic over a waste land. These lost souls hid from themselves in drink, debauchery, and over-tardy death. The less vigorous mooned into a murky Hamletism, vainly (like David in Soupault's *A la dérive*) seeking something to which to attach themselves, isolate misfits, square pegs of a rounding generation.

Along with those thus rendered hors du combat, the period retreated, snuggling to any spurious comfort. Infantile manifestations increased; still today, adults incapable of looking full at life open their tabloids first to what in some dim hope they call "the comics". Of the postwar decade Alice in her Wonderland was a frequent symbol. Charlie Chaplin reached out to the mature through the child in us. Anita Loos, conversely, showed the naive within the adult. Numerous radio programs still indicate the childish level of our entertainment. Popular songs—"A tisket, a tasket"—drew their themes from Mother Goose; bands played "boogie-woogie" for mental babies. At the New York Winter Garden, sedate business men left their wives, at the chorus girls' invitation, to step into the aisle, clap hands with the chorines, gently bump hips, and roguishly cry "Boomps-a-daisy!" The faithful spouse applauded her husband's skill.

More maturely, as minutely with Proust, men delved into the hidden chambers of the past. By whatever means, they must not look ahead. Live in the moment only, or look back. Adolescent sophisticates therefore whirled glinting through life and the pages of F. Scott Fitzgerald, gulping the instant's champagne. In less untutored cloaking of despair they fulgurate in Philip Barry's *Hotel Universe*. The sense of vainly seeking forever lost goals haunted the young *déraciné*, the *heimatlos*, the expatriate. They nursed a nostalgia for the shores of the ideal. Like wraiths they linger in the pages of many books: Kaestner's *Fabien, Bankruptcy* by Pierre Bost, Moravia's *The Indifferent*—of which the hero wants "some goal, even a false one": anything to end the aimless drift of life. Later, as in the cry for belief, even if in "nonsense", that wish comes out of the books.

Out of this waste land many have clutched at supports. T. S. Eliot has climbed to secure authority and single guidance, in aesthetic as in religious universal law. The conclusion of Barry's *Hotel Universe,* beyond a mystic application of Freudian theory, points toward a new recognition of a central pur-

OTHER FIELDS

pose and value in life. The youth of Russia are working toward the salvation they are told waits in a world union of soviets, with the individual straitly bound to his social duty. In equal bowing of the many to the one, Germany strove to create the legend of a pure race, a single strain of thoroughbred Aryans, to dominate the world. There is, allowing for all compulsion, a voluntary march of millions, wherever headed and however misled, in the totalitarian lands. The vote, the voice, is not so much forced as persuaded. Their *Duce,* their *Fuehrer,* their *Comrade-in-Chief,* are less personal heroes than the symbol of their ends. These leaders made believe—made the nation believe —that they would lead it beyond deliverance to glory. Fascism, said its chief English advocate, Lord Oswald E. Moseley, "above all rests on teamwork, the readiness to sacrifice every interest of person or section to the nation as a whole." Every American that has had contact with sports knows the strong appeal in words about team play. This sense that it is highly meritorious for each to give his best, to give himself, for the success of the team (or nation) is thus no poison spreading from one foul source, but a natural outgrowth of our age's emphasis. The problem of racial groups rises wherever men herd in "races". "The white man's burden" grows heavier year by year. If he does not let it learn to walk alone, some day it may crush him. Yet Madison Grant, in *The Conquest of a Continent,* makes a vigorous appeal for the preservation of a Nordic, Protestant America. Henry Fairfield Osborn echoes that call, describing this strain in the population as a precious heritage we should not impair or dilute. Meanwhile "the chosen people" wistfully rebuilds its ancient home. In Spain, in broken France and rebounding England, more embracingly in Pan-American conferences and United Nation hopes—everywhere the feeling surges that "we must all get together", that each must be ready to make personal sacrifice for the general good. The trouble lies only in finding a common definition of the common good.

Ours, says that logical thinker Morris R. Cohen, is "an

age that has pushed the claims of the 'social' in all possible and impossible realms." He himself, however, pushes on the claims of our collective era, with the remark that a true synthesis of classic rationalism and the inspiring sweep of romanticism is "the great desideratum of our age".

Another of the communal fields is ploughed by that partly literary movement known as back-to-the-soil. Like Antaeus, these rootless ones try to gain strength from mother earth. The general agrarian stir is of course also economic, especially when in the United States the government decided to pay farmers for not growing cotton, not raising hogs. Its literary phase differs from the Romantic return to nature in that it seeks not solitude but social movement. It results in the study of folk-ways and the production of regional art. Percy Mackaye, Virgil Geddes, Erskine Caldwell are a few of the many that have grazed in these pastures. Thomas Benton is but one of the many artists that moved from New York back to their native hills. Onya Latour, once in charge of the New York City gallery of the Federal artists' project, opened a cooperative gallery on a farm in the middle west. Sherwood Anderson (almost like Anthony Adverse) settled down to be just one of the small town folks. If much of what these earnest folk discover is arid soil, ground sown out of harvest, dust-bowl land: under the rain of the artist's inspiration it may again prove fertile for spiritual growth. In the meantime, the people more widely grow aware of the physical needs of the land.

In other ways and many lands interest in the common people grew more widespread. The school of populism, especially in France, produced critics as well as novelists. Albert Clouard demanded the rejection of Freud, of writers who pick their souls as others pick their teeth. Leon Lemonnier in his manifesto hailed the refreshing return of the common man, after the snobbery of a Proust, the analytical immoralism of a Gide, the preciosity of a Giraudoux. There is in these populist writers none of the pessimism of the naturalistic novelists; many of them—though Barbusse mocked, and Eugene Dabit, as in

OTHER FIELDS

Hotel du Nord, rebelled—sought to refrain from taking sides in politics. But all of them—those named, and André Thérive, Pierre Hamp for industry, C. F. Ramuz of the peasants, F. Mauriac and more, and such as Alfred Doeblin in Germany, Nora Hoult in England, Frank O'Connor in Ireland—show a concern for the people, a feeling that society is rooted in the common man, that has given populism its name.

It must be recognized—as it was to be expected—that amidst this general chorus ring some discordant cries. Voices not interested in espousing one or another of the totalitarian drives rise against the ever more insistent hand of sovereign control. H. M. Tomlinson, beginning with a stern indictment of *Mars His Idiot,* rails upon the stultifying rule of the Moloch State. As though Hobbes had come to life in the machine age, the new Leviathan sees little good in government. The State, it avers, has as much selective care for mind as a mastodon. Eternal vigilance is the price of individual liberty, with the State always ready to sacrifice good sense for present power. Hilaire Belloc, in *The Servile State,* declares that socialism's unwitting goal is the creation of a permanent slave-class. More than one reports its growth in Russia.

Among the remaining exponents and exemplars of individualism thunders Benjamin De Casseres. His insistence on the personal discards even the common bond of logic. He too sees the State exacting its blood-sacrifices as of old, though called by curious new names; marching relentlessly toward an Automatism that will swallow the individual.

De Casseres joins the perennial few that hail Lucifer as the first individualist. Milton would have liked to join; Andreyev's *Anathema* sets him in the band. These rebels hail the arch-rebel as their champion. He catches in symbol the eternal struggle of the separate psyche against the collective forces that would herd each man into the fold. Keep step; conform. After all, life's problems are simplified not merely for the pastor, but for the docile flock. "The State will take care of you from the cradle to the grave," says De Casseres, "in return for which you become a robot."

Another individual holding out against the machine pressure to conformity, as deftly shown in his screen play *Modern Times,* is the astute genius of the films, Charlie Chaplin. Other voices occasionally rise. An editorial in the (London) *Times Literary Supplement* (May 12, 1945) declares that insistence on the rule of law is beginning to shift. Sidney Hook's *The Hero in History,* declaring that "outstanding figures so transcend their environment that they do not merely shape the issue of an event but ordain its occurrence," takes us back to Carlyle's *Heroes and Hero-Worship.*

While the tightening grip of the state does squeeze forth some protesting cries, it retains secure control. Not only is the current "ideology" completely social, but in many practical ways the state slips into the people's lives. Even in this country, increasing regulatory bodies force awareness of its power; but more, collective bargaining, unemployment insurance, old-age pensions, and other safeguards set by government fiat not individual charity—the immeasurable spread of "relief", then projects of the P.W.A. and W.P.A., the whole alphabetical spree of a drunken typographer—made countless folk welcome the protective hand of the state. There is, for many, deep comfort in such submission to security. Life's worries are tossed onto the back of that collective anonymity, the government. The pioneers fought for freedom; their grandchildren ask for freedom from fear. Let the State tell them a nursery story, and pat them to sleep.

The tension between the spirit and the letter of the law, which *The Times* (London; editorial in the *Literary Supplement,* Aug. 7, 1948) calls "a permanent quality in the soul of Europe", is another aspect of this polarity of the individual and the general. The law should be universal, the same for all; its regularity and predictability are essential for man's proper functioning. It should, at the same time, be flexible enough to allow for individual differences, for particular cases

OTHER FIELDS

and the persons involved in them. Between justice and legality, therefore, a tug develops—with a stronger pull toward the individual allowance or toward the juridical fixity, according to the tenor of the times. In our own period, generalization has carried so far as to establish the crime of "genocide", and for the first time in history, before killing the leaders of the vanquished, to try them for crimes "against humanity".—But war itself has likewise become all-embracing; there are no noncombatants, there are no neutral lands. Even in destruction mankind is reaching toward the universal.

In other regions, the unifying impetus is equally pervasive. Our city herding allows millions to take their exercise vicariously, eating "hot dogs" and drinking "soda pop" in "gardens", stadiums, arenas, watching a few indulge in violent conflict. Our recreations grow decreasingly active while increasingly collective. Cinema houses are not only more numerous than theatres, but larger. Golf, tennis, badminton, and bathing, it is true, crowd our beaches, courts, and courses; but more than all the players are the spectators even of these sports, and especially of boxing, hockey, and the ball games—base, foot, and basket —which bring a nation of fans to the bleachers and uncounted more to the radio. But even on the radio, even with television, their greatest thrill is in sharing the excitement, in rousing with the common roar of the crowd.

The radio, and the fence-boards of the athletic fields, remind us also of advertising, that helps drive into a mass collectivity the purchasing power of the nation. Useless commodities that all must use are drummed into our habits. Some industries owe their very existence to shrewd action upon the principle evoked in the comedy *It Pays To Advertise*. The most spectacular sights of New York's Great White Way are the block-long multicolored electric signs (one, especially vivid, of bubbling fish, five stories high upon a low roof, which irrelevantly named a brand of chewing gum). No woman along that Way would wear a dress unsanctified by the season's style chart. And even the lone cowboy on the far prair-ee drinks Coca-Cola with unnumbered millions more. The family is no longer the social unit. The factory sets the fashion.

The collective emphasis is manifest in architecture, not merely in the large-scale housing projects, public or private. The architect Paul Goodman states (*New Republic*, July 16, 1945): "In recent works on city planning . . . the main cry has come to be for general Integration—integration of living, work, culture, transportation, leisure, etc. . . . The great men proceed from a concrete integrating principle . . . The new integrators cry out for integration in the abstract."

In the less marketable realms of scientific pursuits, we find the same emphasis on general principles. The fields of greatest concentration and advance today are mathematics and stellar and sub-atomic physics. The whole history of mathematics, declares E. T. Bell, may be interpreted as a battle for supremacy between the two concepts of discreteness and continuity—which is the conflict this book presents on a wider scale. Discreteness is emphasized in the theory of numbers, in algebra, in—more specifically—analytical mechanics as advanced by Lagrange (1736-1813). Continuity is manifest in geometry (form vs. number) and in the applications of mathematics to science and industry. The abstract, completely general attack in mathematics was begun in the eighteenth century, but its adequate realization was delayed until our own, which has made the fullest use of the one universally intelligible language. The mathematics of the twentieth century differs significantly from that of the nineteenth, says Bell, because of "a marked increase in abstractness, with a consequent gain in generality, and a growing preoccupation with the morphology and comparative anatomy of mathematical structures."

Bell's language reminds us that even within the range most reliant upon individual observation, courses are given in "theoretical biology", and research increases in biochemistry and biophysics. There are even discussions of biomathematics, the final subjection of the experimental science to general law.

The chemist points out that (as in the glucose, dextrose,

OTHER FIELDS

fruit sugar group, $C_6 H_{12} O_6$) over seventy compounds may have one formula. The atom-bomb has publicized the isotope: various aspects but one element.

Chemistry and physics, indeed, have been spectacular in their success, both in advancing man's explanation of how nature works and in bending nature to man's will. They have consequently imposed their methods as tyrants over man's ways, and have largely impressed upon man's thinking their quest of, if not belief in, a central law. Lancelot Hogben's warning against the interference of the metaphysician (as the science popularizer scornfully calls the philosopher) shows that here, too, the paths are merging. Not only is the specialist reaching into other fields—Hogben defends the scientist by pointing out that the taxonomist must be a geologist, the geneticist must be a mathematician—but the interrelationships in themselves have become subjects of study. The water-tight compartments are being pooled. A group of scholars, over a period of years, has been issuing *The International Encyclopedia of Unified Science*. *The Journal of the History of Ideas* takes a similar coordination as its province. C. E. M. Joad declares (Hogben notwithstanding) that philosophy is the clearing-house of science.

It has more than once been suggested that, if persons opposed in argument were but to define their terms, they would find themselves in essential agreement. Never before, however, has the "science of meaning" been advanced as a general panacea for the ills of the world, as now in the "general semantics" of Alfred Korzybski. First intimated in his *Manhood of Humanity* (1921), then developed in his *Science and Sanity* (1933; 1941), as "a new extensional discipline which explains and trains us to use our nervous systems most efficiently . . . a new, non-Aristotelian system of orientation which affects every branch of science and life", this body of thought now boasts a school, an institute, a periodical (*ETC.*), and ardent disciples among teachers, doctors, dentists, lawyers, publicists, agriculturalists, who believe that "general semantics" provides the essential help for the troubled world, from the problems of "harmonious mating" to those that hold apart the United Nations.

Educational theory and practice have their share in the collective drive. Hogben, lashing out in several directions, attacks "experimental education" as having replaced braincraft divorced from handwork with handicraft divorced from brainwork. But the basic impetus of progressive education is the desire to create of the children a social whole, to fashion them as rounded and serviceable members of the community, who will enjoy "living together." Meanwhile, if school crowding has the individual desperately struggling to keep afloat, the cold hand of scientific method calmly drowns him in the mass. He is categorized and codified and listed by average and quotient in intelligence tests and reaction records of all sorts. Bewildered parents who want to know why their little Willie has such a low I. Q. are reassured (or further puzzled) by the statement that these results are valid statistically, in the aggregate, according to the "laws of probability," but without individual worth.

Psychology must prove itself a science by tagging along. The individual mind is probed for its unconscious orderings, for complexes and inhibitions and censors and taboos. Libido impulses are unearthed beneath socially ordained repressions. All these characterize the *Masse-Mensch* rather than the uniquely individual personality. Indeed, we are told that these all-pervasive qualities are best observed in the diseased. Psychoanalysis owes much of its appeal to its sex-exploitation (thus partly corroborating its claim!) and to the first-aid to authors it extends, far beyond any sanction of the philosopher and the scientist. But, in every variant sect, it seeks invariably for general tendencies that bind the generations and guide their common way—so that a man is individualized but by the chafing of his chains; while his actions are determined in what Jung calls "the collective unconscious." Others similarly picture the control of all conscious thought by "the social mind."

In ultimate unity, Einstein overpassed his formula of relativity and attained the great series of equations indicating the

OTHER FIELDS

harmonious conjunction of the electromagnetic and the gravitational fields, holding all space, time, energy, and matter, in single law. No alchemist-astrologer in his dream of the philosophers' stone ever dared so aweful a union! We hear, indeed, that the conversion of energy into matter has finally been traced in the laboratory, nature's greatest gap seen bridged.

What union yet remains? The scientist sticks to his last. But the wistful popularizers turn their expert eyes upon still alien fields. With electric eye they pierce the metaphysical mist, to assure us that manifestly somewhere "this universal frame is not without a mind." If radiation is the result of electronic orbit-jumping within the atom of matter, and if matter is the consequence of probabilities of concentration of energy whorls—what matter, since

> *Within this vast creation*
> *Of law and deep accord,*
> *These infinite pulsations are*
> *The throbbing heart of God!*

2. *He restoreth the soul.*

To be alive in such an age,
To live in it,
To give to it!
Rise, soul, from thy despairing knees.
What if thy lips have drunk the lees?
Fling forth thy sorrows to the wind—
And link thy hope with humankind—
The passion of a larger claim
Will put thy puny grief to shame.
Breathe the world thought, do the world deed.

THE philosophers and poets of a period that remain to posterity as its pride, are seldom the best evidence of its spirit. They survive, as I have said, precisely because they bear within them something more permanent than their day; they shelter their expression of the *Zeitgeist* within more solid walls of form. It is in the popularizers and the pamphleteers (and their contemporary offspring, the columnists) that a time's prevailing emphasis may best be seen.

But our age is hypochondriac. It is therefore self-conscious, prone to detailed self-analysis. The world seems sorely ailing; an era is at its death's door; propounded panaceas quack on every side. However they agree as to the virulence of the disease, no two medicasters concur in the diagnosis. Confused in their conceptions, they spend more time in detailing the symptoms, which abound, than in probing to their source. Or, struck with what seems a sovereign cure, they lump in a common condemnation all they deem wrong in the world today, and preach their one salvation. Pursuing our trail, we see that the main division still marks those that consider man as bound by natural law from those that hold mankind high above all else in creation.

OTHER FIELDS

This opposition is of course most evident in the contrasting views of science and religion, which nonetheless, it must be kept in mind, both today emphasize not the separate unit but a vast unity. The notion of a central essence brings one close to religion, which in times of collective emphasis is therefore likely to gain strength. In many portions of the world, this renewal of religious fervor is manifest. It appears in the form of conversions to Catholicism, of the Oxford movement, of adherence to an Aimee MacPherson or a Father Divine; it is implicit in the zeal of the young Nazis and Communists, who must have "some belief, even a false one." The most earnest testimony of faith-healing by Christian Scientists, the most pious abandoning of crutches before Sainte Anne de Beaupré, are paralleled in such declarations as that of Professor J. B. S. Haldane, that he was cured of serious gastric disturbances upon embracing Leninism.

"An attitude by our churches of unconcerned neutrality toward the State now belongs to the past!" thundered Reichsbischof Mueller on his election in Germany; "We must all give loyal service to the State." Similarly, when in 1945 Joseph Stalin admitted religion into the official Soviet scheme of things, the Moscow Patriarchy, in its decree to the Russian Orthodox Churches in the Americas, called for "abstention from political activities against the U. S. S. R." Contrariwise, Lambert Fairchild in New York organized *The National Committee for Religious Recovery* because of the feeling that even in this country worship of State was beginning to supplant worship of God. But apart from any political creeds, religion is in people's minds again, and in their hearts.

Science will relinquish none of its gains. It may apply its analytical method to religion itself, finding faith to be a consequence of primitive man's fears, with prayer the modern substitute for sorcery. Or religion may be dismissed—at least, Protestant Christianity—as a mere offshoot of romanticism, to which it tends to return. Conversely, romanticism is derided as "spilt religion", leaving the overflow to muddy the gutters of the spirit. But most writers on science, save in casual references, refrain from such attacks. They either content themselves with exalting the power of science, or in the collective tone of the age link its control with faith.

> There may be millions of different points of view in the universe—each of which may be correct in itself, and each of which may measure true by all local observation—but there is an equation which blends all of these viewpoints into a standard that is universal.

Thus the father of relativity, Albert Einstein. He does not, however, bow to the concept of unbroken causality; for in physics itself the chain of law seems to break. The quantum theory, the concept of statistical probability—an event will occur once in say fifty times, but no one can tell which of the fifty will be the one: an idea long familiar in gambling, but now applied within the electron and thus at the base of life—and the Heisenberg principle of uncertainty, have undermined faith in the regularity of natural processes. But from this very element of accident (or is it choice?) Professor Einstein advances toward "the intelligence manifested in nature," and sees beyond:

> I am of the opinion that all the finer speculations in the realm of science spring from a deep religious feeling . . . Modern scientific theory is working toward a sort of transcendental synthesis in which the scientific mind will work in harmony with man's religious instincts and sense of beauty.

The psychologist might ridicule if not riddle this use of the word instincts. Indeed, many a scientist has declared that his fellows leap off their private docks into deep waters when they pronounce upon religion. But Einstein clearly does not subscribe to the present-day growth of the materialistic point of view, as enunciated, for an instance, by Dr. George W. Crile:

OTHER FIELDS

As radical researches have progressed, it has become increasingly evident that the phenomena of life, like the phenomena of the inanimate world, are dependent upon physical and chemical laws—that is, that protoplasm is not a specialized structure requiring special laws for its control. Advancement in the biological sciences must, therefore, in the future depend upon the fundamental sciences of physics and chemistry. Already a rapid penetration into the mysteries of protoplasm has been made by the application of physical and chemical laws, and we may believe that this advance will not stop until we are able to define, simply and clearly, what a living thing is and the principles by which it is governed . . . In the advance of the frontiers of medicine along these lines it has been necessary to get rid of mysticism, superstition and fundamentalism, not alone among laymen, but among scientific men themselves, as it was when they were confusing religion and fatalism with science. Either protoplasm and the living beings constructed of protoplasm are mechanisms which derive their energy from the ordinary forces in nature, or they are not. The present trend of thought regarding the nature of protoplasm is strongly mechanistic and has been so especially since the strange medley of mysticism and mechanics has begun to be separated into its component parts.

Already we know that the phenomena of life are only phenomena of energy; already we know that all energy is interpreted by the known laws of physics and chemistry; already we know that no living thing can exist in the absence of chemical activity; already we know that drugs, anaesthetics, narcotics and poisons act upon the living molecule chemically and not mystically; already we know that bacteria are merely forms of protoplasm which are organized to attack this or that tissue as the result of adaptation; already we know that the interactions of the tissues are chemical and physical in nature; already we know that the agents that kill bacteria—the antitoxins—are purely physical and chemical; that growth and development are purely physical and chemical; that the ductless glands have the power of influencing chemical and physical processes in the body. All of these things we know already, and having these facts before us, we can predict with certainty the future trend of medical investigation.

Here is the challenge, flat.

Other voices in similar tones take up the cry. Taine earlier declared that vice and virtue are products, like sugar and vitriol. Seventy years later, Professor Norman C. Wetzel told the National Academy of Science that the growth of the human infant, of the chick in the egg, of bacteria, and of the toad, can all be expressed by the same mathematical equation.

In his study of *Nutrition and Physical Degeneration* (1940), W. A. Price declares: "Thinking is as biological as digestion." And Erwin Schrödinger (*What is life?* 1945) seeks to indicate that "the events *in space and time* (italics his) which take place within the spatial boundary of a living organism can be accounted for by physics and chemistry." We are, he believes, just beginning to acquire reliable material for welding together the sum-total of all that is known, into a whole. Waldemar Kaempffert (science expert of the *New York Times,* in *Science Today and Tomorrow,* Second Series, 1945) sees, in virtually every field of man's activity, an increasing mechanization, mass-production, standardization. Reminding us of the chemical achievement noted in Carlyle's remark that gunpowder made all men the same height, Kaempffert observes that the leveling process continues in all the other dimensions. In the sciences he finds an increasing tendency to consider man a complex of physical, chemical, and electrical forces. The problem of the gene, the basis of continuing life,

OTHER FIELDS

he sees as one with the problem of the atom. (This idea Schrödinger elaborates.) And Kaempffert quotes physicists (F. G. Donnan; L. L. Whyte) as looking toward the creation of life in the laboratory, with mammals, including man, unfeasible only because the synthetic processes of nature, though we can set them on their way, we cannot as yet speed up sufficiently.

Bernard Jaffe, in *Crucibles,* tries to straddle. First declaring that "our bodies are organic chemical factories", he points to Alexis Carrel's experiments in keeping cells alive for fifteen years and more, then to the speculations of Oliver Lodge and others that some day laboratory compounds may be infused with life. Immediately thereafter he turns coat, and though adducing no new evidence positively declares: "Man is more than a chemical concatenation of a lump of coal, a whiff of air, and a beaker of water. . . . Beyond the chemist's widest synthetic horizon lies some mysterious life force."

Most in this group are more uncompromising. James Harvey Robinson, in *The Mind In the Making,* assumes that science and the scientific method are the only tools that can pave the road to reality; he admits philosophy only of the instrumental variety, such as Dewey's. Even the *Encyclopaedia Britannica,* in the article on Evolution, by E. S. Goodrich, declares:

> A living organism, then, from the point of view of the scientific observer, is a self-regulating, self-repairing, physico-chemical complex mechanism. What, from this point of view, we call "life" is the sum of its physico-chemical processes, forming a continuous interdependent series without break, and without the interference of any mysterious extraneous force.

The behaviorist, of course, flowers along this way.

Even a scientist, however, finds it hard to look complacently on a picture of the universe that equates him with the flea in his dog's ear. Certainly human nature permits such an attitude no lengthy sway. The spirit of man insists on its own superiority. (It may be argued that such an affirming helps make its assumption come true. By claiming to be like the angels, man may soar near them. There is more danger to mankind when separate "races" assert themselves in the same insistence.) Somehow man must comfort himself by thinking himself important.

At first the objection to this physical view is based on its likely consequences. Science, protest exclaims, by equating all things eliminates values; by setting quantitative (physical) standards of measurement it dismisses values as illusions. The scientific method overshot its mark, declared William E. Hocking, and Lin Yutang quotes the statement in *Between Tears and Laughter,* when it dismissed purposes and values from the universe. "Man has become meaningless." Since man cannot live without values, science must be deposed.

A few scientists protest that because a fact is unpleasant it is not necessarily untrue. Others counter with their own emotional appeal. Edward L. Thorndike, in his speech on retiring from the presidency of *The American Association For The Advancement of Science,* in 1935 (printed in *Science,* Jan. 3, 1936 and reprinted in *ETC* vol. I, 1, 1943) declared:

> If and as the world is determined, there is hope of controlling it in the interest of human values. Every regularity or law that science can discover in the consequences of events will be a step toward the only freedom that is of the slightest use to man, and an aid in the good life. If values did not reside in the orderly world of nature, but depended on chance and caprice, it would be vain to try to increase them.

The "logical positivists" should recall the Devil's Dictionary definition—positive: mistaken at the top of one's voice.

Planck marshals a more reasoned attack upon the basic fortifications of the unbending scientists. He asserts that analy-

OTHER FIELDS

sis of a process is incapable of representing it fully: in physics as in biology the concept of "wholeness" must be introduced. In *The Philosophy of a Biologist* J. B. S. Haldane rushes through the breach thus made:

> Except quite superficially, the phenomena observed in living organisms cannot be interpreted as mere physical and chemical processes . . . the quite evidently manifested coordination or wholeness of life cannot be expressed in terms of them.

Haldane, however, is not satisfied with the vitalist stand. This claimed exemption for man, but abandoned the non-human elements of existence to the sole operation of physical and chemical laws. Upon such an opposition Haldane brings down Crash! the principle of polarity. He insists that it is impossible to separate organism and environment. Indeed, the complexity of these interrelationships is so great we have but glimpsed their strands. The change of a few degrees in temperature, for example, can alter the sex of a living organism. While some may see in such facts evidence of the tyranny of physico-chemical laws, Haldane moves to a more pleasing assumption. He sees, in the entire universe, a personality as pervasive as our own throughout our own body. The beauty that we see in the world is an expression of the wholeness of this personality. The step to religion is now inevitable:

> But when we see this beauty it is not as an expression of our mere individual personality—as what is useful or pleasing to me—but as revealing, perhaps only as a glimpse, all-embracing personality, just as it is revealed in a good action or a demonstration of a fuller truth. . . . The outcome of the foregoing discussion (so Haldane's book ends) is that we find in our experience a manifestation of the personality of God.

[341]

Here the age's quest of an embracing unity leads not to the mechanization of man but to the personifying of the universe. Instead of denying humanity a spirit, nature is endowed with a soul. Not man as superior monkey, but matter as manifest God.

Among authors, the attack is more direct. Dostoievsky believes bad if true—but not true—the priority of reason over will; he deems the great evils of the day caused by man's thwarted will to freedom. The intellect of Bernard Shaw reaches the conclusion that in all life with "energy enough to be interesting", intellect is the merest tool of subjective volition and passion.

Such an attack strikes at mechanism with understanding, if not use, of its own weapons. Other voices are more strident. Benjamin De Casseres declares (in a magazine called *The Thinker!*):

> We are related (if we must speak earthwise) to super-organisms, or a super-organism, which, however, being itself only a part of some other super-organism, is not to be confused with God or Absolute . . . And I say this after forty years of mature consideration: *Science is the greatest of human superstitions.*

Charles Fort, whom De Casseres follows, packed into four crowded volumes the collection that was his life-work: of countless incidents, showers of strange objects from the sky, astronomical and earth-born phenomena, that challenge the explanations of science. A Fortean Society continues his research.

D. H. Lawrence rejected not only science, but that aspect of man's functioning which guides him to reason:

> My great religion is a belief in the blood, the flesh, as being wiser than the intellect. We can go wrong in our minds. But what my blood feels, and believes, and says, is always true.

OTHER FIELDS

And Aldous Huxley reports that, discussing evolution, Lawrence declared:

> 'Evidence doesn't mean anything to me. I don't feel it *here*.'
> And he pressed his two hands on his solar plexus.

In *The Social Basis of Consciousness,* Trigant Burrow declares (with Alfred Korzybski in *Science and Sanity,* and the consequent General Semantics movement) that we have confused signs (including words) with things; hence, all our values are false, whether of logic or ethics or science. And the influential Pareto builds *The Mind and Society* on the premise that the prime social fact is man's nonlogical behavior.

Gabriele D'Annunzio, hailing instinct not intellect as guide to truth, led his disciples to Trieste, established a fortnight's kingdom there, and proudly blew his bubble of the superman.

Artist and scientist alike thus recoil from their own contemplations. G. K. Chesterton takes advantage of the turn blandly to remark:

> The man of science, the hero of the modern world, has suddenly and dramatically abandoned the dreary business of nibbling negation and come back to religious faith.

Evidence of the truth of Chesterton's words is spread in many volumes.

The new psychologies take "uncritically for granted" their basis in mechanistic materialism, declares one of their founders, C. G. Jung. He adds, however, that the neurotic seems often to hesitate between physician and priest. And when he chose the psychiatrist, it was still the minister he sought:

> During the past thirty years, persons from all the countries of the earth have consulted me. I have treated hundreds of patients, the larger number being Protestants, a smaller number Jews, and not more than five or six believing Catholics. Among all my pa-

tients aged over thirty-five, there was not one whose problem in the final analysis was not that of finding a religious outlook on life.

The cohesive strain that a creed provides, the psychanalysts find in "the unconscious". The inventors of this convenient compartment of our selves declare it is not an individual reservoir but a collective stream. Beneath our own flotsam is the rich sediment of the past. It holds rocks of social repressions, but also golden veins of ideals and social will.

That collective unconscious, as Irwin Edman describes it, is for Jung

> the subterranean, ageless, and obscure voice of the spirit, deeper and more pervasive than either body or mind. It is the murmur of the immortal memory of mankind which it is the psychiatrist's task to help the neurotic to overhear. In those depths, he suggests, is salvation.

The artist himself, of course, is not exempt from the unconscious. In fact, in the upspringing surge of this presentation, he both commands and obeys its unseen impulses. For in his creative hours, the artist, Jung declares,

> is objective and impersonal—even inhuman—for as an artist he is his work and not a human being. . . . Art is a kind of innate drive that seizes a human being and makes him its instrument. . . . As a human being he may have moods and a will and personal aims, but as an artist he is 'man' in a higher sense—he is 'collective man'—one who carries and shapes the unconscious, psychic life of mankind.

Thus the unconscious is both the motor and the crank.

The current schools of psychology, however else they differ, all agree in seeking a universal substratum. Most of them have discarded the old "faculties"—intellect, will, reason, and the rest—and indeed deprecate all separation of the processes

OTHER FIELDS

of human functioning. Kurt Koffka advances Gestalt Psychology as the field where life and science most fully meet. Not only are all the however curious activities of a human being closely interrelated, he maintains, but they flow in a single system with the behavior of a chimpanzee, a white rat, an atom. The organism is a whole that acts and reacts in an indivisible unit. The chemist and the physicist may divide it, and the objects that environ it, into atoms, electrons, protons, neutrons, whatnons; even these they must, however, hold in universal rhythms. But what the organism feels and sees are not whirling particles or forces but gathered forms, not isolate points but continuous movement. The living being, and the objects in its universe, have again become societies, organisms. Their reality consists in their functioning in terms of the whole. The "integrated personality" is the quest of the research psychologist as of the young man that takes a correspondence course to get a job.

The various new psychologies all assuming this universal essence, their validity is taken for granted by many who then use them as arguments for the collective emphasis. Eric Gutkind suggests on this basis an analysis of the function of art and thought. Macaulay remarks that, as civilization advances, art declines. Bernard Shaw is one of many that have pictured poetry as lasting only through mankind's adolescence, as doomed to fade with our maturing. The lives of many poets give this a personal emphasis; their writing fades with the lyric matecall. Gutkind proceeds to a subtler consideration. Art is a manifestation of a mind that thinks in pictures. Our true growth, Gutkind insists, depends upon our increasing power to think in concepts. Concepts concern not so much objects in themselves as interrelationships. Not the concrete specific image, but the abstract, general idea: thus his thought is in the flow of our age's emphasis. But Gutkind finds it also in the contrast between the Greeks and the Hebrews. Aesthetic absorption, and ethical concern. The one leads to contemplation; the other places all emphasis upon the deed. Contemplation may grow to idolatry;

notice that the injunction: "Thou shalt not make thee any graven image" is not limited to representations of a god, but forbids any likeness of any thing that is in heaven above, or that is in the earth beneath, or that is in the waters beneath the earth.

Farthest of all human movements from such figures are the processes of mathematics. Again surging in the emphasis of our time, mathematics—which is the science of general relations—has become not only a basic study but a best seller: *Men of Mathematics; Mathematics For the Million; Mathematics and the Imagination; The River Mathematics;* and more. Gutkind sees in this science a parallel for the growth of proletarian culture, which must (like the Soviet peasant) abandon the icon for the idea.

There may be measure of truth in this presentation. The wise Frenchman Alain reminds us that man first made his idols, then worshipped them. Gutkind opposes the pagan's joy, which carves the forms for its devotion, to the prophet's wisdom. The Greeks were not the only people that created their gods in their own image. The Germans more recently proved adept at the same job.

Precisely there, lies a danger Gutkind does not escape. He overlooks in the commandment the word *graven* before *image*, and includes in his condemnation the images of literature as well as of plastic art. Indeed they must be included; and indeed there the whole case falls. Gutkind would distinguish between the figures of art and literature, and the symbols of religion. The pretty pictures of the lay books are to be observed and enjoyed—but guarded against; the parables of the world's bibles (Aaron's rod that becomes a serpent; Balaam's ass; figs and thistles and the other growth) are to be heeded and obeyed. But this is precisely where one must be most on guard. For it is in persuasion and propaganda (social, political, religious, or any other sort) that the image can most deftly lure us against ourselves. For illustrations of this, reread Marc Antony's speech in *Julius Caesar,* or listen to any political harangue.

OTHER FIELDS

The iconoclast—image smasher—belongs in this field, not running around breaking statues. The most dreadful gods are those we make with words. It is on the altars of such idols that we find human sacrifice today. We project our fears and passions into images, then beseech them as gods or curse them as devils. Fanatics in every age create these idols; but in such a time as ours, they grow world-spread. What we desire must be the universal good. Our personal phobia is the evil in the world. And destruction stalks abroad.

It may be—who has grown enough to tell?—that as mankind matures the use of art will die. But today civilization, if not in its infancy, is surely in second childhood. And for such days as men have thus far stumbled through, art is no mere plaything. It is man's flash of imagination through the surrounding dark. It makes beautiful pictures of the truths we but surmise. In its train, groping toward life's great mysteries, philosophy lunges and science probes. Hare and tortoise of man's race against death, these twain shall at last prove twin. Meanwhile they capture mites of truth, cocoon them in logic, chalice them in equations. But the more philosophy fixes of science's gains, the greater the need of art. If a fire illuminates the ground for a radius of three feet, the circumference of twilight is about nineteen. Build a bigger fire: you may see twice as far, but you have twice as considerable a contact with the darkness. The farther we advance upon the endless unknown, the more extensive stretch the frontiers of our ignorance. Until that bright impossible day when all knowledge is compassed within man's mind, the happiest gains of science but enrich the field for art. Thus ever the various high functionings of the human spirit are one concordant drive. And thus ever, in conscious direction and in spontaneous urge, in platform ideologies and in basic philosophic systems, our time moves within the sphere of collective endeavor and comprehensive law.

The organic impulsions common to the various psychological schools have surface variations, however, that lead to many confusions in current thought. To trace these would be as far-winding as futile; we may instance the attitude of that wide symposiast, Samuel D. Schmalhausen. His longing for social betterment, his concern over material misery, leads him to link with the enemy—the individual!—all that is aimed at the spirit:

The total effect of the psychologies that rule in the market place these exuberant days is the instilling in the individual (mediocrity, moron, or mutt, as your generosity inclines) of an exhilarated sense of the comparative insignificance of facts and conditions and objective realities—business panics are merely a state of mind!—and the central significance of the individual's own mind (what's that?) as a controller of destiny; destiny concretely meaning will-to-power, success, competitive rating, self-confidence, getting-there. The individual is captain of his soul and master of his fate. Consolations of philosophy in psychological garb!

What irony! Precisely at the moment in the world's history when the individual has become an unmeaning cog in a meaningless machine, when life is being suffocated by super-organizations that mass themselves graphically against the sky like giants hideously mocking the small stature of man, when the only conceivable salvation in sight is the recognition and glad acceptance of the prepotency, in our newly emerging civilization, of the social and communal psychology of life, we confront a scene in which schools of psychology still continue shamelessly to make their deepest appeal to the individualism and egoism and power-mania dangerously alive in the hearts of competitive men. . . .

While civilization is committing suicide, a distinguished philosopher beguiles us with this lullaby:

"All unhappiness depends upon some kind of disintegration or lack of integration; there is disintegration within the self through lack of coordination between the conscious and the unconscious mind; there

OTHER FIELDS

is lack of integration between the self and society, where the two are not knit together by the force of objective interest and affections. The happy man is the man who does not suffer from either of these failures of unity, whose personality is neither divided against itself nor pitted against the world. Such a man feels himself a citizen of the universe, enjoying freely the spectacle that it offers and the joys that it affords, untroubled by the thought of death because he feels himself not really separate from those who will come after him. It is in such profound instinctive union with the stream of life that the greatest joy is to be found."

This is the most expert definition yet attempted of the Perfect Idiot—as he may be observed at Randall's Island or any other distinguished center for congenital idiots and imbeciles. . . . Shades of Pithecanthropus Erectus!!

More than one distinguished philosopher, however, is probing for this "profound instinctive union" between nature and the human spirit. It may be the failure to achieve that basic harmony that produces the material muddle over which Schmalhausen grieves.

Science, to these men, is but one of several ways of approaching reality. Eddington deems religious experience as revealing as the discovery of Newton's laws of motion. By tucking the external world within the mind (where Berkeley, remember, had also stowed it) Eddington makes human consciousness the prime reality. Here is comfort against those scientists that announce that thought is an inessential complication—a disease of the star—that crops out occasionally in the wide range of inorganic nature, whirling in its galaxies.

On the same pathway, Millikan in *Time, Matter, and Value* declares that something must give meaning to existence. Accepting this as axiomatic, he goes on to state that significance cannot possibly be bestowed by mere lumps of dead matter interacting according to purely mechanical laws. If you ask Why? to either of these statements, the unspoken answer is that it flatters man to have it so. Lest you presume to ask such a question, Planck rushes in. Equally positive in his rejection of positivism, he calls it a stupid sacrilege for man to hope to understand as clearly as the divine spirit understands. Jeans—and all these men are sound scientists, who have made rich contributions to their fields—Jeans says that among physical scientists there is agreement approaching unanimity, that the stream of knowledge is flowing to an ocean of non-mechanistic reality. He too feels that the old duality will disappear not through matter's becoming more insubstantial nor through mind's being revealed as a mere function of matter but through substantial matter's being disclosed as the creation and manifestation of mind.

Other scientists try to be scientific, even in this field, which asks not How? but Why? A. N. Whitehead, especially in his *Process and Reality*, seeks to make such speculations more than wishful thinking. Instead of giving preeminence either to matter or to mind, he advances the idea of an organic synthesis—from which, in the "ism" eagerness of our time, his notion is known as Organism. Arthur H. Compton drives against mechanism along another flank. Behind the barrage of the Heisenberg principle of uncertainty he presses the charge that the old meaningless but unbreakable laws have been repealed; nature has reached forth her conscious hand; purpose once more is effective in the world, and "life again has human meaning."

I might pause here—as I shall again with the philosophers—to show how the scientists here tangle themselves in words. Having no facts, they resort to figures—pretty pictures as useful as a toy. Compton's utterance advances us no whit: life has always had "human meaning"—significance to us mortals that pass through it; the question at issue (which Compton means to face but loses in the language) is whether life has meaning in some larger scheme. This, scientists have not more than asserted: assertion is not science. Scientists, nonetheless, continue

OTHER FIELDS

to flow in the collective current of our time. The editor of *Isis* quotes Origen: *Universus mundus velut animal quoddam immensum* (the whole world is like some enormous animal), then ingeniously elaborates the figure of all humanity, past, present, future, as but one growing man.

The Bishop of Birmingham, in *Scientific Theory and Religion,* with historic approach to modern views, looks across the wide field from light-radiation to galaxies, from electron to man. Out of this range he extracts what he calls a moderate realism. The world is so full of a number of things, he avers, that a single mind can stay in it only for a brief space at a time; our objectivity is interspersed with spells of subjective retreat. Not even the totality of finite minds can grasp and continuously hold reality. We must therefore conclude, concludes the Bishop, that "such objectvity is only constituted by a Universal Mind for Whom all objects are always present."

Others otherwise seek to circumvent the all-embracing claims of science. Dr. William Ralph Inge, in *God and the Astronomers,* says that Dust thou art, to dust returnest, was not spoken of the soul. The law of entropy (the second law of thermodynamics) pictures the world as running down. Energy is constantly dissipated into unavailable forms, until in a billion years, more or less, our sun, as ultimately all suns, will be a frozen lump falling endlessly through cold space. From this picture Inge withholds the eternal values; above that lifeless cold still hearty and warm shines the trinity of goodness and beauty and truth. J. W. N. Sullivan, in *Limitations of Science,* strives to extricate even more of the world from the grim grip of the law of entropy. He reminds us that reality may seem mathematical merely because our minds have learned how to juggle figures; because we are expert public accountants we believe that the universe can be checked by our double-entry books. Sullivan seeks to demonstrate that science sees but one side of things. Somewhat earlier, Gustave Geley, in *From the Unconscious to the Conscious,* had vigorously challenged the wide application of detailed analysis. Suited to the laboratory, he declared, this scientific method, if used to reach beyond, is very like to lead mankind astray. In scientific philosophy, according to Geley, the only valuable procedure is general synthesis.

Wyndham Lewis, especially in *Time and Western Man,* blasts at the whole idea of a mechanistic universe. He sees the blight blown across the world from the "time-mind" of our day—proclaimed in the Einsteinian relativity and the Bergsonian flux, in the "fluid reality" of Alexander, Gentile, Croce, Whitehead, and the rest: a sense of relative values, therefore indeterminate, therefore shifty, therefore false values, propped by a philosophy leaning on a science that begins to doubt its own presuppositions.

Whereupon G. H. Hardy reaffirms "the immutable and unconditional validity of mathematical truth."

Each of these doctors is a specialist of high repute. Fortunately, the patient, nature, is immune to their prescriptions.

In calm but cogent challenge, Bertrand Russell—mathematician and philosopher, speculator upon morals and education, popularizer widely popular—sums up the point of view of those that maintain the prepotency of science. At the various explanations of electronic caprice, he smiles as on those that would use a fly-swatter to kill a stork. It's ludicrous to try to explain doings within the electron by laws of average, statistical laws, that may apply to large-scale behavior. But neither is it necessary, Russell adds, to summon a Jinni, or a God, to establish order. Just be patient: controlling the supposed freedom of the atom, new laws will be found. Freedom, of atom or mind, Russell continues, is a notion repugnant to science. For not only do the findings of psychology, physiology, and physics tend to make free will seem improbable, but science is in its very essence a search for causal laws. Hence science must always assume determinism as a working hypothesis. The very notion of "will" is unscientific. "Value" itself is an echo of desire. What we want, what we will, is the conscious end of a long series of the workings of unchangeable law. Unperturbed

OTHER FIELDS

by the increasing host of modern theists, pantheists, and proponents (Bergson, Lloyd Morgan, Alexander) of a creative evolution and an "emergent" divinity, Russell proclaims the ultimacy of the scientific quest:

> I conclude that, while it is true that science cannot decide questions of value, that is because they cannot be intellectually decided at all, and lie outside the realm of truth and falsehood. Whatever knowledge is attainable, must be attained by scientific methods; and what science cannot discover, mankind cannot know.

Despite Russell's firm stand, and Kaempffert's wide summation, most men pursue other roads toward ultimate knowledge. In bland unconcern for denials of its very existence, they seek to build highways of the human spirit. Dr. Bernard Bavinck, at the conclusion of his lengthy study of *The Natural Sciences,* turns to art for the restoration of the soul:

> Go on Good Friday to hear Bach's *Passion of St. Matthew* and the *Missa Solemnis* and the B minor mass, the greatest works produced by human, nay superhuman, inspiration. When you hear the angels in heaven singing *Sanctus, sanctus, Dominus, Deus Sabaoth*—with Beethoven in mystery far removed from all earthly things; with Bach in endless rejoicing rising ever higher and higher—then you get a faint inkling of the reason why God did not remain God alone, but created a world with joy, life, and love, but also with pain, death, and sin; and of where the solution of this contradiction is to be found. No philosopher in the world can tell you more about it than Bach, Beethoven, and Brahms.

From his studies of symbolism in Shakespeare, G. Wilson Knight turns, in *The Christian Renaissance,* to declare that only poetry can save the world. As the sense-world and the soul, erotic paganism and medieval Christianity, were fused through the Helen of Goethe's *Faust,* so today we require a poetic rebirth that is also an incarnation. The material and the spiritual, too long divorced, must be remated. Hugh l'Anson Fausset first in *The Proving of Psyche* deplored this diseased dualism of modern life; then in *A Modern Prelude* pictures how there came to him, through mystical experiences of unification, a sense of the spiritual wholeness of the universe.

Santayana somewhat vaguely—though he intends a fuller description of his journey—walks the same path. In *Some Turns of Thought in Modern Philosophy* he observes that in the last half-century British opinion (also manifesting the embracing spread of the time!) has passed from insular dogmatism to universal bewilderment. The new physics, which today dominates science, seems to Santayana to rest partly upon the assumptions of a philosophy that is utterly insecure. Its point of view identifies the object with the mental act of experiencing or knowing the object. And this Santayana dismisses as "a subjective, psychological, Protestant"—he might have added Romantic—philosophy.

Having thus, by loosing its underpinnings, unsettled omnipotent science, Santayana glances at the realm of spirit, where what he finds he clothes in a mouthy figure:

> The spiritual man, insofar as he has intellectually passed into the eternal world, no longer endures unwillingly the continued death involved in living or the final death involved in having been born.

Some years before, Van Wyck Brooks, in *Letters and Leadership,* cried out that our greatest need is a collective spiritual life. Today, that need is so urgent that it has carried Augustus Ralli (in *Later Critiques*) to declare that not all facts are part of the universe: only those are truly real that can be used for soul-building.

Let us pause in our manifold listings, to see round what center these attitudes turn. Here is a group of scientists declaring that of course man is but one link in the long chain of mechanic

OTHER FIELDS

forces and phenomena. And all around, other scientists, with a glad seconding of churchmen, philosophers, artists, in various ways set men supreme upon the earth, even to the extent of erecting all the universe within the mind.

Here is the old duality that philosophy has always sought to fuse. Must mind gulp down matter? Or matter swallow mind? Is man supreme or nature? Are they the eternal snake and tail? Here are the two attitudes this volume sees in every time.

3. Time brings the existentialist.

IN the last half-century, our ideas have swung full span. A while ago, the mechanistic theory of the universe was dominant; and over this law-bound realm of matter roamed the free mind of man. Today, matter has escaped from its bondage. We alternate between the four-dimensional space of relativity and the multi-dimensional time of the quantum theory. We can state either the path or the position of an electron, but not both at once. If we locate it in space, it eludes us in time. The free mind of fifty years ago, on the other hand, has in the new psychologies been tightly bound. Deep in the "unconscious" they all find fixatives that control thought and action, that determine the movements of humankind.

Thus the reversal is complete. Instead of free minds exploring a bound universe, an indeterminate world floats before fixed minds. Yet this is no such upheaval as it may seem. In the equation of the universe, which we humans are trying to solve, we have just transferred a term from one side to the other. Until we have unlocked the final door, there must be an unknown—an x—in the calculations. What matter to the mathematician on which side he sets the unknown, so long as the terms balance, and the signs accord?

To the mathematician; not to the man.

Comfortably man worked along, lord of creation. Now behold! *Things* are in the saddle, and ride *us*. What goal is left, to justify human existence? What pride, to sustain man's step? Thus even the scientist wriggles to escape his own conclusions, and in the impulse of the day gropes beyond matter for a supermind.

But energy and substance, matter and mind, are themselves teeterwise joined over another fulcrum of present-day thought. The already mentioned principle of polarity asserts that opposites are in truth inseparable aspects of one rela-

OTHER FIELDS

tionship. Try to sever top from bottom of a stick; you double your problem. And the more you persist in your efforts, the more closely you bring together what you are striving to part. Lancelot Hogben, declaring that his *Science For the Citizen* is the first British handbook to Scientific Humanism, emphasizes that science cannot be divorced from history, that man must endeavor to coordinate science, government, and social welfare, into one coherent scheme of human living. Thus, in the spotlight of our age's vision, all things are basically conjoined.

Among the many fields where the quest for fundamental laws has led to changing views, we may further instance the aesthetic regard for permanence and time. Through the ages, immortality has been looked upon not only as mankind's goal but also, in one sense, as the artist's bestowal. The Egyptian Pharaoh's first official act was to order his tomb. Therein, his embalmed body, surrounded with arms, provisions, and slaves, might rest forever, secure, through submission to nature's movements: to death, in the royal mummy; to the casual drift of the wind-formed sand pile, in the slope of the pyramid.

The Greeks also sought to outlast the ages, but through defiance: still today amid the ruins of countless wars there stand against the sky the marble pillars of their temples for the living spirit. The cathedrals of the middle ages made firm with arch and flying buttress their beauty, which has endured, which not nature's storms, but only man's bombings, can crumble. In the cities of today, however, there is not even the expectancy of such endurance. In the business section, the skyscrapers have an estimated life of two generations. In the residential districts, there is no practical sense in building apartment houses to endure, because new sanitary devices, more living comforts, shifting populations, will soon debase them to slums.

The ancient Roman triumph was perpetuated with statues and arches. In 1836 the Arc de Triomphe for Napoleon cost ten millions of francs. At the turn of the century, the triumphal arch New York City raised for Admiral Dewey (at the junction of two of the world's most famous streets) was elaborately erected—of papier mâché. Millions are spent on great plots marked off (in New York, on land reclaimed from the washing tides) for our universal expositions and world's fairs: crowds come to gape; typewriters and perfumes are awarded their medals; in two years all is razed and sold as junk. A column and a half of the Classified Directory of the Borough of Manhattan in New York City is taken by names of housewreckers, industrial wreckers, demolition corporations, and others whose business it is to keep our works emphemeral. Not only in war do we destroy ourselves!

Contrasted with this continuous dying is a desperate struggle for continuance, as though we feared our imminent end. Gutzon Borglum is hewing stone faces in the bulge of a mountainside, so that only the slow process of nature's erosion will wear them away. Down a fifty foot concrete shaft at Flushing Meadows, New York, under a stone asking that it be opened in the year 6940, lies buried a metal shell, a "time capsule". It contains golf balls, an electric razor, a microfilm of the King James *Bible,* a copy of *True Confessions,* and other tokens of the attainments of our culture, so that future man may have some inkling of this civilization that expects not to endure.

These are, of course, outcropping symptoms. Life as a whole goes on dying without such self-concern. But the drop from permanence to transience is clear enough in our writers. I need not give examples down the earlier ages of boasting about earthly immortality, from Horace, Dante, Spenser, Shakespeare, Milton. Let Goethe sum up their stand:

> What we see in nature is power, devouring power, nothing stationary, everything transitory; a thousand germs destroyed, a thousand born, every moment . . . And art is the exact opposite: it springs from the individual's effort to maintain himself against the destructive power of the all.

"Relativity" is not the single cause, but one outgrowth of the general shift, that has upset all this. Paul Claudel declares that the universe is a machine for marking time. To its ticks, we die. André Gide writes that his problem is not to succeed but to endure. This, to the growing generation, marks him as already a creature of the past. Permanence is a pre-war delusion, as perfection was a pre-war dream.

Some writers, no longer trying to fix the moment for eternity, abandon art for the deliberate death of reportage, seeking still an ephemeral permanence in history's train. This use of the strictly contemporary incident and intimate autobiographical detail may also mark an indifference to contemporary understanding. The moment matters not, nor they that dwell therein. Forget others, sink into the instant—and you at once are history. Two big volumes (by other men) have been written to explain the incidents of the Dublin day that is the span of Joyce's *Ulysses*. Edith Sitwell's line—

With eyes like Mary's when she smiled—

refers, we are told, not to one of the biblical three, but to a nurse that Edith remembers out of her childhood. John V. A. Weaver's verses *In American* display the columnist's capture of the morning's platitude in the week's wording. The dominant arts of the United States, the comic strip and the movies, run their daily course to oblivion. Time has us on its tail. Our age is perhaps seeking to apply the new notion that the one way to attain timelessness is to equal the speed of light. The mass of an object at that speed should give the artist halt.

Complete identification with the time is sought by those whose attitude is labeled existentialism. This springs, along the avenues of our age, from the earlier individualistic approach of Sören Aabye Kierkegaard (1813-55). This Danish thinker, challenging the ability of logic to define reality, declared that all valid thought is concrete thought. It must not be speculative, but must seek to clarify the issues of life, paving the way for a decisive personal commitment, a fundamental and therefore a passionate choice.

Language itself, Kierkegaard continues, is mainly the vehicle of the abstract and the universal, whereas reality is essentially concrete and particular. Reality is grasped by the senses, and by intuition, in what Korzybski later calls the "unspeakable" realm. A man must, therefore, seek to understand himself "as an existing human being." Existence however, is absurd without belief; the individual must recognize himself in absolute self-abasement before God, then realize himself in action. He must not seek to hide in the crowd; mass movements inevitably debase the individual thought and conscience: each man must find, then act, his faith.

The philosophy of Kierkegaard strongly influenced Henrik Ibsen (1828-1906). It constitutes the battleground in his drama *Brand,* wherein the priest, Brand, doomed by his motto "All or nothing", forever fights the spirit of compromise and in his dying moments cries "man must struggle till he falls", while the Invisible Choir bids the "earth-born creature, live for Earth!"

Although just beginning to awaken interest in America, existentialism has found staunch disciples in Europe. It is the basic drive in all the work of Franz Kafka (1883-1924), whose characters seek their true place in the community, there to act in accord with the heavenly will. In his comments on Kafka, Philip Rahv indicates, in the emphasis of our time, the general nature of this attitude. He declares that existentialism seeks "the melody of spontaneous and irresistible being", and that "truth" is neither an abstract truth of the world in general, nor a personal truth, but "an existential truth, of the race, in which all knowledge is contained."

The basic interdependence pictured in these words, building on the individualism of Kierkegaard, is further stressed in the existentialism of Jean-Paul Sartre, foremost proponent of the trend in France, whose novels, plays, and essays are spreading the ideas in England and the United States as well. Sartre maintains most firmly the approach by way of the concrete fact and action. Declaring, for example, that the "absolute Descartes", who was a soldier, and got a servant girl with child, "rises out of his time, disarmed and unconquered, like

OTHER FIELDS

a landmark", while the relative cartesianism is no more than a "coster's barrow philosophy", in which every age finds what it has dumped in, Sartre develops his ideas: "It is not by chasing after immortality that we will make ourselves eternal: we will not make ourselves absolute by reflecting in our work desiccated principles that are sufficiently empty and negative to pass from one century to another, but by fighting passionately in our time, by loving it passionately, and by consenting to perish entirely with it." He nonetheless moves, in his basic holdings, along with our age, from the individual to the mass.

Sartre outlines this position in a defence against charges, from the Communists and Catholics alike, that existentialism ignores human solidarity, considers man as an isolated being. He points out, first, that there are religious existentialists, like Kierkegaard and the French Catholic Gabriel Marcel; and also atheistic existentialists, like the German Martin Heidigger and himself. He then develops the ideas of the latter group. These ideas seem in their field, like democracy in politics, to give scope to individual action in a social world.

The first—and only basic—reality, they affirm, is man's awareness of himself. We start with Descartes' *Cogito, ergo sum.* I think, therefore I am. There are, consequently, no essences, no values, prior to this subjectivity. Man is, therefore, free. Without God, without standards, many men may lapse to indifference, cynicism, hopelessness; to the existentialist, on the contrary, "human life begins on the far side of despair." For man is here first, then he defines himself; he himself will have made what he will be.

Each man, furthermore—and here is our age's train—decides not only what he is to be, but what all others are. Each by his action shapes them all. Every man is responsible for all men. Value is the meaning that man chooses, as he emerges more fully, a plan aware of itself. Every human configuration, no matter how individual, thus has a universal value. Every choice involves all mankind. In choosing oneself, one chooses man. And there is no reality except in action. "What counts is total involvement."

Existentialism has been linked, in the minds of many, with violence and ruthlessness, with depravity. There is some reason for the tie. In Sartre's play *The Graveless Dead* (*The Victors*), members of the French Underground, about to be captured, before the eyes of the audience strangle a loyal fifteen year old boy because they recognize he will not be able to keep their secrets under torture. The characters in *No Exit* have all earned their room in hell.

Sartre himself, in mild self-satire, tells of a woman that, every time she spoke a coarse word in anger, declared "I believe I'm becoming an existentialist". Others have more bluntly remarked that existentialism takes the accent right in the middle —on the stench.

A similar charge was leveled against Zola, and against Ibsen. Compared with Zola, Ibsen retorted: "Save that Zola descends into the cesspool to take a bath; I, to cleanse it". (One victim of philistine abuse should seek a more sympathetic understanding of another.) Whereas Ibsen pictures a descent into the cesspool, however, Sartre sees the cesspool within each man. From abulia, from refusal of freedom, from unwillingness to choose. When he chooses, each man may have within him, instead, a swamp, or a stony field, or a wilderness—but a stretch that he can work to fertile farmland.

First he must recognize that he is free. Then (like Orestes in Sartre's play *The Flies*) he must accept the responsibility of his freedom. He must know that his every act involves all men; what he does is fateful to mankind. Then he must choose to act. In anguish, in defiance (again like Orestes) of the man-made gods, his action, on the far side of despair—without personal hope, only with personal dignity and self-respect—will be a step toward the ultimate validity of things human. In this drive, existentialism is the most promising attitude to rise from the debris of two World Wars.

While some belabor, others belittle this new outlook on the world. "Existentialism?" queries the report from France in the April 19, 1947 issue of *The Saturday Review of Litera-*

OTHER FIELDS

ture: "Born not quite two years ago, it is already passé, a fashion of yesterday. A few plays by Jean-Paul Sartre and a few novels, or rather novelettes, by Camus are all that has remained from this so heralded 'spiritual revolution'." The writer of these words is perhaps as incorrect about its future as he is ignorant of its past. The vogue has ended; the values may begin.

Sartre declares emphatically that his is no philosophy for the market-place. Many, more practically bent, recognizing the individual's insufficiency in the struggle with his time, have turned from any stark personal acceptance of responsibility for all, to the easier avenues of group cooperation. Far-spread in all sorts of industrial unions and social enterprises, this tendency of our age has also become manifest in the banding together of artists in the construction of cooperative works. Some may seek through individual anonymity for group survival. Folk tales and folk poems, now not sprung fresh from the artists of a simple people, are lengthily hunted or deliberately educed. Cooperative paintings have been hung at the Independent Artists shows (*See Twain Turmoil of Today,* Section 6.) In the field of performance, there is spreading the new practice of choral speaking. In addition to the great number of symposiums, and volumes with many contributors, novels have been written with successive chapters by different authors. It is as though the artists were saying: If we all pull together, we may hold back oblivion.

Our age has suggested still another way to challenge time. Unable to erect ourselves against death, we need not resign ourselves to the moment or the group; we can assume the wider fusion with all the ages. Balderston, in *Berkeley Square,* presents a dramatic fantasy of the intermingling of an earlier century with our own. For public comprehension, he tells his audience to imagine a river shoreline, winding through meadows and wooded banks, as seen from a boat—what will the next bend reveal?—then as viewed from an airplane, with all together disclosed: similarly what we view as present, past, and future is really one single spread of coetaneous time. Priestley, in *Time and the Conways,* conversely projects the future into our present moving. A character in this play points out that at each moment we are only a cross-section of ourself; at the end of our life we reassemble our whole being, immortal. Maxwell Anderson, in *The Star-Wagon,* produces a machine that can transport us to any period we may desire. James M. Barrie, in *Dear Brutus,* asks what difference it would make; we'd only do the same things over: it is not time, but character, that determines our fate. The Wellsian time-machine for a journey to any reach of space has carried us not only in philosophical dramas like Shaw's *Back To Methusaleh* to the prehistoric Garden of Eden and ahead "as far as thought can reach"; but even in motion pictures into various realms of the future, and the Hollywood conception of *One Million B.C.* Such time-trips have become commonplace of children's-hour programs on the radio (along with interplanetary conflicts and Buck Rogers' "disintegrating ray"); they are the basic fodder of the "scientifiction" pulp magazines.

Thus the swift passing moment is blent with all time—even though it dwarfs the instant in the eternal hold. In further blending, time becomes to the physicist a fourth attribute in space; along with length, breadth, and thickness (or latitude, longitude, and ascension) it serves to fix the locus of an apple or a star. Space itself has become coherent, not merely a diffuse spread; within its boundless but finite curve the galaxies whirl —as though inside the shell of a supersphere (do not ask what is without!). And within this space dwells the constant, time. It is our passing that we interpret as its flow. Therefore the instant, enduring forever, need not be feverishly clutched and reluctantly relinquished as it dies. The present, through its permanence, loses its importance. Likewise we, that walk in its rays. It is eternity, it is mankind, that count.

OTHER FIELDS

4. *The state swallows the man.*

AMONG the social sciences, in studies and in the practical working of governments today, the impulse toward individualism is virtually stifled between the heaving forces of the two collective attitudes that contend. Even, nay, predominantly and permanently in submarine society, we are today reminded, under water where life is more abundant than either on land or in the air, beyond the death of individuals in the ceaseless round of slaughter the continuity of the race is manifest—seals to their nursing grounds, salmon spawning up the selfsame stream—the constant urge of energy, the single flow of life.

The orthodox historian of an earlier age might declare it an illusion to suppose that great public happenings "have something more fatally necessary about them than ordinary private events." The historian of today also equates the minor and the major events of history—by seeking the general laws that determine them all. In a survey of recent writing in the field, Ingram Bander concludes:

> The "new history" which has taken such far-reaching strides during the past few decades has certainly been marked by a depreciation of chance and by the search for deep-seated causal explanations.

In his well known study of *The New History,* James Harvey Robinson denied the possibility of abrupt change through the accident of a battle's outcome or a tyrant's growth to power. History has never shown, he states, such single circumstance altering more than a small portion of human institutions and ways. The prevailing religious, intellectual, artistic, scientific, linguistic, military, and political ideas and habits (he does not mention economic) rather produce than reflect these seemingly sudden changes in historic events.

Edward P. Cheyney, whose textbooks have influenced a generation of American students, in his celebrated paper on *Law In History,* affirms the existence of basic laws of human movement:

> I do not conceive of these generalizations as principles which it would be well for us to accept or as ideals which we may hope to attain; but as natural laws which we must accept whether we want to or not, whose workings we cannot obviate, however much we may thwart them to our own failure and disadvantage; laws to be reckoned with, much as are the laws of gravitation, or of chemical affinity, or of organic evolution, or psychology.

Historians now feel impelled, Oliver Wendell Holmes sums up the attitude, to make plainer the way from one thing to the whole of things. No longer content with merely recording, they seek behind events for their intermingled causes and fundamental unity.

There are some, nonetheless, that feel there is more than any man's life-time work in "merely recording". Thus the new "scientific history" is divided into two schools. The rebels against the quest for law, without reasserting the power of chance over human destiny, insist that the task of the historian is to record the objective fact, without interpretation or opinion. The psychologists would retort that such men merely remain unaware of their inevitable subjective bias. Thus Sidney Hook objects to one law but makes final obeisance to another:

> What "social" or "literary" necessity guided the union of the sperm and egg out of which the child Shakespeare was born? If Shakespeare hadn't been born would someone else have been Shakespeare? Mystical connections of this sort can be asserted only by the philosophy of absolute idealism, not by dialectical materialism.

OTHER FIELDS

If not such an implicit acceptance, most of the sociological writers of today show at least ritual-fealty to Freud or Marx. History has careened from Carlyle to Calverton, from the soul of the mighty man to the surge of the murmuring mass.

The current theories in anthropology, of eugenics and racial purity, concerned with the breeding of a better race regardless of the individual, are likewise rooted in the belief that man is governed by the laws that have permitted the production of the race horse and golden bantam corn. The ideological movement of the great national dictators is unanimously away from freedom of individual initiative toward authoritarian absolutism. Many whom the dictators would coerce need not that urging; they are swept in the same onrushing tide.

So strong, in these days, is the impulse toward group effort—cooperative buying, trade union bargaining, racial rivalry, team play—that there seems even a stigma upon those that do not align themselves with a movement or a group. How many a Hairy Ape feels an imperious urge to belong! The groups gather, the opposition intensifies; cheers for a gallant foe fade into a chivalrous past, against the cloud of hate: woe to the would-be neutral! Those that would select the best, and reject the worst, of both views find themselves in a spiritual no-man's land, bombarded from both sides. "By not helping me you aid my foe!" the cry rings, denouncing—until even to himself the unattached man begins to seem cut off, isolate, a bit futile. Such a lone liberal is pictured in Robert E. Sherwood's play *The Petrified Forest,* a lad "too young for the war, too old for the revolution", who is hitch-hiking his way to suicide in the west. In the play, a personal weakness flaws the young man; a more representative example of this "social compulsive" may be found in the career of Norman Thomas. This churchman, at first an unattached liberal, became a leader of the Socialist Party, then stood for a united front with the Communists. (And, as often, the cry for greater unity led to wider schism.)

These are impatient hours, demanding that men take sides—

TRENDS IN LITERATURE

To live is to act; all deeds are partisan; why not be aware
Of the current that drives you? Drift not, fellow; swim!—

—demanding that on the brink of decision men move together to the deed.

With the title of "Under Which King"—"Under which king, Bezonian? Speak, or die!"—the lead article in *The Times Literary Supplement* (London, May 31, 1947) declares: "The process of reintegration in British thinking has gone much farther in the collectivist direction than many imagine. It is now half a century since Sir William Harcourt said 'We are all Socialists now!' Today collectivism of one brand or another . . . has virtually killed individualism." One is asked to choose —between two totalitarian modes.

But once again the opposition within the collective urge is rooted in the basic assumption, either that man is the moulder of his days, or that man is the product of his environment, which surrounding him shapes him. As John Strachey sums it up—his title *The Menace of Fascism* showing his side—government planned individualism (as in our N. R. A.) is oxygen to the dying; the alternative of the years ahead is Fascism or Socialism. In the eyes of L. Hausleiter (whose *Revolution in the World Economic System* is issued in the United States as *The Machine Unchained*):

> The nineteenth century developed individual freedom, individuality, nationality; and the twentieth century has embarked on the task of setting a standard for the individual and creating the mass, the international system. Mass inventions, mass commerce, mass production, mass requirements, mass capital, mass cities, mass armies.

In this march of the masses he deems America the culmination of the old order, mass in private enterprise; Russia, the beginning of the new, mass in State enterprise. Along this road,

[368]

OTHER FIELDS

however, we have not far to go, passing Toller's mass-man, to reach the realm of the robots. The motion picture that shows future generations of mankind hatched from a laid egg is plain retrogression; it lacks the machine efficiency of Aldous Huxley's *Brave New World,* wherein the human race is a mass-product of factories.

A few writers avoid the basic opposition within our age, for other aspects of the struggle. Thus William Kay Wallace is perturbed by the persistence of the individual. After *The Passing of Politics,* and *The Scientific World-View,* in a third study, *Our Obsolete Constitution,* he produces what might seem but is not a piece of Swiftian irony, advocating the complete abolition of individual concern. Today's unions and giant corporations, he declares, are no longer economic devices, but the structural units of the nation. They are still extra-constitutional; his aim is to set them legally in control. Personal freedom? "Our constitution is not to be framed to insure the liberties of the individual against the encroachment of government. Such a problem cannot even arise under the new order. For in industrial society government takes, and can only take, cognizance of groups; it has no direct dealings with the individual." This is the logical extreme, if not the reductio ad absurdum, of the collective emphasis. Yet already the United States, by Supreme Court decision, has not merely sanctioned but compelled collective bargaining. The individual still may vote; but he must move with the group. There is no minority action. Under the Wagner Act every shop may become a closed shop; keep out of the union and you are kept out of a job. Like the realist Johnson, our individualists will soon be pinching themselves to prove that they exist!

Albert Jay Nock, though he abandons the individual, sets society against *Our Enemy, the State.* A non-political grouping seems to him, rather gloomily, the one hope against a state collectivism that is moving toward military despotism. In his dark vision the State takes over one "essential industry" after another, manages them with a steady increase in corruption, inefficiency, and prodigality, until it must resort to forced labor —of which slavery Communism and Fascism yield examples. More recently, and to a wider alarm, the same trend is pictured by Friedrich A. Hayek (whose warning reechoed in the April, 1945 *Readers Digest*), as *The Road to Serfdom.*

The two systems thus lumped are in theory opposite. The Marxian attitude relies on economic determinism — historic necessity. The Fascist sees mankind (politically, in terms of one race or one nation) as free to dictate human destiny and to impose human will. Perhaps the fullest exposition of the Marxian point of view, outside of Russian documents and studies limited to that land, is *The Intelligent Man's Review of Europe Today,* by G. D. H. and Margaret Cole; as the most vigorous presentation of the Fascist claims is of course Hitler's *Mein Kampf.*

Many thinkers today are unwilling to subscribe to either of these formularized modes of social living. Thus Ludwig Lewisohn, in *Expression In America,* attributes the protest and despair of contemporary literature largely to the suppression of individual impulses in industrialized society. He emphatically rejects "the religion, the binding principle, of mechanistic Communism"—but he looks ahead dimly to "other dawns", when the breakdown of the materialistic conception of the universe will have aftergrowth of new "wholeness and coherence". (We might trust more fully in this vague future, had we less clearly observed Ludwig Lewisohn. He speaks of the inability of T. S. Eliot to bear his "adolescent disappointment", and attacks the poet's retreat "into the bosom of a fictive father-image and force, in this case Royalism and Anglo-Catholicism." How easy to find one's own faults in others! In *Upstream,* Lewisohn pictures his sorry buffeting in the Christian world. In *The Creative Impulse,* he says America stifles the artist. In *The Case of Mrs. Crump,* most thinly veiled autobiography, he wails that an unwise marriage may ruin a man's career. Whereafter Lewisohn "retreated", to draw solace and new strength from the waters of his fathers' Zion, in this case Judaism.)

OTHER FIELDS

The Russian experiment is dismissed as irrelevant to a western land, in *Economic Equality in the Co-operative Commonwealth,* by Professor H. Stanley Jevons, who instead approves the prospect of a socialism growing naturally from our needs. J. Middleton Murry, though he uses the title *The Necessity for Communism* and calls the Soviet idea "the one living religion in the world today", is also wise enough to ask for an indigenous form.

The fullest of the social and economic prophecies is naturally that proffered by H. G. Wells, inveterate optimist of the world society, in *The Shape of Things To Come.* With Basic English as universal tongue and with the "air-dollar" as the basic unit of world currency, Wells proceeds to equip the future. He calls a conference of scientific and technical workers, in the early year of 1978. This establishes a World Council, an autocratic group; with its Thirty Year Plan, it reorganizes the world's educational system for the elimination of egotism and the sublimation of individuality. Then the world-state, "socialistic, cosmopolitan, and creative", may bring happiness to a collective universe. This goal, of course, was set much earlier in the career of H. G. Wells. It colors his *Outline of History;* it dominates *The World of William Clissold,* the second volume of which is entitled *The World State,* and which pictures the coming of an international directorate of the best minds, coordinating human activities in a world republic.

Having reached the happy age at which an author sets down his autobiography, Wells is content with no such individual task. He offers his as "a sample life", its clue to be found in viewing it as a process of "escape from individual immediacies into the less personal activities now increasing in human society." He reaches toward a participation in the greater life of the race as a whole. "My individual story merges into the story of the handicapped intelligence of our species." Similarly Jacob Wasserman, who in *The World's Illusion* presents Christian Wahnschaffe renouncing his great wealth to grow in humility and universal love, in his autobiographical *My Path As German and Jew* declares:

I am only seemingly an exception. I represent all. I am the expression of a definite will inherent in our age, our generation, our fate. In me are all, even the resisting; I clear the path for all; I sweep away the lie for all.

More moderately the aged Bernard Shaw reminds us: "We are all members one of another."

In this country, Professor Harry A. Overstreet, fluent interpreter of the times, devotes his book *We Move In New Directions* to pointing out the "social immaturities" that delay the coming socialization of economic forces and postpone the achievement of an international world.

Among these economists, sociologists, and political thinkers, a few look beyond the mere body of the State. Paul Cohen-Portheim, in *The Discovery of Europe,* which emphasizes England's role, and in *The Spirit Of France,* declares that the sense of material multiplicity can be overcome only by a renewed recognition of our cultural unity. Even more broadly K. Jaspers, in *Man In the Modern Age,* presents as our one hope a spiritual union over the binding material union of our age. So fully has the individual been merged in the group, he feels, that a person thinks of himself, today, only in terms of his social relationships, only as "we". Essential humanity is reduced to the general. This sapping of the soul must cease; there must arise a brotherhood of cultivated consciousness, a band of self-hoods bound in ties with other self-hoods, a union and communion of souls. On such a path alone, these fervent prophets cry, can mankind soar above the binding subjection of the mass.

OTHER FIELDS

5. Men point the way.

THE collective spirit is everywhere dominant today. Benedetto Croce, in *A History of Europe In the Nineteenth Century,* pictures the world as moving from strife to communal coordination. We still have the strife, but even that is a more collective working. "Certainly never since the French Revolution", says Martha Gruening in *Hound and Horn,* and the editor of *The New York Times Book Review* "cannot do better than quote her words":

> Certainly never since the French Revolution has the individual been so powerless, so insignificant, and so aware of his insignificance. Not only modern industry with its mass production and its regimentation of the human material employed in this production, but the social and political movements which accept this condition or protest against it alike impose conformity, *Gleichschaltung,* class consciousness, mass consciousness, race consciousness, every form of consciousness, indeed, but the individual.

And elsewhere in that section of the *Times* is the remark: "Poetry has gone social if not Socialist."

Couched in current slang, this remark embodies the current feeling. Not only through science and politics; the collective attitude spreads over the more cultural fields of man's endeavor. It shapes his educational and his aesthetic theory, it colors his literary criticism, it informs his many-sided works of art.

Law, which has for one function the protection of the individual, has always found abler advocates to safeguard the corporation and that corporate unity, the state. There is no novelty in such a remark as Morris Ernst's, that today "the corporate soul is respected more than the human body." Paul

Elmer More presents weighty arguments, indeed, that the rights of property are more precious than life: we would give up our lives for our country, which means our laws and the institutions they protect, at the basis of which rests security, which means stability and protection of property. Surely More's archenemies, the proponents of the economic basis of history, must agree. Stalin concurs; Hitler died of it. Follow More's logic rigorously, and perhaps the only one to demur can be the pacifist.

In child-training also, even within "progressive" consideration of freedom and individual initiative, social adjustment is the goal. The end of education is the production of good citizens. The Associate Superintendent of the public schools of New York City emphasizes what he calls the new conception of the school as a builder of children for social usefulness. The Regents' tests, he declares, do not measure its effectiveness as a social instrument. And he concludes: "Never was there a time when the schoolmaster could turn with greater profit to the encyclical on the reconstruction of the social order."

Seventeen leaders in education are studied in Norman Woelfel's *Molders of the American Mind*. He sets them in three groups: those that stress the values inherent in American historical traditions; those that accept as foundation of their practice the ultimacy of science; and those that follow the implications of modern experimental naturalism. The second and third both assume the basic validity of natural law. Woelfel's adherence is to the third group, where he places the most prominent figure in the whole field, John Dewey.

[Dewey's pupil Irwin Edman, however, reaches out to the first group, with a sharp warning against the abandonment of self-discipline and the loss of cultural ties that much of modern education hazards or entails. Edman has proclaimed that "the great tradition is still alive, more alive by far than the passing fashions in current literature and art." It is a surprise that so careful a thinker as Professor Edman should beg the question with the word "passing"; but I have long wished that the auth-

OTHER FIELDS

ors of such statements would take the next step, and show us while it flourishes how to distinguish between a passing fashion and a valid development of the great tradition. Instead of generalizing, if only they would bring 'em back alive! John Erskine (another of Edman's teachers, I believe) once set up what he deemed the basic criterion of good art: "it must be alive." Years later he recognized that this was an empty phrase.]

Woelfel's book concludes that American social ideals must fuse in a Higher Partisanship, wherethrough only productive labor for the common good will have value, and man's goal will be a wide, true synthesis.

The European Center of the Carnegie Foundation published a quarterly called *The International Mind*. When educators in their declarations of principle, when college presidents in public address, announce that the age of rugged individualism is at an end, we may expect that a communal vision will color the outlook of the generations just ahead.

The generations just past are considered in wide cultural survey in several books of Nicholas Berdyaev. In *The Meaning of Creativeness,* he emphasizes man's need of a spiritual centering, such as one may find in social or international ideals, or in God. In *The End of Our Time,* he draws the familiar picture of the Renaissance as an age of emerging sense of personality, individuality, when first European man strutted upon the stage of modern history full of confidence in himself and his creative powers. From that period Berdyaev traces the increasing stress upon the individual until man was ready to dispense with God, supplanting Him with the man-god of Dostoievsky or the superman of Nietzsche or, in horrid reaction, with the abstract collective religion of Marx or the inward Satanism of Freud. Thus, in the very act of affirming himself, man lost himself; for when he abandoned the spiritual center of being, he threw away his own and only compass. Abstract individualism (Nietzsche) and abstract collectivism (Marx), Berdyaev declares, spring from one and the same cause, the withdrawal of man from the divine foundations of his life, his cleavage from the concrete.—Where there is no God, there is no man. In both socialism and futurist art, as Berdyaev sees them (and we should note that his linkage, if not his conclusion, is logical) the face of man is hidden in the dark shadow of a collectivism that has no face. He considers that, indeed, man is weary and ready to sink for rest into the anonymous bosom of any kind of collectivism; that the individual can be strong, in truth, only so long as it recognizes and subdues itself to "superindividualities", to superhuman realities and values. And finally, in *The Meaning of History,* Berdyaev draws from this idea of God the concept of a single design, a growing but unbroken pattern, in all the movement of mankind.

With a less religious cast, and with eyes rather toward the future, William A. Orton, in *America In Search Of Culture,* declares that what men require, even more than the bread of livelihood, is a reason for staying alive. Life must have significance. Most of all in hard times, men need something to believe in. They should be able to find it in their collective image, which they call their country. Hence the intense jingoism of desperate peoples; hence, also the fierce revolt of those that look into this national mirror and cannot like the image. But men are lost unless they can believe in something larger than themselves. Against Herbert Hoover's atavistic picture of the United States as consisting of "fluid human particles", therefore, Orton sets his ideal of membership in a corporate whole. He sees true freedom only where men "find themselves fitting, without strain, into a comprehensive social pattern." This is of course a basic tenet of the religious as well. Through submission to the dogma they win a sense at once of safety and of higher freedom. They that lose themselves in the group shall find themselves.

It follows that art is possible only as a reaching out of the individual to something beyond himself.

Great art, the greatest, demands a frightful intensity, an awful catholicity of living. Individual talent, individual experience, brilliant idiosyncrasy, cannot of themselves alone sustain it. The great artist has truly eaten the flesh and drunk the blood of the Son of Man.

The artist must feel that he *belongs*. I would not question the artist's quest of universality; unfortunately, however, many persons would have the artist belong to this or to that, would thus limit, not enlarge his sympathetic grasp. Newton Arvin characterizes what he deems the valid author: "since he will have abandoned all mysticism he will write in the secular spirit of historical materialism." Per contra, Arthur Colton declares: "Though we want to be concrete, we are realists and must be mystical too because life is mysterious." The John Reed Club's echo of Diego Rivera's cry: "I want to be a propagandist and I want to be nothing else" marks these folk as belonging indeed. Such deliberate joining, for ends mainly social and economic, may be an urgent need, this side Utopia; but the products of such persons, with all their fire flaming for their cause, are likely to prove less art than propaganda.

6. *Propaganda rears.*

PROPAGANDA! Fearful word! The dread of the innocent, who must not succumb to its poison. The flail of the emotional, who drive off argument with the cry. The dump-heap for what one dislikes, and sweeps away with his scorn. The shibboleth by which the clamant advocates of art as a weapon in the class war separate the live artists from those helplessly unaware of their time's urgings. Clarion-call, and sneer: Propaganda!

The difficulty lies in the definition. The term propaganda is currently used in at least three senses. Most of the heat in arguments over the question is generated by the friction of these various meanings, which rub violently as the speaker shifts from one to another to support his points. It may not be good for a bibbler to mix his drinks; but he should at least know the ingredients!

The first, and simplest, sense of the word propaganda is, the presentation of a point of view. In this sense, beyond cavil, every work of art is propaganda. If a man declares that propaganda has no place in art, or protests that some particular work is propaganda, he manifestly has a different definition in mind; to retort to him that all art must show the artist's attitude is ignorance if not equivocation. There is no argument save on common ground. Outside the oral English classroom in the better taught schools, it is too often forgotten that both sides in a debate must "join issue", must face the same basic questions of truth—which one side affirms, the other denies. A lad, called upon in class to distinguish between *bear* and *carry*, once boldly replied: "Carrie is a girl's name, and bare means she has nothing on her!" One meaning of a sound at a time, if you please!—But the all-inclusiveness of this first meaning of propaganda makes it of little use in the critical field.

OTHER FIELDS

Some, instead of declaring that propaganda is universal, use the term as a label for what they disapprove. Every period develops its derogatory epithet, an emotive phrase to sweep opposition aside. Thus Bolshevik came to mean, not a member of the Russian majority party, opposed—remember? to the Mensheviki, but any objectionable radical. Similarly the cry Propaganda! disposes of an objectionable point of view. The emotional evocation is sought, not any thoughtful weighing. As a term of validity in criticism, this use of the word requires no more than mention, for dismissal. Those that thus use it are less readily removed.

There remains, as alone of value in discussions of art, propaganda as not mere presentation but advocacy of a point of view. Conscious promotion of an idea; the attempt to manipulate attitudes. The supplanting of the all-around observer by the one-sided pleader.

Such a purpose, naturally, works beneath disguise. Just as the advertising man on the scent of big game calls himself a public relations counsel, thus would cover his special concern, so the subtlest propaganda would masquerade as art. And indeed, the borderline (as with many distinctions in aesthetics) is often difficult to draw. Art, we have been told, should contemplate not argue. It should lead to heightened understanding, not to deeds. But what of the social novels of Dickens, what of Stowe's *Uncle Tom's Cabin*, Galsworthy's *Justice?* Many books are so strongly steeped in their times as to preclude artistic judgment until their issues have softened with the years. We may cry Propaganda! when the work rouses us, as Virginia Woolf is provoked by Galsworthy and Wells, "to join a society or, more desperately, to write a check." We may protest when we catch a glimpse of the author's finger—however nimbly, however lightly!—pressing the scales upon our eyes. It is significant that in Galsworthy's *Loyalties* De Levis is not merely a Jew but a cad. In his *Fugitive*, by a similar tilting, the fleeing convict, a gentleman, is aided by all the gentlefolk; all the commoners that recognize him seek to return him to the authorities. And

[379]

just as this gentleman was jailed for a crime of honor, so William Falder in *Justice* commits his crime, not to get money and have a good time, but to rescue a good woman from her cruel husband.

The usual "propaganda play" is even less subtle. As in Lillian Hellman's prize-winning *Watch On the Rhine,* the hero is almost a saint, the villain has not one ray of virtue to redeem his pitch-black soul. Through many volumes dealing with the class-truggle, Upton Sinclair pictures even the shopkeeper, the newspaperman, the teacher, as a conscious enemy of progress. All these agents of the capitalist, in his books, deliberately seek to press the worker into a pattern of conformity, into submission beneath the profit-sucking system. In his novel *Oil,* however, Sinclair tells the story of the Teapot Dome scandal through the eyes of the protagonist's son. We watch the lad growing to recognize that this father he loves and admires is nonetheless "the enemy"; his practices, unlike his personality, are antisocial. With the son, the reader notes that there stalks no singled villain, but a man who, by his and his associates' standards, is a real "good fellow". Capitalist and proletarian seem alike inevitable products of the social disorder; hatred is an irrelevant emotion. Thus, instead of trying to change others, we change. Which is the only lasting revolution. . . . Whatever the success in the particular instance, the first is the method of propaganda; the second, the way of art.

You may, turning my words upon me, protest that the second is but subtler propaganda. And perhaps you are right. The author, being a man, has a point of view; the work will show it. In his day those that disagree may cry Propaganda!—And thus we confront definition One with definition Two. The cry is as crude as the work that deserves it. For—the protest at least serves as reminder—the test is subjective: what the reader feels as partial, is to him propaganda; what he feels is unbiased, may be art.

If a bias is felt, at once all are alienated that seek not spur to their desires nor bolstering of their beliefs, but the stim-

OTHER FIELDS

ulation of art. Dismiss from this consideration those that wish, in novels and plays, nothing more than entertainment; there remains a great body of readers and theatregoers that want, in addition, a mirror held to nature. They turn to art for an honest, impartial, full consideration of whatever phase of life the work presents, for a rich stimulation of their spiritual, emotional, intellectual potentialities. "Every character is in the right" is a maxim for art that probes to the core of the matter. If we see Judge Thayer only as the presiding officer that several times doomed the men he called "those sons-of-b . . . . . s" Sacco and Vanzetti, that even sat as judge to pronounce his own impartiality—we doubtless denigrate a respected and respectable member of New England society, who honestly envisaged himself as standing steadfast for the ideals of our threatened democracy. Does Ford, did Hitler, deem himself a villain?

Surely in this best of all possible worlds, moreover, there is little need of applied stress or weighted emphasis. More convincing than any partisan preachment, more blasting than explosive fabrications, is the quiet, impartial, implacable truth. To see life steadily and to see it whole is no mean, as it is no easy, aspiration. The fact that failure is likely is no argument for not trying, surely no reason for substituting a deliberately one-sided picture. This is not portrayal but betrayal.

In a sociological essay, the direct advocacy of a point of view may be refuted, but is likely to be respected. From its insinuation in the guise of fiction, recognition turns in scorn. Seen through, its usefulness is over—save among those that want signatures to a petition or a check. Propaganda may inflame, but it cannot convince. Here is the ball that knocks the prop from under it; not as art, which is self-sustained, but even as argument, as more than piped parade. The audience at a radical play consists of professional critics and radicals. Eugene O'Neill's *Days Without End*, felt to be argument for a return to Catholicism, could not draw enough Catholics to maintain it a fortnight after the subscription weeks. Most of the anti-Nazi plays languished for lack even of interested Jews. When the author's personality comes, vivid and vigorous, into his work, his presentation of an important social problem may draw many readers, interested in his analysis and possible solution. When an event has wakened widespread indignation, a rousing drama may picture it to continuing throngs. The plays of Bernard Shaw are instances of the first appeal; Robert E. Sherwood's *There Shall Be No Night,* starring Alfred Lunt and Lynn Fontanne in a story of the invasion of Finland—with profits donated to war relief—illustrates the second. The work is then, however, to be judged by two criteria: its fulness and fairness in presenting the social situation; and its quality as a work of art. The first of these determines whether it is propaganda. But the cleverest ruse of the devil is to persuade us he doesn't exist: propaganda is effective only when we think it isn't there.

The frequent opposition of propaganda and art might lead one to expect that the more there is of the one, the less there will be of the other. As I have just indicated, however, they may co-exist. Among the many impulses that set an artist creating—love, curiosity, hunger or a more spiritual want—surely indignation is not the least worthy, the least compelling. It may contribute vitality, though it disturb measure, in the result. What is of consequence to the receptor is not the initiating urge but the completed product. In this there will be discerned a residue of the personal emotions and desires of the artist. A blotch of his anger, a playing to the public out of his hopes for sales, a quirk of his predilection for puns, a pressure of his urge to remodel the world: any of these, as fly in amber, may variously impair or enhance the work.

The distinction between art and propaganda is one basically, therefore, neither of expression (which should be moulded by the aim) nor of intention (which may be distorted in the work) but of effect upon the receptor. Upton Sinclair's *The Jungle,* written to win sympathy for the downtrodden workers of the Chicago stockyards, roused a noble nation to an angry awareness that it was being fed foul meat. Much material in-

OTHER FIELDS

tended as propaganda fails because its pleading is not artfully disguised; much intended as art seems partial and biased because the creator was no more skilful than the advocate. Such limitations doubtless determine the nature of most of the stories in *The New Masses* and *The Saturday Evening Post* that are not the result of deliberate pandering to their readers' conventions and prejudices. But what is intended and what is accidental we cannot always trust even the artist himself to tell, when he does vouchsafe word. The social vision Rodin pictures as rough-hewing his work, for an instance, may be little more than a rationalization of a method originally imposed by his extreme myopia. We finally must judge, and can judge only, by the impact of the work upon our sensibility. If it rouses us roundly and deeply, we shall not call it propaganda; if it continues thus to exalt us, we call it art.

The second set of criteria will probably not be applied until the first is immaterial; as now to Stowe and Swift and Rabelais, some day to Sinclair and Shaw and Wells. Virginia Woolf's disposal of the question by a signature unwittingly shirks the issue, but illustrates my point: she sets her opposed authors in different ages. As her contemporaries move her to action, so the first readers of Jane Austen (who stirs in Miss Woolf only a desire to read again) wished to wring her neck, or to put a weapon in her hand. We are involved in the issues of our day; as a work embodies these it may enlist or alienate our sympathy. This aspect of our concern, as in our perusal of a news-article or an editorial, is irrelevant to the work as art.

We may examine a yacht as the boat on which we expect to grow seasick, or as a far-off trim craft atilt in beauty on the waters. An automobile or a piston has also two such aspects; an airplane may soar in beauty, or dive with a bomb. Even so, the painting or the book. A social document; a work of art. The one work may be either—but at different times.

Usually the work moves from the contemporary to the timeless verdict. A few creations leap as by an act of grace at once into the realm of the elect; most that win to salvation follow the longer human course of death and resurrection. A Dickens, a Dreiser, a Thackeray, an Ibsen, is in his day derided, denounced, hailed, eulogized; then, as the pendulum of the years swings beyond his temporal treatment of the eternal themes, he is belittled, accepted with condescension, tolerated, ignored, by an age that deems itself far in advance of the mid-Victorian dogmatism, smugness, hypocrisy, compromise, of its predecessor: finally—to shift the figure to an older time—if he have proper coin to cross the Stygian waves (let them prove not Lethe!), if in his handling of a vital problem the artist has given expression to more than a moment's mood, not ever (as an Orpheus) in the first ruddy vigor of active life, but like an Elysian shade the work of art takes its fit place amid the immortals.

It is not only inevitable that art shall reflect its age; it is a source of strength in the work. Thus T. S. Eliot declares that the "greatness" of literature cannot be determined by literary standards alone — though first such standards must decide whether or not it is literature. Without such a duality, Eliot believes, "great" art would deal only in abstractions and meaningless designs.

Others find the same difficulty, but seek to resolve it by withdrawing art from contemporary considerations. Such men as the early Thornton Wilder and James Branch Cabell look obliquely on their time from remote or fancied realms. John Erskine, in an essay on the subjects "proper" to art (of which I have seen no later repudiation) frowns most decidedly upon the contemporary, suggesting rather Maya than Mae West; King Arthur than Edward VIII; Troy, Ilium, instead of Troy, New York. Erskine sought to illustrate his thesis by a series of books, the best known of which is *The Private Life Of Helen Of Troy*. And in his own writings he disproved his point. For by attitude and analogy, any theme is brought home; as does not escape the motion picture vendors, who in advertising their version of Erskine's book capitalized in large red type the first letters of the last three words!

OTHER FIELDS

Withdrawal from the affairs of life was preached by Oscar Wilde:

> The only beautiful things, as somebody once said, are the things that do not concern us. As long as a thing is useful or necessary to us, or affects us in any way, either for pain or for pleasure, or appeals strongly to our sympathies, or is a vital part of the environment in which we live, it is outside of the proper sphere of art.

Yet Wilde also wrote *The Ballad of Reading Gaol.*

The sociological writers and painters cling to the other end of the pole—which they try to use as a crowbar. Aristotle knew how the two extremes are joined. For he observed that all works of art will be viewed didactically by the immature mind, which insists on extracting a lesson. Perhaps, conversely, we may declare that all propaganda is written by the adolescent. But who among us is wholly and always mature?

In a note to his exhaustive study, *Art and Prudence,* Mortimer J. Adler defines propaganda by indicating three ways in which writing may be didactic:

> (1) the logical sense, in which it is construed as containing syllogisms and as aiming to establish conclusions by evidence or premises; (2) the rhetorical sense, in which it is construed as aiming, not to prove, but to persuade by quasi-arguments and emotional appeals; (3) the analogical sense, in which it is construed as "teaching" in the same way in which life or experience is said to teach. Everything that is knowable is didactic in the last sense.

These three aspects distinguish science, oratory, and art. Neither proof nor persuasion is relevant to art. Propaganda, Professor Adler classes as writing didactic in the second sense. He must admit, however, in art as full as a play or a novel or a motion picture (his immediate theme), incidental application of the other emphases. The detective reasons deftly; the villain lures the maiden to her fall. But—even beyond this concession—the purpose of the author to convince or to persuade is by no means necessarily destructive of the work as art. Surely art has no lack of emotional appeals!

An emphasis may rise so strongly from contemporary concerns as to obliterate aesthetic judgment, deferring to later times the decision as to whether the work's value was social, then historical, or is also and enduringly literary. If one behold a fly squirming in sticky capture, one merely notes the destruction of a pest; seeing a dog in a quicksand, one may stretch forth a plank for its rescue; finding our fellows—ourselves—sunken in quagmires of poverty and injustice, we may toil in mutual help. But we may preserve as a curio, or cast away, the insect imbedded in amber; those ancient bones, the scientist studies or waves aside; this book of another battle, another age, the youth may resent in school study, or never find, the lover of literature may deem of historic interest, or cherish as one of the living works in which with lasting validity an aspect of human concern is recorded. Propaganda, clashing in the conflicts of life, is fleeting; art, poised like Helen above the battlements of a warring world, endures.

Herein the pattern is named.

A name given before a description is a mere label — often accepted as a substitute for the description, thereby supplanting thought and understanding. Onomagic is widely prevalent, even today.

Having our description, let us repeat the bald pattern, now that the names have meaning. Let us also repeat that no period is unmixed; every age is transitional, hence bears holdovers of the age before and anticipations of the age to come.

Attitudes A and B (as on pages 11 and 12) mark the main emphasis of successive periods, a polarity in pendulum swing through time. Attitudes 1 and 2 are a second polarity, within every period, ateeter on the pendulum:

A. Emphasis on oneself; the individual; the separate item; variety.

    1. All things, including man, in one order or flux (or grab-bag, or chaos) of nature ....*Realism*

    2. A man as different, prime, free ....*Romanticism*

B. Emphasis on the collective; the integrating law; the essence; unity.

    1. Natural law or basic essence the same in all things, including mankind ....*Ultraism*

    2. Mankind as different, superior, with common conscience ....*Humanism*

Thus move the major attitudes, beneath our acts and works.

NOTES

Notes

These notes contain:

    1. Titles of books or names of persons alluded to in the text.

    2. The original version of poems quoted from other languages.

    3. Development of points pertinent to the book's thesis, but not relevant in such detail in the body of the book.

* * *

In order to leave the main flow unbroken, no indication of these notes is given in the text. They are intended to supplement rather than complement the main material.

HISTORY REPEATS ITSELF

Notes

(*The prescript before each item indicates the page to which it has reference.*)

7. Sir William Bragg: *The Universe of Light.*
8. Morris R. Cohen: *Reason and Nature: an essay on the meaning of scientific method.*
10. Kenneth Burke: *Counterstatement.*
11. "History repeats itself".
    The saying finds so many examples, in the petty details of anyone's life, that very few seek beyond it. Those that do are likely to remain content with some such remark as: New times but reshuffle the old cards. In his introduction to the first issue of *The Journal of the History of Ideas*, editor Arthur O. Lovejoy declares that no thoughtful person can deny such oscillation.
    He is properly taken to task by Frederick J. Teggart, who in the fourth issue of the *Journal* upholds the claims of progress. These two notions have indeed been opposed through the ages. Aristotle remarked: "Empedocles supposes the course of nature to return upon itself, coming around again periodically to the starting-point; while Anaxagoras makes it move continuously without repeating itself."
    Teggart scatters examples down the ages, of noted thinkers that see history moving in an orbit, around cycles, and of others that view it as moving along a trajectory, an unreturning path. He quotes Bacon's observation that wise and serious men come to feel that "in the revolution of time and of the ages of the world the sciences have their ebbs and flows; that at one season they grow and flourish, at another wither and decay, yet in such sort that when they have reached a certain point and con-

dition they can advance no further." Then Teggart reminds us that Bacon presents this not as valid, but as "by far the greatest obstacle to the advancement of knowledge and to the undertaking of new tasks therein."

For the notion of a cyclic return of conditions breeds resignation, cynicism, eagerness to snatch what one can. The idea of progress, on the other hand, Teggart declares, quoting Comte, Dewey, and Whitehead ("Progress consists in modifying the laws of nature") incites men to study, then to act. Discern the path to the coming day, then hasten its arrival. Thus against the oscillatory theory of history Teggart ranges the followers of Kant, Hegel, and Marx, of Rousseau and Comte, of Darwin, as well as all that still keep the Christian faith. He might have added that the Romantic conception of the power of the human will breeds the notion of the infinite possibility of progress. He should observe, however, that science posits the advancement of the group; religion, of the individual. In this regard too, the "Age of Reason"—the eighteenth century—was anti-Christian. There is no reference to the progress of mankind in either Oriental or Christian doctrine; each sees betterment, in every generation, as an individual achievement.

Progress, to Epictetus (*Discourses* 1, Chap. 4), consists in acting in harmony with nature. The notion of progress as an increasing command over nature, as a development of society, came into being with the "scientific attitude". "Two words", says Macaulay, "are the key to the Baconian doctrine: Utility and Progress." More and more, with industrial and mechanical concentration, with the mass activity of our time, the earnest exhortation that the individual make himself a better man is being drowned in the clanking chorus of collective urgings toward the betterment of mankind.

The notion of progress, not only because of its bondage to science, fares best among measurable things. Its sturdiest claims, therefore, are those that seek to reduce all qualitative "values" to quantitative portions. Such an attempt is summarized by Anatol Rapoport (*ETC*, vol. ii,

3, Spring 1945) in *The Criterion of Predictability*. He remarks that, as it is the positivists' goal to reduce all knowledge to measurements of quantities (reduction indeed!), so is all truth based on the criterion of predictability, which fundamentally means on order and structure and their logical development, i.e., mathematics. (Waldemar Kaempffert also finds that many scientists expect the ultimate recognition that all "reality" is composed of forces that can be measured quantitatively. Less optimistic voices deplore the loss of quality in the world.) From the "early classical examples" of such reduction, wherein pitch and color were shown to be not qualities but quantities, Rapoport points to similar growths in modern mechanics, in chemistry, and beneath the "qualitative" differences of the chemical elements the structural formulations of subatomic physics; beyond these, he indicates the application of the statistical method (laws of average, probability, etc.) to large-scale consideration of human affairs, and looks forward to the time when emotions, and the "verbalizations commonly called ethics", will be traced as changes of colloidal structure within the human cells.

Thus religion and philosophy have failed, Rapoport avers, because they cannot submit to the criterion of predictability, the *"only* yardstick of truth" (italics his) not alone in the fields of natural science but throughout the entire range of meaningful knowledge.

"Happiness, which a hero of *War and Peace* defines negatively as 'the absence of illness and remorse', may constantly approach more precise definitions as the physical, colloidal nature of both illness and remorse becomes known. Social science may then become a study of conditions which will guarantee this state to a maximum number of individuals. It will merge with medical science, simply dividing with the latter the spheres of influence." Such a consideration of man and nature, though it wipes away all the "ethical values" as such, may admit them as quantitative aspects of a scientific approach toward progress. For the goal of progress is ever "higher" civilization, and the highest civilization, Rapoport affirms, "is a state of affairs among human beings where a minimum of conflict, a maximum of freedom, and a maximum of knowledge, prevail."

This attitude—whether one accept it or reject—manifestly shares the unifying spirit of our age, subsuming every aspect of man's functions under the norms of science. And more—since freedom is defined as "maximum predictability of one's own behavior"; and knowledge, as "maximum predictability, with minimum assumptions, about the external world"—we have all that is, or can be, confined in a single pattern of order, and all criteria of reality and truth made one.

The movement of mankind, I suppose, can be envisaged in three ways. The historian Arthur M. Schlesinger, Jr. says that one decides on chaos, cycles, or progress, by an act of faith. Despite the mad mess of the world today, however, most persons feel that the first of these was eliminated when, by the primal act, out of chaos came cosmos. While scientists in the main choose progress as the movement they see, at least in scientific fields, H. T. Pledge, Librarian of the Science Museum of London, in *Science Since 1500* (1947) declares that "we can observe the alternation of continuity and discreteness among the key ideas in the history of science." This alternation, he continues, is not intrinsic to science, but occurs because of the operation of social and economic factors. In other words, it appears in science because it is intrinsic to life. George Sarton, professor of the history of science, speculates in the same fashion: "Not only are the old ideas restored to vogue, but it sometimes seems that a kind of rhythm brings them back to light periodically" (*The Life of Science,* 1948).

The two conceptions, of recurrent cycles and of continuous progress, are examined in many fields, in the provocative study of Ellsworth Huntington (*Mainsprings of Civilization,* 1945; esp. chaps. 24-30), with indication that the two types of motion in human affairs may co-exist. They must, in truth, coalesce. For history turns upon itself, but not in circles: *in a spiral,* thus ever moving onward, traversing old attitudes at higher levels. Or—in the favorite figure of oscillation—mankind abides (where Poe's tale takes one man) in a pit beneath a pendulum. The walls of the pit are nature; the pendulum span is from the One to the many. Only (for those that believe in progress) with man's onward growth the walls recede, and the pendulum rises. Thus time's pattern seems unchanging, if one judge by the shadows on the wall. Yet actually man is driving natural barriers ever farther back, is commanding ever a wider view of nature's powers; and ever the span between individual freedom and social good (to mention but the sociological aspect of the pendulum swing) grows more narrow. And men may look forward to that far yet finite day when the walls of ignorance have dropped beyond the horizon; and the urges of the many are blended with the harmony of the One.

In the meantime, it may be worth pointing to some manifestations, especially in art, along a few turns of the spiral. Nor need we be discouraged if the tale is not new. Everything's been said—but nobody listens. History teaches, if nothing else, man's unwillingness to learn from it.— Which considerations give me courage to rush in.

[Far more frequently than the notion of progress, the notion of man's retrogression has held sway: that we are, indeed, moving along, or along a spiral—but down. The Jews and the Christians picture the primordial Garden of Eden, from which accursed man has been damned to sweat and tears. The Greeks, as in Homer and Hesiod, trace man's descent from the earlier Golden Age of pristine innocence and general good. So commonplace has this idea of a glorious past become that in every generation the senescent voice lament for "the good old days".

More specifically and more historically, the disintegration and death of civilizations has been traced—with fullest body in Edward Gibbon's famous study of *The History of the Decline and Fall of the Roman Empire* (1776-1788). Since this work, the survey of past societies has been widened. Comte Joseph de Gobineau, in his

Essay on the Inequality of Human Races (1854) weighed the problems of the fall of successive societies, and saw a solution in the supremacy of the Aryan race, as that which could create and sustain the highest civilization. But he felt that the superior Aryans were bound to be absorbed by admixture with inferior races, and that every culture is destined to die. Flinders Petrie, in *The Revolutions of Civilization* (1911), presented eight great epochs of Mediterranean life, averaging 1330 years in duration, and each passing through the same successive stages of culture. First came a flowering of sculpture, then of painting, of literature, of music; finally, marking the decline, a surge of mechanical accomplishment, then of wealth before the doom.

Without the racial emphasis of Gobineau, Oswald Spengler, in *The Decline of the West* (1911-1914) combined these pictures into the hypothesis that all societies inevitably pass through an identical succession of stages (he calls the highest stage "culture", and the decline "civilization") to a final rigidity and death. Looking across the Egyptian, Classical, Chinese, and Arabian racial-life-stories to our own, Spengler declared that western culture had exhausted its values by 1800, and that we are now in the "civilization" stage, moving toward our imminent end. Such a prospect, of course, is hailed by the Soviet Communists, who deem their own the dawning culture of the epoch ahead.

The inevitability of this downward movement has been challenged, however, by various historians and other thinkers, who state that the analogy between racial life and human life has been pressed too far, that by self-examination and self-correction a society may escape the ultimate doom. Doubtless, in every culture, most persons took its permanence for granted. Ozymandias (in Shelley's sonnet; but also in history: Fourteenth Century B.C.) sets the mood. In the moribund years of the impending death of a society, its claims of perdurance probably grow more frenetic. We have seen (page 356f) the various ways in which the artists of our time attack the problem of their passing.

Historians look more directly at the issues involved. Thus Arnold J. Toynbee, in *A Study of History* (begun 1934, still incomplete; a one-volume condensation became a "best seller" in 1947), studies the twenty-six civilizations of which history tells, and finds sixteen already buried, and all the remaining ones disintegrating, save possibly our own. This, he feels, may be saved by great leaders who will persuade (not force) the people to their ideals. Along the same path Richard M. Weaver (in *Ideas Have Consequences,* University of Chicago Press, 1948) has set up warning signposts. When the consumer, that is, the mass, becomes the criterion, Weaver avers, knowledge is power in the service of appetite. A lack of respect toward nature, toward individual personality, toward the past, characterizes our time, along with the supergrowth of the machine; equally cause and consequence of this disrespect are both the "scientific" rationalism that, beginning with religion, would sweep aside all abstractions, all a priori or permanent ideals, and the neo-mysticism—warp of ignorance, woof of Freud—that would sweep aside all reliance on reason. The denial of distinctions, mistakenly made in the names of equality and democracy, may lead to the death of distinction. The passion for immediacy, the impatience and rebelliousness of many in our time, are symptoms of the speed with which we rush to our undoing.

Toynbee, Weaver, and many more, feel that modern man's descent into chaos—facilis descensus!—can be checked only by the hard climb of disciplined endeavor on the upward trail of man's ideals. To those for whom religion still has meaning, this will seem self-evident. Their most moderate yet cogent voice has been raised by Rosalind Murray, in *The Good Pagan's Failure,* unanswerable if faith is in your marrow. Those without such faith may find lean sustenance in the ideas of existentialism (See page 359f).

The scientist will frown and say that social prophecy is out of his sphere—which is an admission that the study of society is not yet a science. The Communist will smile and say "The future is mine". And indeed, if we do not heed the portents, this may for a time seem true—which will mean that man must again begin, athwart the new tyrannies, his life-long march toward freedom.]

What most persons that discuss "progress" overlook is that the idea has pertinence only in the field of science. "Scientific activities", says George Sarton (in *The Life of Science,* 1948) "are the only ones which are cumulative and progressive." Furthermore, he adds, "Science is progressive and therefore ephemeral; art is non-progressive and eternal." In truth, "progress" is not a criterion in other fields.

"The great story which cries to be told," Sarton emphasizes, "is that of the rhythm of the mutual interrelationships between science, art, and religion. The story is very difficult to tell, because it is not a story of progress like the history of science, but of vacillations and vicissitudes, of harmony followed by chaos, and beauty mixed with horrors. It would be the story of man's sensitiveness to the fundamental problems and main values of life . . . Beauty is there for all to see, and truth, and virtue, but how few realize that they are but different aspects of the same mystery!" More and more of us, I believe, are recognizing the essential unity of that story; and in its creation, this book is the preliminary study for a chapter. "It is necessary," Sarton concludes, and thereby shows himself a child of his age, "to create a new synthesis." Others put it that we have rather to reawaken the soul.

16. "Aristidization": Henry Hazlitt: *The Nation.* vol. 130; No. 3371.

Doubtless Hazlitt is merely utilizing a legend; politics clanks with other chains than boredom. The only allusion the *Encyclopaedia Britannica* makes to the story of the "famous victim", is a note in the appended bibliography: "In the absence of positive information the fourth century writers (on whom Plutarch and Nepos mainly rely) wove around his surname of *Just* a number of anecdotes." The

NOTES

main encyclopedia discussion of Aristides states: "It is certain that the period following the Persian wars during which he shaped Athenian policy was one of conservative reaction." This should seem, to *The Nation,* sufficient reason for his overthrow! Indeed, in his book *The Anatomy of Criticism* Hazlitt later applies the term more moderately.

17. Most often, writers seem in accord with the main currents of their time and place. The rebel here that sneers at the "bourgeois artists" of America for praising the status quo should note that in Soviet Russia there are no rebels to sneer; *every* artist follows the "party line".

22. See section *Propaganda rears,* in *Other Fields.*

23. Edith Hamilton: *The Roman Way.*

26. Elie Faure: *L'Esprit des formes.*

32. Edmund Spenser-Gabriel Harvey correspondence. The poet Spenser, during the period of his classical experiments, more straitly insisted upon the classical rules of quantity than did the scholar Harvey.

36. En vain contre *Le Cid* un ministre se ligue,
Tout Paris pour Chimène a les yeux de Rodrigue.
L'Académie en corps a beau le censurer:
Le public révolté s'obstine à l'admirer.

38. "The business of the poet ... is to examine, not the individual, but the species . . . he does not number the streaks of the tulip, or describe the different shades in the verdure of the forest."—Samuel Johnson, *Rasselas,* Chap. 10.

40. Laurie Magnus: *English literature in its foreign relations.*

57. Uber allen Gipfeln ist Ruh.

57. Die Phantasie, in ihren hochsten Flug,
Sie strengt sich an und tut sich nie genug;
Doch fassen Geister, wurdig tief zu schauen,
Zum Grenzenlosen grenzenlos Vertrauen.

60. There can be no expectation, in suggesting a basic char-

[399]

acteristic of Romanticism, of wiping away all prior applications of the term. Arthur O. Lovejoy (*On the Discrimination of Romanticisms, PMLA* xxxix, 1924; reprinted in *Essays in the History of Ideas,* 1948) declares that one had best use the word in the plural: Romanticisms. This is of course historically true—without affecting the validity of the present distinction. The fact that romanticism is a multivalued word, indeed, encourages me to assign what seems at present the most serviceable significance.

61. The word nature, Lovejoy reminds us, has been used in some sixty different significancies. In *Nature as Aesthetic Norm* (*Modern Language Notes,* 1927; reprinted in *Essays in the History of Ideas,* 1948) he presents a score of these, as applied in man's estimation of beauty.

61. Le poète s'en va dans les champs; il admire,
Il adore, il écoute en lui-même un lyre,
Et le voyant venir, les fleurs, toutes les fleurs,
Celles qui des rubis font pâlir les couleurs,
Celles qui des paons méme èclipseraient les queues,
Les petites fleurs d'or, les petites fleurs bleues,
Prennent, pour l'acceuillir agitants leurs bouquets,
De petits airs penchés ou de grands airs coquets,
Et, familièrement, car cela sied bien aux belles:
—Tiens! c'est notre amoureux qui passe! disent-elles.

Hugo

63. Ainsi, nature! abri de toute créature!
O mère universelle! indulgente nature!
Ainsi, tous à la fois, mystiques et charnels,
Cherchant l'ombre et le lait sous tes flancs éternels,
Nous sommes là, savants, poètes, pêle-mêle,
Pendus de toutes parts à ta forte mamelle.

Hugo

65. Mais à ces douces beautés mon âme indifferente . . .

Lamartine

65. Quoi donc! c'est vainement qu'ici nous aimâmes!
Rien ne nous restera de ces coteaux fleuris

NOTES

Où nous fondions notre être en y mêlant nos flammes!
L'impossible nature a déjà tout repris.
Hugo

72. Byron and Scott were for a few years (about 1825) fertile ground for subjects for French painters, playwrights, and composers; and costumes for the masquerades of the period were chosen among their characters. The French conservatives found their best answer to Byron in quoting him:

> Brightest in dungeons, Liberty, thou art,
> For there thy habitation is the heart—

the true dwelling-place of freedom is indeed the heart; but the heart of Byron (and, they added, of every Romantic) is slave to his passions.

77. Aus meinen grosses Schmerzen
Mach' ich die kleine Lieder.
Heine

77. Anfange wollt ich fast verzagen,
Und ich glaubt, ich trüg es nie;
Und ich hab es doch getragen,—
Aber fragt mir nur nicht: Wie?
Heine

77. Examples could of course be multiplied:
L'art ne fait que des vers, le coeur seul est poète.
Merely verse is made by art,
The only poet is the heart.
André Chenier

Alfred de Musset:
Ah! frappe-toi le coeur, c'est là qu'est le génie.
C'est là qu'est la pitié, la souffrance et l'amour.
Ah! Strike to your heart; it's there that genius lies;
It's there lie pity, suffering, and love.

Ce que l'homme ici-bas appelle le génie,
C'est le besoin d'aimer; hors de là tout est vain.
What man down here calls genius
Is the need to love; all else is vain.

Aimer est le grand point, qu'importe la maîtresse?
Qu'importe le flacon pourvu qu'on ait l'ivresse!

[401]

To love's the essential; what matters the mistress?
What matters the flask if the drunkenness comes!

78. Reason, however, it should be noted, can recognize truth, can indeed combine truths; but it cannot create them. Observation of this fact led Renan to seek to unite science, the quest of truth, with religion, the quest of good. He remarked: "Reason alone cannot create truth . . . It is philology, or erudition, that will provide the thinker with that forest of things (*silva rerum ac sententiarum,* as Cicero puts it) without which philosophy will never be more than a Penelope's weaving always to be recommenced." Then, in the last preface to *The Future of Science* (1888 edition), Renan crossed the bridge: "My religion is still the progress of reason, that is, of science . . . For us idealists, one single doctrine is true, the transcendent doctrine according to which the purpose of mankind is the creation of a superior conscience, or, as they put it in the old days, the greatest glory of God."

81. Qui de nous, Lamartine, et de notre jeunesse,
Ne sait par coeur ce chant, des amants adoré,
Qu'un soir, au bord du lac, tu nous as soupiré?
Which of us, Lamartine, from our very youth,
Hasn't known by heart the song, adored of lovers,
That one evening, by the lake, you sighed to us?
Alfred de Musset

81-82. Le Lac (The Lake)
Alphonse Marie Louis de Prat de Lamartine

Ainsi, toujours poussés vers de nouveaux rivages,
Dans la nuit éternelle emportés sans retour,
Ne pourrons-nous jamais sur l'océan des ages
   Jeter l'ancre un seul jour? . . .

"O temps, suspends ton vol! et vous, heures propices,
   Suspendez votre cours!
Laissez-nous savourer les rapides délices
   Des plus beaux de nos jours!

"Assez de malheurex ici-bas vous implorent:
   Coulez, coulez pour eux;

NOTES

> Prenez avec leurs jours les soins qui les dévorent;
>   Oubliez les heureux" . . .
>
> Temps jaloux, se peut-il que ces moments d'ivresse,
> Ou l'amour à longs flots nous verse le bonheur,
> S'envolent loin de nous de la même vitesse
>   Que les jours de malheur?
>
> Hé quoi! n'en pourrons-nous fixer au moins la trace?
> Quoi! passés pour jamais? quoi! tout entiers perdus?
> Ce temps qui les donna, ce temps qui les efface,
>   Ne nous les rendra plus?
>
> Eternité, néant, passé, sombres abîmes,
> Que faites-vous des jours que vous engloutissez?
> Parlez: nous rendrez-vous ces extases sublimes
>   Que vous nous ravissez? . . .

85. (88). Naturally, as I wish the reader to have always in mind, this pressing on the emotions is by no means a purely literary development. Events in the late eighteenth century turned many of the reading public (as in our time to detective stories) to seek distraction in the terror novel, which became the current vogue.

86. Alfred de Vigny begins one of his best-known poems:
J'aime le son du cor, le soir, au fond des bois . . .
I love the sound of the horn, at dusk, in the depths of the woods . . .

and ends it:

Dieu! que le son du cor est triste au fond des bois!
God! how sad is the sound of the horn in the depths of the woods!

Alphonse de Lamartine:
Mon coeur, lassé de tout, même de l'espérance,
N'ira plus de ses voeux importuner le sort.
My heart, weary of all things, even of hope,
Will no longer go with its vows to importune fate.

[403]

Alfred de Musset:
Les plus désesperés sonts les chants les plus beaux
Et j'en sais d'immortels qui sonts des purs sanglots.
The most despairing songs are the most beautiful;
I know some immortal ones that are pure sobs.

(which is French for Shelley's "Our sweetest songs are those that tell of saddest thought".)

Rien ne nous rend si grands qu'une grande douleur.
Nothing makes us so great as a great sorrow.

L'homme est un apprenti, la douleur est son maître,
Et nul ne se connaît tant il n'a pas souffert . . .
Pour vivre et pour sentir, l'homme a besoin des pleurs.
Man's an apprentice, his master is grief,
And no one knows himself that has not suffered . . .
To live and to feel, a man has need of tears.

Le seul bien qui me reste au monde
Est d'avoir quelquefois pleuré.
The one thing good in the world that's left to me
Is that I have sometimes wept.

The cure for all this mooning melancholy, this sad sweet sipping of mellow mournfulness, is implicit in a line of Musset's own *Fantasio*:

Il n'y a point de maître d'armes mélancolique.
There's no such thing as a doleful fencing-master!

90.   La tombe dit à la rose:
—Des pleurs dont l'aube t'arrose
Que fais-tu, fleur des amours?
La rose dit à la tombe:
—Que fais-tu de ce qui tombe
Dans ton gouffre ouvert toujours?

La rose dit:—Tombeau sombre,
De ces pleurs je fais dans l'ombre
Un parfum d'ambre et de miel.
La tombe dit:—Fleur plaintive,
De chaque âme qui m'arrive,
Je fais un ange du ciel.

Hugo

NOTES

90. Les uns vont courbés sous le fardeau des peines;
Au banquet de bonheur bien peu sonts conviés.
Tous n'y sont point assis également à l'aise.
Une loi, qui d'en bas semble injuste et mauvaise,
Dit aux uns: Jouissez! aux autres: Enviez! . . .
Hugo

91. Votre aile en le heurtant ne fera rien répandre
Du vase où je m'abreuve et que j'ai bien rempli.
Mon âme a plus de feu que vous n'avez de cendre!
Mon coeur a plus d'amour que vous n'avez d'oubli!
Hugo

95. "a short round-trip". In many moods death and love have served as reciprocal imagery. The association of religion and love, widespread beyond any need of present noting, often bears post-mortem emphasis. The "bride of Christ" was somehow to be united with her mate in the happy realm where there is neither marriage nor giving in marriage; it is in heaven that Lycidas hears the unexpressive nuptial song. But more directly, and often, love turns metaphor for death, or death serves as symbol for mating. *Mors erotica;* "death thy bride". When Thomas Nash declares

    I come, I come, sweet Death, rock me asleep! . . .
    The whiles I sleep my soul is stealing hence
    And life forsakes his earthly residence—

    he means what Dryden makes more plain:

    The youth, though in haste
    And breathing his last
    In pity died slowly, while she died more fast;
    Till at length she cry'd Now, my dear, let us go,
    Now die, my Alexis, and I will die too.

    Emily Dickinson in more sober mood reverses the imagery:

    A wife at daybreak I shall be;
    Sunrise, hast thou a flag for me?
    At midnight I am yet a maid—
    How short it takes to make it bride!

[405]

Then, Midnight, I have passed from thee
Unto the East and Victory.

Midnight, "Good night!"
I hear them call,
The angels bustle in the hall,
Softly my Future climbs the stair,
I fumble at my childhood's prayer—
So soon to be a child no more!
Eternity, I'm coming, Sir—
Master, I've seen that face before.

96. Plonger au fond du gouffre, Enfer, ou Ciel, qu'importe?
Au fond de l'inconnu pour trouver du *nouveau!*

99. The Clavilux, or Color Organ, is an electrical device for breaking light and throwing on a screen patterns of color in harmonies of shifting design and hue. Or see the Walt Disney film *Fantasia*.

105. The journey, of course, serves other purposes as well, such as permitting essential description to be borne in the narrative flow, and through eyes as new to the land as the reader's.

107-8. Readers of today, with *Forever Amber, The Chinese Room,* and the rest of their own breed of aphrodisiac teasers, may have forgotten the *Three Weeks* of Elinor Sutherland Glyn, *The Gadfly* of Ethel Lillian Boole Voynich.

These tit-bits of suggestion were memorialized in many a romping rhyme, of which the milder are printable; for instance:

Would you like to sin   On a tiger skin   With Elinor Glyn?
Or would you prefer   To err   On some other fur?

If you wanna be bad fly   To follow *The Gadfly,*
And feel your groin itch   With Ethel Boole Voynich.

No doubt the same sorts of versifier with agile feet and risqué laughter clamber after *Forever Amber;* there

NOTES

are those that with ribald whimsy distort the honest intent of the *Kinsey Report*.

112. There is a hint of our insistence on man's supremacy, in our habit of using animals as symbols of the worst in man. There are more men than dogs like "the dog in the manger"; the viper that bites its benefactor is to be condemned only if human. We exceed other animals in vice, as in virtue—because these are human attributes, extended to the beasts only by our presumption. We choose, even in our imagery, to hold superior.

115. The loss of fear through faith (without the balance of reason) is another hold of Communism upon its adherents. For those that embrace its creed without reservations, that manifest themselves as loyal disciples, unquestioning through every change in the party line, there is the reward of security. Not only does Communism remove the uncertainties of life for its devout, but it holds against the backsliding the counter-fear of the purge. Do not think; do not deviate: believe. There is safety within the sickle; the hammer is for those outside.

In times of widespread insecurity and fear, not only is there a fresh surging of belief (or at any rate of avowed believers) in the various religions, but many persons in different fields make an idol of faith. See pages 227; 237; and especially 302. It is thus characteristic of our age that it should add to the ideals a new "freedom": freedom from fear (page 328).

120-1. Julien Benda: *Belphegor*.

121. G. K. Chesterton: *The Victorian age in literature*.

121-2. That Shakespeare was not wholly bemused in the romantic glamour of wooing may be judged from the couples he sets as foils to the happy Rosalind and Orlando, in *As You Like It*. Touchstone takes up with Audrey: "Oh, well, I suppose it has to be some one; come along, wench, here's what may pass for a parson." To this casual cohabitation is added another doomed match, when Rosalind, disguised as a man, tricks young Phoebe into marrying the doddering Silvius, whom she detests. Finally: Oliver repents, Celia is nearby and unattached: let's hitch them! Cynical counter-currents in the stream of happy love!

124. More causes (here irrelevant) of the liking for originality and the far seeking for novelty might of course be mentioned. Those interested will find some of them developed in the author's *The Quest For Literature,* pages 389 f. and 414 f.

131. "Procrustean bed". In *my* bed, with its four crossed slats, at least you can play tic-tac-toe!

142. *Early Victorian England,* 1830-1865. Two volumes issued by the Oxford University Press, under the general editorship of G. M. Young.

152. Sonnet For a Picture

(parody of Dante Gabriel Rossetti,
leader of the Pre-Raphaelites)

That nose is out of drawing. With a gasp
She pants upon the passionate lips that ache
With the red drain of her own mouth, and make
A monochord of colour. Like an asp
One lithe lock wriggles in his rutilant grasp.
Her bosom is an oven of myrrh, to bake
Love's warm white shewbread to a browner cake.
The lock his fingers clench has burst its clasp.
The legs are absolutely abominable.
Ah! what keen overgust of wild-eyed woes
Flags in that bosom, flushes in that nose?
Nay, death sets riddles for desire to spell,
Responsive. What red hem earth's passion sews,
But may be ravenously unripped in hell?

Swinburne

This is suggests, too, the efforts of the decadents among the French.

157. La nature est un temple où de vivants piliers
Laissent parfois sortir de confuses paroles;

NOTES

L'homme y passe à travers des forêts de symboles
Qui l'observent avec des regards familiers.

Comme de longs échos qui de loin se confondent
Dans une ténébreuse et profonde unité,
Vaste comme la nuit et comme la clarté,
Les parfums, les couleurs et les sons se répondent.
Baudelaire

159. "titbits": Glenway Westcott: *A Calendar of Saints for Unbelievers.*

159. Ce soir, la lune rêve avec plus de paresse;
Ainsi qu'un beauté, sur de nombreux coussins,
Qui d'une main distraite et légère caresse,
Avant de s'endormir, le contour de ses seins . . .
Baudelaire

160. Vous êtes un beau ciel d'automne, clair et rose!
Mais la tristesse en moi monte comme la mer,
Et laisse, en refluant, sur ma lèvre morose
Le souvenir cuisant de son limon amer.
Baudelaire

160. Vainement ma raison voulait prendre la barre;
La tempête en jouant déroutait ses efforts,
Et mon âme dansait, dansait, vieille gabarre
Sans mâts; sur une mer monstrueuse et sans bords!
Baudelaire

160-1. Quand le ciel bas et lourd pèse comme un couvercle
Sur l'esprit gémissant en proie aux longs ennuis,
Et que de l'horizon embrassant tout le cercle
Il nous verse un jour noir plus triste que les nuits;

Quand la terre est changée en un cachot humide,
Où l'espérance, comme une chauve-souris,
S'en va battant les murs de son aile timide
Et se cognant la tête à des plafonds pourris;

Quand la pluie étalant ses immenses trainées
D'une vaste prison imite les barreaux,
Et qu'un peuple muet d'infâmes araignées
Vient tendre ses filets au fond de nos cerveaux,

Des cloches tout à coup sautent avec furie
Et lancent vers le ciel un affreux hurlement,
Ainsi que des esprits errants et sans patrie
Qui se mettent á geindre opiniâtrement.

—Et de longs corbillards, sans tambours ni musique,
Défilent lentement dans mon âme: l'Espoir,
Vaincu, pleure, et l'Angoisse atroce, despotique,
Sur mon crâne incliné plante son drapeau noir.
Baudelaire

161. . . . plongé dans cette volupté
D'évoquer le Printemps avec ma volonté,
De tirer un soleil de mon coeur et de faire
De mes pensers brûlants une tiède atmosphère.
Baudelaire

165. For Hugo Blümner and Gertrude Stein, see pages 260 f.

166. Et l'harmonie est trop exquise,
Qui gouverne tout son beau corps,
Pour que l'impuissante analyse
En note les nombreux accords.

O metamorphose mystique
De tous mes sens fondus en un!
Son haleine fait la musique,
Comme sa voix fait le parfum!
Baudelaire

166. *A* noir, *E* blanc, *I* rouge, *U* vert, *O* bleu, voyelles.

168. *The Sorcerer's Apprentice,* Dukas; Debussy; Cadman; Debussy; Rimsky-Korsakoff; Richard Strauss.
      Program music playfully climbs to its apogee—which in serious mood would be its reductio ad absurdum, or would send it back home to opera—in *Peter and the Wolf,* by Prokofieff. In this, the story is told not on the program but by a narrator, whose comments the conductor directs over and between the notes of the music.

169. Mark Van Doren: *The Poetry of John Dryden.*

NOTES

169-70. It is interesting to observe that the passage from Coleridge's *Cristabel* which Ruskin quotes as his "horrible example" of pathetic fallacy:—

> The one red leaf, the last of its clan,
> That dances as often as dance it can,
> Hanging so light, and hanging so high,
> On the topmost twig that looks up at the sky—

is quoted twice by George Moore, in his essay on pure poetry, with the highest praise: *"Time cannot wither nor custom stale* a dream-flower like this one; creating out of itself, the mind gave birth belike to immortality."

170. Frère, de ces deux voix étranges, inouïes,
San cesse renaissantes, sans cesse évanouies,
Qu'écoute l'Eternel durant l'éternité,
L'une disait Nature! et l'autre, Humanité!
Hugo

170. . . . pourquoi le Seigneur, qui seul lit à son livre,
Mêle éternellement dans un fatal hymen
Le chant de la nature au cri du genre humain?
Hugo

170-1. H. Flanders Dunbar: *Symbolism in Medieval Thought.*

173. La laine des moutons sinistres de la mer.
Hugo

La chair est triste, hélas, et j'ai lu tous les livres.
Fuir! là-bas fuir! Je sense que des oiseaux sont ivres
D'être parmi l'écume inconnue et les cieux!
Mallarmé

    Cimitière marin

Ce toit tranquille, où marchent des colombes,
Entre les pins palpite, entre les tombes.
Valéry

The beginnings of obscurity, in extravagance of roundabout figured phrases, are parodied by Lewis Carroll in *Poeta Fit Non Nascitur* (1863):

Next, when you are describing
A shape or sound, or tint,
Don't state the matter plainly
But put it in a hint;
And learn to look at all things
With a sort of mental squint.

"For instance, if I wished, Sir,
Of mutton pies to tell
Should I say 'dreams of fleecy flocks
Pent in a wheaten cell'?"
"Why, yes," the old man said, "that phrase
Would answer very well."

In our years, however, these are sought, not as the Euphuists or Carroll's victims sought fine periphrastic figures, but for the unique and quintessential capture of an experience in space-time.

173-4.   Un jour, je vis passer une femme inconnue.
Cette femme semblait descendre de la nue;
Elle avait sur le dos des ailes, et du miel
Sur sa bouche entr'ouverte, et dans ses yeux le ciel.
A des voyageurs las, à des errants sans nombre,
Elle montrait du doigt une route dans l'ombre,
Et semblait dire: On peut se tromper de chemin.
Son regard faisait grace à tout le genre humain;
Elle était radieuse et douce; et, derrière elle,
Des monstres attendris venaient, baisant son aile,
Des lions graciés, des tigres repentants,
Nemrod sauvé, Néron en pleurs; et par instants
A force d'être bonne elle paraissait folle.
Et, tombant à genoux, sans dire une parole,
Je l'adorai, croyant déviner qui c'était.
Mais elle—devant l'ange en vain l'homme se tait—
Vit ma pensée, et dit: Faut-il qu'on t'avertisse?
Tu me crois la pitié; fils, je suis la justice.
Hugo

174-5.   Tout Orgueil fume-t-il du soir,
Torche dans un branle etouffée

NOTES

> Sans que l'immortelle bouffée
> Ne puisse à l'abandon surseoir!
>
> La chambre ancienne de l'hoir
> De mainte riche mais chu trophée
> Ne serait pas même chauffée
> S'il survenait par le couloir.
>
> Affres du passé necessaires
> Agrippant comme avec des serres
> Le sépulcre de désaveu,
>
> Sous un marbre lourd qu'elle isole
> Ne s'allume pas d'autre feu
> Que la fulgurante console.
>
> Mallarmé

175. L'univers n'est qu'un défaut
  Dans la pureté du non-être.
  Valéry

179. "a jumping back and forth" from prose to poetry: William M. Patterson: *The Rhythm of Prose*.

180. Dujardin's title reminds us that the successive schools are themselves a steady flow: the title is drawn from the famous refrain of a poem by Theodore de Banville:

    Nous n'irons plus aux bois; les lauriers sonts coupés.
    We'll to the woods no more, the laurels are felled.

186. The change may be noted even in the place-names across the continent. The States early colonized draw village and town names largely from four sources, three of them backward-looking:

  1) The home country: New England, New Amsterdam, New York; Greenwich; there is a Plymouth in Maine, New Hampshire, Vermont, Massachusetts, Connecticut, New York, and Pennsylvania.
  2) The *Bible*: Bethlehem, Zion, Canaan, Hebron, Sabbath Day Point.
  3) The seats of classical culture and legend: Syracuse, Ithaca, Rome, Troy.

[Abounding in the States of the expansion westward, on the other hand, are village and town names drawn wholly from local conditions or geography or events:
Bunkerville, Dry Lake, Steamboat, Rawhide, Roundup; Butte Creek, Chalk Butte, Four Buttes, Square Butte, Goldbutte, Heart Butte; Homesteak, Mill Iron; Red Barn, Red Oak, Red Springs, Red Bluff, Redwater (all these Reds, in Texas); Devil's Slide, Devil's Elbow, Devil's Lake, Devil's Tower; Big Horn, Big Piney, Big Sandy, Bigtrails (all these Bigs, in Wyoming); Dull Center, Lost Cabin, Jitney, Broken Hills, Camp Stool, Lame Deer, Lone Grave; Bitter Creek (in Sweetwater County, Wyoming).]

4) The one similarity in names, in the eastern and the westward States, lies in those (like the land itself) taken from the Indians.

194-5.   Chanson D'Automne

    Les sanglots longs
    Des violons
      De l'automne
    Blessent mon coeur
    D'une langueur
      Monotone.

    Tout suffocant
    Et blême, quand
      Sonne l'heure,
    Je me souviens
    Des jours anciens,
      Et je pleure.

    Et je m'en vais
    Au vent mauvais
      Qui m'emporte
    Deçà, delà,
    Pareil à la
      Feuille morte.
            Verlaine

209. The fate of this very play of Sherwood's, *There Shall Be*

No Night, illustrates how far we are from such assertive individualism. As soon as Hitler attacked Russia, and the Soviets thus perforce became our allies, *There Shall Be No Night* — which was a picture of Soviet aggression against Finland—was hush-hushed away. Individual protest against injustice was stilled in a common cause.

210. Especially observers (visitors or "refugees") from Europe announce the coming era of mass-control in America. Thus Max Glass-Pleshing, in *Liberation from Yesterday* (N. Y., The Beechhurst Press, 1947; pages 656-7) speaks of "out-of-date democracy", and declares dogmatically: "It is no longer a question of whether the Americans want or do not want to adopt a kind of communistic political formula, they will be obliged to do so . . ." He states that the United States will create "an American brand of national communism", leaving certain individual possibilities "as an illusion", but exacting "the same personal discipline and social sense" as the Russian brand. His gloomy but embracing vision, indeed, pictures the "faith" of Russia (Europe) and America joined against the "fanaticism" of a Japanized Asia.

216. Alfred Korzybski: *Science and Sanity* (1933; 1941), around which has been built the wide structure and school of "general semantics", which calls its quarterly *ETC*.

221, 223. New York Times, Oct. 22, 1933; April 7, 1940.

229. Trigant Burrow: *Phylobiology,* paper read at the twentieth annual meeting of the American Psychopathological Association, June 1930; printed in *Psyche,* xi, 1930; reprinted with foreword by A. Rapoport in *ETC,* iii, 1946.

233. Calverton's comment on Sinclair Lewis is from *The Modern Monthly,* March, 1934.

Calverton's *The Passing of the Gods* is an analysis of the "cultural compulsive". He too announces that "ultimately speaking, there is no such thing as an individual mind." He twice quotes H. G. Wells' remark that the brain of man, like the nose of a pig, is a food-getting instrument. He refers to Ernest Sutherland Bates and Trigant Burrow, apparently on the principle that whoso has given utterance to one's own opinion is an authority. With these cohorts gathered about him, Calverton is bold to declare that all, even the "new", psychology has gone astray because it maintains an individualistic emphasis instead of a social concern. The neurotic mind, he declares, "is fundamentally a reflection of maladjustment on the part of the group rather than on the part of the individual." Hence it is absurd to seek to cure the individual "without stressing the more basic necessity of changing the society of which he is an inevitable product." Yet Calverton can hardly imagine a society to which every individual will be adjusted. When he is appeased by Communism, his own logic must overthrow such a society to readjust Rockefeller, Hoover, and Ford.

For religion, the great social glue, as Calverton describes it has lost its cohesive power. That "vast ego-absorbing instrument of the community" — notice the scientific tone sought by Calverton's repeated use of such terms as "instrument" — must be replaced by a new ego-solvent. The poor artist, lacking such a paste to hold him to his group, has been converted "into a spiritual sport". What aesthetic fly-paper will Calverton spread? — "It should be obvious, therefore, that the only satisfactory and lasting solution to the ego problem of our age is to be found in Communism."

This conclusion Calverton reaches through a study of which these are the climactic words:

> The more closely the individual identifies his interests with those of the group, the more willing he is to sacrifice his personal ambitions for a social objective, and the less subject he is to the fears and the frustrations that he would be bound to suffer as an isolated individual, a separate ego, unsupported by such an identificatory alliance. Of course, when that identification is at all complete, as in the case of countless thousands of men who have died in wars or the

still more countless myriads who have enlisted as soldiers in the class war, there is no consciousness of sacrifice involved. What, judged from an individualistic point of view, is considered sacrifice becomes, from a social point of view, merely a form of duty. In large part, it is the conjunction effected by such an alliance between the ego and society that endows the individual in varying degrees with the power to become more than an individual, to become a Phidias, a Cincinnatus, a Michelangelo, a Thomas Munzer, a Thomas Paine, a Richard Wagner, a Diego Rivera, a Nicolai Lenin.

Permit a fuller regard of this closing paragraph, into which the author has poured all his arguments, not noticing that they dissolve one another, to leave a disquieting void. For if the individual should identify his interests with those of the group, why didn't Calverton enroll in the capitalist army? Having turned from the dominant attitude of his time and country, he counters by declaring that the prevailing point of view is dead. But how does he reconcile the sacrifice of personal ambitions for a social objective — which is thereupon not sacrifice but merely a form of duty — with the demand that, if an individual is out of alignment, society be changed? Perhaps we are all out of step but Joe!

The neatest trick of the skilled argufier comes in Calverton's choice of names. These men, he lists as having effected "an identificatory alliance between the ego and society." Pheidias. The *Encyclopaedia Britannica* says "of his life we know little apart from his works." And not one of his unquestioned works survives. About all we do know is that the sculptor was a close follower of Pericles, the Mussolini of his day, who forced passage of a law restricting the Athenian vote to males whose mother and father were both natives, and who "frankly endeavored to turn allies into subjects". Is it because Pheidias proved a most willing subject that he won renown as a sculptor? Cincinnatus. Largely legendary; undoubtedly reactionary.

Again *Britannica*: "a persistent opponent of the plebeians . . . the story of his success, related five times under five different years, possibly rests upon historical basis, but the account given in Livy is incredible." Michelangelo. Allied with his age? He fought it all his life! Several times exiled. Reached Rome through trying to palm off one of his own works as an antique. Fled Rome time and time again, in fury, in fear of the wrathful Pope. Ordered by that Pope, against his raging protests that he was a sculptor, to paint the ceiling of the Sistine chapel. (Many consider the result his masterpiece.) Eight of his ripest years — from thirty-nine till he was forty-seven — harassed beyond power to produce a single statue. His life (like Wagner's) an example of unending struggle, of wretchedness, disappointment, triumph over greatest odds. Thomas Munzer. Do you remember him? Calverton dug him out. He may not be well known, but he is in one sense a forerunner of Calverton's last two figures. Munzer rebelled against the Church, refused its collective authority, proclaimed that he was under the direct influence of the Holy Spirit. So violently did this work in him — such a nuisance, or a rebel, did he prove — that Luther disavowed him. Whereupon Munzer took the town of Mühlhausen, set up a communistic theocracy, and with a peasant band plundered the countryside, until he was caught and killed. Thomas Paine. An all-around rebel. Richard Wagner. I need not review his life, as bitter as Beethoven's, almost as ravaged as Rodin's. Diego Rivera, Nicolai Lenin. These are the supermen from Calverton's "still more countless myriads who have enlisted as soldiers in the class war". Surely there should be more artists! Though the death of more than Trotzky warns us not to expect many Lenins. But identificatory alliance of the ego and society, to which they sacrificed personal aims? Lenin moulded the Russian Revolution; instead of sacrificing himself, he shaped society.

These are the men who, Calverton says, became more than men because they identified their interests with those of the group. Not, manifestly, the majority group.

Then which group? Evidently there are as many of Calverton's groups as of Hazlitt's "social minds". Scar-Face Capone might gloat: "Me and me buddies is in cahoots. That makes me more than an individual. Like Butch Nero; like Blitz Hitler." The point — which Calverton cannot conceal by mixing artists and rebels and myths — the point is that artists are inevitably opposed to the group. At least, the group is invariably opposed to its artists. They are different; they insist upon asserting their ego instead of sacrificing their personal ambitions. The artists that endure transcend their group, their age. Their age, therefore, is likely to misunderstand and to fight them. Even Calverton's choice examples prove precisely the point he would wave aside. Communists often write as though history began with Marx; perhaps Calverton relied on equal background in his readers. Or hoped his readers would be social, and sacrifice their personal information for his communal objective. Not the artist, but his art, achieves the nice balance between the ego and society, the expression of the immanent unity of all things through the multifold variety of their manifestations.

Such blithe ignorance or cavalier scorn or dismissal of the past has grown in every field. Seeking basic, general, pervasive characteristics, our time has tried to peel the onion, man. Going back as well as within, it has copied the primitive, deeming it also prime. But earlier bindings, though studied by some and by a few acclaimed, are spurned by many in an age that must achieve the ultimate synthesis. Thus in our educational systems Hutchins and his scholastic discipline are condescendingly smiled down; students are proffered but overall views, in "survey" courses: general science; world literature. While quizzicasters tickle our fancy with far-flung insignificant facts, splash of the Pierian spring, the rest of us are coddled on a journey that reverses the specialist's path, as we learn less and less about more and more. How soon shall we attain the goal, and know nothing about everything?

Like the Knownothings, we are a positive folk, in our opposed attitudes. While a learned few assure us that (like space and time) all values are relative, the more, who have always assumed values, have been jolted back to their direct avowal by the War. Indeed, as we have seen with the humanists, and in the final pages, values are central to our theme. Yet here too, while the search for or study of values appears not only in art but in every field from thermodynamics to post-War Planning, there is the same tendency to scorn the past. At the Fifty-sixth Meeting of the *American Economic Association* — not held, in 1943, because of the War; but printed — the first paper is on *Political Science, Political Economy, and Values*. And in his discussion of this paper, Frank H. Knight declares:

> Historically speaking, the active ethical mores of our culture are not derived from Greek thought, and even less from the Jewish-Christian religious tradition. They arose in modern times, specifically, in the movement called "rationalism" and "the enlightenment" . . .

Thus, Walt Whitman's "democratic" desire to post *To Let* signs on Parnassus, our realtors of the social scene would spread to Plato's Academy and to Bethlehem.

One phase of the return to values, as well as the somewhat naive process of a literary generation's growing aware of its rebellion, is illustrated in Leslie A. Fiedler's *The State of American Writing,* 1948 (in the symposium in *Partisan Review,* August, 1948). Fiedler is speaking of Americans born at the time of World War I or the Russian Revolution. They grew through the heedlessness of childhood during the exceptionally heedless "roaring twenties", the speakeasy spendthrift gangster time. In adolescence, they were slapped aware of the world by the depression; the wretchedness they felt, they saw around them, gave an added glow to the mirage of an ideal world in Soviet Russia. Russia the dream soon became Russia the ally and "friend"; in the surge of what seemed a common fight, the youth did not notice that Russia was taking all we offered and giving nothing. Only after the Nazi downfall did they gradually recognize that the aims of Russia were dangerously opposed to their own goals. Thus in 1948 Fiedler can declare:

> When we were kids becoming a writer seemed, if not synonymous with, at least an aspect of, becoming a Communist; abandoning oneself to the proletariat and finding oneself as an artist seemed a single act—and there was a covert moral satisfaction (we did not have those words then, of course) in what was at once a self-sacrifice and a self-assertion. Our awakening was gradual, though a little faster than our political disenchantment, toward a realization of the enormous *contempt* for art just below the culture-vulturish surface of the John Reed Clubs.

In those early days when they "were kids", the writers Fiedler calls "naturalists" were the saints of their devotion; the "New Humanists" — who dared talk of individual responsibility — were manifestly their foul fiends. And today, though these young men have grown mature enough to desanctify their saints, they cannot yet bring themselves to grant respectability to the erstwhile devils. Fiedler begins:

> It becomes easier and easier to *say* these days (we have known it for a long time) that the writer in the forties is essentially concerned with establishing alternatives to naturalism ("a 'scientific' equation of the individual with the sum of his environmental causes"). This involves the reinstatement in his vocabulary of such words as 'freedom', 'responsibility', and 'guilt', words which a little while ago he regarded as obscenities, and which even yet he cannot manage without uneasiness. All the better — that uneasiness redeems him from the possibilities of sentimentality, from the sterile certainty of the New Humanists, whose im-

pertinent attacks on naturalism delayed for years the legitimate revolt of creative writers. It was necessary that we be able honestly to say of Babbitt and More, "Who the hell are *they?*" before a reassertion of the autonomy of the individual could seem anything but a slogan of the White Terror. It is a help, too, that our leading naturalists have become middle aged, ripe for ritual slaughter.

Down with the gods of our childhood! The hour approaches for the new neophytes to set incense at *our* shrines.

This "legitimate revolt of creative writers", however, is but returning them toward the traditional pathway along time's spiral, to which the "New Humanists" had continued to point. To speak of the revolt's having been "delayed for years" betrays an impatience that must still be curbed. So far as the general public is concerned Fiedler's order does not apply: the political disenchantment with Russia is the first awakening; there is yet little consequent revulsion against the collective impetus — rather, an opposed collectivism tightens against the Soviet loom. To the fundamental pressure of this emphasis on the state, the collective, the universal — the roots of ultraism, of Fiedler's "naturalism", of materialism, in an attitude that equates man and nature in a lawbound age — the public perforce responds, but with little knowledge. The public, by and large, has Christianly continued to give lip service to the notions of personal "responsibility" and "guilt"; though enough of the rationalist, 'scientific' dismissal of these has seeped into various cultural levels to weaken their general hold. In the train of war there is, by way of reaction against its loosening of restraints and passions, a counter-call for a return to morals and faith; the response to this must not be construed as a reversal of the major trend of our time. For the notions of freedom and responsibility and guilt rest upon not social but individual emphasis; and in spite of the awakening and "revolt" of the sensitive (the artists)

NOTES

among the ripening generation, the philosophical, political, social, even aesthetic, reach toward an emphasis upon the individual is still a groping tendril far up the spiral of time.

234. The story of the R A P P is told by Max Eastman in *The Modern Monthly* for November, 1933. "Fellow-travelers" is the euphemism for non-members of the Communist Party who were in general sympathy with its aims, and forwarded its program. They have by now either been "purged" or been drawn into the main body.

236. Maud Bodkin: *Archetypal Patterns in Poetry.*

236-7. Archibald MacLeish: preface to the *Anthology of the Younger Poets.*

237. Eda Lou Walton: *Unity,* leading article in the *Saturday Review of Literature,* Oct. 26, 1933.

240. Man as the battleground of Ariel and Caliban: Dostoievsky has said: "Beauty is not only a mysterious but a terrible thing. There God and the Devil strive for mastery. And their battleground is the human soul."

244. Bergen Evans: *The Natural History of Nonsense* (1946).

246. La personnalité de m'am'selle n'intéresse qu'à maman!

247. "This something not ourselves . . ." Aldous Huxley in the introduction to *Letters of D. H. Lawrence.*

249. Kasimir Edschmid: *Expressionism in Literature and the New Poetry.*

249. Oskar Pfister: *Expressionism in Art: Its Psychological and Biological Basis.*

249. The expressionistic technique must not be confused with the elaborate theory of Expressionism developed by Benedetto Croce. Yet this also is a true product of the time. It builds into a general system the Romantic emphasis on feeling, on intuition. For it declares that the intuition of a thing is the authentic aesthetic fact; but that, since this

[423]

can be grasped only when expressed, all art is expression, and all expression is art.

250. Reasoned arguments denying reason may be found both on scientific explorations, as those of Freud (Gide; surrealism) and along the faith-full pathways of religion (T. S. Eliot; Ludwig Lewisohn; G. K. Chesterton, as in his notable *Defence of Nonsense* in *The Defendant*).

MODERN ART

248f. The position of the modern artist (in this collective world, which—see note above—denies the supremacy of reason) has been variously interpreted and appraised. S. I. Hayakawa sees the modern artist as champion of a new, non-Aristotelian orientation. In *The Revision of Vision* (*ETC*, vol. iv, 4, Summer, 1947), after summarizing the Korzybskian attack on "the semantics of identification", Hayakawa declares that such identification—an individualist concern with the particular subject—has been since Greek times "consciously or unconsciously the public ideal of western art". This ideal Hayakawa finds symbolized in the story of Pygmalion, "semantic nitwit", fallen in love with a statue. Since (to the Greeks, and to the ages after) identification is admirable, Aphrodite rewards Pygmalion by changing the statue into a woman, giving divine sanction to the notion that "that art is greatest that is most likely to cause the beholder to have an identification reaction of confusing the symbol with the thing symbolized." Few critics, I fancy, would follow Hayakawa in assigning the ages this definition, which presents the aim rather of advertising, pornography, and propaganda than of art.

Yet the attitude comes naturally from Hayakawa's point of view, for—like the Communists—he sees art as primarily weapon. Thus he views modern art—"cubism, abstractionism, surrealism, dadaism, fauvism" (this indiscriminate bunching gives little sign of historical knowledge or aesthetic sensibility)—modern art as in revolt against this semantics of identification and as seeking to establish a dynamic semantics of non-identification and of "time-and-relation-mindedness".

Surrealism, for example, as Hayakawa views it, may begin by seeming to show a concrete object, then suddenly doing it violence—fair flesh greening to putrescence—"to make a mockery of your identification reactions". Abstract artists may distort, may ignore conventional perspective, make their brush stroke visible or leave bare spots on the canvas, create non-existent objects, or indulge in other eccentricities, because they are "engaged in the most difficult kind of educational endeavor":—to win the receptor from identification patterns to "the visual relationships that are necessarily the main point of art." Hayakawa seems to think that this end justifies the means, as the receptor is swept into the more embracing modern world of space-time, in which objects and entities have been largely supplanted by relations, and as the receptor loses, in his social experience, "the deluded self-importance of absolute individualism".

Less justification for the distortions and abstractions of modern art is found by T. H. Robsjohn-Gibbings, who (in *Mona Lisa's Moustache;* 1947) attacks art for doing the very things for which Hayakawa sings its praises. With much the same lumping, he emphasizes that futurism, cubism, dadaism, surrealism, and the rest are directed against the individual, against the power of reason, against the bases of the liberal, bourgeois traditions of democracy. (Did not Mussolini call the leader of futurism, Marinetti, "the John the Baptist of Fascism"!) Robsjohn Gibbings—like many in controversy—overpresses his point. Where Hayakawa finds an educational campaign, he discovers a power-seeking conspiracy; but there can be little doubt of the truth of his major claim: that modern art has been availing itself of the devices of magic and other non-rational drives, to reach beyond the conscious mind to deeper, and what it assumes to be more universal, impulsions.

More objectively—neither as challengers nor as champions, but as interpreters—others (such as Gyorgy

Kepes, in *The Language of Vision*, 1944; C. Law Watkins, in *The Language of Design*, Phillips Memorial Gallery, Washington, D. C., 1946; most fully, Charles Biederman, in *Art as the Evolution of Visual Knowledge*, Red Wing, Minn., 1948) have tried to examine the pathway of modern art. It may be accepted as a truism that most artists will seek to interpret, or unconsciously will reflect, their time. The new vistas of our age, emphasizing dynamic and structural patterns of interrelationships, in space-time events, manifestly have brought a quest for a new, dynamic pictorial art.

The spatial organization of a picture depends upon proximity and similarity, and their interaction. Every line, hue, value, chroma, by the general law of inertia sets up an expectancy of its continuance; the satisfaction of this, according to our habits of spatial organization, tends to shape the optical units into a closed, compact whole. This closed, compact whole is the framed picture, the work of art.

The new sense of dynamic relations demands that this static whole be given motion. The idea that time is interwoven with space, as a fourth dimension, calls for such indication on the canvas. In response to such demands came the superimposed images and other speed presentations of the Futurists, such paintings as Marcel Duchamp's "Nude Descending a Staircase" (1913), which seeks to give the impression of the woman in motion, on successive steps; and Giacomo Balla's "Dog on a Leash" (1912), with its several tails, to suggest the wagging, and its interwoven, partly blurred pattern for the moving leash. Out of these urges, too, has grown the new "art form" called Mobile, of bits of metal and other materials wired in a design that can be shifted by hand or transformed by the whimsied wind—developed by Laszlo Moholy-Nagy and Alexander Calder.

In order to emphasize the dynamic rhythm of his work, the artist may reduce his picture surface to the basic oppositions—of pure colors, elementary shapes (squares, circles, opposed oblongs), horizontal and vertical directions, instead of attempting to reproduce the subtleties and particularities of a specific object. By thus avoiding representation, he seeks—Pieter Mondriaan says he has achieved—"the clear realization of liberal and universal rhythm distorted and hidden in the individual rhythm of the limiting form."

The painter or the sculptor of abstract forms may claim that he is exercising, for the first time in art, the age-old privilege of the mathematician. When the multiplication table assures us that 7 times 4 are 28, it little recks whether we accept that generalization, or multiply oranges, monkeys, or millions of dollars. When the algebraist tells us that the relations expressed in the equations $3x$ plus $2y$ equals 38, and x plus $5y$ equals 30, are satisfied when x equals 10 and y equals 4, he would deem it irrelevant, if not impertinent, for us to ask "Ten what? Four what? For what?" The mathematician works on, equably, in higher powers and dimensions, with complete unconcern as to concrete attachments. And in geometry as in machinery there are many, if not abstract, surely general patterns. Now at length, after ages of ships and shoes and madonnas and sealing-wax, the artist is putting onto canvas his belief that such-and-such relations of form and of color make satisfying equations (even of the fifth power or the fourth dimension); he too prefers that the receptors understand these as essences, as general or universal values; but he smiles tolerantly if their imagination peoples the forms with peonies, palaces, or parades. Thus we may perhaps most pleasantly picture the abstract artist as seeking equations and general formulations of beauty, just as the mathematician seeks equations and general formulations of truth.

Throughout may be observed the quest of the universal, of the essence-in-all, the quest that is central to our age. Contemporary artists, says Gyorgy Kepes, "throw away all conscious control... The artist acts the role of the midwife. He only assists at the birth of a living form that grows from deeper strata than his conscious efforts could reach. He invents techniques that give the fewest obstacles to the free flow of organic formation."

"Invents"—because this is a conscious quest of the unconscious. I have mentioned the reliance on chance in Duchamp's "Three Standard Stops" (page 252. Surrealism is discussed, page 250f.). Kepes tells us how Hans Arp, with deliberate abandon, cut out bits of paper, tossed them on a cardboard, jounced them around, and pasted on the cardboard the pattern that they formed by chance. He continues: "Such chance has in it, however, more reason than we, with our present blinkers and confused senses, can see. The resulting order shows an organic understanding far more embracing than the formal logic-sharpened-in-static-object concept. It is natural that these automatic expressions resemble the biomorphic realms of nature. They have the same order as the visible forms of mutations, transformations, the perpetual asymmetric rhythm of the processes not yet fossilized in terms of things."

Persons not ready to admit that they are fossils may feel that Kepes' assertions here are somewhat misty. A more reasoned approach may, however, be made to some of the devices or techniques of the modern artist. What to the uninitiate may seem senseless aberrations will often be revealed as—if not artistic products—at least purposeful endeavors. As man seemed to be losing his status as an individual, the artist had to reexamine his position in society, in space-time.

One place the artist sought help was from the primitive. He found, in primitive art, various planes in a single work, full-face and profile together. Perhaps a simultaneous presentation of various planes would combine dynamic directions into an integrated whole that would vibrate with a sense of motion. In its simplest forms, this technique, like the art of primitives and children, represents objects and persons full-face and profile in the same picture; the more complex attempts to work with shifting planes are manifest in Cubism.

It is clear, too, that a single observation, even long

consideration from a single point of view, does not give either a full representation of an object, or what we might call its spatial essence. Accordingly, the artist may seek this fulness, or this essence, by several paths. He may, within the one picture, increase the number of points of reference; he may use various perspective lines; he may indicate several vanishing points—to give a sense of three-dimensional space and of movement, as though the beholder were seeing all around the object. He may reverse perspective, and make parallel lines (as of a road, or two rows of trees) diverge as they recede, to suggest the amplitude of space; or like the Chinese leave the lines parallel and mark distance by overlapping planes and smaller size; or adopt the convention accepted by the Egyptians for several thousand years, of using smaller size for less important persons, indicating distance by having the remoter groups just as large, but over the heads of those in the foreground. The artist may, on the other hand, try to combine in one unit what would be the result of several observations from different points of view, as when Picasso puts both eyes into a profile. He may, finally, make a selection, among the many things to be seen from all angles of vision, of what seems to him most worthy of retention. As Franz Boas puts it, in *Primitive Art,* "those features are represented that are considered permanent and essential, and there is no attempt on the part of the draftsman to confine himself to reproduction of what he actually sees at a given moment."

What one "actually sees at a given moment" is of course, as our age has emphatically demonstrated, far from the quintessential reality. One aspect of the order of our time is the sense of the interpenetration of formerly dissociated fields—we combine the sciences, as in biophysics, biochemistry; it is the mathematics of the electron that led to the atomic bomb—and the kneading together of scientific and technical knowledge. As interpenetration has become a device of integration in the sciences, as gases or ripples on water may interpenetrate, so does the painter attempt interpenetration of his figures —his planes, lines, colors—on the canvas. Figures on the canvas may thus directly flow into and through one another, as though endowed with transparency; or they may seem to fluctuate, now close at hand, now far away; now inside, now out. To these ends, the artist may utilize equivocal contour lines, lines that are at the one time part of two objects. We are all familiar with the continuous pattern of diamond-shaped boxes, of which we seem to see now the tops, and now the bottoms. Within the forms of a picture, there may be an at first invisible man, his shape implicit in the landscape: clouds form his hair, lines of the buildings include his profile, the statue on the street outlines his arm and shoulder. This device recalls, for serious purposes, the hidden figures in the forest which children hunted for in the comics of forty years ago. Or a keyhole may be a keyhole, but also the silhouette of a man, the outline of a church tower, and the limiting edge of the horizon. The artist, also, may fuse the foreground and the background, by arbitrary extension and variation of light and shade, or size of objects. By such devices, the artist seeks to draw together and unify different spatial data, and also to add to the rhythmic flow (and therefore the sensuous intensity) of the picture surface. And as the shapes interpenetrate and expand, so do the ideas suggested: one picture may have many interpretations. These devices are all in the collective current of our age.

A further avenue of enrichment, the artist may seek, in the embracing emphasis of the time, in a fuller exploitation of texture differences and values. Exploring this range, he blends touch with sight; he adds to color, to light and dark, such sensations as softness, coldness, roughness. The texture of our surroundings plays a part in our recognition and evaluation of, and response to, our environment, largely neglected by the painter. In the counteremphasis to this neglect, came first such techniques as stippling and pointilism, applying various thicknesses of pigment, and other ways of giving the paint itself depth and a "feel" on the canvas; then the wide variety of "collage" offerings—match-sticks, newspapers, buttons, stones, sandpaper, string, varieties of cloth, alone or with paint on canvas creating a work—and such painted objects as cup and spoon made of fur, and the drooped and melting watches of Dali.

The artist today strives constantly to create graphic symbols for the invisible aspects of things. He seeks to suggest storm and calm; he tries to convey heat and cold, the impulsions of sound (as in Charles Burckfield's "Song of the Katydids") and other radiations. Atmospheric vibration, the movement of light and heat, may be felt in "Public Gardens at Arles" and other landscapes of Van Gogh.

It is of course not only in primitive art that the moderns find precedent for their devices. I have mentioned the treatment of distance by the Chinese and by the Egyptians, peoples of complex cultures. Simultaneity in different places, or the essence of movement, is also earlier to be found: the Roman Janus, god of the gateway, is two-headed, looking both inward and out; while the Hindu Brahma has four heads, to see at once to the four corners of the world, and his fellow-deity Siva—perhaps the most familiar figure in Hindu art—is many-armed. "The Droll Dreams of Pantagruel" (supposedly printed in 1565, twelve years after Rabelais' death, but extant from the Variorum edition of 1823; available in the three volume edition in English published by Covici Friede in 1929) consists of 120 satiric drawings that (along with such artists as Breughel and Bosch) anticipate the surrealists. Friar Hackem (Plate V) wears a woman's leg for a head-piece. The King of the Island of Sly (Plate XVII) has a pitcher for a head, with a brush sticking out; from the elongated pitcher handle hangs what looks like a toilet flush-chain. Grandgousier, in Plate XLIV, has become one with his soup-pot, eating from himself as he walks. For Plate XCVI—a man with a stifled mouth, whose body is a lute played with a strand of wheat by a priapus growing out of a plant—a Variorum note explains: "The author identifies him with his instrument in order to indicate the great application he gave to it." Plate CXII shows one of the queerly "deformed fellows" begotten of Pantagruel by the emission of anal wind. In these 120 figures, the phantasmagoria of surrealism, even to the ants and other antics of Dali, have apt antecedents.

[As with the romantics, as with all rebellious youth, much of the machinery of the surrealists is used *épater le bourgeois*, to shock the middle class. Access to one surrealist exhibition in Paris was through a public urinal. In Picasso's play *Desire* (Philosophical Library, 1948), the four-lettered scatological terms are frequent; and two female characters, Fat Anguish and Skinny Anguish, live in a "sewer bedroom kitchen and bathroom" and talk from the "man-hole of their bed". On a reproduction of the Mona Lisa, Marcel Duchamp drew a moustache (whence the title of Robsjohn-Gibbbings' book) and added the letters "L H O O Q"—which pronounced in French, say "Elle a chaud au cul: She has a hot bottom." —But these are scrapings from the bottom of the surrealist barrel. Their serious effort is to fish up the universal essence, hidden below consciousness in the individual.]

In two other ways, less device than doctrine, modern art may differ from earlier work. The first of these is involved in the general composition of the picture; the second, in the artist's choice of subject.

There have been many styles, many theories, of composition, of the arrangement of the material on the canvas. The Japanese, for example, balance the occupied space and the empty space. In western art, the masses in a picture may be balanced about a central focus. Or the groupings may be made to assume the outlines of a pyramid, or of a Roman or of a Gothic arch. Early German and Flemish art (as in Dürer) may set all vertical, horizontal, diagonal lines so that, if extended, they meet at the picture frame and thus by joining lead back into the picture. Greek dynamic symmetry (borrowed extensively by today's commercial artists; see page 289) makes the picture a pattern of mathematical proportions, especially of the square roots of 2, 3, and 5. The modern artist may, of course, avail himself of any of these styles of composition, or find still other ways of achieving balance and unity within the picture frame. Or, indeed, he may use converse devices, to make the painting stretch beyond, or seek beyond, its frame limitations, to become part of the larger life beyond the canvas. Increasingly, however, the modern artist has worked upon a quite different principle, enunciated first by the impressionists. This principle, of "unified surface tension", substitutes for the principle of balanced unity the idea that every cubic centimeter of the picture must be equally interesting. Such an approach to the picture, instead of drawing the eye to a central or unified design, is likely to spread or spot a diversity of lines, colors, forms, widely across the canvas, every inch of it separately claiming the beholder's attention.

The attitude toward the subject, too, has changed. The artist today seldom feels that his subject matter is a vase of flowers, a spread of countryside, or the features of Mrs. I Hava Million. Following the impulse toward abstraction, he finds subject matter (especially if he is a surrealist) in Freudian symbolism; or, in his search for ideas among other periods and places, he may come to take as his subject itself the evocation of a style. The Pre-Raphaelites (with whom Robsjohn-Gibbings begins his excoriation of modern art) first consciously made this evocation their goal; but today painters may move from copying their instructors or masters to seeking to recapture the primitive or the exotic, or any other spirit than the (ugly, mechanical, inhuman, superficial, moribund!) spirit of our time. Thus—in his witty and often illuminating but unreliable volume, *Painting in Public* (Knopf, 1948)—Maurice Richard Grosser tells us that Picasso's "actual subject has never been, since the jugglers and mountebanks of his Blue Period, the objects on his canvas. His subject is rather how some particular school or race or time would have envisaged these objects." This characterization of Picasso's work may be extreme; but it is a fact that the quest of the modern artist carries him frequently and far afield. We must ask, of any modern painting, whether its subject is an object, an order or arrangement, an idea, an emotion, a suggestion, or a style.

While all these modernist devices and doctrines may rise from the particular urges of our time, or serve particular ends, as just indicated, they of course also fuse into a general technique with a wider intention. (Nothing has yet been said, for example, of the use of these devices for their effect on the emotions, as in the eerie erotic suggestions of Dali; or as in the eager-jawed skulls and frantically clutching body fragments of such a work as Picasso's "Guernica".) The distortions, the contradictions, the compressions, all the differences from the expected, from the representational or the traditional, create a new set of tensions in the beholder. For the work to succeed as art, these tensions must be dissolved, must be resolved into a new emotion-and-meaning-full configuration. The traditional meaningful unity of the rational mind has been disintegrated; the fixed pattern of expectancy has been as decisively outblown as by atomic fission. There is, thence, a release and a rush of energy. Man's mind, like the electrons, demands associative structure. There must, therefore, come a new integration of the emotion-and-meaning elements, of lines and lights and love and social essences, to establish the thing we are beholding, as a work of art.

This—in the embracing movement of our time—re-emphasizes another fusion, for it adds to the endeavors of the artist the dynamic participation of the receptor—the receptor, who inevitably searches for order, who strives to gather his impressions into a unified whole.

Such concerns animate the drive of the modern artist, caught in, striving to understand, to capture, to utilize, the urges of our time.

The true artist retains, more than the less sensitive citizen, the sense of his individual being. Some of the characteristics of art that we have just observed rise, in part at least, from the need the artist may feel of asserting that individuality, in these days when it is threatened. Such activity is welcomed by H. W. Janson, professor of art at Washington University (in the "Round Table on Modern Art" held by *Life* magazine, Oct. 11, 1948): "I feel that the modern artist, in insisting upon the highly individual experiences that have been emphasized today, is fulfilling a very valuable function. He is preserving something that is in great danger—namely, our ability to remain individuals."

Many artists, however, feel uncomfortable, even traitorous, in thus traipsing along an individual trail. Not fully aware (how many of us analyze our relation to the age?) of the contemporary drive toward universals, they do what they see is being done—they "express their personality"; they strive to be different, unique; they think that they paint in "the idiom of the times". While they persist in an obscurity, an abstraction, they themselves do not comprehend, they are not truly happy in their work. This state of affairs is deplored by the acute Meyer Schapiro (professor of fine arts at Columbia University, and one of the keenest observers in the field). In the *Life* "Round Table" discussion, Professor Schapiro states:

> In recent years, there has been much uneasiness among artists. I have talked with few good artists who have not admitted their dissatisfaction and sometimes a nostalgia for certain older things. There are people who have been bold enough to advise these artists to paint religious or political pictures, or to represent the familiar environment, in order to solve their problem. Why haven't these constantly proposed goals been realized? Serious artists are concerned with the question. They want to create an art that is more fully human, more public, more universal."

Thus the critic urges the collective emphasis of our time upon the artist, who is already uneasy under its pressure. What neither (at least in Professor Schapiro's

[435]

picture) seems to have realized is that these very abstractions and soul-barings and exposures of neurosis patterns and dream images are part of the quest of the universal, the essence beneath or within all things, that marks our time. The uneasiness may, in truth, rise from the artist's sense of waste, of self-betrayal: he is betraying his unique self for an imaginary race-self, mankind-self—for a false abstraction. Whatever the polarity of his particular unifying quest—an object vs. an essence; an idea vs. an emotion; a person vs. the sense of personality; an individual pattern vs. generalized form—the artist must make us see the entire pole, not seek to perch on a single end.

What the protestants against abstract art are seeking is not a return to the individual, but a turn from the quest of a general essence or law to the quest of a general spirit—from ultraism to humanism. Thus in 1948 *The Boston Institute of Modern Art,* observing that the word *modern* is beginning to bear derogatory connotations, changed its name to *The Boston Institute of Contemporary Art.* At the same time, it denounced today's art products as replete with unintelligibility, exploitation, double-talk, and chicanery, and urged the artist to make "a strong, clear affirmation for humanity". This is akin to Sandburg's cry in poetry: *The People, Yes!* Similarly, Francis Henry Taylor (in the Dec. 1948 *Atlantic Monthly*) and Alfred Frankfurter (in various issues of *Art News*) have been pointing a movement away from aesthetic towards ethical judgments.

By a flick of coincidence, two avenues of modern painting were anticipated by the writer of the world's greatest nonsense. He looks toward abstract art when one of his characters inquires: "Did you ever see such a thing as a drawing of a muchness?" And he suggests a second venture, in the conversation that ensues when one character says he'll not recognize another, should they meet again, "you're so exactly like other people."

MODERN ART

"The face is what one goes by, generally," Alice remarked in a thoughtful tone.

"That's just what I complain of," said Humpty Dumpty. "Your face is the same as everybody has—the two eyes, so"—(marking their places in the air with his thumb) "nose in the middle, mouth under. It's always the same. Now if you had the two eyes on the same side of the nose, for instance—or the mouth at the top—that would be *some* help."

"It wouldn't look nice," Alice objected. Humpty Dumpty only shut his eyes and said, "Wait till you've tried."

Picasso tried.

And I'm not sure whether it's a "shaggy-dog story" or a daddling toward Dali wherein the witness at the trial of the Knave of Hearts, in his confusion, "bit a large piece out of his teacup instead of the bread-and-butter." The muchness of today fuses, or confuses, the container and the content. Art fortunately, never rests content, but always seeks new pathways and patterns of beauty.

252. Biography shows further strain of this impulse toward social inclusion, beyond H. G. Wells' calling his own "a sample life": the book called *The Autobiography of Alice B. Toklas* is really the autobiography of her boon-companion, Gertrude Stein; Hans Zinsser calls his own life story *As I Remember Him: The Biography of R. S.*

252. The belief of Paul Eluard in "the collective of poetic activity" (says Julien Levy in *Surrealism*, 1936) was the moving impetus toward most of the joint surrealist enterprises. Eluard insisted that it was both possible and desirable to exploit double, plural, or communal invention.

An old and amusing parlor game, among literate children, is for one to write a line of verse, pass the paper to the next, who writes a second line; likewise to the third; and around until each in the room has added whatever came into his head as his further line.

[437]

When the sheet thus returns to the first writer, he reads the product aloud. The results are, often, even more diverting if each one folds the paper after writing, so that no one sees any line except his own.—Some of the verses signed "Paul Eluard" sound as though they had been written in such a fashion. Only the children do not issue their game-creation as poetry.

258. Pour ses yeux,—pour nager dans ces lacs, dont les quais
Sont plantés de beaux cils qu'un matin bleu pénètre,
J'ai, Muse, moi, ton pitre,—enjambé la fenêtre,
Et fui notre baraque où fument tes quinquets . . .
Le Pitre Chatié, 1864
Yeux, lacs avec ma simple ivresse de renaître
Autre que l'histrion qui du geste évoquais
Comme plume la suie ignoble des quinquets,
J'ai troué dans le mur de toile une fenêtre . . .
Le Pitre Chatié, 1887

260. "proletarian poet": Stanley Burnshaw, *The Iron Land.*

260. The collective urge of our time has enticed many artists towards Communism, which affords them a greater sense of their social importance. That wise and keen thinker, Ananda K. Coomaraswamy, indicated, as one deep defect of our civilization, the sense of luxury—of uselessness, of independence from other aspects of living—that the western world feels in poetry, or painting, or the other fine arts. Communism in its way restores the artist to a place in the social scheme: he is, as much as the tailor and the engineer, a worker for the good of the state. Thus we find the practical Diego Rivera declaring that certain of his frescoes are best because they are "the best constructed, the most correct in historical dialectic, the richest in materialistic synthesis." Similarly, in theory, Herbert Read wished "to do for the realm of art, on the basis of Hegel's dialectic, something analogous to what Marx on the same basis did for the realm of economics." Thus the artist is at least fortified by the thought that he is accepted; he "belongs".

NOTES

260f. Readers may be interested in a further example of "structures of meaningless sound":

> Utopos ha Boccas peula chama polta chamaan.
> Bargol he maglomi Baccan soma gymnosophaon.
> Agrama gymnosophon labarem bacha bodamilomin.
> Voluala barchin heman la lauoluala dramme pagloni.

This is, actually, not a modern experiment in sound patterns, but a quatrain in "Utopian", first published in 1556. The "translation" into English may be found in Thomas More's *Utopia*, where the Utopian language was created for the poem.

261. Leon N. Solomons and Gertrude Stein: *Psychological Review*, Sept. 1896. These automatic writings and early studies are related to her poetry by B. F. Skinner, in *The Atlantic Monthly*, Jan. 1934.

269. L'air qu'on respire a comme un goût mental. Les hommes Ressemblent aux idées qui longent un esprit.
D'eux à moi, rien ne cesse d'être intérieur;
Rien ne m'est étranger de leur joue à ma joue,
Et l'espace nous lie en pensant avec nous.
Romains

271. H. G. Wells, *The Bulpington of Blup*: esp. p. 68 f.

277. The Nazis erected "a logical structure upon an irrational premise". Communism has built an even firmer house. By the compulsion of its edicts and enforcing acts, every phase of Soviet life is an active outgrowth and proponent of its philosophy. The collective emphasis of our age reaches its extreme in the Communist criterion.

"Art is a weapon", judged by its efficacy in advancing the Communist creed. (See page 234). Likewise, all work in every field. The geneticist and Nobel Prize Winner H. J. Muller has detailed (*Saturday Review of Literature*, Dec. 4 and 11, 1948) political perversions of science in the U.S.S.R., and the possible consequences of such interpretations, enforced by the Communist creed. In truth, the peace of the world may hang upon this Communist conception.—What if its premise is false!

285. *Skyscraper,* Carpenter; Grofe; Honegger; *The Story of a Soldier,* Stravinsky; Gershwin; *The Races,* Satie.

285-6. Soviet dancers: Vecheslova and Chabukani, of the Marinsky Theatre, Leningrad. American debut at Carnegie Hall, New York, Jan. 13, 1934.

286. *The Sunken Cathedral,* Debussy; *Station W G Z B X,* James. The other two, Hindemith and Schoenberg. The Roth Quartet played works by Roussel, Casella, Ravel, Prokofieff, Milhaud, Copland, Dohnanyi, Bartok, and others.

286. Concert in honor of Arnold Schoenberg, Town Hall, New York, Oct. 11, 1933.

286. Ich bin nur ein Funke vom himmelischen Feuer, Ich bin nur ein Ton der himmelischen Stimme.

290. Sheldon Cheney: *Expressionism in Art.*

297. Bernard de Voto, in *Harper's Magazine,* Jan. 1934.

307. Thus Robert Shafer, in a volume expounding and extolling Paul Elmer More, declares: "Mr. More's work from first to last has been an attempt to conserve and revivify what some historians and critics regard as the romantic conception of human nature."

307. Eugene O'Neill: (short story) *Tomorrow,* in *Seven Arts,* June 1917.

307. *The New Yorker,* May 7, June 6, Aug. 26, 1944. Quoted in Bergen Evans, *The Natural History of Nonsense,* which reminds us that the migration of the lemmings is a result of over-production; and their mass suicide in the ocean, a folk myth.

308. "Politics are destiny . . . beginning of the nineteenth century. Economics are destiny . . . twentieth century." Here again is shift from the inner, individual control to the outer drive of law. But note that truth itself may not be an absolute; rather, it may be swung on the psychic seesaw of the years. In the early nineteenth century, it was widely believed that the individual has determining power

NOTES

in the movements of history. In the twentieth century, it is still more widely believed that the social, the group, force predominates and prescribes. As each age acts in line with its beliefs, it promotes the accordant trends of our living, thus helps to make them, for their period, come true. "Right you are, if you think you are." And time weaves its pattern.

309-10. Robert Frost: *Swinging Birches.*

311. John Masefield: *The Everlasting Mercy.*

330. E. T. Bell: *The Development of Mathematics.*

332. The attention of our time to sex has been viewed as a consequence of other lack, of the failure of the period to satisfy other needs: the old associations, the old faiths and loyalties and traditions, are gone: for want of a spiritual bond, man clings in a fleshly union. While, however, it is true that Freud has encouraged conversation on the subject, and an earlier frankness has somewhat returned, permitting the use of "the four-letter words" in fiction; and the general publication of such documents as "the Kinsey Report", 1948, and *A Research In Marriage,* by G. V. Hamilton, 1948—the latter of which was first published for professional workers only, then generally released), it has yet to be established that this age is particularly, or peculiarly, devoted to erotic concerns.

332-3. The fact that Einstein had later to discard these equations has but increased the ardor of his integrating quest. "The idea that there are two structures of space independent of each other," he remarked, "the metric-gravitational and the electromagnetic, is intolerable to the human spirit." He has made his life's goal the attainment of the formula that binds them.

An expositor of Einstein, Lincoln Barnett (in *The Universe and Dr. Einstein,* 1948, for which Dr. Einstein has written the *Foreword*), presses the point that this is, as Einstein declares, "the grand aim of all science. . . Completion of the United Field Theory will climax the long march of science towards unification of concepts,"

—And the goal in other fields, too, in the eyes of our unity-seeking age. "The philosopher and mystic, as well as the scientist, have always sought through their various disciplines of introspection to arrive at a knowledge of the ultimate immutable essence that undergirds the mutable illusory world." And note how this sentence of Barnett's assumes that such a single essence exists! (See also pages 352-3, and Note thereto.)

335. While Protestantism, with its insistence on the right of individual interpretation of Holy Writ, and its consequent many sects and sub-divisions, has been characterized as a "Romantic aberration", it is different from most other religions only in its fuller allowance of individual judgment, not in any greater measure of individual concern. In spite of the frequent association of Church and State, from ancient empires whereof the ruler was god to present ones wherein the ruler is, or appoints, the head of the Church; in spite also of the occasional opposition of Church and State, with religion setting up a hierarchy of its own, the emphasis of most religions in upon the single soul.

The Catholic faith, for instance, notwithstanding current objections that it is "totalitarian", will in another sense not admit but proclaim its totalitarian nature: it is concerned with the individual entire, with every aspect of his being, with—indeed—his pilgrimage through life and his eternal salvation. But this total concern rests upon a belief in the individual's free will, and the individual's own responsibility for his choice between good and evil. And the Catholic Church, however it may encourage charity and bring succor to the unfortunate, deems the clearing of the slums of less consequence than, at most incidental to, the cleansing and the straightening of the individual soul. Each is to strive to make and keep himself righteous; that is a life-struggle for any man.

In our collective day, the notion of individual charity seems to many quaint and far out-moded; it is, indeed, officially discouraged. And even the hope of and striving for individual salvation seems to many a delusive ana-

NOTES

chronism, opposed to work for the good and the growth of society or the state. This attitude marks the study of *Western Political Thought* by John Bowle, for which he is taken to task in *The Traditions of the West* (*The Times*, London; lead in *Literary Supplement*, Dec. 27, 1947. It may be that the tradition of the English, less tugged than our own by intermingling European strains, even in the socialist urge of the epoch preserves a strong individualistic core.). Remarking that in, and ever since, the Gospels the individual has been the Christian unit of salvation, *The Times* challenges Mr. Bowle's belief that this is a less lofty view than that of whole-hearted devotion to society as a whole. It states, rather, that "it is surely this belief in the individual as the unit of salvation which has been very largely responsible, in the secular sphere, for the demand for personal liberty in the Western world. It is a mere matter of history, as Mr. Bowle amply shows, that the first demands for liberty were almost always religious, made by men and women who were emboldened by the conviction that a good infinitely precious beyond anything in the power of the secular sovereign, to wit their eternal salvation, depended on their demand. Where the belief in individual salvation has declined, liberty also has declined." This final fact has wide illustration in the "totalitarian" world of today. It is, as I have said, deeply significant that both Fascism and Communism are anti-Christian.

338. Hippolyte Taine: *History of English Literature* (1863).

338. Prof. Norman C. Wetzel: Address at Annual meeting, *National Academy of Sciences,* Cleveland, Ohio, Nov. 20, 1934.

340. William E. Hocking, *What Man Can Make of Man;* Lin Yutang, *Between Tears and Laughter.* The arguments as to whether or not the world has a purpose are summarized in *Teleological Arguments,* by Archie J. Bahm, in the *Scientific Monthly* of May, 1944.

345. Kurt Koffka: *Principles of Gestalt Psychology.*

[443]

345. This contrast between the image and the idea is manifest in other fields as well. Thus to the Greeks, to whom algebra was a necessary evil, the pictures of geometry were a joy; negative numbers, of which they could not make images, they rejected. The Hindus, even before the Christian era, although they were weak in geometry, worked with negative numbers. Similarly today, abstract mathematical ideas (relativity; the quantum; multi-dimensional space; space "finite but boundless"; orders of infinity) beyond the reach of diagrams, pictures, or everyday metaphors, attract the scientist.

351. "editor of *Isis*": George Sarton: *The History of Science and the New Humanism.*

352-3. Although the mathematician-philosopher Bertrand Russell discards deity while the mathematician-physicist-philosopher Albert Einstein does not, they agree in distrusting such things as quantum jumps-on-the-average and Heisenbergian uncertainty. Russell attributes such devices to the dodges of present ignorance; Einstein adds: "I cannot believe that God plays dice with the world". Both believe in a universe of order and harmony and fundamental, unitary law. There seems a confusion, however, if not a contradiction, in Dr. Einstein's effort to bind the concept of a unitary law to the notions of spiritual life and "religious instincts"; see page 336. (See also pages 332-3, and Note thereto.)

359 f. Sören A. Kierkegaard, *Either-Or; Unscientific Postscript.* The fullest discussion in English is in *Something about Kierkegaard,* by David F. Swenson (Augsburg Publishing House, Minneapolis, 1945). Jean-Paul Sartre, *Huis Clos; La Nausée; The Case for Responsible Literature,* in *Partisan Review,* Summer, 1946; *Existentialism* (Philosophical Library, 1947). For further facets, see *The Death of Tragedy,* leading article in *The Times Literary Supplement* (London, Oct. 5, 1946). *Huis Clos* has been translated as *No Exit,* in one volume with *The Flies,* which in the guise of a Greek drama more fully embodies existentialist ideas.

NOTES

365. Louis Roule: *Fishes and Their Ways of Life.*

365. Ingram Bander: *Notes on Chance in History, The City College Alumnus,* April, 1935. The historian of an earlier age is Seeley.

377. It may be an urge to greater one-ness with the group that leads a Jean Papadiamantopoulos to become Jean Moreas; a George Goetz, V. F. Calverton; a Louis Farigoule, Jules Romains — to mention but these of the many not pen-names but life-names adopted.

379, 382, 385. Propaganda, says F. E. Lumley, in *The Propaganda Menace,* is promotion that is veiled, as to (1) its origin or sources, (2) its promulgators' intention, (3) the methods used for its inculcation, (4) the truth of its contents, and/or (5) the consequences of acting in accord with its urgings. But the whole art of persuasion (which the Greeks called rhetoric) demands a veiling; we call it "propaganda" only when we see, and lift, the veil.

NOTES

365. Louis Roule, *Fishes and Their Ways of Life*.

365. Ingrith Deyrup-Olsen, Bander, Notes on Chance in History, *The City College Alumnus*, April, 1937. The historian of an earlier age is Seeley.

371. It may be an urge to greater one-ness with the group that leads a Jean Papadiamantopoulos to become Jean Moréas; a George Goetz, V. F. Calverton; a Louis Farigoule, Jules Romains — to mention but these of the many not pen-names but life-names adopted.

379, 387, 388. Propaganda, says F. E. Lumley, in *The Propaganda Menace*, is promotion that is veiled, as to (1) its origin or sources, (2) its promulgators' intention, (3) the methods used for its inculcation, (4) the truth of its contents, and/or (5) the consequences of acting in accord with its urgings. But the whole art of persuasion, which the Greeks called rhetoric, demands a veiling; we call it "propaganda" only when we see, and lift, the veil.

[443]

INDEX

Index

(Subjects that receive major consideration are not listed here, e.g., art, realism, romanticism, symbolism, poetry. For these, consult the table of contents; or read the book.)

A la recherche du temps perdu—267f, 270
abstract forms—427
Academy, French—35, 120
Adding Machine, The—246, 306
Adler, Alfred—74, 114f, 236
Adler, Mortimer J.—385f
aesthetics—3
Ah Wilderness—301
Alain—114, 346
Alice in Wonderland—106, 324
Allen, Hervey—102f, 107
Ambush—268
Ame enchantée, L'—305
anarchy—203f
Anathema—108, 327
Anaxagoras—391
Ancient Mariner—88
Anderson, Maxwell—226, 364
Anderson, Sherwood—309
Andreyev, Leonid N.—327
animals—407
Another Language—23
Anthony Adverse—102f, 107, 197f
antithesis—47
Apology for Poetry—32
Apuleius—121
Aristides—16, 398f
Aristotle—6, 39f, 162, 225, 255, 303
Arnold, Matthew—151f
Arp, Hans—428
art for art's sake—92, 162f
art, limits of—99
art, modern—424f
art, movements in—17
art, work of—14
Arvin, Newton—377
As You Like It—31, 51, 407f
Asch, Sholom—221f
Assyrian attitude toward art—4
Augustan Age—37

Austen, Jane—383
autobiography—371f
Avare, L'—39

Babbitt, Irving—96, 243, 422
Bach, Johann Sebastian—353
Bacon, Francis—391f
Balderston, John L.—363f
Balla, Giacomo—426
ballet—287f
Balzac, Honoré de—196, 270
Bander, Ingram—365, 445
Banville, Théodore de—413
Barbusse, Henri—233f
Barnett, Lincoln—441f
Barren Ground—268
Barrie, James M.—314, 364
Barry, Philip—299f, 307, 324
Baudelaire, Charles—90, 96, 154f, 158f, 165f, 169, 178, 242, 408f
Bavinck, Bernard—353
beauty—271f, 423
Beethoven, Ludwig van—353
Beggars on Horseback—249
behaviorism—114
Behrman, S. N.—276f
Bell, Clive—290f
Bell, E. T.—330
Belloc, Hilaire—327
Benda, Julien—120f, 407
Benét, Wm. Rose—236f
Berdyaev, Nikolai A.—375f
Berge, André—226f
Bergerac, Cyrano de—105, 109
Bergson, Henri—176f, 272, 352
Berkeley, George—349
Bible, The—358
Biederman, Charles—426
Birmingham, Bishop of—351
Blake, Wm.—42, 43, 44f, 49, 76, 84, 129

[449]

Blankfort, Michael—232f
Blümner, Hugo—165, 260f
Bly Market—266
Boas, Franz—429
Bodenheim, Maxwell—279
Bodkin, Maud—236
Boileau-Despréaux, Nicolas—35
Bonsels, Waldemar—304
Bourgeois Gentilhomme, Le—39
Bowle, John—443
Bragg, Wm.—7, 391
Brahms, Johannes—353
Brancusi, Constantin—246, 291
Brand—360
Brave and the Blind, The—232f
Brecht, Bertholt—225
Breton, André—250
Bridge of San Luis Rey, The—298
Bridges, Robert—195, 232
Browning, Robert—147f, 156, 264, 284
Brunngraber, R.—308
Buck, Pearl—301
Buffon, Georges L. L. de—42
Burckfield, Charles—431
Burke, Kenneth—10, 21, 391
Burns, Robert—64
Burrow, Trigant—343, 415, 416
Butler, Samuel—38, 39, 195
Byron, George Gordon—62, 72, 74, 84, 130, 132, 144, 401

Cabell, James Branch—16, 91, 118, 155, 159, 196f, 247, 384
Calder, Alexander—426
Calverton, V. F.—220, 233, 367, 415f, 445
Calvin, John—99
Campion, Thomas—31f
Canby, Henry S.—197, 227
Carlyle, Thomas—72, 100, 328, 338, 367
Carroll, Lewis—411f, 436f
Castle of Otranto, The—88
catharsis—95
Cavalier—34
censorship—107f
Cervantes Saavedra, Miguel de—3
Chaplin, Charlie—324, 328
character, the—39
Chateaubriand, François Réné de—78
Chaucer, Geoffrey—87, 121, 128
chemistry—27, 330f

Cheney, Sheldon—290
Chénier, André—401
Chesterton, Gilbert K.— 121, 231, 298, 343, 407
Cheyney, Edward P.—366
Chopin, Frédéric F.—181
Christian attitude toward art—4
Cicero, Marcus Tullius—402
Cid, Le—35f
Cincinnatus, Lucius Quintus—417f
civilization, epochs of—396f
Clarissa Harlowe—42
Claudel, Paul—258, 271, 303, 358f
clavilux, the—99, 261, 406
Clitandre—36
Coates, Robert M.—265
Cohen, Morris R.—8, 207, 325f, 391
Cohen-Portheim, Paul—372
Coleridge, Samuel T.—53, 64, 71, 72f, 75, 84, 88, 89, 129f, 411
collages—252
color organ—406
Colton, Arthur—377
Comédie humaine, La—270
comedy, Roman—23
Communism—139, 203f, 234f, 237, 239, 308f, 316, 396f, 407, 416f, 438f, 443
compromise—317f
Compton, Arthur H.—350
Comte, Auguste—155, 392
confessions—39
conscience—241f
contemporary, the—21f
Coomaraswamy, A. K.—438
Cooper Hill—35
Corneille, Pierre—35f
Counterfeiters, The—266f
Cradle Will Rock, The—225
Crane, Hart—185, 237
Cranford—42f
Craven, Thomas—224
Crile, George W.—336f
Cristabel—411
Croce, Benedetto — 78, 126, 373, 423f
cubism—424f, 428
cummings, e e—195, 217f
cycles—391f

da-da—101, 249f
Daiches, David—162
Dali, Salvador — 253, 277f, 431f, 434, 437

[450]

INDEX

dance, the—286f
Dane, Clemence—196
Daniel, Samuel—77
D'Annunzio, Gabriele—343
Dante Alighieri—22, 117f, 135, 296, 358
Darwin, Charles—392
Davenant, Wm.—78
Davidson, Donald—227
Days Without End—300f
death and love—405f
Debs, Eugene Victor—79
De Casseres, Benjamin—254f, 327f, 342
Decline of the West, The—396
Defoe, Daniel—41, 46f
de la Mare, Walter—167
de la Roche, Mazo—196
democracy—203f, 311, 316f
Demosthenes—212
Denham, John—35
Dennet, Mary Ware—109f
De Quincey, Thomas—84
Descartes, Réné—36, 360f
Desire—432
Desire Under the Elms—224f
Devil's Dictionary, The—340
De Voto, Bernard—297
Dewey, John—244, 339, 374, 392
diabolism—90
Dickens, Charles—102f, 142f, 144f, 379, 384
Dickinson, Emily—405f
Diderot, Denis — 40, 42, 67, 73, 156f
Discourse on Method—36
Disney Walt—406
Divine Comedy, The—22
Doll's House, A—22
Don Quixote—22
Donne, John—3
Dos Passos, John—308
Dostoievsky, Fedor M. — 144, 342, 375, 423
drama, Greek—27
dream—131f
Dreiser, Theodore — 16, 196, 305f, 384
Dryden, John—35, 38, 40, 41, 46, 127f, 169, 405
Du Bellay, Joachim—31
Ducasse, Curt J.—286

Duchamp, Marcel — 252, 426, 428, 432
Dujardin, Edouard—180, 413
Duncan, Isadora—287f
Dürer, Albrecht—432
dynamic symmetry—289
Dynamo—300

E S P—269
Eastman, Max—423
Eddington, A. S.—349
Eddy, Mary Baker—9
Edman, Irwin—272, 344, 374f
Edschmid, Kasimir—249
education—374f
Egyptian attitude toward art—4
Einfühlung—271f
Einstein, Albert—91, 332f, 336, 352, 441f, 444
Elegy in a Country Churchyard—47f
Eliot, George—143
Eliot, T. S. — 93f, 185, 207f, 220, 240f, 255, 258, 298, 319, 324, 384
Eluard, Paul—437f
Emerson, Ralph Waldo—149f, 233
emotion—79f
empathy—271f
Empedocles—391
Endymion—49f
England, Elizabethan—34
entropy—351
Epictetus—392
Epstein, Jacob—22, 111
Erewhon—195
Ernst, Morris—373f
Erskine, John—384
escape, art as—93f
Essay of Dramatic Poetry—35
Essay on the Inequality of Human Races—395f
Euripides—119
Evans, Bergen—244, 440
excess—84f
existentialism—100, 359f
expressionism—78, 248f, 423f

Faerie Queene, The—118
Fairchild, Lambert—335
faith—115f, 407, 442f
Fascism—203f, 239, 275f, 316, 425, 443

[451]

Faure, Elie—26, 399
fear—114f, 297f, 407
fellow-traveler—423
Femmes savantes, Les—39
Fernandez, Ramon—21
Fiedler, Leslie A.—420f
Fielding, Henry—40f
Finnegans Wake—266
Flaubert, Gustave — 86, 132, 181, 183
Fleurs du mal, Les—90
Flies, The—444
Flight to the West—275f
folk psychology—259
Fontanne, Lynn—273
For Whom the Bell Tolls—265
form—126f
Fort, Charles—255f, 342
Fountain, The—301
France, Anatole—34f, 70, 166, 175, 215
Frank, Waldo—308f
Frankfurter, Alfred—436
freedom—394
"freedom from fear"—407
frein vital—241f
Freud, Sigmund—9, 114, 131f, 207, 221, 244, 250, 256, 305, 307, 367, 375, 433, 441
From Morn to Midnight—269
Frost, Robert—165, 309f, 313
frottages—252
Fugitive, The—379f
Fuller, Margaret—151

Galsworthy, John—196, 249, 291, 309, 379f
Garçonne, La—110
Gautier, Théophile—163
Geley, Gustave—351f
generalization—38, 42
Gestalt psychology—345
Ghil, Réné—166
Gibbon, Edward—395
Gide, André—266f, 309, 359
Gilbert, Bernard—266
Gilbert, W. S.—89, 140f, 143, 282
Glasgow, Ellen—268
Glass-Pleshing, Max—415
Glyn, Elinor—107f, 406f
Gobineau, Joseph de—395f
Godwin, Wm.—7
Glyn, Elinor—107f, 406f

Goethe, Johann W. von—21, 57, 70, 126, 135f, 156, 358
Gogol, Nikolai V.—144
Golden Bird, The—246, 291
Good Earth, The—301
Good Pagan's Failure, The—397
Goodman, Paul—330
Gorelik, Mordecai—224
Gorki, Maxim—225
Gothic cathedral—25
Gourmont, Remy de—162, 169, 314
Grapes of Wrath, The—22
Gray, Thomas—47f, 87, 129, 272
Greek art—25
Greek attitude toward art—4f, 8
Grosser, M. R.—433f
Gruening, Martha—373
Gulliver's Travels—38
Gutkind, Eric—345f

Hairy Ape, The—299f
Haldane, J. B. S.—335, 341f
Hamilton, Edith—399
happiness—393
Harding, Ann—272f
Hardy, G. H.—352
Hardy, Thomas—74, 108
Harvey, Gabriel—399
Hayakawa, S. I.—424f
Hayek, Fr. A.—370
Hazlitt, Henry—16, 67, 228f, 398f
Hegel, Georg W. F.—57, 176, 219, 392
Heine, Heinrich—77, 101, 156, 401
Heliodorus—121
Hellman, Lillian—380
Hemingway, Ernest—247, 265
Henley, Wm. E.—144
Heroes and Hero Worship—72
Hesiod—395
Hesse, Herman—304
Hicks, Granville—227f
history, the "new"—365
Hitler, Adolf—124, 133, 308, 370, 374, 381
Hogben, Lancelot—331f, 357
Homer—24, 395
Hood, Thomas—13
Hook, Sidney—328, 366f
Hoover, Herbert—376
Hopkins, Gerard Manly—195
Hotel Universe—324f
housewreckers—358

[452]

INDEX

Housman, A. E.—274
Howard, Sidney—224
Hudibras—38
Hugo, Victor—13, 15, 53, 57, 62f, 65, 90f, 92, 158, 400f, 404f, 411, 412
humanism, the new—421f
humanitarianism—139
Hunt, Leigh—67
Huntington, Ellsworth—394f
Huxley, Aldous—245f, 343, 369
Huysmans, Joris K.—159, 167

Ibsen, Henrik—119, 144, 360, 362, 384
Iceman Cometh, The—307
idea vs image—345, 444
Ideas Have Consequences—397
image vs idea—345, 444
imagination—75f
imitation—4
impartiality—277f
impossible, the—105f
impressionism—433
Inge, Wm. Ralph—351
inner check—241f
inspiration—75f
interpenetration—429f
Isis—351

Jaffe, Bernard—339
James, Henry—180, 295f
James-Lange theory—259
James, Wm.—180
Jammes, Francis—301
Jaspers, K.—372
Jean-Christophe—270, 340f
Jeans, James H.—350
Jeffers, Robinson—279
Jevons, H. Stanley—371
Jewish attitude toward art—4, 345f
Joad, C. E. M.—331
Johannes Kreisler—268f
Johnson, Samuel — 43, 47, 54, 58, 231, 399
Jolas, Eugène—264
Jonson, Ben—34, 76
Joseph Andrews—40
Joyce, James—180, 185, 217, 219, 264, 266, 359
Julius Caesar—225
Jung, Carl G.—238, 343f
Justice—379f

Kaempffert, Waldemar—338f, 353, 393
Kafka, Franz—304, 360
Kaiser, Georg—269
Kant, Immanuel—392
Keats, John—16, 42f, 49f, 69f, 72, 76, 78, 87, 91, 96, 129
Kepes, Gyorgy—425f, 427f
Keyserling, Hermann—271
Kierkegaard, S. A.—359f, 444
King James (I of England)—31
King Lear—225
Kipling, Rudyard—149
Knight, Frank H.—420
Knight, G. Wilson—353f
knowledge—394
Koffka, Kurt—345
Korzybski, Alfred—216f, 331f, 343, 360
Kreymborg, Alfred—279
Kukryniksi—252

La Bruyere, Jean de—39
la Fayette, Mme. de—120
Lake, The—81
Lamartine, Alphonse — 65, 78, 81, 86, 400, 402f
Lamb, Charles—88
La Meri—287
Landor, W. S.—79, 151
law—373f
Lawrence, D. H. — 134, 153, 187, 245f, 259f, 342f
Lee, Vernon—272
lemmings—307
Lenin, Nikolai—417f
Lenore—88
Lessing, Gotthold E.—157
Leviathan—204
Lewis, Sinclair—16, 279, 308
Lewis, Wyndham—352
Lewisohn, Ludwig — 240, 247, 302, 370
liberal, Ione—367f
Lin Yutang—124, 340
Lindsay, Vachel—301f
Lippmann, Walter—243
Liszt, Franz von—181f
literacy—316f
Living Newspaper, The—225f
Longus—121
Loos, Anita—324
Lotze, Rudolf H.—272

[453]

love—115f, 117f
love and death—405f
Lovejoy, Arthur O.—391f, 400
Lowell, Amy—179
Lower Depths, The—225
Loyalties—379
Lucas, F. L.—131f
Lucy—48f
Luther, Martin—99

Macaulay, Thomas B.—345, 392
Macbeth—31
MacLeish, Archibald—236f
Magnus, Laurie—40, 399
Malherbe, François de—35
Mallarmé, Stéphane—156, 160, 163, 174f, 257f, 279, 411, 412f
Man Who Came To Dinner, The—295
Mann, Thomas—233
March of Time, The—225f
Margueritte, Victor—110
Marlowe, Christopher—118
Marx, Karl — 156, 207, 233, 250, 305, 367, 370, 375, 392
Masefield, John—3, 307, 311
mathematics—330f
Mather, Jr., Frank J.—293f
Maugham, Somerset—196, 309
Maxims—39
Mayakovski, Vladimir—234f
mechanism—349f
Melville, Herman—74
memoirs—39
Men of Good Will—269
Mencken, H. L.—247, 294f
Merchant of Venice, The—24
Meredith, George—295
Michelangelo Buonarroti—417f
Millay, Edna St. V.—303
Millikan, R. A.—349f
Milton, John—32, 126, 327, 358
Milton—44
Misanthrope, Le—39
Misérables, Les—270
mobile—426
modern art—424f
Moholy-Nagy, L.—426
Molière (J. B. Poquelin)—39
Mona Lisa's Moustache—425f
Mondriaan, Pieter—427
monodrama—268f
Monroe, Harriet—303

TRENDS IN LITERATURE

Moore, George—411
More, Hannah—88f
More, Paul Elmer—170f, 295, 373f, 422, 439, 440
Moréas, Jean—445
Morgan, Charles—246, 301
Morgenstern, Christian—261
Morris, Wm.—144, 149
mot juste, le—92
Mourning Becomes Electra—300
Muller, H. J.—439
Mumford, Lewis—297, 308f
Munson, Gorham B.—242
Münsterberg, Hugo—272
Munzer, Thomas—417f
Murder In the Cathedral—298
Murray, Rosalind—397
Murry, J. M.—228, 371
music—98f, 165f, 292
Musset, Alfred de—64, 78, 81, 84, 86, 181, 401f, 404
Mutability—49

Napoleon Bonaparte—101, 124, 135, 139, 308, 357
Nash, Thomas—405
nature—10, 48f, 60, 400
Nazism—275f, 439
negative (attitude)—241f
neo-classical—31f
Nock, Albert J.—369f
Nouvelle Heloise, La—42
Nouvelle revue française—298
Novalis (von Hardenberg)—63, 77
Novecentismo—234
novelty—408

Objectivists Anthology—281f
oblivion—259f
Ode to the West Wind—75
O'Neill, Eugene—224f, 283f, 299f, 307, 381, 440
Organism—350
Oriental art—25
Origen—351
originality—3, 408
Orton, Wm. A.—376f
Our Town—225, 298
Overstreet, Harry A.—372
Ovid—121
Ozymandias—396

Paine, Thomas—417f
painting—165f

[454]

INDEX

Pamela—39, 40, 120
Pater, Walter — 84, 87f, 96, 126, 152f, 162
pathetic fallacy—411
Pepys, Samuel—40
permanence—357f
persistence of attitudes—13
Petrie, Flinders—396
Petrified Forest, The—367
Pfister, Oskar—249
Pheidias—417f
Picabia, Francis—249f
Picasso, Pablo—261, 432, 433f, 436f
Pierce, Frederick—244f
Pins and Needles—224
Piscator, Erwin—225f
place-names, American—413f
Planck, Max K. E. L.—340f, 350
Plato—26, 255
Pledge, H. T.—394
plot—128f
Poe, Edgar A.—75, 80, 158f
poetry, Elizabethan—31f
polarity, principle of—7
politics—14
Pope, Alexander—35, 38, 40, 45, 47
science—58, 98f, 140
populism—326f
Pound, Ezra—96, 264f, 271, 279f
Précieuses ridicules, Les—39
Pre-Raphaelites—152, 433
Price, W. A.—338
Priestly, J. B.—363f
primitive art—428f
program music—168, 285f, 410
progress—391f
propaganda — 22, 377f, 382, 385, 445
propaganda analysis—310f
Proust, Marcel—267f, 324
psychology—332f, 343f
Puritan—34
Pushkin, A. S.—144
Pygmalion—424

Quiller-Couch, Arthur—51, 102

Rabelais, François — 22, 203, 383, 431f
Racine, Jean—39, 45, 73, 119f
"radical" form—278f
Rapin, René—35
Rapoport, Anatol—392f, 415

Rascoe, Burton—294f
Rasselas—399
Raven, The—75
Read, Herbert—98, 438
reason — 78f, 100, 115, 131, 248f, 274f, 402
recreations—329
religion—7, 98f, 140, 442f
religion, return to—297f
Reliques of English Poetry—87
Renaissance—31f, 34
Renan, Joseph E.—155f, 402
Retz, Cardinal de—40
Reynolds, Joshua—42
Rice, Elmer—246, 275f, 299, 306
Richards, I. A.—311
Richardson, Samuel—39
Richelieu, Cardinal—35f
Richman, Arthur—268
Rimbaud, Arthur — 13, 133, 166, 176, 178
Rivera, Diego—377, 417f, 438
Robinson, E. A.—3, 282f
Robinson, James H.—339, 365
Robinson Crusoe—42
Robsjohn-Gibbings, T. H. — 425f, 432
Rochefoucauld, Duc de la—39
Rodin, Auguste—22, 111, 168, 175f
Rolland, Romain—304f
Romains, Jules—168f, 196, 269f, 439, 445
roman à clef—38
Roman art—25
Ronsard, Pierre de—31
Rossetti, D. G.—408
Rougon-Macquart series—270
Roundhead—34
Rousseau, J. J.—40, 42, 57f, 73, 77, 89, 99f, 392
Rowe, Nicholas—119
Royce, Josiah—74, 236
Ruskin, John—64, 144, 149, 169f
Russell, Bertrand—110f, 258f, 352f, 444
Rymer, Thomas—35

St. Denis, Ruth—287
Sainte-Beuve, Charles A.—157, 182
Saint-Evremond, Seigneur de—35
Saint-Simon, Louis, duc de—40
Sand, George—64, 181f
Sandburg, Carl—309, 436

[455]

Sanine—13
Santayana, George—94f
Saroyan, Wm.—265, 288
Sarton, George—351, 394f, 398
Sartre, Jean-Paul—360f, 363, 444
Schapiro, Meyer—435f
Schelling, F. W. von—67, 70
Schlesinger, Jr., A. M.—394
Schmalhausen, S. D.—348f
Schneider, Isidor—235f, 298
Schoenberg, Arnold—286
school (literary)—14
Schopenhauer, Arthur—74, 76
Schrödinger, Erwin—338f
Schubert, Franz—77
Scott, Walter—102, 143, 401
Scudéry, Mme. de—120
sculpture—166f, 175f
"semantics of identification"—424f
Sevigné, Mme. de—120
Shadow and Substance—298
Shakespeare, Wm.—24, 27, 31f, 34, 50f, 87, 105, 121f, 157, 358, 407f
Shan-Kar, Uday—287
Shaw, G. B.—140, 195, 196, 231, 308, 342, 345, 364, 372, 382f
Shelley, P. B.—41, 63, 76, 78, 80f, 84, 87, 101, 114f, 130, 132, 272
Sherwood, Robert E. — 209, 275, 367, 382
Shoemakers' Holiday, The—225
Sidney, Philip—32
Sinclair, Upton—308, 380, 382f
Sitwell, Edith—359
solitary, the—80f
Somebody's Death—269
Song For St. Cecilia's Day, A—46
Soupault, Philippe—323
Souriau, Maurice—272
Southey, Robert—71, 80
Soviet dancers—285f
Spectra—294
Spender, Stephen—237, 260
Spengler, Oswald—167, 396
Spenser, Edmund—32, 358, 399
Staël, Mme. de—57, 124
Stalin, Joseph—234, 335, 374
Stein, Gertrude — 165, 185, 261f, 437, 439
Stendhal—21
Stern, G. B.—196
Stevenson, R. L.—79, 134, 193f
Stowe, H. B.—379, 383

Strachey, John—368
Strange Interlude—300
stream of consciousness—180
Study of History, A—397
style—*See* form
subject matter—126f
Sullivan, J. W. N.—351
summum bonum—314f
surrealism — 101, 176, 250f, 432, 437f
Swift, Jonathan—47, 383
Swinburne, Algernon C.—152f, 160, 165, 408
synaesthesis—76

Taine, Hippolyte—338
Tale of Two Cities, A—102f
Talley Method, The—276f
Taylor, Francis H.—436
Teggart, Frederick J.—391f
Tempest, The—34
Tennyson, Alfred, Lord — 13, 42f, 141, 144f
Testament of Beauty, The—232
texture in art—430f
Thackery, Wm. M.—142f, 384
There Shall Be No Night—275, 382, 414f
Thompson, Francis—7, 64, 152f, 160
Thorndike, Ed. L.—340
Three Cities—221f
Tieck, Ludwig—156f
time—357f
To Spring—49
Toller, Ernst—308, 368f
Tolstoi, Leo N.—144
Tom Jones—41
Tomlinson, H. M.—327
Toynbee, Arnold J.—397
Transition—264
True Confessions—358
Turgenev, Ivan S.—144
tyranny—203f
Tzara, Tristan—249

Ulysses—266, 293
unanimism—70, 269f
Uncle Tom's Cabin—22, 155
"unified field theory"—441f
Untermeyer, Louis—303
Utopia—439

INDEX

Valéry, Paul—169, 174f, 257f, 279, 309, 411, 413
Valley Forge—226
value—352f
Van Doren, Mark—410
Van Gogh, Vincent—431
Vergil—24
Verlaine, Paul—194f, 414
Verne, Jules—105
vers de société—38
verse, free—178f
Victorian—141f
Vigny, Alfred de—78, 86, 403
Voltaire—57
Voynich, Ethel L. B.—108, 406f

Wagner, Richard—417f
Wallace, Wm. K.—369
Waller, Edmund—35
Walpole, Horace—88
Walpole, Hugh—196, 246
Walton, Eda Lou—237, 274, 279, 302f
Wasserman, Jacob—371f
Waste Land, The—264
Watkins, C. Law—426
Weaver, John V. A.—359
Weaver, Richard M.—397
Wells, H. G.—105f, 271, 308, 323, 364, 371, 379, 383, 437, 439

Weltschmerz—74
Werfel, Franz—265, 301
West, Rebecca—248
Wetzel, Norman C.—338
Wharton, Edith—227
Whitehead, A. N.—350, 392
Whitman, Walt—79, 154, 165, 178f, 185f, 227f, 233, 420
Wilde, Oscar—152, 162, 167, 303, 385
Wilder, Thornton—298, 384
Wilenski, R. H.—290f, 293f
Wilfred, Thomas—261
will, the—240f
will, free—112f, 140
Woelfel, Norman—374f
Wolfe, Humbert—248
woman—117f
Woodberry, George Ed.—271
Woolf, Virgina—379, 383
Woollcott, Alexander—294f
wonder—91
Wordsworth, Wm.—43, 44, 45, 48f, 53, 64, 65f, 70f, 75, 78, 130

Yeats, Wm. Butler—260, 304
Yesterday's Burden—265

Zinsser, Hans—437
Zola, Emile—144, 196, 233f, 270, 362

INDEX

Valéry, Paul—109, 1741, 2371, 379, 395, 411, 413
Valley Forge—226
value—352†
Van Doren, Mark—110
Van Gogh, Vincent—131
Vergil—84
Verhaine, Paul—1941, 414
Verne, Jules—109
vers de société—38
verso, free—1781
Victorian—1711
Vigny, Alfred de—78, 86, 405
Voltaire—57
Voynich, Ethel L. B.—108, 1061

Wagner, Richard—1171
Wallace, Wm. K.—368
Waller, Edmund—85
Walpole, Horace—88
Walpole, Hugh—196, 246
Walton, Izaak—132, 274, 275, 302†
Wassermann, Jacob—371†
Watts-Lund, The—261
Watkins, G. Law.—126
Weaver, John V. A.—330
Weaver, Richard M.—387
Wells, H. G.—1081, 271, 306, 323, 361, 371, 379, 383, 431, 439

Wahlmacht—74
Wedel, Franz—243, 301
Weis, Rebecca—248
Wendt, Herman C.—338
Wharton, Edith—227
Whitehead, A. N.—382, 392
Whitman, Walt—79, 131, 165, 1761, 1801, 2171, 285, 410
Wilde, Oscar—152, 162, 167, 303, 382
Wilder, Thornton—208, 384
Wilenski, R. H.—2301, 2951
Wilfred, Thomas—261
will, the—2401
will, free—112, 140
Woerfel, Normao—3741
Wolfe, Humbert—212
woman—1171
Woodberry, George Ed.—271
Woolf, Virginia—379, 383
Woolnoth, Alexander—2911
wonder—91
Wordsworth, Wm.—43, 44, 45, 161, 53, 64, 65†, 70†, 75, 78, 150

Yeats, Wm. Butler—260, 304
Yesterday's Burden—265

Zimmer, Hans—437
Zola, Emile—144, 196, 235†, 270, 362

[457]